Man Cannot Speak for Her

6

When the telegraphic wires
brought us the news last
winter of a proposition
before your Legislature
to take the words white
male from your con-
-stitution, we were hold-
-ing meetings all through
New York preparatory
to our constitutional
convention, patiently
labouring in the faith that
the efforts of our lives, if
never realized to ourselves
would descend in blessings
to our children's children

This is a page in Elizabeth Cady Stanton's own hand of the text of a speech that was given in the 1867 referendum campaign in Kansas. It reads:

When the telegraphic wires brought us the news last winter of a proposition before your Legislature to take the words white male from your constitution, we were holding meetings all through New York preparatory to our constitutional convention, patiently labouring in the faith that the efforts of our lives, if never realized to ourselves, would descend in blessings to our children's children.

Kansas Collection, University of Kansas Libraries.

MAN CANNOT SPEAK FOR HER

VOLUME II

KEY TEXTS OF THE EARLY FEMINISTS

Compiled by

Karlyn Kohrs Campbell

Contributions in Women's Studies, Number 102

GREENWOOD PRESS
NEW YORK • WESTPORT, CONNECTICUT • LONDON

Library of Congress Cataloging-in-Publication Data

Campbell, Karlyn Kohrs.
Man cannot speak for her.
(Contributions in women's studies, ISSN 0147-104X; no. 102)
Bibliography: p.
Includes index.
Contents: v. 1. A critical study of early feminist rhetoric.—v. 2. Key texts of the early feminists.
1. Feminism—United States—History—Sources. 2. Speeches, addresses, etc., American—Women authors—History and Criticism. 3. Political oratory—United States—History. 4. Women's rights—United States—History. 5. Rhetoric—Political aspects—United States—History. 6. Rhetoric—Social aspects—United States—History. 7. Women orators—United States—History.
I. Title. II. Series.
HQ1154.C28 1989 305.4'2'0973 88-32825
ISBN 0-313-26668-9 (set)
ISBN 0-313-25649-7 (v. 1 : lib. bdg. : alk. paper)
ISBN 0-313-25650-0 (v. 2 : lib. bdg. : alk. paper)

British Library Cataloguing in Publication Data is available.

A paperback edition of *Man Cannot Speak For Her: Volume II Key Texts of the Early Feminists* is available from Praeger Publishers; ISBN: 0-275-93267-2.

Library of Congress Catalog Card Number: 88-32825
ISBN: 0-313-26668-9 (set)
ISBN: 0-313-25649-7 (v. 1)
ISBN: 0-313-25650-0 (v. 2)
ISSN: 0147-104X

First published in 1989

Greenwood Press, Inc.
88 Post Road West, Westport, Connecticut 06881

Printed in the United States of America

The paper used in this book complies with the Permanent Paper Standard issued by the National Information Standards Organization (Z39.48-1984).

10 9 8 7 6 5 4 3 2 1

Contents

Introduction

This is the second volume of a two-part study of the rhetoric of early feminists. What follows attempts to survey very briefly the history of the woman's rights/woman suffrage movement and to outline the critical concepts developed at length in the first volume. Those who have volume I available may wish to skip immediately to the texts.

Social movements arise and develop through the interaction of many factors, but rhetoric is a key constituent. In rhetoric, activists define their ideology, urge their demands upon outsiders, refute their opposition, maintain the morale of stalwarts, struggle to enliven familiar arguments, and attempt to keep their concerns high on the political agenda.

This volume is a collection of works of the U.S. woman's rights/woman suffrage movement from its beginnings through 1920. Those items included are key works in the history of the movement that reflect its origins and growth and represent the diversity of issues and styles that characterized it. Each work is preceded by a headnote identifying the author(s) and describing the occasion on which it appeared. The works included were created by figures of national importance and reflect the concerns of the mainstream movement; I have omitted discourse from such distinct but related efforts as those for birth control and improving the conditions of women workers. Each work is complete; each is annotated to identify individuals and to provide historical information likely to be unfamiliar to contemporary readers. Collectively, these works are a documentary history of what became the social movement for woman's rights/ woman suffrage.

More important, these are the movement's key rhetorical works. Through these works scholars can see the processes by which the movement came into existence, its ideology developed and conflicts arose, its arguments were laid out, evidence was marshaled and presented, opposing views were answered, obstacles were transcended, and appeals were adapted to varied audiences. In other words, these works form the core of the persuasive message of early feminism. They are the basis for describing the challenges women faced and for evaluating the resourcefulness with which women deployed the available means of persuasion to encompass and transcend the obstacles they confronted.

I refer to early activists as feminists only in the sense that they worked to improve the conditions of women. To themselves, they were woman's rights advocates or suffragists; in the United States, only their opponents called them "suffragettes." In Great Britain, by contrast, the radicals of the Women's Social and Political Union, led by Emmeline and Christabel Pankhurst, adopted this epithet as their own.

Early woman's rights activists faced many rhetorical challenges, some of which were unique. Most fundamentally, they struggled for the right to use the power of rhetoric--for the right to act in the public sphere by speaking, organizing, publishing newspapers, and lobbying. Women justified their right to rhetorical activism on several grounds. A major source of their ideology was natural rights philosophy, a body of belief refined in the Enlightenment and summed up in the

American Declaration of Independence. At base, particularly as expressed in the Seneca Falls "Declaration of Sentiments," a reworking of the Declaration of Independence, woman's rights was a demand for personhood. That is, women wanted inclusion in the cultural values proclaiming that individuals had inalienable rights because they were persons, that it was government's function to protect those rights, and that to do so, government had to rest on the consent of the governed, expressed through the ballot. Natural rights affirmed the right of individuals to equality of opportunity, and it presupposed that the highest good was the full development of each person's rational faculties.

Women's earliest demand was for education, the key element in Mary Wollstonecraft's *A Vindication of the Rights of Woman*, published in England in 1792. Addressed to Talleyrand, a leader of the French Revolution, and responding to Edmund Burke's *Reflections on the French Revolution* (1790) and to Jean-Jacques Rousseau's *Emile, ou l'Éducation* (1762), it was rationalistic both in content and style. Wollstonecraft presumed that humans were distinctively rational, and thus, creatures with souls. As rational creatures with souls, then, women were created not merely for the comfort and pleasure of men but to develop their understanding and, hence, their virtue. Following Plato, Wollstonecraft held that there was no morality without knowledge or virtue without understanding. Wollstonecraft made two great demands: for education to develop woman's understanding, and for a change in attitude proclaiming a woman's duty to be development of her reason rather than pursuit of beauty and pleasure. She argued that, in addition to increasing her virtue, woman's mental development would enable her to better educate her children, to perform her household duties more systematically, to discover that true pleasure is the reward of labor, and to care for herself if left without support. The book was influential; it was read by early movement leaders such as Lucretia Coffin Mott, and after the Civil War it was reprinted in the *Revolution*, published by Elizabeth Cady Stanton, Parker Pillsbury, and Susan Anthony.

Because of dominant views of woman's nature, demands for educational opportunities were controversial even when linked to women's traditional roles. In 1819, for example, educational pioneer Emma Hart Willard proposed "A Plan for Improving Female Education" to the New York legislature, urging its members to provide funds to endow a school for young women. Conscious of controversy, she was careful to state that the education offered would be "as different from those appropriate to the other sex as the female character and duties are from the male" (Willard 1819, 2). Willard did not say that education was a woman's right as a rational being, only that it was preparation to enable her to perform her special *duties*. Willard linked the duties to patriotism: "And who knows how great and good a race of men may yet arise from the forming hand of mothers, enlightened by the bounty of that beloved country, to defend her liberties, to plan her future improvement, and to raise her to unparaleled glory?" (46). Although her case was cogently argued, and although she was careful to remain seated in order to avoid any hint that she was violating taboos against speaking publicly, the Legislature responded with praise and a charter, but no money (Lutz 1931, 28). Private donors finally endowed Troy Female Seminary, which opened its doors in 1821 and offered education on the secondary level to women for the first time; the movement leader Elizabeth Cady Stanton was one of its graduates.

Resistance to woman's rights, including education, arose out of the concept of True Womanhood or the cult of domesticity, which defined females as "other," as suited only to be wives and mothers. By 1850, distinct ideas about the natures of men and women had emerged. Man's nature was thought to be violent, lustful, and competitive; his place was public sphere, encompassing all that involved the mechanical, political, and monetary. By contrast, woman's nature was defined as pure, pious, submissive, and domestic; her place was the private sphere of the home, a haven from amoral capitalism and dirty politics. As a "ministering angel," she tended the spiritual and emotional needs of husband and children. However, woman retained her purity and moral superiority only so long as she remained at home (Welter 1976, 21).

The concept of woman contained a contradiction that became apparent as pious women responded to the moral evils of prostitution, alcohol abuse, and slavery. Despite their supposed natural moral superiority, women were attacked for public efforts to eliminate these evils. Women who joined moral reform, temperance, and abolition societies and made speeches, held conventions, and published newspapers entered the public sphere; thereby, in the eyes of society, they lost their "womanliness" and their claim to purity. The woman's rights movement arose out of this contradiction.

The careers of early women reformers illustrate how woman's rights agitation emerged from other reform efforts. Abolitionists Maria W. Miller Stewart, Sojourner Truth, and Sarah and Angelina Grimké discovered that being a woman and speaking publicly were seen as mutually exclusive. A woman who spoke violated her nature. Maria W. Miller Stewart, for example, acknowledged that by speaking publicly to men and women, she had made herself "a hissing and a reproach." A major source of criticism was the clergy, who used the Bible, particularly the epistles of Paul, to argue that pure and pious women should remain silent.

Despite theological resistance to women's public reform activities, Protestantism was an important source of woman's rights ideology. The core of Protestantism is the notion that worshipers need no one to intercede for them with God; they can read and interpret the Scriptures for themselves. Instead of a limited priesthood, there is a priesthood of all believers. That notion is consistent with the individualism implicit in natural rights philosophy, and women used it to justify their right to speak on moral questions and to challenge scriptural interpretations that reduced woman's sphere of activities.

The struggle for the right to speak was hindered by biological misinformation, which was used to buttress arguments for excluding woman from higher education and political activity. On average, women were smaller then men. It was assumed that they also had smaller brains, brains presumably too small to sustain the rational deliberation required in politics and business. Moreover, their smaller, and, presumably more delicate and excitable nerves, it was held, could not tolerate the pressures of public debate or the marketplace. Menarche, the onset of menstruation, was viewed as a physical cataclysm that rendered women unfit for normal activity. Harvard medical professor Dr. Edward Clarke (1873) argued against higher education for women on the grounds that the blood needed to sustain development of the ovaries and womb would be diverted to the brain, which he believed was a major cause of serious illness in women.

In a rare deviation from individualistic principles, opponents sometimes argued that women should be excluded from public life on the grounds that the family rather than the individual was the fundamental unit of society. The family was to be represented in public by the husband, while the wife confined herself to domestic concerns. Women responded that, according to natural rights theory, no one could be represented by another without her consent, and they pointed to the laws that oppressed married women as evidence of how poorly husbands had represented the interests of their wives.

Problems created by the need to justify their right to speak were compounded by the powerlessness of their female listeners. Women speakers faced the dual challenge of empowering women and of appealing to males, who held virtually all political and economic power. In responding to the contradictory demands involved in appearing womanly while speaking, advocates sometimes used a "feminine" style that mirrored the experiences of women. Women learned the arts of housewifery and child-rearing from other women in supervised internships that combined expert advice with trial and error. In the same way, women speakers relied on personal experience coupled with examples to recreate the processes by which they had arrived at conclusions; they invited women in the audience to collaborate in making arguments and to test claims against their knowledge. In this type of rhetorical style, the speaker adopted a personal tone, audience members were treated as peers, with an emphasis on identification, and arguments unfolded inductively. Such a style had the advantage of making the speaker appear conventionally feminine; it appealed to women in audiences even as it encouraged them to participate actively in reaching conclusions instead of accepting claims passively.

Woman's rights activism was constrained by the legal reality. In New York in 1848, at the time of the first woman's rights convention at Seneca Falls, a married woman had no right to retain her own earnings, to control her children, to make a contract, to bring a lawsuit, or to make a will. She owned only what she inherited or received as a gift, but she could not bequeath her property, and if it was sold, the proceeds belonged to her husband. Her husband had absolute control of their children; in the rare case of divorce, they belonged to him, no matter how unfit he might be and regardless of fault. He might will them to another guardian, along with the entirety of the estate amassed in marriage. If a husband died without leaving a will, the law was ruthless. The survivor received a "widow's portion," at best, one-third of the estate. The remainder reverted to trustees, if there were children, or to the state, if there were none.

In the period prior to the Civil War, these oppressive laws were the major target of woman's rights activities. The laws were attacked at their conventions, which called public attention to the vulnerabilities of wives. Through exercise of the power to petition, women gained hearings from state legislatures and struggled to appeal to males, sometimes by arguing that improving the lot of wives and mothers would greatly increase their ability to perform their traditional duties, sometimes by arguing from natural rights principles. The legal changes that some states enacted were not due solely to the efforts of woman's rights activists. Rapid industrialization, for example, created pressure for legal reforms that would ease commercial transactions. However, most states made no such changes, and the temperance movement that caught fire after 1874 was fueled by the problems of married women who were legally and economically at the mercy of their drunkard husbands.

From its earliest beginnings, there were conflicts between those who saw woman's rights as a struggle for a broad array of causes leading to woman's emancipation and those whose chief concern was woman suffrage, illustrated by the debate at the national woman's rights convention of 1860. These ideological differences were exacerbated by events following the Civil War.

When war came in 1861, women ceased their agitation to devote themselves to ending slavery and supporting the Union effort. Elizabeth Cady Stanton and Susan B. Anthony headed a drive to gather signatures on petitions in support of what became the Thirteenth Amendment to the Constitution abolishing slavery. The U.S. Sanitary Commission was organized to provide for the "comfort, security, and health of the Army." Dorothea Dix, prison reformer and advocate for the insane, became Superintendent of Nurses. Dr. Elizabeth Blackwell, the first U.S. woman physician, helped recruit and train nurses. Clara Barton, who would later establish the American Red Cross, and Mary Ann "Mother" Bickerdyke went directly to the battlefields, bringing supplies and nursing the wounded. The Sanitary Commission established and ran hospitals and convalescent homes, inspected army camps and medical facilities, provided clothing, bandages, medicine, and extra food, all of which were inadequately supplied to the poorly provisioned Army. To carry on this work, some 7,000 branches of the Sanitary Commission raised some fifty million dollars and managed its disbursement.

Women believed that their Republican and abolitionist allies would reward their efforts with enfranchisement. Instead, a Fourteenth Amendment was proposed that, for the first time, inserted the word "male" into the U.S. Constitution, a change that would require passage of a constitutional amendment to effect woman suffrage. Women felt deeply betrayed when their former allies abandoned them, deferring woman's enfranchisement on the grounds that it was "the Negro's hour." The issue was political expediency. Suffrage for freedmen was controversial; suffrage for women was even more controversial. Republicans desired the political power they would gain from the votes of newly enfranchised Afro-American men in Southern and border states. They feared that if suffrage for freedmen were linked to woman suffrage, both would fail. The Fourteenth Amendment was ratified in 1868; the Fifteenth Amendment, prohibiting denial or abridgement of the right of citizens to vote, based on race, color, or previous condition of servitude, was ratified in 1870, without the inclusion of "sex."

Republicans and abolitionists saw their fears confirmed by the 1867 vote in Kansas on the first state referenda proposing enfranchisement for freedmen and for women. Both referenda failed, but the margin of defeat for woman suffrage was larger. These defeats were particularly noteworthy, given Kansas's special anti-slavery history and the campaigning of such renowned suffragists as Elizabeth Cady Stanton, Susan B. Anthony, and Lucy Stone. These advocates linked abolitionist appeals and natural rights principles to woman suffrage, but their persuasive impact was minimized when national and local Republican newspapers refused to support woman suffrage efforts and suppressed coverage of suffragists' speeches.

Frustration and anger led Anthony and Cady Stanton to make a momentous decision. During the Kansas campaign, they met southern dandy George Francis Train, a pro-slavery Democrat who campaigned for woman suffrage and against votes for Afro-American men. He offered them money to publish their own newspaper, the *Revolution*, and their former abolitionist allies in the woman's rights effort saw their acceptance as betrayal.

As a result, in 1869 the movement split. Cady Stanton, Anthony, and their supporters formed the National Woman Suffrage Association (NWSA), an all-woman organization with a broad and somewhat radical agenda. In response, Lucy Stone, Henry Blackwell, Julia Ward Howe, and others formed the American Woman Suffrage Association (AWSA), a more conservative group that devoted itself exclusively to woman suffrage. The NWSA retained its commitment to universal suffrage--rejecting the logic behind the Fourteenth Amendment and "the Negro's hour." The AWSA accepted that logic. The NWSA, located in New York City, believed the route to suffrage was a federal amendment; the AWSA, located in Boston, concentrated on achieving suffrage state by state. When in 1870 the AWSA began publishing the *Woman's Journal*, the more radical journal, the *Revolution*, was driven out of business. Until their merger as the National American Woman Suffrage Association (NAWSA) in 1890, these two groups would divide efforts for woman's advancement.

However, the activists did not surrender meekly in the face of defeats on the Fourteenth and Fifteenth Amendments. Based on arguments developed by attorney Francis Minor, spouse of Virginia Minor, president of the Missouri Woman Suffrage Association, women claimed their right to the ballot based on the definition of citizenship in the Fourteenth Amendment: "All persons born or naturalized in the United States and subject to the jurisdiction thereof, are citizens of the United States and of the state wherein they reside." Women claimed the ballot as a privilege of citizenship and argued that state laws prohibiting women from voting violated the amendment's provisions. To test their case, they attempted to register and vote in the 1872 election. When they were refused, as happened in most instances, they sued.

Susan B. Anthony persuaded registrars to accept her vote by promising to pay all court costs and fines if legal action were taken against them, but she was arrested and indicted under a law designed to prevent former supporters of the Confederacy from voting. In response, because she could not defend herself in court or testify on her own behalf, she began a speaking tour that took her to every postal district in the county in which her trial was to be held (Anthony 1874). She was so effective in making her case that the prosecutor requested and was granted a change of venue to the next county, but with the help of Matilda Joslyn Gage, her case was made to potential jurors in every postal district there as well. She was defeated when the judge, specially appointed for this trial, directed a verdict of guilty and fined her only one hundred dollars, a sum she publicly refused to pay.

When the argument that women had the votes was tested before the Supreme Court in *Minor v. Happersett* in 1875, the Court declared that the right to vote was not entailed in citizenship. In discussing that case, Carrie Chapman Catt, who led the final campaign for passage and ratification of the Nineteenth Amendment, wrote:

> To get the word "male" in effect out of the Constitution cost the women of the country 52 years of pauseless campaign thereafter. During that time they were forced to conduct 56 campaigns of referenda to male voters; 480 campaigns to get Legislatures to submit suffrage amendments to voters; 47 campaigns to get State Constitutional Conventions to write woman suffrage into State Constitutions; 277 campaigns to get state party platforms to include woman suffrage planks; 30 campaigns to get presidential party conventions to adopt woman suffrage planks in party platforms; and 19 campaigns with 19 successive Congresses. . . . It was a continuous, seemingly endless, chain of activity. (Walker 1951, 229)

The failures reflected in those statistics came because suffrage remained unpopular with a majority of men and women.

For the most part, men and women espoused the tenets of true womanhood and viewed the efforts of reformers with displeasure. True women were unselfish, devoting themselves to others; women activists were selfishly working for themselves, and although nearly all were married with many children, they were attacked as sour old maids who wanted to wear the pants and consign men to the kitchen and the nursery. As long as women relied primarily on natural rights arguments in defense of their cause, resistance remained high. However, from the beginning, there was a second line of argument, an argument based on benefits or expediency, that became more prominent after 1880 and made woman suffrage popular by making it more acceptable to conservative women and men. The woman who effected this change was Frances E. Willard, president of the Woman's Christian Temperance Union (WCTU) from 1879 to 1898 (Bordin 1980, 1986).

The argument from expediency or benefits treated woman suffrage as a means to good ends rather than a natural right. Willard called woman suffrage "home protection," the means by which women would protect themselves and their loved ones from the ravages of King Alcohol. The expediency argument presupposed that women as wives and mothers were essentially different from men--purer, more spiritual, concerned for others, and naturally domestic. These distinctive qualities meant that women would use their votes to purify politics (some called this "public housekeeping") and to protect wives and children. Most particularly, their votes would close the saloon and eliminate the brothels frequently housed above them. From this perspective, women were not moving into the public sphere, they were simply claiming as theirs what was necessary to protect the home and family. Obviously, arguments based on the benefits of women's enfranchisement contradicted arguments based on natural rights, a conflict that would become bitter in the 1920s in the struggle over an equal rights amendment.

During Frances Willard's tenure as president, the WCTU grew to be the largest women's organization in the United States, with 250,000 adult members and branches in every state and territory, all cities, and most local communities. This was in contrast to an estimated membership of 13,000 in the combined NAWSA in 1890. The WCTU was popular as an all-female organization in which women did not compete with men, as an organization that promoted goals approved by the Protestant clergy, and as an association committed to traditional values and traditional gender roles. The contradictions embedded in Willard's arguments exacerbated differences between Afro-American and white women activists. As segregation became law in the 1890s and lynchings of Afro-American men accused of raping white women became epidemic, Willard decried the lawlessness and violence, but she accepted the rape charges as true. Her straddling of the issue prompted Ida B. Wells, an Afro-American journalist, to attack Willard in the press.

Willard's stand on lynching exemplified the racism that pervaded much of the early women's movement. At the outset, the strong links to abolitionism created identification between women and Afro-Americans. Freed slave Sojourner Truth, for instance, spoke in support of the abolition of slavery and for woman's rights. In her *Appeal to Christian Women of the Southern States* (1836), Angelina Grimké called on the white women of the South to work against slavery because of its terrible effects on both slave and free women. The Grimké sisters, along with Lucretia Coffin Mott, were noteworthy as abolitionists who worked for full integration of Afro-Americans.

With passage of the Fourteenth Amendment, many suffragists, including Cady Stanton and Anthony, in frustration and anger, made highly racist statements that attacked Afro-Americans as well as recent immigrants (Davis 1981). As the movement focused on passage of a federal suffrage amendment, its racism increased. In their efforts not to alienate Southerners, needed for passage and ratification, suffragists rejected the appeals of Afro-American women for support against segregation and asked Afro-Americans not to appear at conventions or to march in parades. Although some, such as Ida B. Wells and Mary Church Terrell, were active in promoting woman suffrage, Afro-American experience with the Fourteenth and Fifteenth Amendments made them recognize that suffrage was no panacea. Afro-Americans supported the woman's ballot but directed most of their efforts to fighting against the evils of lynch law and segregation. They struggled to make the concerns of Afro-American women part of the larger effort for woman's rights.

Afro-American women led the fight against lynching, guided by Ida B. Wells. Sponsored by Afro-American women's clubs, she spoke, beginning in New York City in 1892, to reveal the facts she had uncovered in her investigation. Wells used facts gathered by the *Chicago Tribune* to show that only a tiny percentage of those lynched were even accused of rape; she used the statements of Southern white newspapers to demonstrate that the true motives were prevention of the growth of Afro-American economic and political power. The defense of white womanhood was merely an excuse, and the soundness of her analysis was reaffirmed in the 1930s by the all-white Association of Southern Women for the Prevention of Lynching (ASWPL), headed by Jessie Daniel Ames (Hall 1978, 1979).

Like Wells, Mary Church Terrell combined support of rights for women with support of rights for all Afro-Americans. She made a career of speaking and organizing against segregation, lynching, the sharecropping and tenant system that reduced Afro-Americans to peonage, and the convict lease system. In her speeches, she reviewed Afro-American women's incredible progress since slavery and attempted to reach out to white women for their help and support. Although she articulated and publicized Afro-American women's problems, and asked white women for their support, little was forthcoming.

The period from 1890 to 1915 has been called the "doldrums" of the movement because suffragists made little progress. Their arguments had become familiar, and they struggled to rejuvenate their appeals. During this period the great leaders of the early period died (Lucy Stone in 1893; Elizabeth Cady Stanton in 1902; Susan B. Anthony in 1906), and anti-suffrage organizations reached their greatest strength between 1896 and 1907 (Camhi 1973). Woman suffrage advocates were compelled to respond to opposition claims, for example, that suffrage would lead to child neglect and divorce and that because women could not fight they should not vote. Only when the Progressive movement began to flourish, particularly in the West, did the tide against woman suffrage turn.

Ultimately, women gained suffrage through their own varied exertions, aided by the climate created during World War I. Suffrage came because of long-term endeavors to persuade ordinary citizens of its rightness, epitomized by the speaking tours of the Rev. Dr. Anna Howard Shaw. Suffrage came because women organized to maximize the pressure on Congress to pass a federal amendment, symbolized by the administrative genius of Carrie Chapman Catt. Finally, suffrage came because militant agitation, exemplified by the work of Alice Paul and the National Woman's Party (NWP), put that issue at the top of the political agenda.

Anna Howard Shaw began her work for woman's rights in 1881 as a lecturer for the Massachusetts Woman Suffrage Association. In 1887 she became a paid speaker for the AWSA and continued in that role for the NAWSA until her death in 1919. During the last forty years of her life, Shaw spoke in every state, delivering hundreds of speeches each year, often speaking eight times a day. The NAWSA's own history claimed that Shaw won more people to woman suffrage than any other advocate (Catt and Shuler 1923, 268-269).

Like many others, Shaw based her arguments on the three key sources of suffragist ideology: natural rights, the Judeo-Christian tradition, and evolutionary progress. As a public advocate, Shaw had to be a skilled entertainer as well as a forceful persuader, and her speeches are full of fascinating stories and humorous anecdotes. For instance, in her 1913 presidential address, she responded to the notion that women were too emotional to vote:

> I had heard so much about our emotionalism that I went to the last Democratic national convention . . .

> to observe the calm repose of the male politicians. I saw some men take a picture of one gentleman whom they wanted elected . . . they were followed by hundreds of other men screaming and yelling, shouting and singing the "Houn' Dawg.". . . I saw men jump upon the seats and throw their hats in the air and shout. . . . No hysteria about it--just patriotic loyalty, splendid manly devotion to principle. And so they went on and on until 5 o'clock in the morning--the whole night long. . . . I have been to many women's conventions in my day but I never saw a woman leap on a chair and take off her bonnet and toss it up in the air and shout. . . . I never heard a body of women whooping and yelling for five minutes when somebody's name was mentioned in the convention. But we are willing to admit that we are emotional. I have actually seen women stand up and wave their handkerchiefs. I have even seen them take hold of hands and sing, "Blest be the tie that binds." (HWS 5:371)

Shaw's speeches made the idea of woman suffrage less threatening to ordinary male voters and their wives.

However, persuasive individuals were not enough. The movement needed skilled leadership, which it found in Carrie Chapman Catt, NAWSA president from 1900 to 1904 and from 1915 to 1920. In 1916 she announced her "Winning Plan" to trusted lieutenants and swore them to secrecy to prevent arousing the opposition. Her plan was based on a hard-nosed assessment of what was possible, and it combined precinct-level organization, state-by-state efforts, and lobbying Congress for passage of a federal amendment. Catt was deeply influenced by ideas of evolutionary progress drawn from Charles Darwin and Herbert Spencer. She believed that because self-government was right, its spread was inevitable, and she believed that because opposition to woman's rights was irrational, based on ignorance and prejudice, it would be overcome.

During the doldrums of the movement, politicians ignored suffrage because their constituents seemed not to support it. In 1912, Alice Paul organized what became the National Woman's Party (NWP) to demonstrate how strongly women wanted the vote and to demand that a federal amendment be passed immediately. She brought to the suffrage movement a belief in the value of militant agitation that she had learned in England working with radical "suffragettes" Emmeline and Christabel Pankhurst. She and her cohorts organized parades, picketed the White House and Congress, and burned a paper effigy of President Wilson as well as copies of his speeches. These tactics demonstrated women's intense desire for the ballot; they captured and held the attention of the public, the President, and the Congress; and they highlighted the contrast between the democratic principles for which the war was being fought and the nation's treatment of women. They also provoked harsh reprisals; more than 300 women were arrested, detained, tried, and imprisoned during the second Wilson administration. However, because no legal basis for the arrests existed (Flexner 1959, 287), and because imprisoned women, demanding to be treated as political prisoners, refused to eat and were brutally force-fed, their actions generated considerable public attention and sympathy.

Ultimately, women's varied efforts succeeded. President Wilson addressed Congress to urge passage, and, after a number of delays, occasioned by defeats in the Senate, on May 21, 1919, the House re-passed the amendment, this time followed by Senate passage on June 4. The ratification campaign quickly followed, facilitated by the exceptional organizing of the NAWSA. The Nineteenth Amendment was ratified on August 26, and all U.S. women were eligible to vote in the 1920 election.

Tragically, suffrage turned out to be only a minor victory. Most women did not vote; those who voted did not vote as a bloc and so had little political leverage. As the Depression eroded most of the gains women had made in higher education and the professions, women learned how little they had gained through the ballot. Women's legal and economic oppression continued, and the second, modern movement became inevitable.

Although earlier activists worked for the advancement of women, the first group to claim "feminism" as a label was the National Woman's Party. A 1927 editorial in *Equal Rights* affirmed: "Feminism is the only word in the language that precisely describes the purpose of our own organism" (Nelson 1976, 245). In this respect as in others, the NWP is a direct link between the early and the contemporary women's movements. In 1923, on the seventy-fifth anniversary of the Seneca Falls convention, the NWP introduced an equal rights amendment in Congress, an amendment regularly reintroduced until its passage in 1972. In 1985, the amendment failed ratification, but efforts to obtain its passage continue.

One of the most visionary members of the NWP was Crystal Eastman, a lawyer and socialist. She argued against the NWP's focus on passage of an equal rights amendment and for a broad feminist agenda. In a lecture delivered in 1920 after women had won the vote, she set forth basic goals:

> What is the problem of women's freedom? It seems to me to be this: how to arrange the world so that women can be human beings, with a chance to exercise their infinitely varied gifts in infinitely varied ways, instead of being destined by

> the accident of their sex to one field of activity--housework and child-raising. And second, if and when they choose housework and child-raising, to have that occupation recognized by the world as work, requiring a definite economic reward and not merely entitling the performer to be dependent on some man. (1920, 24)

The aims she described continue to challenge contemporary feminists.

The works collected in this volume are offered in order to make a significant body of U.S. women's rhetoric available to scholars, and to challenge those who explore rhetorical literature to incorporate our mothers as well as our fathers into their studies.

Man Cannot Speak for Her

1

Maria W. Miller Stewart, Lecture Delivered at the Franklin Hall, 1832

By her own account, Maria Miller was born in 1803, orphaned and "bound out" to a clergyman's family five years later, married to James W. Stewart in 1826, and widowed three years later. Shortly after her religious conversion in 1831, she brought a manuscript to the Boston office of William Lloyd Garrison and Isaac Knapp, publishers of the **Liberator.** *This was excerpted in their paper but printed in its entirety as a pamphlet, "Religion And The Pure Principles of Morality, The Sure Foundation On Which We Must Build"* (1831). *A year later they printed "Meditations from the Pen of Mrs. Maria W. Stewart." During 1832 and 1833, Miller Stewart made three public lectures in Boston,*[1] *each of which was reprinted in the* **Liberator.** *In 1835, Garrison published the collected* **Productions of Mrs. Maria W. Stewart.** *After her farewell address, delivered on September 21, 1832, she left Boston for New York, where she was tutored by young Afro-American women intellectuals and became a member of a Female Literary Society* (**Meditations** 1879, 10)*; eventually she became*

---

1 "Franklin Hall, at No. 16 Franklin Street in Boston, was the site of regular monthly meetings of the New England Anti-Slavery Society" (Richardson 1987, 45).

a public school teacher. After losing her job in 1852, she moved to Baltimore, where she opened a school that later failed. During the Civil War she went to Washington, D.C., where she opened another school, but after the Freedmen's Hospital opened, she worked there as a matron; in 1871, she opened a Sunday school. In 1879, she brought out a new edition of her **Meditations** *adding a preface that included testimonial letters and biographical data. She died on December 17, 1879, 50 years to the day after the death of her husband.*

This lecture was probably her second public speech (Richardson 1987, xix), *and as the text itself makes clear, it was addressed to an audience of mixed race and sex, although a majority of those who heard it and who subscribed to the* **Liberator** *were Afro-Americans* (Quarles 1969, 20). *Her message, here and elsewhere, exhorted Afro-Americans to self-help, appealed to white women for sympathetic identification, and to one and all refuted colonization as a solution to slavery and relentlessly described the racism that made the lives of free Afro-Americans in the North little different from those of slaves.*

While her language strongly reflected the period in which she spoke, her views prefigured those of later speakers. Her descriptions of the obstacles thrown up by racism were very like those described by Mary Church Terrell in 1906, and while she advocated "plead[ing] our cause before the whites", she was as adamant as Ida B. Wells in 1892 in urging Afro-Americans to help themselves. Finally, like many Afro-American speakers throughout history, her speeches evinced intense religious commitments, including belief in God's special promises to "Ethiopia." Like Angelina Grimké [Weld] and others of the period, she relied heavily on the authority of the Bible; as she wrote: "I have borrowed much of my language from the holy Bible." The criticism she braved as a woman speaker, to which she referred in this speech, is evidence of the link between women's reform efforts in other causes, such as abolitionism, and their recognition that such efforts were indivisible from a struggle for woman's rights, particularly her right to speak and agitate for moral reform. The text is from **Productions of Mrs. Maria W. Stewart** (1835, 51-56).

Why sit ye here and die? If we say we will go to a foreign land, the famine and the pestilence are there, and there we shall die. If we sit here, we shall die. Come let us plead our cause before the whites: if they save us alive, we shall live--and if they kill us, we shall but die.[2]

Methinks I hear a spiritual interrogation--'Who shall go forward, and take off the reproach that is cast upon the people of color? Shall it be a woman?'[3] And my heart made this reply--'If it is thy will, be it even so, Lord Jesus!'

I have heard much respecting the horrors of slavery; but may Heaven forbid that the generality of my color throughout these United States should experience any more of its horrors than to be a servant of servants, or

---

[2] This is a paraphrase of 2 Kings 7:3-4, in which four leprous men ask, "Why sit we here until we die? If we say, We will enter into the city, then the famine is in the city, and we shall die there: and if we sit still here, we die also. Now therefore come, and let us fall unto the host of the Syrians: if they save us alive, we shall live; and if they kill us, we shall but die." Miraculously, they discovered that the Lord had frightened the Syrians who had all departed.

[3] "And David spake to the men that stood by him, saying, What shall be done to the man that killeth this Philistine [Goliath], and taketh away the reproach from Israel?" (1 Sam. 17:26).

hewers of wood and drawers of water![4] Tell us no more of southern slavery; for with few exceptions, although I may be very erroneous in my opinion, yet I consider our condition but little better than that. Yet, after all, methinks there are no chains so galling as the chains of ignorance--no fetters so binding as those that bind the soul, and exclude it from the vast field of useful and scientific knowledge. O, had I received the advantages of early education, my ideas would, ere now, have expanded far and wide; but, alas! I possess nothing but moral capability--no teachings but the teachings of the Holy Spirit.

I have asked several individuals of my sex, who transact business for themselves, if providing our girls were to give them the most satisfactory references, they would not be willing to grant them an equal opportunity with others? Their reply has been--for their own part, they had no objection; but as it was not the custom, were they to take them into their employ, they would be in danger of losing the public patronage.

And such is the powerful force of prejudice. Let our girls possess what amiable qualities of soul they may; let their characters be fair and spotless as innocence itself; let their natural taste and ingenuity be what they may; it is impossible for scarce an individual of them to rise above the condition of servants. Ah! why is this cruel and unfeeling distinction? Is it merely because God has made our complexion to vary? If it be, O shame to soft, relenting humanity! "Tell it not in Gath! publish it not in the

---

[4] "And Joshua made them [the men of Gideon, Hivites] that day hewers of wood and drawers of water for the congregation, and for the altar of the Lord, even unto this day, in the place which he should choose" (Josh. 9:27). See also the curse of Noah on his younger son Ham (Gen. 9:25).

streets of Askelon!"[5] Yet, after all, methinks were the American free people of color to turn their attention more assiduously to moral worth and intellectual improvement, this would be the result: prejudice would gradually diminish, and the whites would be compelled to say, unloose those fetters!

> Though black their skins as shades
> of night,
> Their hearts are pure, their souls
> are white.

Few white persons of either sex, who are calculated for anything else, are willing to spend their lives and bury their talents[6] in performing mean, servile labor. And such is the horrible idea that I entertain respecting a life of servitude, that if I conceived of there being no possibility of my rising above the condition of a servant, I would gladly hail death as a welcome messenger. O, horrible idea, indeed! to possess noble souls aspiring after high and honorable acquirements, yet confined by the chains of ignorance and poverty to lives of continual drudgery and toil. Neither do I know of any who have enriched themselves by spending their lives as house-domestics, washing windows, shaking carpets, brushing boots, or tending upon gentlemen's tables. I can but die but expressing my sentiments; and I am as willing

---

[5] "The beauty of Israel is slain upon thy high places: how are the mighty fallen! Tell it not in Gath, publish it not in the streets of Askelon; lest the daughters of the Philistines rejoice, lest the daughters of the uncircumcised triumph" (2 Sam. 1:19-20).

[6] Refers to the parable of the talents in Matt. 25:14-30.

to die by the sword as the pestilence;[7] for I am a true born American; your blood flows in my veins, and your spirit fires my breast.

I observed a piece in the *Liberator* a few months since, stating that the colonizationists had published a work respecting us, asserting that we were lazy and idle. I confute them on that point. Take us generally as a people, we are neither lazy nor idle; and considering how little we have to excite or stimulate us, I am almost astonished that there are so many industrious and ambitious ones to be found; although I acknowledge, with extreme sorrow, that there are some who never were and never will be serviceable to society. And have you not a similar class among yourselves?

Again. It was asserted that we were "a ragged set, crying for liberty." I reply to it, the whites have so long and so loudly proclaimed the theme of equal rights and privileges, that our souls have caught the flame also, ragged as we are. As far as our merit deserves, we feel a common desire to rise above the condition of servants and drudges. I have learnt, by bitter experience, that continual hard labor deadens the energies of the soul, and benumbs the faculties of the mind; the ideas become confined, the mind barren, and, like the scorching sands of Arabia, produces nothing; or, like the uncultivated soil, brings forth thorns and thistles.[8]

---

[7] Penalties for Israelite disobedience are described this way: "And I will bring a sword upon you, that shall avenge the quarrel of my covenant: and when ye are gathered together within your cities, I will send the pestilence among you; and ye shall be delivered into the hand of the enemy" (Lev. 26:25).

[8] "And thorns shall come up in her places, nettles and brambles in the fortresses thereof: and it shall be an habitation of

Again, continual hard labor irritates our tempers and sours our dispositions; the whole system becomes worn out with toil and fatigue; nature herself becomes almost exhausted, and we care but little whether we live or die. It is true, that the free people of color throughout these United States are neither bought nor sold, nor under the lash of the cruel driver; many obtain a comfortable support; but few, if any, have an opportunity of becoming rich and independent; and the employments we most pursue are as unprofitable to us as the spider's web or the floating bubbles that vanish into air. As servants, we are respected; but let us presume to aspire any higher, our employer regards us no longer. And were it not that the King eternal has declared that Ethiopia shall stretch forth her hands unto God,[9] I should indeed despair.

I do not consider it derogatory, my friends, for persons to live out to service. There are many whose inclination leads them to aspire no higher; and I would highly commend the performance of almost any thing for an honest livelihood; but where constitutional strength is wanting, labor of this kind, in its mildest form, is painful. And doubtless many are the prayers that have ascended to Heaven from Afric's daughters for strength to perform their work. Oh, many are the tears that have been shed for the want of that strength! Most of our color have dragged out a miserable existence of servitude from the cradle to the grave. And what literary acquirements can be made, or useful knowledge derived, from either maps, books, or charts, by those who continually drudge from Monday morning until Sunday noon? O, ye fairer sisters, whose hands are never soiled, whose nerves and muscles are never strained, go

---

dragons, and a court for owls" (Isa. 34:13).

[9] Ps. 68:31 reads "Ethiopia shall soon stretch out her hands unto God."

learn by experience! Had we had the opportunity that you have had, to improve our moral and mental faculties, what would have hindered our intellects from being as bright, and our manners from being as dignified as yours? Had it been our lot to have been nursed in the lap of affluence and ease, and to have basked beneath the smiles and sunshine of fortune, should we not have naturally supposed that we were never made to toil? And why are not our forms as delicate, and our constitutions as slender, as yours? Is not the workmanship as curious and complete? Have pity upon us, have pity upon us, O ye who have hearts to feel for others' woes; for the hand of God has touched us. Owing to the disadvantages under which we labor, there are many flowers among us that are

> ----born to bloom unseen,
> And waste their fragrance on the desert air.[10]

My beloved brethren, as Christ has died in vain for those who will not accept of offered mercy, so will it be vain for the advocates of freedom to spend their breath in our behalf, unless with united hearts and souls you make some mighty efforts to raise your sons and daughters from the horrible state of servitude and degradation in which they are placed. It is upon you that woman depends; she can do but little besides using her influence: and it is for her sake and yours that I have come forward and made myself a hissing and a reproach among the people;[11]

---

[10] "Full many a flower is born to bloom unseen,/ And waste its sweetness on the desert air" (Thomas Gray, "Elegy Written in a Country Churchyard," 1751).

[11] "Because for thy sake I have borne reproach; shame hath covered my face" (Ps. 69:7); "Jerusalem, and the cities of Judah,

for I am also one of the wretched and miserable daughters of the descendants of fallen Africa. Do you ask, why are you wretched and miserable? I reply, look at many of the most worthy and interesting of us doomed to spend our lives in gentlemen's kitchens. Look at our young men, smart, active, and energetic, with souls filled with ambitious fire; if they look forward, alas! what are their prospects? They can be nothing but the humblest laborers, on account of their dark complexions; hence many of them lose their ambition, and become worthless. Look at our middle-aged men, clad in their rusty plaids and coats; in winter, every cent they earn goes to buy their wood and pay their rents; their poor wives also toil beyond their strength, to held support their families. Look at our aged sires, whose heads are whitened with the frosts of seventy winters, with their old wood-saws on their backs. Alas, what keeps us so? Prejudice, ignorance, and poverty. But ah! methinks our oppression is soon to come to an end; yea, before the Majesty of heaven, our groans and cries have reached the ears of the Lord of Sabaoth.[12] As the prayers and tears of Christians will avail the finally impenitent nothing; neither will the prayers and tears of the friends of humanity avail us any thing, unless we possess a spirit of virtuous

---

and the kings thereof, and the princes thereof, to make them a desolation, an astonishment, an hissing, and a curse, as it is this day" (Jer. 25:18).

[12] "And as Esaias said before, Except the Lord of Sabaoth had left us a seed, we had been as Sodoma and been made like unto Gomorrha" (Rom. 9:29); "Behold the hire of the labourers who have reaped down your fields, which is of you kept back by fraud, crieth: and the cries of them which have reaped are entered into the ears of the Lord of sabaoth" (James 5:4).

emulation within our breasts. Did the pilgrims, when they first landed on these shores, quietly compose themselves, and say, "the Britons have all the money and all the power, and we must continue their servants forever?" No; they first made powerful efforts to raise themselves, and then God raised up those illustrious patriots, WASHINGTON and LAFAYETTE, to assist and defend them. And, my brethren, have you made a powerful effort? Have you prayed the Legislature for mercy's sake to grant you all the rights and privileges of free citizens, that your daughters may rise to that degree of respectability which true merit deserves, and your sons above the service situations which most of them fill?

2

Address, Convention of Anti-Slavery Women, 1838

On Thursday afternoon, May 17, 1838, Sara T. Smith, on behalf of the Business Committee, presented this address, which was read and adopted, to the second Anti-Slavery Convention of American Women. The convention was meeting in Pennsylvania Hall in Philadelphia, a hall built by abolitionists when they were refused the right to use churches or to rent halls for their meetings. The Anti-Slavery Convention of American Women was interracial, a practice so inflammatory that the mayor of Philadelphia asked them to cease, but his request was refused. The evening after the speech was delivered, a mob burned Pennsylvania Hall to the ground. The Convention of American Women continued its interracial meetings in the home of one of its members. This speech was printed in the **History of Pennsylvania Hall,** (*History* 1838, 131-134), *and published separately as* **Address To Anti-Slavery Societies in Behalf of the Anti-Slavery Convention of American Women Assembled at Philadelphia, 1838** (1838, 3-14), *from which this text is taken.*

Dear Friends:--In that love for our cause which knows not the fear of man, we address you, in confidence that our motives will be understood and regarded. We fear not censure from you for going beyond the circle which has been drawn around us by physical force, by mental usurpation, by the usages of ages--not any one of which, can we admit, gives the right to prescribe it; else might the monarchs of the old world sit firmly on their thrones--the nobility of Europe lord it over the man of low degree--the chains we are now seeking to break continue riveted on the neck of the slave. Our faith goes not back to the wigwam of the savage, or to the castle of the feudal chief, but would rather soar with hope to that period when "*right* alone shall make *might*"--when the truncheon and the sword shall lie useless--when the intellect and the heart shall speak and be obeyed--when "He alone whose right it is, shall rule and reign in the hearts of the children of men."

We are told that it is not within the "province of woman," to discuss the subject of slavery; that it is a "political question," and we are "stepping out of our sphere," when we take part in its discussion. It is not true that it is *merely* a political question,--it is likewise a question of justice, of humanity, of morality, of religion; a question which, while it involves considerations of immense importance to the welfare and prosperity of our country, enters deeply into the home-concerns, the every-day feelings of millions of our fellow beings. Whether the laborer shall receive the reward of his labor, or be driven daily to *unrequited* toil--whether he shall walk erect in the dignity of conscious manhood, or be reckoned among the beasts which perish--whether his bones and sinews shall be his own, or another's--whether his child shall receive the protection of its natural guardian, or be ranked among the live-stock of the estate, to be disposed of as the caprice or interest of the master may dictate--whether the sun of knowledge shall irradiate the hut of the peasant, or the murky cloud of ignorance brood darkly over it--whether "every one shall have liberty to worship God according to the dictates of his own conscience," or man assume the prerogative of Jehovah, and impiously seek to plant himself upon the throne of the Almighty; these considerations are all involved in the question of liberty or slavery.

And is a subject comprehending interests of such magnitude, merely a "political question," and one in which woman "can take no part without losing something of the modesty and gentleness which are her most appropriate ornaments"? May not the "ornament of a meek and quiet spirit" [1 Pet. 3:4] exist with an upright mind and enlightened intellect, and must woman necessarily be less gentle because her heart is open to the claims of humanity, or less modest because she feels for the degradation of her enslaved sisters, and would stretch forth her hand for their rescue?

By the Constitution of the United States, the whole physical power of the North is pledged for the suppression of domestic insurrections, and should the slaves, maddened by oppression, endeavor to shake off the yoke of the task-master, the men of the North are bound to make common cause with the tyrant, and put down, at the point of the bayonet, every effort on the part of the slave, for the attainment of his freedom. And when the father, husband, son, and brother shall have left their homes to mingle in the unholy warfare, "to become the executioners of their brethren, or to fall themselves by their hands," will the mother, wife, daughter, and sister feel that they have no interest in this subject? Will it be easy to convince them that it is no concern of theirs, that their homes are rendered desolate, and their habitations the abodes of wretchedness? Surely this consideration is of itself sufficient to arouse the slumbering energies of woman, for the overthrow of a system which thus threatens to lay in ruins the fabric of her domestic happiness; and she will not be deterred from the performance of her duty to herself, her family, and her country, by the cry of "political question."

But admitting it to be a political

question, have we no interest in the welfare of our country? May we not permit a thought to stray beyond the narrow limits of our own family circle, and of the present hour? May we not breathe a sigh over the miseries of our countrymen, nor utter a word of remonstrance against the unjust laws that are crushing them to the earth? Must we witness "the headlong rage or heedless folly," with which our nation is rushing onward to destruction, and not seek to arrest its downward course? Shall we silently behold the land which we love with all the heart-warm affection of children, rendered a hissing and a reproach throughout the world, by this system which is already "tolling the death-bell of her decease among the nations?" No: the events of the last two years have "cast their dark shadows before," overclouding the bright prospects of the future, and shrouding the destinies of our country in more than midnight gloom, and we cannot remain inactive. Our country is as dear to us as to the proudest statesman, and the more closely our hearts cling to "our altars and our homes," the more fervent are our aspirations that every inhabitant of our land may be protected in his fireside enjoyments by just and equal laws; that the foot of the tyrant may no longer invade the domestic sanctuary, nor his hand tear asunder those whom God himself has united by the most holy ties. Let our course, then, still be *onward*! Justice, humanity, patriotism, every high and every holy motive urge us forward, and we dare not refuse to obey. The way of duty lies open before us, and though no pillar of fire[1] be visible to the outward sense, yet an unerring light shall illumine our pathway, guiding us through the sea of persecution and the wilderness of prejudice and error, to the promised land of freedom where "every man

---

[1] In their exodus, the Israelites were guided by a pillar of cloud by day and a pillar of fire by night (Exod. 13:21).

shall sit under his own vine and under his own fig-tree, and none shall make him afraid" [Micah 4:4].

The numerous small societies, scattered over the various districts of our extended country, we would greet with affectionate interest, with assured hope.

Though you are now only as glimmering lights on the hilltops, few and far between, yet if with all diligence these fires be kept burning, the surrounding country shall catch into flame--the chains fall from our brethren, and they unite with us in the jubilee song of thanksgiving. To bring about this glorious consummation of our hopes, we must be diligent in business, fervent in spirit; there must be the patient continuance in well doing of those who have been battling for the world's freedom, and who have counted nothing too near or too dear to sacrifice for their brethren in bonds; there must be an increase of energy and zeal in the many who have enlisted in the ranks of the friends of freedom. In joining an Anti-Slavery Society, we have set our names to no idle pledge. Let not any one member feel released from individual action; though by association we gain strength, yet it is strength to be used by each individual. The day, the hour calls imperatively for "doing with all our might" [Eccles. 9:10] what our hands find to do; the means are various. To some among us may be given the head to devise, to others the hand to execute; one may have time to devote, another money; let each give liberally of that which he or she possesses. Time, talents, influence, wealth, all are required, all will aid in the great enterprise. Let each one seriously inquire how he or she can availingly promote the cause, and in that department faithfully work. Let the aged counsel, the young execute; plead not inability: we much fear that many among us rest satisfied with "the name to live and yet are dead" [Rev. 3:1]. We give in our names as members of a society, pay a small annual subscription, and attend the meetings of the society. So far is well, but much more is needed for the accomplishment of our work. Ignorance yet remains to be enlightened, prejudice to be removed, injustice to be overthrown; and daily, almost hourly opportunities may offer to exert our strength where it can be availingly applied; and in order to do this keep yourselves informed of every Anti-Slavery movement. The editor of the *Emancipator* says: "Other things being equal, those are the most efficient abolitionists who are the most intelligent; and, commonly, the most good is done in those places where our books and publications are most circulated and read."

Another editor, commenting on the above, says:

> Every word of this is true. We know a society of 120 members. Forty-one Anti-Slavery papers are taken by them, and well circulated. The result is, it has had a rapid increase, it exerts a decisive influence on the community in which it is located, its prospects are most flattering, and no society has acted more efficiently in the petition of business. We know of another society of forty-six members, of whom only two or three take an Anti-Slavery paper. Societies will not act efficiently, they cannot act intelligently, they must backslide, if they do not supply themselves well with Anti-Slavery publications. Is it not a shame, that within the limits of societies numbering forty, sixty, seventy members, but two or three numbers of our paper should be taken? Nay, we have been told of one large society, that not only took no Anti-Slavery papers, but had never sent up delegates to our anniversaries, and, in fact, knew nothing about them. In the name of

> common sense, what good does such a society propose to accomplish? A light under a bushel might as well be put out. Organization without effort is all a farce. An artificial skeleton of dry bones has no more power, than the same bones had before they were jointed, wired, and so arranged as to constitute a *form* of life.

The taunting question heard so long and so untiringly repeated, "What has the North to do with slavery?" is most triumphantly answered by the practice of any one active, consistent member of an Anti-Slavery Society, as "we remember them in bonds as bound with them" [Heb. 13:3]. We find we have much to do, much even for ourselves. How slowly, yet how surely, do we feel the loosening of those bonds of prejudice wherewith we have been bound; how slow are we to feel the truth that all men are indeed "born free and equal?" How much do we find to do in acting up to this doctrine, in our closets, in our families, in our intercourse with the world, and by the wayside! The attentive consideration of what we owe to our colored brethren will dispose us to manifest our sympathy with them; and to show them by our conduct that we do not consider them as strangers and aliens; that we appreciate their manly struggles for the advancement of their race; and when favorable circumstances permit the escape of any beyond the prescribed length of the chain which has bound them, we cannot, we dare not join in the rude ridicule of the vulgar, the sneering contempt of the supercilious, or the mistaken kindness of the benevolent, who say that to awaken their sensibilities to their grievances would be cruelty in the extreme; that "where ignorance is bliss 'tis folly to be wise."[2] We

---

[2] From Thomas Gray, "On A Distant Prospect of Eton College" (1742).

see the fallacy of this hackneyed sentiment. Ignorance is not bliss--insensibility is not enjoyment. The objector little knows how tightly these fetters of caste have been drawn around, how deeply they have scarred their victim! how bitterly the injustice has been felt, and the more intensely, as it has been borne in silence, without either the solace of sympathy or the hope of relief.

The education of colored children recommends itself to abolitionists, as the most efficient means of raising them from their present despised condition. Many societies have established schools, (ought not all to do it?) wherein their younger members cheerfully devote a portion of their leisure time to the instruction, not only of the children, but of adults. The eagerness for learning manifested by most escaped from the house of bondage, their anxiety to improve the intervals of labor in acquiring knowledge, is too touching to be unnoticed or disregarded; it proves that their ignorance is not natural stupidity, that their degradation is the work of the oppressor, that the darkness in which they have been shrouded is a darkness to be felt. Let us, then, encourage and aid their earnest efforts, and though in many instances little can be done towards repairing their deep wrong in their own persons, yet we can incite them to provide by industry, frugality, and enterprise, all the blessings of freedom for their children. While we thus labor to restore to our colored brethren the rights of which they have been so long and so unjustly deprived, let us endeavor to come to the work with pure hearts and clean hands. Let us refuse to participate in the guilt of him "who useth his neighbor's service without wages and giveth him not for his work" [Jer. 22:13]. Whether we are guiltless of such participation while we continue to purchase and use the products of unrequited toil; becomes a question of serious import, and one which we recommend to your attentive consideration.

It is not necessary to enter into a

labored argument to prove that one of the main props of the system of slavery is the price paid by the inhabitants of non-slaveholding states and countries for the productions of the states in which slavery prevails. This is so evident that we presume none will dispute it. Considering the fact, then, as admitted, we would ask, what is the slaveholder but our agent, holding and using his human chattels for our benefit? and if it be true that "what a man does by another, he does himself" are we not partners with him in guilt? With what consistency, then, can we demand that he "undo the heavy burdens, and let the oppressed go free" [Isa. 58:6], while we continue to pay him for retaining them in bondage?

Our inconsistency, in this respect, does not escape the vigilant eyes of our opponents. Said a slaveholder to an abolitionist, "we make the sugar, and you buy it," thus plainly intimating that if they were culpable, we were far from blameless. We feel that on this point we have been verily guilty, and though the scales are falling from the eyes of many, yet much remains to be done among ourselves. And what are the motives that restrain us from acting consistently on this subject?

Are we unwilling to forego a few sensual gratifications in such a cause? Will we not consent to be somewhat more coarsely clothed and to deny the palate some of its wonted gratifications, rather than contribute to swell the burden of sighs and groans which unceasingly ascend from breaking hearts to the throne of Him "who executeth righteousness and judgment for all that are oppressed?" [Ps. 103:6].

In presenting to your consideration a few remarks on the subject of peace, we would not be understood as wishing to identify the anti-slavery cause with that of peace. We no more desire that the Anti-Slavery Society should become a Peace Society, than we wish it to be a Temperance, Bible, or Missionary Society. We believe that each of these objects may be best promoted by a distinct organization of its friends. Nor have we any intention of discussing the abstract question of the lawfulness of war, or the *right* of using violence in self defence. We would only suggest to you, the importance of carefully examining how far abolitionists are restrained from the use of such methods of defence, by their declaration of sentiments, issued at the time of the formation of the American Anti-Slavery Society; and what the influence of its use would probably be upon our cause. From these two positions only, do we feel at liberty to present the subject.

The declaration of sentiments of the Anti-Slavery Convention, assembled in Philadelphia in 1833, contrasts the principles and measures of abolitionists, and those of our revolutionary fathers, in the following language:

> *Their* principles led them to wage war against their oppressors, and to spill human blood, like water, in order to be free. *Ours* forbid the doing of evil that good may come, and lead us to reject and to entreat the oppressed to reject, the use of all carnal weapons for deliverance from bondage; relying solely upon those which are spiritual, and mighty, through God, to the pulling down of strong holds.
>
> *Their* measures were physical resistance--the marshalling in arms--the hostile array--the mortal encounter. *Ours* shall be such only as the opposition of moral purity to moral corruption--the destruction of error by the potency of truth, &c. (*Declaration* 1835).

Sentiments analogous to these have been incorporated into the constitutions of many Anti-Slavery Societies and are supposed to be adopted by abolitionists generally. Are we not, by them, bound utterly to reject the use of weapons of physical resistance, in our efforts to promote the emancipation of the slave? How far the restriction is applicable to cases of defence against invasion of the personal rights of abolitionists, while acting as such, each must decide for himself. We regard such a decision of so much importance, that we would urge upon you a serious reconsideration of the subject.

Without entering at all into a discussion of the *right* to adopt such measures, we think it may be shown that their use would injure rather than aid our cause. In the few instances where the lives of abolitionists have been in immediate peril, has it not been seen that non-resistance has as effectually shielded the individual, as an opposite course of conduct, while it won more honor to his principles? And has it not in all ages, among all classes of men, been established as a general truth, that, while physical strength and violence may be foiled or overcome, unresisting and forbearing meekness is almost omnipotent in the propagation of truth. The "wisdom of this world" [1 Cor.3:19] has never understood "the philosophy of forgiveness."[3] The patient endurance of injuries, the returning of good for evil, exert an influence on the human soul, so silent that it cannot be believed in, until it is felt, and yet so mighty, that it has been compared, by Him who "knew what was in man" [John 2:22], to heaping coals of fire on the head.[4] We deem it very desirable and important that so powerful an influence should be enlisted in behalf of the anti-slavery cause. The work that we have to perform is an *Herculean* task, and we would gladly avail ourselves of all righteous means of hastening its accomplishment.

It is a universally admitted truth, that opposition strengthens human purpose, unless

---

[3] See, for example, Luke 6:27-28.

[4] Prov. 25; 22; Rom. 12:20.

the judgment and conscience are convinced that the course pursued is wrong or inexpedient. Such conviction is not produced, is not designed to be produced, by the measures which we are discussing; therefore, they unfit the mind for the reception of truth, and the heart for righteous action. Thus the only influence which their use exerts upon the progress of anti-slavery principles, is deleterious. And even if it were admitted that they are sometimes necessary for the preservation of life, are there not those who love the cause of freedom and of God, with an ardor sufficient to induce them to suffer the loss of life, rather than injure the prosperity of that cause?

To pursue the discussion of this subject farther, would perhaps be to transcend our prescribed limits. We earnestly and respectfully commend it to the attention of our fellow laborers, especially to that portion of them who believe that Christianity justifies a resort to arms for self-preservation. Those who do not thus believe, of course, need not such arguments as we have presented.

Aware that a disposition to "prove all things" [1 Thess. 5:21], has ever been characteristic of abolitionists, we feel assured that by careful study, and fervent prayer, they will be enabled to choose right paths for their feet, and that, in the accomplishment of a work upon which God has so manifestly set his seal of approbation, his servants will not be left unaided by the illuminations of that Holy Spirit who was sent to guide them "into all truth" [John 16:13].

In looking back on the past, have we not much to encourage us to persevere in the work set before us? For a long period a solitary voice was heard crying in the wilderness;[5] now there is the shouting of a host. Then was demanded a little more sleep, a little more slumber; now there is the awakening of the

---

[5] Isa. 40:3; Matt. 3:3.

nation; and though not yet sufficiently aroused to discern friends in those who have shaken this false rest, yet if we fail not in our duty, there can be no more "folding of the hands to sleep" [Prov. 6:10], but our country will arise and go forth, clothed with majesty, and girded with power.

In behalf of the Anti-Slavery Convention of American Women, assembled in Philadelphia.

MARY S. PARKER,[6] *President*

ANNE W. WESTON[7],
MARTHA V. BALL[8],
JULIANA A. TAPPAN[9],
SARAH LEWIS, *Secretaries*

---

[6] Mary S. Parker, president of the Boston Female Anti-Slavery Society to whom Sarah Moore Grimké's *Letters on the Equality of the Sexes* were addressed.

[7] Ann W. Weston, teacher and sister of Maria Weston Chapman, who with her sisters Caroline, Deborah, and Maria ran a succession of anti-slavery fairs in Boston, beginning in 1834.

[8] Martha V. Ball, secretary of the Boston Female Anti-Slavery Society.

[9] Juliana A. Tappan, daughter of Lewis Tappan, wealthy New York merchant and financial backer of the anti-slavery movement, and an active member of the Ladies New York City Anti-Slavery Society.

3

Angelina Grimké [Weld], Address at Pennsylvania Hall, 1838

Angelina Grimké (1805-79) was the daughter of a South Carolina slaveowner. She and her sister Sarah came North and joined the abolitionist cause, speaking for anti-slavery in New York and Massachusetts. Their lectures were the beginning of major efforts to break the barriers against women speaking in public. Conflict over women's role in the movement would split the abolitionists, but this speech was given at a general meeting of male and female abolitionist societies, the first meeting at which "men and women acted together as moral beings" (Birney 1885, 24). *Two days before this address, Angelina was married to Theodore Weld, a prominent abolitionist, and this hour-long speech ended her meteoric career as a speaker. What follows are described as notes on the speech, a description contradicted by the finished artistry of the text. The comments in parenthesis are by the contemporary reporter and describe the scene inside and outside the hall during the speech. The text is from* **History of Pennsylvania Hall, Which Was Destroyed by a Mob on the 17th of May 1838** ed. Samuel Webb (1838, 123-26).

Men, brethren and fathers--mothers, daughters and sisters, what came ye out for to see? A reed shaken with the wind?[1] Is it curiosity merely, or a deep sympathy with the perishing slave, that has brought this large audience together? (*A yell from the mob without the building.*) Those voices without ought to awaken and call out our warmest sympathies. Deluded beings! "they know not what they do" [Luke 23:34]. They know not that they are undermining their own rights and their own happiness, temporal and eternal. Do you ask, "what has the North to do with slavery?" Hear it--hear it. Those voices without tell us that the spirit of slavery is *here*, and has been roused to wrath by our abolition speeches and conventions: for surely liberty would not foam and tear herself with rage,[2] because her friends are multiplied daily, and meetings are held in quick succession to set forth her virtues and extend her peaceful kingdom. This opposition shows that slavery has done its deadliest work in the hearts of our citizens. Do you ask, then, "what has the North to do?" I answer, cast out first the spirit of slavery from your own hearts, and then lend your aid to convert the South.[3] Each one present has a work to do, be his or her situation what it may, however limited their means, or insignificant their supposed influence. The great men of this country will not do this work; the church will never do it. A desire to please the world, to keep the favor or all parties and of all conditions, makes them dumb on this and every other unpopular subject. They have become worldly-wise, and therefore God, in his wisdom, employs them not to carry on his plans of reformation and salvation. He hath chosen the foolish things of the world to confound

---

[1] Matt. 11:7.

[2] Mark 9:18.

[3] Matt. 7:5.

the wise, and the weak to overcome the mighty.[4]

As a Southerner I feel that it is my duty to stand up here to-night and bear testimony against slavery. I have seen it--I have seen it. I know it has horrors that can never be described. I was brought up under its wing: I witnessed for many years its demoralizing influences, and its destructiveness to human happiness. It is admitted by some that the slave is not happy under the *worst* forms of slavery. But I have *never* seen a happy slave. I have seen him dance in his chains, it is true; but he was not happy. There is a wide difference between happiness and mirth. Man cannot enjoy the former while his manhood is destroyed, and that part of the being which is necessary to the making, and to the enjoyment of happiness, is completely blotted out. The slaves, however, may be, and sometimes are, mirthful. When hope is extinguished, they say, "let us eat and drink, for to-morrow we die" [Isa. 22:13]. (*Just then stones were thrown at the windows,--a great noise without, and commotion within.*)

What is a mob? What would the breaking of every window be? What would the levelling of this Hall be? Any evidence that we are wrong, or that slavery is a good and wholesome institution? What if the mob should now burst in upon us, break up our meeting and commit violence upon our persons-- would this be anything compared with what the slaves endure? No, no: and we do not remember them "as bound with them" [Heb. 13:3], if we shrink in the time of peril, or feel unwilling to sacrifice ourselves, if need be, for their sake. (*Great noise.*) I thank the Lord that there is yet life left enough to feel the truth, even though it rages at it--that conscience is not so completely seared as to be unmoved by the truth of the living God.

Many persons go to the South for a

---

[4] 1 Cor. 1:27-28.

season, and are hospitably entertained in the parlor and at the table of the slave-holder. They never enter the huts of the slaves; they know nothing of the dark side of the picture, and they return home with praises on their lips of the generous character of those with whom they had tarried. Or if they have witnessed the cruelties of slavery, by remaining silent spectators they have naturally become callous--an insensibility has ensued which prepares them to apologize even for barbarity. Nothing but the corrupting influence of slavery on the hearts of the Northern people can induce them to apologize for it; and much will have been done for the destruction of Southern slavery when we have so reformed the North that no one here will be willing to risk his reputation by advocating or even excusing the holding of men as property. The South know it, and acknowledge that as fast as our principles prevail, the hold of the master must be relaxed. (*Another outbreak of mobocratic spirit, and some confusion in the house.*)

How wonderfully constituted is the human mind! How it resists, as long as it can, all efforts made to reclaim from error! I feel that all this disturbance is but an evidence that our efforts are the best that could have been adopted, or else the friends of slavery would not care for what we say and do. The South know what we do. I am thankful that they are reached by our efforts. Many times have I wept in the land of my birth, over the system of slavery. I knew of none who sympathized in my feelings--I was unaware that any efforts were made to deliver the oppressed --no voice in the wilderness was heard calling on the people to repent and do works meet for repentance[5]--and my heart sickened within me. Oh, how should I have rejoiced to know that such efforts as these were being made. I only wonder that I had such feelings. I wonder

---

[5] Isa. 40:3; Matt. 3:3.

when I reflect under what influence I was brought up, that my heart is not harder than the nether millstone.[6] But in the midst of temptation I was preserved, and my sympathy grew warmer, and my hatred of slavery more inveterate, until at last I have exiled myself from my native land because I could no longer endure to hear the wailing of the slave. I fled to the land of Penn; for here, thought I, sympathy for the slave will surely be found. But I found it not. The people were kind and hospitable, but the slave had no place in their thoughts. Whenever questions were put to me as to his condition, I felt that they were dictated by an idle curiosity, rather than by that deep feeling which would lead to effort for his rescue. I therefore shut up my grief in my own heart. I remembered that I was a Carolinian, from a state which framed this iniquity by law. I knew that throughout her territory was continual suffering, on the one part, and continual brutality and sin on the other. Every Southern breeze wafted to me the discordant tones of weeping and wailing, shrieks and groans, mingled with prayers and blasphemous curses. I thought there was no hope; that the wicked would go on in his wickedness, until he had destroyed both himself and his country. My heart sunk within me at the abominations in the midst of which I had been born and educated. What will it avail, cried I in bitterness of spirit, to expose to the gaze of strangers the horrors and pollutions of slavery, when there is no ear to hear nor heart to feel and pray for the slave. The language of my soul was, "Oh tell it not in Gath, publish it not in the streets of Askelon" [2 Sam 1:20]. But how different do I feel now! Animated with hope, nay, with an assurance of the triumph of liberty and good will to man, I will lift up my voice like a trumpet, and show this people their trans-

---

[6] See, for example, Ps. 95:8 and Heb. 3:15.

gression,[7] their sins of omission toward the slave, and what they can do towards affecting Southern mind [sic], and overthrowing Southern oppression.

We may talk of occupying neutral ground, but on this subject, in its present attitude, there is no such thing as neutral ground. He that is not for us is against us, and he that gathereth not with us, scattereth abroad.[8] If you are on what you suppose to be neutral ground, the South look upon you as on the side of the oppressor. And is there one who loves his country willing to give his influence, even indirectly, in favor of slavery--that curse of nations? God swept Egypt with the besom of destruction,[9] and punished Judea also with a sore punishment, because of slavery. And have we any reason to believe that he is less just now?--or that he will be more favorable to us than to his own "peculiar people?" (*Shouting, stones thrown against the windows, &c.*)

There is nothing to be feared from those who would stop our mouths, but they themselves should fear and tremble. The current is even now setting fast against them. If the arm of the North had not caused the Bastille of slavery to totter to its foundation, you would not hear those cries. A few years ago, and the South felt secure, and with a contemptuous sneer asked, "Who are the abolitionists? The abolitionists are nothing?"--Ay, in one sense they were nothing, and they are nothing still. But in this we rejoice, that "God has chosen things that are not to bring to nought things that are" [1 Cor. 1:28]. (*Mob again disturbed the meeting.*)

We often hear the question asked, "What shall we do?" Here is an opportunity for

---

[7] Isa. 58:1.

[8] Matt. 12:30.

[9] Isa. 14:23.

doing something now. Every man and every woman present may do something by showing that we fear not a mob, and, in the midst of threatenings and revilings, by opening our mouths for the dumb and pleading the cause of those who are ready to perish.

To work as we should in this cause, we must know what Slavery is. Let me urge you then to buy the books which have been written on this subject and read them, and then lend them to your neighbors. Give your money no longer for things which pander to pride and lust, but aid in scattering "the living coals of truth"[10] upon the naked heart of this nation,--in circulating appeals to the sympathies of Christians in behalf of the outraged and suffering slave. But, it is said by some, our "books and papers do not speak the truth." Why, then, do they not contradict what we say? They cannot. Moreover the South has entreated, nay commanded us to be silent; and what greater evidence of the truth of our publications could be desired?

Women of Philadelphia! allow me as a Southern woman, with much attachment to the land of my birth, to entreat you to come up to this work. Especially let me urge you to petition. *Men* may settle this and other questions at the ballot-box, but you have no such right; it is only through petitions that you can reach the Legislature. It is therefore peculiarly *your* duty to petition. Do you say, "It does no good?" The South already turns pale at the number sent. They have read the reports of the proceedings of Congress, and there have seen that among other petitions were very many from the women of the North on the subject of slavery. This fact has called the attention of the South to the subject. How could we expect to have done more as yet? Men who hold the rod over slaves, rule in the councils of the nation: and they deny our right to petition and to remonstrate against

---

[10] Isa. 6:6-8.

abuses of our sex and of our kind. We have these rights, however, from our God. Only let us exercise them: and though often turned away unanswered, let us remember the influence of importunity upon the unjust judge,[11] and act accordingly. The fact that the South look with jealousy upon our measures shows that they are effectual. There is, therefore, no cause for doubting or despair, but rather for rejoicing.

It was remarked in England that women did much to abolish Slavery in her colonies.[12] Nor are they now idle. Numerous petitions from them have recently been presented to the Queen, to abolish the apprenticeship with its cruelties nearly equal to those of the system whose place it supplies. One petition two miles and a quarter long has been presented. And do you think these labors will be in vain? Let the history of the past answer. When the women of these States send up to Congress such a petition, our legislators will arise as did those of England, and say, "When all the maids and matrons of the land are knocking at our doors we must legislate." Let the zeal and love, the faith and works of our English sisters quicken ours--that while the slaves continue to suffer, and when they shout deliverance, we may feel the satisfaction of *having done what we could*.

---

[11] Luke 18: 1-6.

[12] "Anti-slavery reached its climax in the 1830s, sending over 4000 petitions to Parliament during three separate sessions, a feat unequalled by any other national movement. . . . Women began to petition *en masse* at the beginning of the 1830s. . . . In 1833 a single petition of 187,000 'ladies of England --a huge featherbed of a petition' was hauled into Parliament by four sturdy members" (Drescher 1982, 30, 33).

4

Declaration of Sentiments and Resolutions, 1848

The Declaration of Sentiments, a paraphrase of the Declaration of Independence, was authored by Mary Ann McClintock, Lucretia Coffin Mott, Elizabeth Cady Stanton, and Martha Coffin Wright, who also published the call for the convention. Although the call appeared for only one day in the **Seneca County Courier** *and Frederick Douglass's* **North Star**, *some 300 men and women attended the convention. According to the* **History of Woman Suffrage**, *following a number of speeches on the first day, "The Declaration having been freely discussed by many present, was . . . with some slight amendments adopted, and was signed by one hundred men and women"* (1:69). *Subsequently, after intensely hostile press reaction, many asked to have their names removed. Eleven resolutions were presented initially; at the last session, Coffin Mott proposed and spoke in support of #12. Only resolution #9 on woman suffrage was not unanimously adopted; it passed because of the strenuous efforts of former slave Frederick Douglass, an abolitionist speaker and publisher of the North Star. The texts of the Declaration of Sentiments and resolutions were published in* **HWS** 1:70-73, *and in the convention* **Proceedings** (1870, 4-7).

DECLARATION OF SENTIMENTS

When, in the course of human events, it becomes necessary for one portion of the family of man to assume among the people of the earth a position different from that which they have hitherto occupied, but one to which the laws of nature and of nature's God entitle them, a decent respect to the opinions of mankind requires that they should declare the causes that impel them to such a course.

We hold these truths to be self-evident: that all men and women are created equal; that they are endowed by their Creator with certain inalienable rights, that among these are life, liberty, and the pursuit of happiness; that to secure these rights governments are instituted, deriving their just powers from the consent of the governed. Whenever any form of government becomes destructive of these ends, it is the right of those who suffer from it to refuse allegiance to it, and to insist upon the institution of a new government, laying its foundation on such principles, and organizing its powers in such form as to them shall seem most likely to effect their safety and happiness. Prudence, indeed, will dictate that governments long established should not be changed for light and transient causes; and accordingly, all experience hath shown that mankind are more disposed to suffer, while evils are sufferable, than to right themselves by abolishing the forms to which they were accustomed. But when a long train of abuses and usurpations, pursuing invariably the same object evinces a design to reduce them under absolute despotism, it is their duty to throw off such government and to provide new guards for their future security. Such has been the patient sufferance of the women under this government, and such is now the necessity which constrains them to demand the equal station to which they are entitled.

The history of mankind is a history of repeated injuries and usurpations on the part of man toward woman, having in direct object the establishment of an absolute tyranny over her. To prove this, let facts be submitted to a candid world.

He has never permitted her to exercise her inalienable right to the elective franchise.

He has compelled her to submit to laws, in the formation of which she had no voice.

He has withheld from her rights which are given to the most ignorant and degraded men--both natives and foreigners.

Having deprived her of this first right of a citizen, the elective franchise, thereby leaving her without representation in the halls of legislation, he has oppressed her on all sides.

He has made her, if married, in the eye of the law, civilly dead.

He has taken from her all right in property, even to the wages she earns.

He has made her, morally, an irresponsible being, as she can commit many crimes with impunity, provided they be done in the presence of her husband. In the covenant of marriage, she is compelled to promise obedience to her husband, he becoming, to all intents and purposes, her master--the law giving him power to deprive her of her liberty, and to administer chastisement.

He has so framed the laws of divorce, as to what shall be the proper causes of divorce; in case of separation, to whom the guardianship of the children shall be given; as to be wholly regardless of the happiness of women--the law, in all cases, going upon a false supposition of the supremacy of man, and giving all power into his hands.

After depriving her of all rights as a married woman, if single and the owner of property, he has taxed her to support a government which recognizes her only when her property can be made profitable to it.

He has monopolized nearly all the profitable employments, and from those she is permitted to follow, she receives but a scanty remuneration.

He closes against her all the avenues to wealth and distinction, which he considers most honorable to himself. As a teacher of theology, medicine, or law, she is not known.

He has denied her the facilities for obtaining a thorough education--all colleges being closed against her.

He allows her in Church, as well as State, but a subordinate position, claiming Apostolic authority for her exclusion from the ministry, and, with some exceptions, from any public participation in the affairs of the Church.

He has created a false public sentiment, by giving to the world a different code of morals for men and women, by which moral delinquencies which exclude women from society, are not only tolerated but deemed of little account in man.

He has usurped the prerogative of Jehovah himself, claiming it as his right to assign for her a sphere of action, when that belongs to her conscience and to her God.

He has endeavored, in every way that he could, to destroy her confidence in her own powers, to lessen her self-respect, and to make her willing to lead a dependent and abject life.

Now, in view of this entire disfranchisement of one-half the people of this country, their social and religious degradation,--in view of the unjust laws above mentioned, and because women do feel themselves aggrieved, oppressed, and fraudulently deprived of their most sacred rights, we insist that they have immediate admission to all the rights and privileges which belong to them as citizens of the United States.

In entering upon the great work before us, we anticipate no small amount of misconception, misrepresentation, and ridicule; but we shall use every instrumentality within our power to effect our object. We shall employ agents, circulate tracts, petition the state and national legislatures, and endeavor to enlist the pulpit and the press in our behalf.

We hope this Convention will be followed by a series of Conventions, embracing every part of the country.

Firmly relying upon the final triumph of the Right and True, we do this day affix our signatures to this declaration. [*Names followed.*]

RESOLUTIONS

Whereas, The great precept of nature is conceded to be, "that man shall pursue his own true and substantial happiness." Blackstone,[1] in his *Commentaries* remarks, that this law of Nature being coeval with mankind, and dictated by God himself, is of course superior in obligation to any other. It is binding over all the globe, in all countries, and at all times; no human laws are of any validity if contrary to this, and such of them as are valid, derive all their force, and all their validity, and all their authority, mediately and immediately, from this original; therefore,

1. Resolved, That such laws as conflict, in any way, with the true and substantial happiness of woman, are contrary to the great precept of nature, and of no validity; for this is "superior in obligation to any other."
2. Resolved, That all laws which prevent woman from occupying such a station in society as her conscience shall dictate, or which place her in a position inferior to that of man, are contrary to the great precept of nature, and therefore of no force or authority.
3. Resolved, That woman is man's equal--was intended to be so by the Creator, and the

---

[1] Sir William Blackstone (1723-80), British jurist, author of the *Commentaries on the Laws of England* (4 vols., 1765-69), which ordered and clarified the chaos of English common law.

highest good of the race demands that she should be recognized as such.

4. Resolved, That the women of this country ought to be enlightened in regard to the laws under which they live, that they may no longer publish their degradation, by declaring themselves satisfied with their present position, nor their ignorance, by asserting that they have all the rights they want.

5. Resolved, That inasmuch as man, while claiming for himself intellectual superiority, does not accord to woman moral superiority, it is pre-eminently his duty to encourage her to speak, and teach, as she has an opportunity, in all religious assemblies.

6. Resolved, That the same amount of virtue, delicacy, and refinement of behavior, that is required of woman in the social state, should also be required of man, and the same transgressions should be visited with equal severity on both man and woman.

7. Resolved, That the objection of indelicacy and impropriety, which is so often brought against woman when she addresses a public audience, comes with a very ill-grace from those who encourage, by their attendance, her appearance on the stage, in the concert, or in feats of the circus.

8. Resolved, That woman has too long rested satisfied in the circumscribed limits which corrupt customs and a perverted application of the Scriptures have marked out for her, and that it is time she should move in the enlarged sphere which her great Creator has assigned her.

9. Resolved, That it is the duty of the women of this country to secure to themselves their sacred right to the elective franchise.

10. Resolved, That the equality of human rights results necessarily from the fact of the identity of the race in capabilities and responsibilities.

11. Resolved, therefore, That, being invested by the Creator with the same capabilities, and the same consciousness of responsi-

bility for their exercise, it is demonstrably the right and duty of woman, equally with man, to promote every righteous cause, by every righteous means; and especially in regard to the great subjects of morals and religions, it is self-evidently her right to participate with her brother in teaching them, both in private and in public, by writing and by speaking, by any instrumentalities proper to be used, and in any assemblies proper to be held; and this being a self-evident truth, growing out of the divinely implanted principles of human nature, any custom or authority adverse to it, whether modern or wearing the hoary sanction of antiquity, is to be regarded as a self-evident falsehood, and at war with mankind.

12. Resolved, That the speedy success of our cause depends upon the zealous and untiring efforts of both men and women, for the overthrow of the monopoly of the pulpit, and for the securing to woman an equal participation with men in the various trades, professions, and commerce.

5

Elizabeth Cady Stanton, Speech at the Seneca Falls Convention, 1848

This first speech marked the beginning of Cady Stanton's extraordinary career. Along with Lucretia Coffin Mott and Susan B. Anthony, she was one of the major figures in the early movement for woman's rights. In addition to being the moving force behind the Seneca Falls convention, she was also a founder and president (1851-53) of the New York Woman's Temperance Society, a founder and president (1866-69) of the American Equal Rights Association, a founder and president of the National Woman Suffrage Association (1869-90), and president of the merged National American Woman Suffrage Association (1890-92). She was an editor of the **Revolution** *(1868-70), of the first three volumes of the* **History of Woman Suffrage** *(1881-87), and the editor and chief contributor to the two volumes of the* **Woman's Bible** *(1895, 1898). She also published an autobiography,* **Eighty Years and More** (1898). *Throughout her life she was the movement's philosopher and its chief publicist, speaking and writing constantly. Although others made great contributions, during her lifetime she was the movement's greatest speaker. This speech is taken from the convention* **Proceedings** (1870, 3-19).

I should feel exceedingly diffident to appear before you at this time, having never before spoken in public, were I not nerved by a sense of right and duty, did I not feel the time had fully come for the question of woman's wrongs to be laid before the public, did I not believe that woman herself must do this work; for woman alone can understand the height, the depth, the length, and the breadth of her own degradation. Man cannot speak for her, because he has been educated to believe that she differs from him so materially, that he cannot judge of her thoughts, feelings, and opinions by his own. Moral beings can only judge of others by themselves. The moment they assume a different nature for any of their own kind, they utterly fail. The drunkard was hopelessly lost until it was discovered that he was governed by the same laws of mind as the sober man. Then with what magic power, by kindness and love, was he raised from the slough of despond[1] and placed rejoicing on high land.

Let a man once settle the question that a woman does not think and feel like himself, and he may as well undertake to judge of the amount of intellect and sensation of any of the animal creation as of woman's nature. He can know but little with certainty, and that but by observation.

Among the many important questions which have been brought before the public, there is none that more vitally affects the whole human family than that which is technically called Woman's Rights. Every allusion to the degraded and inferior position occupied by women all over the world has been met by scorn and abuse. From the man of highest mental cultivation to the most degraded wretch who staggers in the streets do we meet ridicule, and coarse jests, freely bestowed upon those

---

[1] The morass that Christian and Christiana had to cross in John Bunyan's *Pilgrim's Progress* (1675).

who dare assert that woman stands by the side of man, his equal, placed here by her God, to enjoy with him the beautiful earth, which is her home as it is his, having the same sense of right and wrong, and looking to the same Being for guidance and support. So long has man exercised tyranny over her, injurious to himself and benumbing to her faculties, that few can nerve themselves to meet the storm; and so long has the chain been about her that she knows not there is a remedy.

The whole social, civil and religious condition of woman is a subject too vast to be brought within the limits of one short lecture. Suffice it to say, for the present, wherever we turn, the history of woman is sad and dark, without any alleviating circumstances, nothing from which we can draw consolation.

As the nations of the earth emerge from a state of barbarism, the sphere of woman gradually becomes wider, but not even under what is thought to be the full blaze of the sun of civilization is it what God designed it to be. In every country and clime does man assume the responsibility of marking out the path for her to tread. In every country does he regard her as a being inferior to himself, and one whom he is to guide and control. From the Arabian Kerek, whose wife is obliged to steal from her husband to supply the necessities of life; from the Mahometan [sic] who forbids pigs, dogs, women, and other impure animals, to enter a Mosque, and does not allow a fool, madman or woman to proclaim the hour of prayer; from the German who complacently smokes his meerschaum, while his wife, yoked with the ox, draws the plough through its furrow; from the delectable carpet-knight, who thinks an inferior style of conversation adapted to woman, to the legislator, who considers her incapable of saying what laws shall govern her, is the same feeling manifested.

In all eastern countries she is a mere slave, bought and sold at pleasure. There are many differences in habits, manners and customs among the heathen nations of the Old World, but there is little change for the better in woman's lot. She is either the drudge of man, to perform all the hard labor of the field, and all the menial duties of the hut, tent or house, or she is the idol of his lust, the mere creature of his varying whims and will. Truly has she herself said in her best estate,

> I am a slave, a favored slave,
> To share his pleasures and seem very blest,
> When weary of these fleeting charms and me
> There yawns the sack, and yonder the rolling sea,
> What, am I then a toy for dotards play
> To wear but till the gilding frets away?

In Christian countries, boasting a more advanced state of civilization and refinement, woman still holds a position infinitely inferior to man.

In France the Salic Law tells much, although it is said that woman there has ever had great influence in all political revolutions.[2] In England she seems to have advanced a little, there she has a right to the throne, and is allowed to hold some other offices, and to vote on some questions. But in the United States of America, in a republic based on the theory that no just government can be formed without the consent of the governed, woman has no right either to hold office, or to the elective franchise. She stands at this moment unrepresented in this government, her rights and interests wholly overlooked.

---

[2] Salic law prohibited a woman from succeeding to the titles or offices of noble families, including the throne.

There is a class of men who believe in their natural, inborn, inbred superiority, and their heaven-descended right to dominion over the fish of the sea, the fowl of the air, and last, though not least, the immortal being called woman. I would recommend this class to the attentive perusal of their Bibles--Gen. 1:27; to historical research, to foreign travel, to a closer observation of the manifestations of mind about them, and to a humble comparison of themselves with such women as Catharine of Russia,[3] Elizabeth of England,[4] distinguished for their statesman-like qualities; Harriet Martineau[5] and Madame De Staël,[6] for their literary attainments; or Caroline Herschel[7] and Mary Somerville[8] for

---

[3] Catherine I (1683-1727), empress of Russia, ruled upon the death of her husband, Peter the Great, in 1725.

[4] Elizabeth I (1533-1603), queen of England from 1558-1603.

[5] Harriet Martineau (1802-1876), English author on religion, economics, and government. *Illustrations of Political Economy* (1832-1834) featured theories of Malthus and Ricardo; *History of Thirty Years Peace, 1816-1846*, was her most famous work.

[6] Anne Louise Germaine Necker De Staël (1766-1817) held salons for leading literary and political figures, authored books on Rousseau, the French Revolution, and *Delphine* and *Corinne*, the first feminist psychological romantic novels.

[7] Caroline Herschel (1750-1848), English astronomer who detected three nebulae and eight comets and received the gold medal of the Royal Astronomical Society in 1828.

their scientific researches; or for physical equality, to that whole nation of famous women, the Amazons. We seldom find this class of objectors among liberally educated persons, who have the advantage of observing the race in different countries, climes and phases. But barbarians though they be, in entertaining such an opinion, they must be met and fairly vanquished. Let us consider, then, man's superiority, intellectually, morally, physically.

Man's intellectual superiority cannot be a question until woman has had a fair trial. When we shall have had our freedom to find out our own sphere, when we shall have had our colleges, our professions, our trades, for a century, a comparison then may be justly instituted. When woman, instead of being taxed to endow colleges where she is forbidden to enter--instead of forming sewing societies to educate "poor, but pious," young men, shall first educate herself, when she shall be just to herself before she is generous to others; improving the talents God has given her, and leaving her neighbor to do the same for himself, we shall not then hear so much about this boasted superiority. How often, now, we see young men carelessly throwing away the intellectual food their sisters crave. A little music, that she may while an hour away pleasantly, a little French, a smattering of the sciences, and in rare instances, some slight classical knowledge, and woman is considered highly educated. She leaves her books and studies just as a young man is entering thoroughly into his. Then comes the gay routine of fashionable life, courtship and marriage, the perplexities of house and children, and she knows nothing beside. Her sphere is home. And whatever yearning her

---

[8] Mary Fairfax Somerville (1780-1872), Scottish mathematician, author of scientific works; Somerville College, Oxford, was named in her honor.

spirit may have felt for a higher existence, whatever may have been the capacity she well knew she possessed for more elevated enjoyments, enjoyments which would not conflict with those holy duties, but add new lustre to them, all, all is buried beneath the weight of these undivided cares.

Men, bless their innocence, are fond of representing themselves as beings of reason, of intellect, while women are mere creatures of the affections. There is a self-conceit that makes the possessor infinitely happy, and we would dislike to dispel the illusion if it were possible to endure it. But so far as we can observe, it is pretty much now-a-days as it was with Adam of old. No doubt you all recollect the account we have given us. A man and a woman were placed in a beautiful garden, with everything about them that could contribute to their enjoyment. Trees and shrubs, fruits and flowers, and gently murmuring streams made glad their hearts. Zephyrs freighted with delicious odors fanned their brows, and the serene stars looked down upon them with eyes of love. The Evil One saw their happiness, and it troubled him, and he set his wits to work to know how he should destroy it. He thought that man could be easily conquered through his affection for the woman, but the woman would require more management, she could be reached only through her intellectual nature. So he promised her the knowledge of good and evil. He told her the sphere of her reason should be enlarged. He promised to gratify the desires she felt for intellectual improvement. So he prevailed and she did eat. Did the Evil One judge rightly in regard to man? Eve took the apple, went to Adam, and said; "Dear Adam, taste this apple. If you love me, eat?" Adam stopped not so much as to ask if the apple were sweet or sour. He knew he was doing wrong, but his love for Eve prevailed, and he did eat.[9] Which, I ask you, was the creature of the affections?

In consideration of man's claim to moral superiority, glance now at our theological seminaries, our divinity students, the long line of descendants from our Apostolic fathers, the immaculate priesthood, and what do we find here? Perfect moral rectitude in every relation of life, a devoted spirit of self-sacrifice, a perfect union of thought, opinion and feeling among those who profess to worship the one God, and whose laws they feel themselves called upon to declare to a fallen race? Far from it. These persons, all so thoroughly acquainted with the character of God, and of His designs, made manifest by His words and works, are greatly divided among themselves. Every sect has its God, every sect has its Bible, and there is as much bitterness, envy, hatred and malice between those contending sects, yea, even more, than in our political parties during the periods of their greatest excitement. Now the leaders of these sects are the priesthood, who are supposed to have passed their lives, almost, in the study of the Bible, in various languages and with various commentaries--in the contemplation of the infinite, the eternal, the glorious future open to the redeemed of earth. Are they distinguished among men for their holy aspirations, their virtue, purity and chastity? Do they keep themselves unspotted from the world? Is the moral and religious life of this class what we might expect from minds said to be fixed on such mighty themes? By no means. Not a year passes but we hear of some sad, soul-sickening

---

[9] "And when the woman saw that the tree was good for food, and that it was pleasant to the eyes, and a tree to be desired to make one wise, she took of the fruit thereof, and did eat, and gave also unto her husband with her; and he did eat" (Gen. 3:6).

deed, perpetrated by some of this class. If such be the state of the most holy, we need not pause now to consider those classes who claim of us less reverence and respect. The lamentable want of principle among our lawyers, generally, is too well known to need comment. The everlasting backbiting and bickering of our physicians is proverbial. The disgraceful riots at our polls, where man, in performing the highest duty of citizenship, and ought surely to be sober-minded the perfect rowdyism that now characterizes the debates in our national Congress,--all these are great facts which rise up against man's claim for moral superiority. In my opinion, he is infinitely woman's inferior in every moral quality, not by nature, but made so by a false education. In carrying out his own selfishness, man has greatly improved woman's moral nature, but by an almost total shipwreck of his own. Woman has now the noble virtues of the martyr. She is early schooled to self-denial and suffering. But man is not so wholly buried in selfishness that he does not sometimes get a glimpse of the narrowness of his soul, as compared with woman. Then he says, by way of an excuse for his degradation, "God made woman more self-denying than man. It is her nature. It does not cost her as much to give up her wishes, her will, her life, even, as it does him. He is naturally selfish. God made him so."

No! think not that He who made the heavens and the earth, the whole planetary world, ever moving in such harmony and order, that He who so bountifully scattered through all nature so much that fills us with admiration and wonder, that He who made the mighty ocean, mountain and cataract, the bright birds and tender flowers, that He who made man in his own image, perfect, noble and pure, loving justice, mercy and truth,--oh say not that he has had any part in the production of that creeping, cringing, crawling, debased, selfish monster, now extant, claiming for himself the name of man. No! God's commands rest upon man as well as woman. It is as much his duty to be kind, self-denying and full of good works, as it is hers. As much his duty to absent himself from scenes of violence as it is hers. A place or position that would require the sacrifice of the delicacy and refinement of woman's nature is unfit for man, for these virtues should be as carefully guarded in him as in her. The false ideas that prevail with regard to the purity necessary to constitute the perfect character in woman, and that requisite for man, has done an infinite deal of mischief in the world. I would not have woman less pure, but I would have man more so. I would have the same code of morals for both. Delinquencies which exclude woman from the society of the true and the good, should assign to man the same place. Our laxity towards him has been the fruitful source of dissipation, drunkenness, debauchery and immorality of all kinds. It has not only affected woman injuriously, but he himself has been the greatest sufferer. It has destroyed the nobility of his character, the transparency of his soul, and all those finer qualities of our nature which raise us above the earth and give us a foretaste of the refined enjoyments of the world to come.

Let us now consider man's claim to physical superiority. Methinks I hear some say, surely, you will not contend for equality here. Yes, we must not give an inch, lest you take an ell. We cannot accord to man even this much, and he has no right to claim it until the fact has been fully demonstrated. Until the physical education of the boy and the girl shall have been the same for many years. If you claim the advantage of size, merely, why, it may be that under any course of training, in ever so perfect a development of physique in woman, man might still be the larger of the two, though we do not grant even this. But the perfection of the physique is great power combined with endurance. Now your strongest men are not always the tallest men, nor the broadest, nor the most corpulent, but very often the small, elastic man, who is well built, tightly put together, and possessed of an indomitable will. Bodily strength depends much on the power of the will. The sight of a small boy thoroughly thrashing a big one, is not rare. Now, would you say the big, fat boy whipped, was superior to the small active boy who conquered him? You do not say the horse is physically superior to man, for although he has more muscular power, yet the power of mind in man renders him his superior, and he guides him wherever he will. The power of mind seems to be in no way connected with the size and strength of body. Many men of herculean powers of mind have been small and weak in body. The late distinguished Dr. Channing,[10] of Boston, was feeble in appearance and voice, yet he has moved the world by the eloquence of his pen. John Quincy Adams was a small man of little muscular power, yet we know he had more courage than all the Northern doughfaces, six feet high and well proportioned, that ever represented us at our capitol. Mental power depends far more on the temperament, than on the size of the head or the size of the body. I never heard that Daniel Lambert was distinguished for any great mental achievements.[11] We cannot say what the woman might be physically, if the girl were allowed all the freedom of the boy in romping, climbing, swimming, playing whoop and ball. Among some of the Tartar tribes of the present day, women manage a horse, hurl a javelin, hunt wild animals, and fight an enemy as well as a man. The Indian women endure fatigues and carry

---

[10] William Ellery Channing (1789-1842), Unitarian minister and author, pastor of the Federal St. Congregational Church in Boston, who supported many reforms and led efforts for religious tolerance.

[11] Daniel Lambert (1770-1800), an Englishman of great size (5'11" and 739 lbs. at his death), whose name was a synonym for immensity.

burdens that some of our fair-faced, soft-handed, moustached young gentlemen would consider quite impossible for them to sustain. The Croatian and Wallachian women perform all the agricultural operations in addition to their domestic labors, and it is no uncommon sight in our cities, to see the German immigrant with his hands in his pockets, walking complacently by the side of his wife, whilst she bears the weight of some huge package or piece of furniture upon her head. Physically, as well as intellectually, it is use that produces growth and development.

But there is a class of objectors, who say they do not claim superiority, they merely assert a difference. But you will find by following them up closely, that they soon run this difference into the old groove of superiority. The phrenologist says that woman's head has just as many organs as man's, and that they are similarly situated. He says, too, that the organs most used are most prominent. They do not divide heads according to sex, but they call all the fine heads masculine, and the inferior feminine. When a woman presents a well-developed intellectual region, they say she has a masculine head, as if there could be nothing remarkable of the feminine gender. When a man has a small head, with little reasoning power, and the affections strongly developed, they say he has a woman's head, thus giving all reasoning power to the masculine gender.

> Some say our heads are less,
> Some men's are small, not they the least of men,
> For often fineness compensates for size,
> Besides the brain is like the hand, and grows with using.

We have met here to-day to discuss our rights and wrongs, civil and political, and not, as some have supposed, to go into the detail of social life alone. We do not propose to petition the legislature to make our husbands just, generous and courteous, to seat every man at the head of a cradle, and to clothe every woman in male attire. None of these points, however important they may be considered by leading men, will be touched in this Convention. As to their costume, the gentlemen need feel no fear of our imitating that, for we think it in violation of every principle of taste, beauty and dignity; notwithstanding all the contempt cast upon our loose, flowing garments, we still admire the graceful folds, and consider our costume far more artistic than theirs. Many of the nobler sex seem to agree with us in this opinion, for the bishops, priests, judges, barristers, and lordmayors of the first nation on the globe, and the Pope of Rome, with his Cardinals, too, all wear the loose flowing robes, thus tacitly acknowledging that the male attire is neither dignified nor imposing. No, we shall not molest you in your philosophical experiments with stocks, pants, high-heeled boots and Russian belts. Yours be the glory to discover, by personal experience, how long the knee-pan can resist the terrible strapping down which you impose, in how short time the well developed muscles of the throat can be reduced to mere threads by the constant pressure of the stock, how high the heel of a boot must be to make a short man tall, and how tight the Russian belt may be drawn and yet have wind enough left to sustain life. But we are assembled to protest against a form of government, existing without the consent of the governed--to declare our right to be free as man is free, to be represented in the government which we are taxed to support, to have such disgraceful laws as give man the power to chastise and imprison his wife, to take the wages which she earns, the property which she inherits, and, in case of separation, the children of her love; laws which make her the mere dependent on his bounty. It is to protest against such unjust laws as these that we are assembled to-day, and to have them, if possible, forever erased from our statute-books, deeming them a shame and a disgrace to a Christian republic in the nineteenth century. We have met

> To uplift woman's fallen divinity
> Upon an even pedestal with man's.

And, strange as it may seem to many, we now demand our right to vote according to the declaration of the government under which we live. This right no one pretends to deny. We need not prove ourselves equal to Daniel Webster to enjoy this privilege, for the ignorant Irishman in the ditch has all the civil rights he has.[12] We need not prove our muscular power equal to this same Irishman to enjoy this privilege, for the most tiny, weak, ill-shaped stripling of twenty-one, has all the civil rights of the Irishman. We have no objection to discuss the question of equality, for we feel that the weight of argument lies wholly with us, but we wish the question of equality kept distinct from the question of rights, for the proof of the one does not determine the truth of the other. All white men in this country have the same rights, however they may differ in mind, body or estate. The right is ours. The question now is, how shall we get possession of what rightfully belongs to us. We should not feel so sorely grieved if no man who had not attained the full stature of a Webster, Clay, Van Buren, or Gerrit Smith could claim the

---

[12] Daniel Webster (1782-1852), American statesman, lawyer, and orator, who won fame in the *Dartmouth College Case* and *McCulloch v. Maryland*, and was a member of Congress, (1813-17, 1823-27) U.S. Senator from MA, (1827-41), and Secretary of State (1841-45, 1850-52).

right of the elective franchise.[13] But to have drunkards, idiots, horse-racing, rumselling rowdies, ignorant foreigners and silly boys fully recognized, while we ourselves are thrust out from all the rights that belong to citizens, it is too grossly insulting to the dignity of woman to be longer quietly submitted to. The right is ours. Have it, we must. Use it, we will. The pens, the tongues, the fortunes, the indomitable wills of many women are already pledged to secure this right. The great truth, that no just government can be formed without the consent of the governed, we shall echo and re-echo in the ears of the unjust judge, until by continual coming we shall weary him.[14]

But, say some, would you have woman vote? What, refined, delicate women at the polls, mingling in such scenes of violence and vulgarity? Most certainly. Where there is so much to be feared for the pure, the innocent, the noble, the mother surely should be there to watch and guard her sons who must encounter such stormy, dangerous scenes at the tender age of twenty-one. Much is said of woman's influence, might not her presence do much toward softening down this violence, refining this vulgarity? Depend upon it, the places that, by their impure atmosphere, are unfit for women, cannot but be dangerous to her sires and sons.

But, if woman claims all the rights of a citizen, will she buckle on her armor and fight in defense of her country? Has not woman already often shown herself as courageous in the field, as wise and patriotic in counsel as man? But for myself, I think all

---

[13] Henry Clay (1777-1852), Kentucky statesman, lawyer, orator; Martin Van Buren (1782-1862), 8th President of the U.S. (1837-41); Gerrit Smith (1797-1874), abolitionist and reformer.

[14] Luke 18: 1-6.

war sinful. I believe in Christ. I believe that command, "resist not evil" [Matt. 5:39], to be divine. "Vengeance is mine, and I will repay, saith the Lord" [Rom. 12:19]. Let frail man, who cannot foresee the consequences of an action, walk humbly with his God, loving his enemies, blessing them who curse him, and always returning good for evil. This is the highest kind of courage that mortal man can attain to. And this moral warfare with our own bad passions requires no physical power to achieve. I would not have man go to war. I can see no glory in fighting with such weapons as guns and swords, whilst man has in his possession the infinitely superior ones of righteousness and truth.

But what would woman gain by voting? Men must know the advantages of voting, for they all seem very tenacious about the right. Think you, if woman had a voice in this government, that all those laws affecting her interests would so entirely violate every principle of right and justice? Had woman a vote to give, might not the office-holders and seekers propose some change in her condition? Might not Woman's Rights become as great a question as free soil?

"But are you not already represented by your fathers, husbands, brothers and sons?" Let your statute books answer the question. We have had enough of such representation. In nothing is woman's true happiness consulted. Men like to call her an angel--to feed her on what they think sweet food--nourishing her vanity; to make her believe that her organization is so much finer than theirs, that she is not fitted to struggle with the tempests of public life, but needs their care and protection!! Care and protection--such as the wolf gives the lamb--such as the eagle the hare he carries to his eyrie!! Most cunningly he entraps her, and then takes from her all those rights which are dearer to him than life itself--rights which have been baptized in blood--and the maintenance of which is even now rocking to their foundations the kingdoms of the Old World.

The most discouraging, the most lamentable aspect our cause wears is the indifference, indeed, the contempt with which women themselves regard the movement. Where the subject is introduced, among those even who claim to be intelligent and educated, it is met by the scornful curl of the lip, and by expression of ridicule and disgust. But we shall hope better things of them when they are enlightened in regard to their present position. When women know the laws and constitutions under which they live, they will not publish their degradation, by declaring themselves satisfied, nor their ignorance, by declaring they have all the rights they want. They are not the only class of beings who glory in their bondage. In the Turkish harem, in those Seraglios, where intellect and soul are buried beneath the sensualism and brutality which are the inevitable results of woman's degradation, even there, she declares herself not only satisfied with her position, but glories in it. Miss Martineau, in her "Travels in the East," recently published, says, referring to the inmates of the harems: "Everywhere they pitied us European women heartily, that we had to go about traveling, and appearing in the streets without being properly taken care of, that is, watched."[15] They think us strangely neglected in being left so free, and boast of their spy system and imprisonment as tokens of the value in which they are held. Can woman here, although her spiritual and intellectual nature is recognized to a somewhat greater degree than among the Turks, and she is allowed the privilege of being in her nursery and kitchen, and although the Christian promises her the ascendancy in heaven as man has it here, while

---

[15] Harriet Martineau, "The Hareem," in *Eastern Life, Present and Past* (1848, 259-70; cited material in Yates 1985, 183). See also p. 45, n 5.

the Mahometan [sic] closes the gates of the celestial city tight against her, can she be content, notwithstanding these good things, to be denied the pure enjoyments arising from a full cultivation of her mind, and an admission into all the rights and privileges which are hers? She must and will, ere long, when her spirit awakens, and she learns to care less for the

> Barren verbiage, current among men,
> Light coin, the tinsel clink of compliment.

She must and will demand everywhere

> Two heads in council--two beside the hearth,
> Two in the tangled business o' the world,
> Two in the liberal offices of life,
> Two plummets dropped to sound the abyss
> Of science, and the secrets of the mind.

Let woman live as she should. Let her feel her accountability to her Maker. Let her know that her spirit is fitted for as high a sphere as man's, and that her soul requires food as pure and exalted as his. Let her live first for God, and she will not make imperfect man an object of reverence and awe. Teach her her responsibility as a being of conscience and reason, that all earthly support is weak and unstable, that her only safe dependence is the arm of omnipotence, and that true happiness springs from duty accomplished. Thus will she learn the lesson of individual responsibility for time and eternity. That neither father, husband, brother or son, however willing they may be, can discharge her high duties of life, or stand in her stead when called into the presence of the great Searcher of Hearts at the last day. Methinks I hear some woman say, "Must we not obey our husbands? Does not the Bible so command us?" No, you have not rightly read your Bible. At the creation of our first parents, God called their name Adam, and gave them dominion over the fish of the sea, the fowls of the air, and every living thing that moved upon the earth, but he says nothing to them of obedience to each other. After the fall, after Noah come out of the ark, he addressed them in like manner. The chief support that man finds for this authority over woman in the Bible, he gets from St. Paul. It needs but little consideration to see how limited this command of St. Paul must be, even if you give it all the weight which is usually claimed. "Wives, obey your husbands in the Lord."[16] Now as the command is given to me, I am of course to be the judge of what is "in the Lord," and this opens a wide field of escape from any troublesome commands. There can be no subordination where the one to whom a command is given is allowed to sit in judgment on the character of the command. The Bible argument on this subject would of itself afford sufficient material for an entire lecture. I shall not, therefore, attempt to go into it at this time, enough to say that that best of Books is ever on the side of freedom, and we shrink not from pleading our cause on its principles of universal justice and love.

Let me here notice one of the greatest humbugs of the day, which has long found for itself the most valuable tool in woman--"The Education Society." The idea to me, is simply absurd, for women, in their present degradation and ignorance, to form sewing societies for the education of young men for the ministry. An order of beings above themselves, claiming to be gifted with superior powers, having all the avenues to learning, wealth and distinction thrown freely open to

---

[16] She has combined the language of Eph. 5:22, addressed to wives, and Eph. 6:1, addressed to children.

them, who, if they had but the energy to avail themselves of all these advantages, could easily secure an education for themselves, while woman herself, poor, friendless, robbed of all her rights, oppressed on all sides, civilly, religiously and socially, must needs go ignorant herself. Now, is not the idea preposterous, for such a being to educate a great, strong, lazy man, by working day and night with her needle, stitch, stitch, and the poor widow always throws in her mite, being taught to believe that all she gives for the decoration of churches and their black-coated gentry, is given unto the Lord.[17] I think a man, who, under such conditions, has the moral hardihood to take an education at the hands of woman, and at such an expense to her, should, as soon as he graduates, with all his honors thick upon him, take the first ship for Turkey, and there pass his days in earnest efforts to rouse the inmates of the harems to a true sense of their degradation, and not, as is his custom, immediately enter our pulpits to tell us of his superiority to us, "weaker vessels"[18]--his prerogative to command, ours to obey--his duty to preach, ours to keep silence. Oh, for the generous promptings of the days of chivalry. Oh, for the poetry of romantic gallantry. May they shine on us once more. Then may we hope that these pious young men, who profess to believe in the golden rule, will clothe and educate themselves and encourage woman to do the same for herself; or perhaps they might conceive the happy thought of reciprocating the benefits so long enjoyed by them. There is something painfully affecting in the self- sacrifice and generosity of women, who can neither read nor write their own language with correctness, going about begging money for the education of men. The last time when an appeal of this kind was

---

[17] Mark 12:42; Luke 21:2-3.

[18] 1 Pet. 3:7.

made to me, I told the young girl that I would send her to school a year, if she would go, but I would never again give one red cent to the Education Society. And I do hope that every Christian woman, who has the least regard for her sex, will make the same resolve. We have worked long enough for man, and at a most unjust and unwarrantable sacrifice of self, yet he gives no evidence of gratitude, but has, thus far, treated his benefactors with scorn, ridicule and neglect. But, say they, you do not need an education as we do. We expect to shine in the great world. Our education is our living. What, let me ask, is the real object of education. Just in proportion as the faculties which God hath given us are harmoniously developed, do we attain our highest happiness. And has not woman an equal right to happiness here as well as hereafter? And should she not have equal facilities with him for making an honest living while on this footstool?

One common objection to this movement is, that if the principles of freedom and equality which we advocate were put into practice, it will destroy all harmony in the domestic circle. Here let me ask, how many truly harmonious households have we now? Look round your circle of friends: on the one hand you will find the meek, sad-looking, thoroughly subdued wife, with no freedom of thought or action, her days passed in the dull routine of household cares, and her nights half perchance in making tattered garments whole, and the other half in slumbers oft disturbed by sick and restless children. She knows nothing of the great world without; she has no time to read, and her husband finds more pleasure in discussing politics with men in groceries, taverns, or depots, than he could in reading or telling his wife the news, whilst she sits mending his stockings and shirts through many a lonely evening; nor dreams he, selfish being, that he owes any duty to the perishing soul by his side, beyond providing a house to cover her head, with food and raiment. As to her little "heaven ordained" world within, she finds not much comfort there, for her will and wishes, should she have any, must be in subjection to that of her tyrant. The comfort of wife, children, servants, one and all, must be given up, wholly disregarded, until the great head of the house has all his wants supplied. No matter what the case may be, he must have his hot dinner. If wife or children are sick, they must look elsewhere for care; he cannot be disturbed at night; it does not agree with him to have his slumbers broken, it gives him the headache and renders him unfit for business; and, worse than all, how often woman's very soul is tortured by the harsh, brutal treatment of fathers toward their children. What mother cannot bear me witness to anguish of this sort. Oh! women, how sadly you have learned your duty to your children, to the holy promptings of your own hearts, to the God that gave you that merciful love for them in all their wanderings, when you stand silent witnesses of the cruel infliction of blows and stripes from angry fathers on the trembling forms of helpless infancy. It is a mother's sacred duty to shield her children from violence, from whatever source it may come. It is woman's mission to resist oppression wherever she may find it, whether at her own fireside, or on a Southern plantation, by every moral power within her reach. Many men, well known for their philanthropy, who hate oppression in the outer world, can play the tyrant right well at home. It is a much easier matter to denounce all the crying sins of the day, most eloquently, too, under the inspiration of applauding thousands, than to endure alone, for an hour, the peevish moaning of a sick child. To know whether a man is truly great and good, you must not judge by his actions in the great world, but follow him to his home, where all restraints are laid aside, and there you see the true man, his virtues and his vices, too.

On the other hand, in these "harmonious households," you sometimes find the so-called "hen-pecked husband" ofttimes a kind, generous, noble-minded man, who hates contention and is willing to do anything for peace. He having unwarily caught a Tartar, tries to make the best of her. He can think his own thoughts, tell them, too, when he feels quite sure that she is not at hand. He can absent himself from home, as much as possible, but he does not feel like a free man. The detail of his suffering I can neither describe or imagine, never having been the confident [sic] of one of these unfortunate beings; but are not his sorrows all written in the book of the immortal Caudle, written by his own hand, that all may read and pity the poor man, though feeling all through that the hapless Mrs. Caudle had, after all, many reasons for her continual wail for substantial grief.[19] Now, in the ordinary households we see there may be no open rupture; they may seemingly glide on without a ripple over the surface; the aggrieved parties having resigned themselves to suffer all things with Christian fortitude, with stern philosophy, but there can be no harmony or happiness there. The only happy households we now see are those in which husband and wife share equally in counsel and government. There can be no true dignity or independence where there is subordination to the absolute will of another, no happiness without freedom. Let us then have no fears that this movement will disturb what is seldom found, a truly united and happy family.

Is it not strange that man--with the pages of history all spread out before him--is so slow to admit the intellectual power, the moral heroism of woman, and her identity with himself. That there have been comparatively a

---

[19] Douglas William Jerrold (1803-1857), English dramatist and author, published humorous works in British periodicals. Among the best known were "Mrs. Caudle's Curtain Lectures" (1846) and "Mr. Caudle's Breakfast Talk" (1846).

greater number of good queens than of good kings is a fact stated by several historians. Zenobia, the celebrated queen of the East, is not exceeded by any king on record for talent, courage and daring ambition.[20] The Emperor Aurelian, while besieging her beautiful city of Palmes, writes thus: "The Roman people speak with contempt of the war I am waging with a woman, but they are ignorant both of the character and power of Zenobia."[21] She was possessed of attainments very unusual in that age, and was a liberal patron of literature and science. No contemporary sovereign is represented as capable of such high pursuits. Margaret, Queen of Denmark, Norway and Sweden,[22] justly called the Semiramis of the North,[23] by her talent, energy, firmness and foresight, raised herself to a degree of power and grandeur then unequaled in Europe. No monarch has ever rivaled Isabella of Spain, in bravery, sagacity, political wisdom, and a proud sense of honor.[24] Yet these charac-

---

[20] Zenobia, Queen of Palmyra, 262-272 C.E., an accomplished linguist to whose wisdom and courage are ascribed her husband Odenathus's (king, 260-267) military successes against Persia. During her reign the Palmyrene kingdom secured Syria, occupied Egypt, and overran nearly the whole of Asia Minor.

[21] Aurelian, Roman emperor, 270-275 C.E.

[22] Margaret I (1353-1412), regent and ruler, in effect, of Denmark (1387-1412), Norway (1388-1412), and Sweden (1389-1412), was perhaps Scandinavia's greatest medieval monarch.

[23] Semiramis, mythical Assyrian queen noted for her beauty and wisdom.

[24] Isabella I (1451-1504) was queen of Castile (1474-1504) and, through marriage to Ferdinand II, of Aragon (1479-1504).

teristics were united with the purest modesty and the warmest feminine affections. Ferdinand, her husband, was her inferior in mind, heart and nobility of character. As a wife and a mother she seems to have been as perfect a model as of a queen. Her treaty with the Queen of Portugal is probably the only one in history of which it could be said: "The fair negotiators experienced none of the embarrassments usually incident to such deliberations, growing out of jealousy, distrust and a mutual desire to overreach. They were conducted in perfect good faith, and a sincere desire on both sides to establish a cordial reconciliation." Austria has produced no wiser or better sovereign than Maria Theresa, to whose strength of character her nobles paid involuntary homage when they unanimously exclaimed, "We will die for our King Maria Theresa."[25] She, too, was an affectionate wife and mother. In England it was common to hear the people talk of King Elizabeth and Queen James.[26] Catherine of Russia bears honorable comparison with Peter the Great. The annals of Africa furnish no example of a monarch equal to the brave, intelligent and proud hearted Tinga, the negro Queen of Angola.[27] Blanche of Castile evinced great ability in administering the government of

---

[25] Maria Theresa (1717-1780), a central figure in the wars and politics of Europe from the death of her father in 1740 until her own death. She was archduchess of Austria, queen of Hungary and Bohemia, and wife of the Holy Roman Emperor Francis I.

[26] James I (1566-1625), king of England (1603-25) and as James VI, of Scotland (1567-1625).

[27] Nzinga Mbande (1582-1663) was queen of part of the Mbundu nation (Angola) from 1624-1663. She was also known as Njinga Pande and Dona Ana de Souza.

France, during the minority of her son,[28] and similar praise is due to Caroline of England during the absence of her husband.[29] What did woman not do? what did she not suffer in our revolutionary struggle? In all great national difficulties, her heart has ever been found to beat in the right place. She has been loyal alike to her country and her tyrants. "He said it, and it must be right," was the remark of Josephine in her happy days, when her own judgment suggested a change of course from the one marked out to her by Napoleon, but she lived long enough to learn that he might both do and say much that was not right.[30] It has happened more than once that in a crisis of national affairs woman has been appealed to for her aid. Hannah Moore, one of the great minds of her day, at a time when French revolutionary and atheistical opinions were spreading, was earnestly besought by many leading men to write something to counteract these destructive influences.[31] Her style was so popular, and she had shown so intimate a knowledge of human nature that they hoped much from her influence. Her Village Politics by

---

[28] Blanche of Castile (1188-1252), wife of Louis VIII, king of France, 1223-26, then regent for her son Louis IX until 1236 and in 1248 during his absence on a crusade.

[29] Caroline (1683-1737) and George II were crowned king and queen of England and Ireland in 1727; she acted as regent on four occasions during the king's absence from England.

[30] Josephine (1763-1814), wife of Napoleon Bonaparte, empress of France from 1804 until he divorced her in 1809.

[31] Hannah Moore (1745-1833), English writer on moral and religious subjects, philanthropist. Her *Village Politics* (1792) was written under the pseudonym of Will Chips.

Will Chip [sic], written in a few hours, showed that she merited the opinion entertained of her powers upon all classes of mind. It had, as was expected, great effect. The tact and intelligence of this woman completely turned the tide of opinion, and many say prevented a revolution. Whether she did old England's poor any essential service by warding off, for a time, what must surely come, is a question; however, she did it, and the wise ones of her day gloried in her success. Where was the spirit found to sustain that mighty discoverer, Christopher Columbus, in the dark hours of his despair? Isabella of Aragon may be truly said to be the mother of this western world. She was the constant friend and protector of Columbus during her life; and although assailed at all sides, yet she steadily and firmly rejected the advice of narrow-minded, timid counselors, and generously bestowed her patronage upon that heroic adventurer. In all those things in which the priests had no interest, consequently did not influence her mind, she was ever the noble woman, loving justice; the Christian, loving mercy. The persecution of the Jews, and the establishment of the Inquisition cannot be said to have been countenanced by her, they were the results of priestly cruelty and impudence. Torquemada, the Confessor of the Queen, did not more fatally mislead her then, than do the priests of our day mislead us; the cry of heretic was not more potent in her day than that of infidel in ours.[32] They burned and tortured the bodies of all who rejected the popular faith, we consign their souls to hell-fire and their lives to misrepresentation and persecution. The feeling of aversion so often expressed at seeing woman in places of publi-

---

[32] Tomas de Torquemada (1420-98), Spanish churchman and inquisitor, confessor to Ferdinand II and Isabella I, instrumental in bringing about the expulsion of the Jews in 1492.

city is merely the effect of custom, very like that prejudice against color, so truly American. White men make no objections to women or negroes to serve or amuse them in public, but the claim of equality is what chagrins the tyrant. Man never rejects the aid of either, when they serve him in the accomplishment of his work. What man or woman has a feeling of disapproval in reading the history of Joan of Arc. The sympathies of every heart are at once enlisted in the success of that extraordinary girl. Her historian tells us that when all human power seemed unavailing, the French no longer despised the supernatural aid of the damsel of Domremy. The last stronghold of the Dauphin Charles was besieged; the discouraged French were about to abandon it when the coming of this simple girl paralyzed the English, and inspired the followers of Charles with the utmost courage. Her success was philosophical, in accordance with the laws of mind. She had a full faith in herself and inspired all those who saw her with the same. Let us cultivate like faith, like enthusiasm, and we, too, shall impress all who see and hear us with the same confidence we ourselves feel in our final success. There seems now to be a kind of moral stagnation in our midst. Philanthropists have done their utmost to rouse the nation to a sense of its sins. War, slavery, drunkenness, licentiousness, gluttony, have been dragged naked before the people, and all their abominations and deformities fully brought to light, yet with idiotic laugh we hug those monsters to our breasts and rush on to destruction. Our churches are multiplying on all sides, our missionary societies, Sunday schools, and prayer meetings and innumerable charitable and reform organizations are all in operation, but still the tide of vice is swelling, and threatens the destruction of everything, and the battlements of righteousness are weak against the raging elements of sin and death.

Verily, the world waits the coming of some new element, some purifying power, some spirit of mercy and love. The voice of woman has been silenced in the state, the church, and the home, but man cannot fulfill his destiny alone, he cannot redeem his race unaided. There are deep and tender chords of sympathy and love in the hearts of the down-fallen and oppressed that woman can touch more skillfully than man. The world has never yet seen a truly great and virtuous nation, because in the degradation of woman the very fountains of life are poisoned at their source. It is vain to look for silver and gold from mines of copper and lead. It is the wise mother that has the wise son. So long as your women are slaves you may throw your colleges and churches to the winds. You can't have scholars and saints so long as your mothers are ground to powder between the upper and nether millstone of tyranny and lust. How seldom, now, is a father's pride gratified, his fond hopes realized, in the budding genius of his son. The wife is degraded, made the mere creature of caprice, and the foolish son is heaviness to his heart. Truly are the sins of the fathers visited upon the children to the third and fourth generation. God, in his wisdom, has so linked the whole human family together, that any violence done at one end of the chain is felt throughout its length, and here, too, is the law of restoration, as in woman all have fallen, so in her elevation shall the race be recreated. "Voices" were the visitors and advisers of Joan of Arc. Do not "voices" come to us daily from the haunts of poverty, sorrow, degradation and despair, already too long unheeded. Now is the time for the women of this country, if they would save our free institutions, to defend the right, to buckle on the armor that can best resist the keenest weapons of the enemy--contempt and ridicule. The same religious enthusiasm that nerved Joan of Arc to her work nerves us to ours. In every generation God calls some men and women for the utterance of truth, a heroic action, and our work to-day is the fulfilling of what has long since been foretold by the Prophet--Joel 2:28: "And it shall come to pass afterward, that I will pour out my spirit upon all flesh, and your sons and your daughters shall prophesy." We do not expect our path will be strewn with the flowers of popular applause, but over the thorns of bigotry and prejudice will be our way, and on our banners will beat the dark storm-clouds of opposition from those who have entrenched themselves behind the stormy bulwarks of custom and authority, and who have fortified their position by every means, holy and unholy. But we will steadfastly abide the result. Unmoved we will bear it aloft. Undauntedly we will unfurl it to the gale, for we know that the storm cannot rend from it a shred, that the electric flash will but more clearly show to us the glorious words inscribed upon it, "Equality of Rights."

Then fear not thou to wind thy horn,
Though elf and gnome thy courage scorn.
Ask for the Castle's King and Queen,
Though rabble rout may rush between,
Beat thee senseless to the ground
And in the dark beset thee round,
Persist to ask and it will come;
Seek not for rest in humbler home,
So shalt thou see what few have seen;
The palace home of King and Queen.

6

Lucretia Coffin Mott, "Discourse on Woman," 1849

Lucretia Coffin Mott (1793-1880) was a Quaker minister, abolitionist, and leader in the movement for woman's rights. In 1837 she was one of the organizers of the Anti-Slavery Convention of American Women, and with the Grimké sisters, she illustrates the link between abolitionism and woman's rights. She signed the call to the first woman's rights convention in Seneca Falls and was advertised as one who would speak there (she made the opening and closing addresses). Her prominence as a reformer and speaker enabled her to attract audiences to the early woman's rights conventions, which she faithfully attended. She continued her work for woman's rights and other causes, such as peace, temperance, and the rights of labor, until her death.

The Bible was a primary source of evidence to justify prohibitions against women's speaking or other reform activity. This speech is an early but sophisticated response to such arguments. It includes rebuttals of such claims based on hermeneutic analysis of biblical texts and proposes a single ethical standard for judging human behavior.

It came into being because Richard Henry Dana (1787-1879), poet, essayist, and founder of the **North American Review**, *toured the country delivering a lecture on womanhood "in which he ridiculed the demands for civil and political rights, and for a larger sphere of action and eulogized Shakespeare's women, especially Desdemona, Ophelia, and Juliet, and recommended them to his countrywomen as models of innocence, tenderness and confiding love in man for their study and imitation"* (HWS 1:367-68). *No text of Dana's lecture exists; "Mr. Dana's Lecture on Woman," from the* [New York] **Literary World** (9 March 1850, 224), *provides the most information about what he said:*

> *The Mercantile Library course closed last week with Mr. Dana's lecture on Woman, one of his series on Shakspeare [sic], that preparatory to the consideration of Desdemona. Though it had been several times before, of late years, delivered in this city it still had a large audience. Nor did it fail of the effect of novelty, its doctrines being, and likely to be for some time to come, strange to the prevailing practice and opinions; perhaps stranger to the latter than the former, as it is easier for men to think against nature than to act against nature. Mr. Dana is not at all of the modern school, who affect to make Woman what she is not, never has been, and never can be, man and woman both, or perhaps we should rather say, simply man for the unsexing philosophy ignores the woman altogether.*
>
> *Mr. Dana is old-fashioned enough to believe in essential differences of sex, mental and moral marked as the physical; which result in corresponding diverse, yet united, healthy development. He thinks with Shakspeare that Lady Macbeth called with propriety upon*

> *the spirits to "unsex" her; a proceeding which would be quite a wasting of words with some of the modern holders of women's rights. Of these rights, as Shakspeare understood them, as Milton understood them, as nature indicates them, as the Bible teaches them, no more resolute chivalric defender can be found than Mr. Dana. His reverence for the sex has the strength, the courtesy which we find so beautifully expressed in the old poets of England, and in such mirrors of knighthood as Sir Philip Sidney.*[1] *Put by the side of this the pedantic schoolmaster labors of the drill sergeant who would force woman into some new walk of life unfitted for her! There has been some cavil at Mr. Dana's lecture, as it has been delivered on other occasions, but we are convinced that the heart of every woman present responded to its beauty and truth; its harmonious position of woman in the scale of creation, not the inferior of man, but his divinely constituted complement, the other half of a perfect whole.*

Liberal Philadelphians invited Coffin Mott to respond, and she delivered "Discourse on Woman" on December 17, 1849, in the Assembly Hall in Philadelphia. A stenographer took down her speech, which she then edited. It was published in Great Britain as well as the United States (1850).

There is nothing of greater importance to the well-being of society at large--of man as well

---

[1] Sir Philip Sidney (1554-86), English courtier, soldier, poet, and essayist, best known for *The Defense of Poesie* (1595).

as woman--than the true and proper position of woman. Much has been said, from time to time, upon this subject. It has been a theme for ridicule, for satire and sarcasm. We might look for this from the ignorant and vulgar; but from the intelligent and refined we have a right to expect that such weapons shall not be resorted to,--that gross comparisons and vulgar epithets shall not be applied, so as to place woman, in a point of view, ridiculous to say the least.

This subject has claimed my earnest interest for many years. I have long wished to see woman occupying a more elevated position than that which custom for ages has allotted to her. It was with great regret, therefore, that I listened a few days ago to a lecture upon this subject, which, though replete with intellectual beauty, and containing much that was true and excellent, was yet fraught with sentiments calculated to retard the progress of woman to the high elevation destined by her Creator. I regretted the more that these sentiments should be presented with such intellectual vigor and beauty, because they would be likely to ensnare the young.

The minds of young people generally, are open to the reception of more exalted views upon this subject. The kind of homage that has been paid to woman, the flattering appeals which have too long satisfied her--appeals to her mere fancy and imagination, are giving place to a more extended recognition of her rights, her important duties and responsibilities in life. Woman is claiming for herself stronger and more profitable food. Various are the indications leading to this conclusion. The increasing attention to female education, the improvement in the literature of the age, especially in what is called the "Ladies' Department," in the periodicals of the day, are among the proofs of a higher estimate of woman in society at large. Therefore we may hope that the intellectual and intelligent are being prepared for the discussion of this question, in a manner which shall tend to ennoble woman and dignify man.

Free discussion upon this, as upon all other subjects, is never to be feared; nor will be, except by such as prefer darkness to light. "Those only who are in the wrong dread discussion. The light alarms those only who feel the need of darkness."[2] It was sound philosophy, uttered by Jesus, "He that doeth truth cometh to the light, that his deeds may be made manifest, that they are wrought in God" [John 3: 21].

I have not come here with a view of answering any particular parts of the lecture alluded to, in order to point out the fallacy of its reasoning. The speaker, however, did not profess to offer anything like argument on that occasion, but rather *a sentiment*. I have no prepared address to deliver to you, being unaccustomed to speak in that way; but I felt a wish to offer some views for your consideration, though in a desultory manner, which may lead to such reflection and discussion as will present the subject in a true light.

In the beginning, man and woman were created equal. "Male and female created he them, and blessed them, and called their name Adam" [Gen. 1:27]. He gave dominion to both over the lower animals, but not to one over the other.

> "Man o'er woman
> He made not lord, such title to himself
> Reserving, human left from human free."[3]

---

[2] The source of this is unclear. The closest biblical version is found in John 3:20.

[3] Coffin Mott is misquoting John Milton's *Paradise Lost*, 12.69-71: "But man over men/ He made not lord; such title to himself/ Reserving, human left from human free." Sarah Grimké also misquotes these

The cause of the subjection of woman to man, was early ascribed to disobedience to the command of God. This would seem to show that she was then regarded as not occupying her true and rightful position in society.[4]

The laws given on Mount Sinai for the government of man and woman were equal, the precepts of Jesus make no distinction. Those who read the Scriptures, and judge for themselves, not resting satisfied with the perverted application of the text, do not find the distinction, that theology and ecclesiastical authorities have made, in the condition of the sexes. In the early ages, Miriam [Exod. 15:20] and Deborah [Judg. 4, 5], conjointly with Aaron and Barak, enlisted themselves on the side which they regarded the right, unitedly going up to their battles, and singing their songs of victory. We regard these with veneration. Deborah judged Israel many years--she went up with Barak against their enemies, with an army of 10,000, assuring him that the honor of the battle should not be to him, but to a woman. Revolting as were the circumstances of their success, the acts of a semi-barbarous people, yet we read with reverence the song of Deborah:

---

lines in the first of her *Letters on the Equality of the Sexes* (Bartlett 1988, 34), which may have been the source of Coffin Mott's misquotation (Nies 1977, 24).

[4] Quakers believed that Christ restored men and women to their original relation of equality (Fell 1667). For a contemporary retelling of the story of Christ, see "The Kenosis of the Father: A Feminist Midrash on the Gospel in Three Acts," in Rosemary Radford Ruether, *Sexism and God-Talk: Toward a Feminist Theology* (Boston: Beacon Press, 1983), 1-11.

> Blessed above woman shall Jael, the wife of Heeber, the Kenite be; blessed shall she be above women in the tent. . . . She put her hand to the nail, and her right hand to the workman's hammer; she smote Sisera through his temples. At her feet he bowed, he fell, he lay down dead" [Judg. 5:24, 26-27].

This circumstance, revolting to Christianity, is recognized as an act befitting woman in that day. Deborah, Huldah [2 Kings 22:14], and other honorable women, were looked up to and consulted in times of exigency, and their counsel was received. In that eastern country, with all the customs tending to degrade woman, some were called to fill great and important stations in society. There were also false prophetesses as well as true. The denunciations of Ezekiel were upon those women who would "prophesy out of their own heart, and sew pillows to all armholes" [14:17], &c.

Coming down to later times, we find Anna [Luke 2:36], a prophetess of four-score years, in the temple day and night, speaking of Christ to all them who looked for redemption in Jerusalem. Numbers of women were the companions of Jesus [Matt.26:55],--one going to the men of the city, saying, "Come, see a man who told me all things that ever I did; is not this the Christ?" [John 4:29]. Another, "Whatsoever he saith unto you, do it" [John 2:5]. Philip had four daughters who did prophesy [Acts 21:8]. Tryphena and Tryphosa [Rom. 16:12] were co-workers with the apostles in their mission, to whom they sent special messages of regard and acknowledgement of their labors in the gospel. A learned Jew, mighty in the Scriptures, was by Priscilla instructed in the way of the Lord more perfectly [Acts 18:2]. Phebe [Rom. 16:1] is mentioned as a *servant* of Christ, and commended as such to the brethren. It is worthy of note, that the word *servant*, when applied to Tychicus [Eph. 6:21; Col. 4:7], is rendered *minister*. Women *professing* godliness, should be translated *preaching*.

The first announcement, on the day of Pentecost, was the fulfillment of ancient prophecy, that God's spirit should be poured out upon *daughters* as well as sons, and they should prophesy [Joel 2:28; Acts 2:17]. It is important that we be familiar with these facts, because woman has been so long circumscribed in her influence by the perverted application of the text, rendering it improper for her to speak in the assemblies of the people, "to edification, to exhortation, and to comfort" [1 Cor. 14:3].

If these scriptures were read intelligently, we should not so learn Christ, as to exclude any from a position, where they might exert an influence for good to their fellow-beings. The epistle to the Corinthian church, where the supposed apostolic prohibition of women's preaching is found, contains express directions how woman shall appear, when she prayeth or prophesyeth [1 Cor. 14]. Judge then whether this admonition, relative to *speaking* and asking questions, in the excited state of that church, should be regarded as a standing injunction on woman's *preaching*, when that word was not used by the apostle. Where is the Scripture authority for the advice given to the early church, under peculiar circumstances, being binding on the church of the present day? Ecclesiastical history informs us, that for two or three hundred years, female ministers suffered martyrdom, in the company with their brethren.

These things are too much lost sight of. They should be known, in order that we may be prepared to meet the assertion, so often made, that woman is stepping out of her appropriate sphere, when she shall attempt to instruct public assemblies. The present time particularly demands such investigation. It requires also, that "of yourselves ye should judge what is right" [Luke 12:57] that you should know the ground whereon you stand. This age is notable for its works of mercy and benevolence

--for the efforts that are made to reform the inebriate and the degraded, to relieve the oppressed and the suffering. Women as well as men are interested in these works of justice and mercy. They are efficient co-workers, their talents are called into profitable exercise, their labors are effective in each department of reform. The blessing to the merciful, to the peacemaker [Matt. 5:7,9] is equal to man and to woman. It is greatly to be deplored, now that she is increasingly qualified for usefulness, that any view should be presented, calculated to retard her labors of love.

Why should not woman seek to be a reformer? If she is to shrink from being such an iconoclast as shall "break the image of man's lower worship," as so long held up to view; if she is to fear to exercise her reason, and her noblest powers, lest she should be thought to "attempt to act the man," and not "acknowledge his supremacy;" if she is to be satisfied with the narrow sphere assigned her by man, nor aspire to a higher, lest she should transcend the bounds of female delicacy; truly it is a mournful prospect for woman. We would admit all the difference, that our great and beneficent Creator has made, in the relation of man and woman, nor would we seek to disturb this relation; but we deny that the present position of woman, is her true sphere of usefulness; nor will she attain to this sphere, until the disabilities and disadvantages, religious, civil, and social, which impede her progress, are removed out of her way. These restrictions have enervated her mind and paralysed her powers. While man assumes, that the present is the original state designed for woman, that the *existing* "differences are not arbitrary nor the result of accident," but grounded in nature; she will not make the necessary effort to obtain her just rights, lest it should subject her to the kind of scorn and contemptuous manner in which she has been spoken of.

So far from her "ambition leading her to

attempt to act the man," she needs all the encouragement she can receive, by the removal of obstacles from her path, in order that she may become a "true woman." As it is desirable that man should act a manly and generous part, not "mannish," so let woman be urged to exercise a dignified and womanly bearing, not womanish. Let her cultivate all the graces and proper accomplishments of her sex, but let not these degenerate into a kind of effeminacy, in which she is satisfied to be the mere plaything or toy of society, content with her outward adornings, and with the tone of flattery and fulsome adulation too often addressed to her. True, nature has made a difference in her configuration, her physical strength, her voice, &c.--and we ask no change, we are satisfied with nature. But how has neglect and mismanagement increased this difference! It is our duty to develop these natural powers by suitable exercise, so that they may be strengthened "by reason of use." In the ruder state of society, woman is made to bear heavy burdens, while her "lord and master" walks idly by her side. In the civilization to which we have attained, if cultivated and refined woman would bring all her powers into use, she might engage in pursuits which she now shrinks from as beneath her proper vocation. The energies of men need not then be wholly devoted to the counting house and common business of life, in order that women in fashionable society may be supported in their daily promenades and nightly visits to the theatre and ball room.

The appeal of Catharine Beecher to woman some years ago, leading her to aim at higher pursuits, was greatly encouraging.[5] It gave

---

[5] Catharine Beecher (1800-78), author and educator. The cited material is from a fund-raising pamphlet, *Suggestions Respecting Improvements in Education* (1829). Pages from which citations are drawn are indicated in parenthesis.

earnest of an improved condition of woman. She says,

> The time is coming, when woman will be taught to understand the construction of the human frame, the philosophical results from restricted exercise, unhealthy modes of dress, improper diet, and other causes, which are continually operating to destroy the health and life of the young (8). . . . Woman has been but little aware of the high incitements which should stimulate to the cultivation of her noblest powers. The world is no longer to be governed by physical force, but by the influence which mind exerts over mind (52). . . . Woman has never wakened to her highest destinies and holiest hopes. (53).
>
> The time is coming when educated females will not be satisfied with the present objects of their low ambition. When a woman now leaves the immediate business of her own education, how often, how generally do we find her, sinking down into almost useless inactivity. To enjoy the social circle, to accomplish a little sewing, a *little* reading, a little domestic duty, to while away her hours in self-indulgence, or to enjoy the pleasures of domestic life,--these are the highest objects at which many a woman of elevated mind, and accomplished education aims. And what does she find of sufficient interest to call forth her cultivated energies, and warm affections? But when the cultivation and development of the immortal mind shall be presented to woman, as her especial and delightful duty, and that too whatever be her

> relations in life; when by example and experience she shall have learned her power over the intellect and the affections, . . then we shall not find woman, returning from the precincts of learning and wisdom, to pass lightly away the bright hours of her maturing youth. We shall not so often see her, seeking the light device to embroider on muslin and lace (and I would add, the fashionable crochet work of the present day); but we shall see her, with the delighted glow of benevolence, seeking for immortal minds, whereon she may fasten durable and holy impressions, that shall never be effaced or wear away. (54-55)

A new generation of women is now upon the stage, improving the increased opportunities furnished for the acquirement of knowledge. Public education is coming to be regarded the right of the children of a republic. The hill of science is not so difficult of ascent as formerly represented by poets and painters; but by fact and demonstration smoothed down, so as to be accessible to the assumed weak capacity of woman. She is rising in the scale of being through this, as well as other means, and finding heightened pleasure and profit on the right hand and on the left. The study of Physiology, now introduced into our common schools, is engaging her attention, impressing the necessity of the observance of the laws of health. The intellectual Lyceum and instructive lecture room are becoming, to many, more attractive than the theatre and the ball room. The sickly and sentimental novel and pernicious romance are giving place to works, calculated to call forth the benevolent affections and higher nature. It is only by comparison that I would speak commendatory of these works of imagination. The frequent issue of them from the press is to be regretted. Their exciting contents, like stimulating drinks, when long indulged in, enervate the mind, unfitting it for the sober duties of life.

These duties are not to be limited by man. Nor will woman fulfill less her domestic relations, as the faithful companion of her chosen husband, and the fitting mother of her children, because she has a right estimate of her position and her responsibilities. Her self-respect will be increased; preserving the dignity of her being, she will not suffer herself to be degraded into a mere dependent. Nor will her feminine character be impaired. Instances are not few, of woman throwing off the encumbrances which bind her, and going forth in a manner worthy of herself, her creation, and her dignified calling. Did Elizabeth Fry lose any of her feminine qualities by the public walk into which she was called?[6] Having performed the duties of a mother to a large family, feeling that she owed a labor of love to the poor prisoner, she was empowered by Him who sent her forth, to go to kings and crowned heads of the earth, and ask audience of these; and it was granted her. Did she lose the delicacy of woman by her acts? No. Her retiring modesty was characteristic of her to the latest period of her life. It was my privilege to enjoy her society some years ago, and I found all that belonged to the feminine in woman--to true nobility, in a refined and purified moral nature. Is Dorothea Dix throwing off her womanly nature and appearance in the course

---

[6] Elizabeth Gurney Fry (1780-1845), English prison reformer and Quaker minister, worked tirelessly to improve the conditions of women in Newgate prison, urging separation by sex and supervision of women prisoners by women.

she is pursuing?[7] In finding duties abroad, has any "refined man felt that something of beauty has gone forth from her?" To use the contemptuous word applied in the lecture alluded to, is she becoming "mannish"? Is she compromising her womanly dignity in going forth to seek to better the condition of the insane and afflicted? Is not a beautiful mind and a retiring modesty still conspicuous in her?

Indeed, I would ask, if this modesty is not attractive also, when manifested in the other sex? It was strikingly marked in Horace Mann when presiding over the late National Educational Convention in this city.[8] The retiring modesty of William Ellery Channing was beautiful, as well as of many others, who have filled dignified stations in society.[9] These virtues, differing as they may in degree in man and woman, are of the same nature and call forth our admiration wherever manifested.

The noble courage of Grace Darling is justly honored, leading her to present herself on the coast of England, during the raging storm, in order to rescue the poor, suffering, shipwrecked mariner.[10] Woman was not wanting in courage, in the early ages. In war and bloodshed this trait was often displayed. Grecian and Roman history have lauded and

---

[7] Dorothea Lynde Dix (1802-1887), prison reformer and pioneer in movement for specialized treatment of the insane.

[8] Horace Mann (1796-1859), educator, lawyer, legislator, first president of Antioch College.

[9] See p. 51, n 10.

[10] Grace Darling (1815-1842), daughter of lighthouse keeper who, with her father, saved stranded passengers of the ship *Farforshire* which foundered on the Farne Islands (Armstrong 1965).

honored her in this character. English history records her courageous women too, for unhappily we have little but the records of war handed down to us. The courage of Joan of Arc was made the subject of a popular lecture not long ago, by one of our intelligent citizens. But more noble, moral daring is marking the female character at the present time, and better worthy of imitation. As these characteristics come to be appreciated in man too, his warlike acts, with all the miseries and horrors of the battle-ground, will sink into their merited oblivion, or be remembered only to be condemned. The heroism displayed in the tented field, must yield to the moral and Christian heroism which is shadowed in the signs of our times.

The lecturer regarded the announcement of woman's achievements, and the offering of appropriate praise through the press, as a gross innovation upon the obscurity of female life--he complained that the exhibition of the attainments of girls, in schools, was now equal to that of boys, and the newspapers announce that "Miss Brown received the first prize for English grammar," &c. If he objected to so much excitement of emulation in schools, it would be well; for the most enlightened teachers discountenance these appeals to love of approbation and self-esteem. But, while prizes continue to be awarded, can any good reason be given, why the name of the girl should not be published as well as that of the boy? He spoke with scorn, that "we hear of Mrs. President so and so; and committees and secretaries of the same sex." But if women can conduct their own business, by means of Presidents and Secretaries of their own sex, can he tell us why they should not? They will never make much progress in any moral movement, while they depend upon men to act for them. Do we shrink from reading the announcement that Mrs. Somerville is made an honorary member of a scientific association?[11] That Miss Herschel has made some discoveries, and is prepared to take her equal part in science?[12] Or that Miss Mitchell of Nantucket has lately discovered a planet, long looked for?[13] I cannot conceive why "honor to whom honor is due" [Rom. 13:7] should not be rendered to a woman as well as man; nor will it necessarily exalt her, or foster feminine pride. This propensity is found alike in male and female, and it should not be ministered to improperly, in either sex.

In treating upon the affections, the lecturer held out the idea, that as manifested in the sexes, they were opposite, if not somewhat antagonistic; and required a union, as in chemistry, to form a perfect whole. The simile appeared to me far from a correct illustration of the true union. Minds that can assimilate, spirits that are congenial, attach themselves to each other. It is the union of similar, not opposite affections, which are necessary for the perfection of the marriage bond. There seemed a want of proper delicacy in his representing man as being bold in the demonstration of the pure affection of love. In persons of refinement, true love seeks concealment in man, as well as in woman. I will not enlarge upon the subject, although it formed so great a part of his lecture. The contrast drawn seemed a fallacy, as has much, very much that has been presented, in the sickly sentimental strains of the poet, from age to age.

The question is often asked, "What does

---

[11] See p. 46, n 8.

[12] See p. 45, n 7.

[13] Maria Mitchell (1818-1889), Coffin Mott's cousin. An astronomer, later professor at Vassar, she discovered Mitchell's comet in 1847. In 1848 she became the first woman elected to the American Academy of Arts and Sciences in Boston.

woman want, more than she enjoys?" What is she seeking to obtain? Of what rights is she deprived? What privileges are withheld from her? I answer, she asks nothing as favor, but as right, she wants to be acknowledged a moral, responsible being. She is seeking not to be governed by laws, in the making of which she has no voice. She is deprived of almost every right in civil society, and is a cypher in the nation, except in the right of presenting a petition. In religious society her disabilities, as already pointed out, have greatly retarded her progress. Her exclusion from the pulpit or ministry--her duties marked out for her by her equal brother man, subject to creeds, rules, and disciplines made for her by him--this is unworthy her true dignity. In marriage, there is assumed superiority, on the part of the husband, and admitted inferiority, with a promise of obedience, on the part of the wife. This subject calls loudly for examination, in order that the wrong may be redressed. Customs suited to darker ages in Eastern countries, are not binding upon enlightened society. The solemn covenant of marriage may be entered into without these lordly assumptions, and humiliating concessions and promises.

There are large Christian denominations who [sic] do not recognize such degrading relations of husband and wife.[14] They ask no magisterial or ministerial aid to legalize or to sanctify this union. But acknowledging themselves in the presence of the Highest, and invoking his assistance, they come under reciprocal obligations of fidelity and affection, before suitable witnesses. Experience and observation go to prove, that there may be as much harmony, to say the least, in such a union, and as great purity and permanency of affection, as can exist

---

[14] The reference is to the Quakers, who conducted their own weddings in a simple ceremony (Bacon 1969, 16).

where the more common custom or form is observed. The distinctive relations of husband and wife, of father and mother of a family are sacredly preserved, without the assumption of authority on the one part, or the promise of obedience on the other. There is nothing in such a marriage degrading to woman. She does not compromise her dignity or self-respect; but enters married life upon equal ground, by the side of her husband. By proper education, she understands her duties, physical, intellectual and moral; and fulfilling these, she is a help meet, in the true sense of the word.

I tread upon delicate ground in alluding to the institutions of religious associations; but the subject is of so much importance, that all which relates to the position of woman, should be examined, apart from the undue veneration which ancient usage receives.

> Such dupes are men to custom, and so prone
> To reverence what is ancient, and can plead
> A course of long observance for its use,
> That even servitude, the worst of ills,
> Because delivered down from sire to son,
> Is kept and guarded as a sacred thing.

So with woman. She has so long been subject to the disabilities and restrictions, with which her progress has been embarrassed, that she has become enervated, her mind to some extent paralysed; and, like those still more degraded by personal bondage, she hugs her chains. Liberty is often presented in its true light, but it is liberty for man.

> Whose freedom is by suffrance, and at will
> Of a superior--he is never free.

> Who lives, and is not weary of a
> life
> Exposed to manacles, deserves them
> well.[15]

I would not, however, go so far, either as regards the abject slave or woman; for in both cases they may be so degraded by the crushing influences around them, that they may not be sensible of the blessing of Freedom. Liberty is not less a blessing, because oppression has so long darkened the mind that it cannot appreciate it. I would therefore urge, that woman be placed in such a situation in society, by the yielding of her rights, and have such opportunities for growth and development, as shall raise her from this low, enervated and paralysed condition, to a full appreciation of the blessing of entire freedom of mind.

It is with reluctance that I make the demand for the political rights of woman, because this claim is so distasteful to the age. Woman shrinks, in the present state of society, from taking any interest in politics. The events of the French Revolution, and the claim for woman's rights are held up to her as a warning. But let us not look at the excesses of women alone, at that period; but remember that the age was marked with extravagances and wickedness in men as well as women. Indeed, political life abounds with these excesses, and with shameful outrage. Who knows, but that if woman acted her part in governmental affairs, there might be an entire change in the turmoil of political life. It becomes man to speak modestly of his ability to act without her. If woman's judgment were exercised, why might she not aid in making the laws by which she is governed? Lord Brougham remarked that the works of Harriet Martineau upon Political Economy were not excelled by

---

[15] These lines and those above are from William Cowper, "The Task" (1835, 126, 128).

those of any political writer of the present time.[16] The first few chapters of her Society in America [1837], her views of a Republic, and of Government generally, furnish evidence of woman's capacity to embrace subjects of universal interest.

Far be it from me to encourage woman to vote, or to take an active part in politics, in the present state of our government. Her right to the elective franchise however, is the same, and should be yielded to her, whether she exercise that right or not. Would that man too, would have no participation in a government based upon the life-taking principle--upon retaliation and the sword. It is unworthy a Christian nation. But when, in the diffusion of light and intelligence, a convention shall be called to make regulations for self-government on Christian, non-resistant principles, I can see no good reason, why woman should not participate in such an assemblage, taking part equally with man.

Walker, of Cincinnati, in his *Introduction to American Law* [1837], says:

> With regard to political rights, females form a positive exception to the general doctrine of equality. They have no part or lot in the formation or administration of government. They cannot vote or hold office. We require them to contribute their share in the ways of taxes, to the support of government, but allow them no voice in its direction. We hold them amenable to the laws when made, but allow them no share in making them. This language, applied to males, would be

---

[16] Henry Peter Brougham (1778-1868), British statesman, a founder of the *Edinburgh Review*, liberal leader in the House of Commons. For information on Harriet Martineau, see p. 43, n 5.

> the exact definition of political slavery; applied to females, custom does not teach us so to regard it.

Woman, however, is beginning so to regard it.

> The law of husband and wife, as you gather it from the books, is a disgrace to any civilized nation. The theory of the law degrades the wife almost to the level of slaves. When a woman marries, we call her condition coverture, and speak of her as a *femme covert*. The old writers call the husband baron, and sometimes, in plain English, lord. . . . The merging of her name in that of her husband is emblematic of the fate of all her legal rights. The torch of Hymen serves but to light the pile, on which these rights are offered up. The legal theory is, that marriage makes the husband and wife one person, and that person is the *husband*. On this subject, reform is loudly called for. There is no foundation in reason or expediency, for the absolute and slavish subjection of the wife to the husband, which forms the foundation of the present legal relations. Were woman, in point of fact, the abject thing which the law, in theory, considers her to be when married, she would not be worthy the companionship of man.[17]

I would ask if such a code of laws does not require change? If such a condition of the wife in society does not claim redress? On no good ground can reform be delayed.

---

[17] Timothy Walker (1802-56), jurist and author.

Blackstone[18] says, "The very being and legal existence of woman is suspended during marriage,--incorporated or consolidated into that of her husband, under whose protection and cover she performs every thing." Hurlbut, in his *Essays upon Human Rights*, says:

> The laws touching the rights of woman are at variance with the laws of the Creator. Rights are human rights, and pertain to human beings, without distinction of sex. Laws should not be made for man or for woman, but for mankind. Man was not born to command, nor woman to obey. . . . The law of France, Spain, and Holland, and one of our own States, Louisiana, recognizes the wife's right to property, more than the common law of England. . . . The law depriving woman of the right of property is handed down to us from dark and feudal times, and not consistent with the wiser, better, purer spirit of the age. The wife is a mere pensioner on the bounty of her husband. Her lost rights are appropriated to himself. But justice and benevolence are abroad in our land, awakening the spirit of inquiry and innovation; and the Gothic fabric of the British law will fall before it, save where it is based upon the foundation of truth and justice (1848, 144-72).[19]

May these statements lead you to reflect upon this subject, that you may know what woman's condition is in society--what her restrictions are, and seek to remove them. In

---

[18] See p. 37, n 1.

[19] Elisha P. Hurlbut, prominent lawyer and judge.

how many cases in our country, the husband and wife begin life together, and by equal industry and united effort accumulate to themselves a comfortable home. In the event of the death of the wife, the household remains undisturbed, his farm or his workshop is not broken up, or in any way molested. But when the husband dies, he either gives his wife a *portion* of their joint accumulation, or the law apportions to her a *share*; the homestead is broken up, and she is dispossessed of that which she earned equally with him; for what she lacked in physical strength, she made up in constancy of labor and toil, day and evening. The sons then coming into possession of the property, as has been the custom until of latter time, speak of having to *keep* their mother, when she in reality is aiding to keep them. Where is the justice of this state of things? The change[s] in the law of this State and of New York, in relation to the property of the wife, go to a limited extent, toward the redress of these wrongs; but they are far more extensive, and involve much more, than I have time this evening to point out.

On no good ground can the legal existence of the wife be suspended during marriage, and her property surrendered to her husband. In the intelligent ranks of society, the wife may not, in point of fact, be so degraded as the law would degrade her; because public sentiment is above the law. Still, while the law stands, she is liable to the disabilities which it imposes. Among the ignorant classes of society, woman is made to bear heavy burdens, and is degraded almost to the level of the slave.

There are many instances now in our city, where the wife suffers much from the power of the husband to claim all that she can earn with her own hands. In my intercourse with the poorer class of people, I have known cases of extreme cruelty, from the hard earnings of the wife being thus robbed by the husband, and no redress at law.

An article in one of the daily papers lately, presented the condition of needle women in England. There might be a presentation of this class in our own country, which would make the heart bleed. Public attention should be turned to this subject, in order that avenues of more profitable employment may be opened to women. There are many kinds of business which women, equally with men, may follow with respectability and success. Their talents and energies should be called forth, and their powers brought into the highest exercise. The efforts of women in France are sometimes pointed to in ridicule and sarcasm, but depend upon it, the opening of profitable employment to women in that country, is doing much for the enfranchisement of the sex. In England also, it is not an uncommon thing for a wife to take up the business of her deceased husband and carry it on with success.

Our respected British Consul stated to me a circumstance which occurred some years ago, of an editor of a political paper having died in England; it was proposed to his wife, an able writer, to take the editorial chair. She accepted. The patronage of the paper was greatly increased, and she, a short time since retired from her labors with a handsome fortune. In that country however, the opportunities are by no means general for woman's elevation.

In visiting the public school in London, a few years since, I noticed that the boys were employed in linear drawing, and instructed upon the black board, in the higher branches of arithmetic and mathematics; while the girls, after a short exercise in the mere elements of arithmetic, were seated, during the bright hours of the morning, *stitching wristbands*. I asked, Why there should be this difference made; why they too should not have the black board? The answer was, that they would not probably fill any station in society requiring such knowledge.

But the demand for a more extended education will not cease, until girls and boys have equal instruction, in all the departments of useful knowledge. We have as yet no high school for girls in this state. The normal school may be a preparation for such an establishment. In the late convention for general education, it was cheering to hear the testimony borne to woman's capabilities for head teachers of the public schools. A resolution there offered for equal salaries to male and female teachers, when equally qualified, as practiced in Louisiana, I regret to say was checked in its passage, by Bishop Potter; by him who has done so much for the encouragement of education, and who gave his countenance and influence to that convention.[20] Still the fact of such a resolution being offered, augurs a time coming for woman, which she may well hail. At the last examination of the public schools in this city, one of the alumni delivered an address on Woman, not as is too common in eulogistic strains, but directing the attention to the injustice done to woman in her position in society, in a variety of ways. The unequal wages she receives for her constant toil, &c., presenting facts calculated to arouse attention to the subject.

Women's property has been taxed, equally with that of men's, to sustain colleges endowed by the states; but they have not been permitted to enter those high seminaries of learning. Within a few years, however, some colleges have been instituted, where young women are admitted, nearly upon equal terms with young men; and numbers are availing themselves of their long denied rights. This is

---

[20] Alonzo Potter (1800-65), Rector of St. Paul's, Boston (1826-31); professor of philosophy and political economy (1831-38) and vice president (1838-45) of Union College; author of *The School and the Schoolmaster* (1842); and Protestant Episcopal Bishop of Pennsylvania (1845-65), he did much to extend and improve public school education.

among the signs of the times, indicative of an advance for women. The book of knowledge is not opened to her in vain. Already is she aiming to occupy important posts of honor and profit in our country. We have three female editors in our state--some in other states of the Union. Numbers are entering the medical profession--one received a diploma last year; others are preparing for a like result.[21]

Let woman then go on--not asking as favor, but claiming as right, the removal of all the hindrances to her elevation in the scale of being--let her receive encouragement for the proper cultivation of all her powers, so that she may enter profitably into the active business of life; employing her own hands, in ministering to her necessities, strengthening her physical being by proper exercise, and observance of the laws of health. Let her not be ambitious to display a fair hand, and to promenade the fashionable streets of our city, but rather, coveting earnestly the best gifts,[22] let her strive to occupy such walks in society, as will befit her true dignity in all the relations of life. No fear that she will then transcend the proper limits of female delicacy. True modesty will be as fully preserved, in acting out those important vocations to which she may be called, as in the nursery or at the fireside, ministering to man's self-indulgence.

Then in the marriage union, the independence of the husband and wife will be equal, their dependence mutual, and their obligations

---

[21] James and Lucretia Coffin Mott raised money to establish the Female Medical College of Pennsylvania, which opened in 1850. In 1852, Lucretia presided over a series of public lectures on women's health and hygiene delivered by Dr. Hannah Longshore, an 1851 graduate (Bacon 1980, 136).

[22] See Luke 10:42.

reciprocal.

In conclusion, let me say, "Credit not the old fashioned absurdity, that woman's is a secondary lot, ministering to the necessities of her lord and master! It is a higher destiny I would award you. If your immortality is as complete, and your gift of mind as capable as ours, of increase and elevation, I would put no wisdom of mine against God's evident allotment. I would charge you to water the undying bud, and give it healthy culture, and open its beauty to the sun--and then you may hope, that when your life is bound up with another, you will go on equally, and in a fellowship that shall pervade every earthly interest."[23]

---

[23] In HWS 1:375, the author of this statement is identified as Nathaniel Parker Willis (1806-67), an author, playwright, and journalist.

7

Sojourner Truth, Speech at the Woman's Rights Convention, Akron, Ohio, 1851

Isabella (c.1797-1883), a slave in upstate New York, was freed by law in 1828, and in 1843 took the name of Sojourner Truth to begin a career of religious and reform speaking. She toured Indiana, Missouri, and Kansas for abolition and subsequently spoke for woman's rights and woman suffrage as well as for the rights of freed slaves. This speech was delivered at one of the early regional conventions, at which woman's rights advocates encountered fierce resistance, particularly from the clergy.

The text is from the **Narrative of Sojourner Truth** (Truth 1878, 133-35), *as recorded by Mrs. Frances D. Gage, who presided at the Akron woman's rights convention. Because Truth grew up speaking Dutch in upstate New York and had no contact with Southerners, white or Afro-American, until her teens, it is unlikely that, although illiterate, she spoke in a substandard Southern dialect, in which the speech was recorded by Mrs. Gage* (Fauset 1938). *Hence, I have removed purely dialectical indicators.*

Mrs. Gage set the scene for the speech this way:

> *I rose and announced "Sojourner Truth," and begged the audience to*

> *keep silence for a few moments. The tumult subsided at once, and every eye was fixed on this almost Amazon form, which stood nearly six feet high, head erect, and eye piercing the upper air, like one in a dream. At her first word, there was a profound hush. She spoke in deep tones, which, though not loud, reached every ear in the house, and away through the throng at the doors and windows:--*

Well, children, where there is so much racket there must be something out o' kilter. I think that 'twixt the Negroes of the South and the women of the North all a-talking about rights, the white men will be in a fix pretty soon.

But what's all this here talking about? That man over there says that women need to be helped into carriages, and lifted over ditches, and to have the best place everywhere. Nobody ever helps me into carriages, or over mud puddles or gives me any best place (*and raising herself to her full height and her voice to a pitch like rolling thunder, she asked*), and aren't I a woman? Look at me! Look at my arm! (*And she bared her right arm to the shoulder, showing her tremendous muscular power.*) I have plowed, and planted, and gathered into barns, and no man could head me--and aren't I a woman? I could work as much and eat as much as a man (when I could get it), and bear the lash as well--and aren't I a woman? I have borne thirteen children[1] and seen them almost all sold off into slavery, and when I cried out with a mother's grief, none but Jesus heard--and aren't I a woman? Then they talk about this thing in the head--what's this they call it? (*"Intellect,"*

---

[1] Another text reads five, a figure that is given in other sources as the actual number of her children.

whispered someone near.) That's it honey. What's that got to do with woman's rights or Negroes' rights? If my cup won't hold but a pint and yours holds a quart, wouldn't you be mean not to let me have my little half-measure full? *(And she pointed her significant finger and sent a keen glance at the minister who had made the argument. The cheering was long and loud.)*

Then that little man in black [a clergy-man] there, he says women can't have as much rights as man, 'cause Christ wasn't a woman. Where did your Christ come from? *(Rolling thunder could not have stilled that crowd as did those deep, wonderful tones, as she stood there with outstretched arms and eye of fire. Raising her voice still louder, she repeated,)* Where did your Christ come from? From God and a woman.[2] Man had nothing to do with him. *(Oh! what a rebuke she gave the little man.)*

(Turning again to another objector, she took up the defense of mother Eve. I cannot follower her through it all. It was pointed, and witty, and solemn, eliciting at almost every sentence deafening applause; and she eneded by asserting that) If the first woman God ever made was strong enough to turn the world upside down, all alone, these together *(and she glanced her eye over us)*, ought to be able to turn it back and get it right side up again; and now they are asking to do it, the men better let them. *(Long-continued cheer-ing.)*

'Bliged to you for hearing on me, and now old Sojourner hasn't got anything more to say.

(Amid roars of applause, she turned to her corner, leaving more than one of us with streaming eyes and hearts beating with gratitude. She had taken us up in her strong

---

[2] Mary's child wipes out Eve's curse: "Christ hath redeemed us from the curse of the law" (Gal. 3:13); "And there shall be no more curse." (Rev. 22:3)

arms and carried us safely over the slough of difficulty, turning the whole tide in our favor. I have never in my life seen anything like the magical influence that subdued the mobbish spirit of the day and turned the jibes and sneers of an excited crowd into notes of respect and admiration. Hundreds rushed up to shake hands, and congratulate the glorious old mother and bid her God speed on her mission of "testifying again concerning the wickedness of this here people.")

8

Ernestine Potowski Rose, Speech at the National Woman's Rights Convention, Worcester, MA, 1851

Ernestine Siismondi Potowski Rose was born in 1810 in Poland, daughter of a rabbi, with whom she studied Talmud and Torah. She left Poland after the death of her mother, traveling throughout Europe and witnessing the events of the 1830 French Revolution firsthand. In England she met Robert Owen and espoused his principles; she married William E. Rose. She and her husband came to the United States in 1836, where she lectured on the evils of the existing social system, against slavery, for the rights of women, for the religious rights of individuals, and on other reform questions, traveling to 23 states. Her lectures and reform efforts laid the foundation for the woman's rights movement, in which she was very active until she returned to England in ill health in 1873. As a foreigner, a radical, and an outspoken agnostic, she was a controversial figure.

Prior to 1866, there was no formal organization for woman's rights; conventions functioned as a substitute. The 1851 convention at Worcester was the second national convention, evidence that interest in woman's rights was geographically widespread. This speech ranks with that of Cady Stanton at Seneca Falls as a statement about movement ideology and concerns. The text is from the convention **Proceedings** (1852, 36-47).

After having heard the letter read from our poor incarcerated sisters of France, well might we exclaim, Alas! poor France! where is thy glory? Where the glory of the Revolution of 1848, in which shone forth the pure and magnanimous spirit of an oppressed nation, struggling for Freedom?[1] Where the fruits of that victory that gave to the world the motto, Liberty, Equality, and Fraternity? A motto destined to hurl the tyranny of kings and priests into the dust, and give freedom to the enslaved millions of the earth. Where, I again ask, is the result of these noble achievements, when Woman, ay, one half of the nation, is deprived of her rights? Has Woman then been idle during the contest between Right and Might? Has she been wanting in ardor and enthusiasm? Has she not mingled her blood with that of her husband, son, and sire? Or has she been recreant in hailing the motto of Liberty floating on your banners as an omen of justice, peace, and freedom to man, that at the first step she takes practically to claim the recognition of her Rights, she is rewarded with the doom of a martyr? But Right has not yet asserted her prerogative, for Might rules the day; and as every good cause must have its martyrs, why should Woman not be a martyr for her cause? But need we wonder that France, governed as she is by Russian and Austrian

---

[1] For detailed information on women's extensive activities in the Revolution of 1848 see Lougee, (1972, ch. 6, esp. 172-78). The hope that an ideal socialist state could be established non-violently was dashed in the general election, which gave over 5 million votes to Louis Napoleon. In July, 1851, a last attempt to establish universal suffrage failed. Napoleon exploited conflicts among the monarchists and republicans and established himself in a *coup d'état*, ratified by plebiscite.on December 2, 1851. One year later a plebiscite conferred supreme power, with the title of emperor, on Napoleon III.

despotism, does not recognize the rights of humanity in the recognition of the Rights of Woman, when even here, in this far-famed land of freedom, under a Republic that has inscribed on its banner the great truth that all men are created free and equal, and endowed with inalienable rights to life, liberty, and the pursuit of happiness,--a declaration borne, like the vision of hope, on wings of light to the remotest parts of the earth, an omen of freedom to the oppressed and downtrodden children of man,--when, even here, in the very face of this eternal truth, woman, the mockingly so called "better half" of man, has yet to plead for her rights, nay, for her life; for what is life without liberty, and what is liberty with out equality of rights? And as for the pursuit of happiness, she is not allowed to pursue any line of life that might promote it; she has only thankfully to accept what man in his magnanimity decides is best for her to do, and this is what he does not choose to do himself. Is she then not included in that declaration? Answer, ye wise men of the nation, and answer truly; add not hypocrisy to oppression! Say that she is not created free and equal, and therefore (for the sequence follows on the premises) that she is not entitled to life, liberty, and the pursuit of happiness. But with all the audacity arising from an assumed superiority, you dare not so libel and insult humanity as to say, that she is not included in that declaration; and if she is, then what right has man, except that of might, to deprive woman of the rights and privileges he claims for himself? And why, in the name of reason and justice, why should she not have the same rights? Because she is woman? Humanity recognizes no sex--virtue recognizes no sex--mind recognizes no sex--life and death, pleasure and pain, happiness and misery recognize no sex. Like man, woman comes involuntarily into existence; like him she possesses physical and mental and moral powers, on the proper cultivation of which depends her happiness; like him she is subject to all the vicissitudes of life; like him she has to pay the penalty for disobeying nature's laws, and far greater penalties has she to suffer from ignorance of her far more complicated nature than he; like him she enjoys or suffers with her country. Yet she is not recognized as his equal! In the laws of the land she has no rights, in government she has no voice. And in spite of another principle, recognized in this Republic, namely, that "taxation without representation is tyranny," yet she is taxed without being represented. Her property may be consumed by taxes to defray the expenses of that unholy, unrighteous custom called war, yet she has no power to give her veto against it. From the cradle to the grave she is subject to the power and control of man. Father, guardian, or husband, one conveys her like some piece of merchandise over to the other. At marriage she loses her entire identity and her being is said to have become merged in her husband. Has nature thus merged it? Has she ceased to exist and feel pleasure and pain? When she violates the laws of her being, does her husband pay the penalty? When she breaks the moral laws, does he suffer the punishment? When he supplies his wants, is it enough to satisfy her nature? And when at his nightly orgies, in the grog-shop and the oyster cellar, or at the gaming-table, he squanders the means she helped by her cooperation and economy to accumulate, and she awakens to penury and destitution, will it supply the wants of her children to tell them, that owing to the superiority of man she had no redress by law; and that as her being was merged in his, so also ought theirs to be? What an inconsistency, that from the moment she enters that compact, in which she assumes the high responsibility of wife and mother, she ceases legally to exist, and becomes a purely submissive being. Blind submission in woman is considered a virtue, while submission to wrong is itself wrong, and resistance to wrong is virtue alike in woman as in man.

But it will be said that the husband provides for the wife, or in other words, he feeds, clothes, and shelters her! I wish I had the power to make every one before me fully realize the degradation contained in that idea. Yes! he *keeps* her, and so he does a favorite horse; by law they are both considered his property. Both may, when the cruelty of the owner compels them to run away, be brought back by the strong arm of the law, and according to a still extant law of England both may be led by the halter to the market-place and sold. This is humiliating indeed, but nevertheless true; and the sooner these things are known and understood, the better for humanity. It is no fancy sketch. I know that some endeavor to throw the mantle of romance over the subject, and treat woman like some ideal existence, not liable to the ills of life. Let such deal in fancy, that have nothing better to deal in; we have to do with sober, sad realities, with stubborn facts.

Again, I shall be told that the law presumes the husband to be kind, affectionate, and ready to provide for and protect his wife. But what right, I ask, has the law to presume at all on the subject? What right has the law to intrust the interest and happiness of one being into the hands of another? And if the merging of the interest of one being into the other is a necessary consequence on marriage, why should woman always remain on the losing side? Turn the tables. Let the identity and interest of the husband be merged in the wife. Think you she would act less generously towards him, than he towards her? Think you she is not capable of as much justice, disinterested devotion, and abiding affection, as he is? Oh, how grossly you misunderstand and wrong her nature! But we desire no such undue power over man; it would be as wrong in her to exercise it as it now is in him. All we claim is an equal legal and social position. We have nothing to do with individual man, be he good or bad, but with the laws that oppress woman. We know that bad and unjust laws must in the nature of things make man so too. If he is kind, affectionate, and consistent, it is because the kindlier feelings, instilled by a mother, kept warm by a sister, and cherished by a wife, will not allow him to carry out those barbarous laws against woman.

But the estimation she is generally held in, is as degrading as it is foolish. Man forgets that woman cannot be degraded without its re-acting on himself. The impress of her mind is stamped on him by nature, and the early education of the mother which no after-training can entirely efface; and therefore, the estimation she is held in falls back with double force upon him. Yet, from the force of prejudice against her, he knows it not. Not long ago, I saw an account of two offenders, brought before a Justice of New York. One was charged with stealing a pair of boots, for which offense he was sentenced to six months' imprisonment; the other crime was assault and battery upon his wife: he was let off with a reprimand from the judge! With my principles, I am entirely opposed to punishment, and hold, that to reform the erring and remove the causes of evil is much more efficient, as well as just, than to punish. But the judge showed us the comparative value which he set on these two kinds of *property*. But then you must remember that the boots were taken by a stranger, while the wife was insulted by her legal owner! Here it will be said, that such degrading cases are but few. For the sake of humanity, I hope they are. But as long as woman shall be oppressed by unequal laws, so long will she be degraded by man. We have hardly an adequate idea how all-powerful law is in forming public opinion, in giving tone and character to the mass of society. To illustrate my point, look at that infamous, detestable law, which was written in human blood, and signed and sealed with life and liberty, that eternal stain on the statute book of this country, the Fugitive Slave Law.[2] Think you that before its passage, you could have found any in the free States--except a few politicians in the market--base enough to desire such a law? No! no! Even those who took no interest in the slave question would have shrunk from so barbarous a thing. But no sooner was it passed, than the ignorant mass, the rabble of the self- styled Union Safety Committee, found out that we were a law-loving, law-abiding people! Such is the magic power of Law. Hence the necessity to guard against bad ones. Hence also the reason why we call on the nation to remove the legal shackles from woman, and it will have a beneficial effect on that still greater tyrant she has to contend with, Public Opinion.

Carry out the republican principle of universal suffrage, or strike it from your banners and substitute "Freedom and Power to one half of society, and submission and slavery to the other." Give woman the elective franchise. Let married women have the same right to property that their husbands have; for whatever the difference in their respective occupations, the duties of the wife are as indispensable and far more arduous than the husband's. Why then should the wife, at the death of her husband, not be his heir to the same extent that he is heir to her? In this inequality there is involved another

---

[2] Federal acts of 1793 and 1850 provided for the return between states of escaped slaves. The more rigorous 1850 law, passed as part of the Compromise of 1850, commanded all good citizens "to aid and assist [Federal marshals and their deputies] in the prompt and efficient execution of this law" and imposed heavy penalties on anyone assisting slaves in escaping. When apprehended, alleged fugitives were denied a jury trial, their testimony was not admitted, while the master's statement claiming ownership, even if the master were absent, was taken as the main evidence.

wrong. When the wife dies, the husband is left in the undisturbed possession of all there is, and the children are left with him; no change is made, no stranger intrudes on his home and his affliction. But when the husband dies, not only is the widow, as too often is the case, deprived of all, and at best receives but a mere pittance, while strangers assume authority denied to the wife. The sanctuary of affliction must be desecrated by executors; everything must be ransacked and assessed, lest she should steal something out of her own house; and to cap the climax, the children must be placed under guardians. When the husband dies poor, to be sure, no guardian is required, and the children are left for the mother to care and toil for them, as best she may. But when anything is left for their maintenance, then it must be placed in the hands of strangers for safe keeping! The bringing up and safety of the children is left with the mother, and safe they are in her hands. But a few hundred or thousand dollars cannot be intrusted with her! But, say they, "in case of a second marriage, the children must be protected in their possession." Does that reason not hold as good in the case of the husband as in that of the wife? Oh, no! When *he* marries again, he still retains his identity and power to act; but *she* becomes merged once more into a mere nonentity; and therefore the first husband must rob her to prevent the second from doing so! Make the laws then, (if any are required,) regulating property between husband and wife, equal for both, and all these difficulties would be removed.

According to a late act, the wife has a right to the property she brings at marriage, or receives in any way after marriage.[3] Here is some provision for the favored few; but for the laboring many, there is none. The mass of

---

[3] New York Married Woman's Property Act of 1848.

the people commence life with no other capital than the union of heads, hearts and hands. To the benefit of this best of capital, the wife has no right. If they are unsuccessful in married life, who suffers more the bitter consequences of poverty than the wife? But if successful, she cannot call a dollar her own. The husband may will away every dollar of the personal property, and leave her destitute and penniless, and she has no redress by law. And even where real estate is left, she receives but a life-interest in a third part of it, and at her death, she cannot leave it to any one belonging to her, it falls back even to the remotest of his relatives. This is law, but where is the justice of it? Well might we say that laws were made to prevent, not to promote, the ends of justice. Or, in case of separation, why should the children be taken from the protecting care of the mother? Who has a better right to them than she? How much do fathers generally do towards the bringing of them up? When he comes home from business, and the child is in good humor and handsome trim, he takes the little darling on his knee and plays with it. But when the wife, with the care of the whole household on her shoulders, with little or no help, is not able to put them in the best order or trim, how much does he do towards it? Oh, no! Fathers like to have children good-natured, well-behaved, and comfortable, but how to put them in that desirable condition is out of their philosophy. Children always depend more on the tender, watchful care of the mother, than of the father. Whether from nature, habit, or both, the mother is much more capable of administering to their health and comfort than the father, and therefore she has the best right to them. And where there is property, it ought to be divided equally between them, with an additional provision from the father towards the maintenance and education of the children. Much is said about the burdens and responsibilities of married men. Responsibilities indeed there are, if they but felt them;

but as to burdens, what are they? The sole province of man seems to be centered in that one thing, attending to some business. I grant that owing to the present unjust and unequal reward for labor, many have to work too hard for a subsistence; but whatever his vocation, he has to attend as much to it before as after marriage. Look at your bachelors, and see if they do not strive as much for wealth, and attend as steadily to business, as married men. No! the husband has little or no increase of burden, and every increase of comfort after marriage; while most of the burdens, cares, pains, and penalties of married life fall on the wife. How unjust and cruel, then, to have all the laws in his favor! If any difference should be made, by law, between husband and wife, reason, justice, and humanity--if their voices were heard--would dictate that it should be in her favor.

It is high time to denounce such gross injustice, to compel man by the might of right to give to woman her political, legal, and social rights. Open to her all the avenues of emolument, distinction, and greatness; give her an object for which to cultivate her powers, and a fair chance to do so, and there will be no need to speculate as to her proper sphere. She will find her own sphere in accordance with her capacities, powers, and tastes; and yet she will be woman still. Her rights will not change, but strengthen, develop, and elevate her nature. Away, then, with that folly and absurdity, that a possession of her rights would be detrimental to her character; that if she is recognized as the equal to man, she would cease to be woman. Have his rights as citizen of a republic, the elective franchise with all its advantages, so changed man's nature, that he has ceased to be man? Oh, no! But woman could not bear such a degree of power; what has benefited him, would injure her; what has strengthened him, would weaken her; what has prompted him to the performance of his duties, would make her neglect hers! Such is the superficial mode of reasoning--if it deserves that name--which is brought against the doctrine of woman's equality with man. It reminds me of two reasons given by a minister of Milton, on the North River. Having heard that I had spoken on the Rights of Woman, he took the subject up on the following Sunday; and in order to prove that woman should not have equal rights with man, he argued, first, that Adam was created before Eve, and secondly, that man was compared to the fore wheels, and woman to the hind wheels of a wagon. These reasons are about as philosophical as any that can be brought against the views we advocate.

But here is another difficulty. In point of principle, some say it is true that woman ought to have the same rights as man; but in carrying out this principle in practice, would you expose her to the contact of rough, rude, drinking, swearing, fighting men at the ballot-box? What a humiliating confession lies in this plea for keeping woman in the background! Is the brutality of some men, then, a reason why woman should be kept from her rights? If man, in his superior wisdom, cannot devise means to enable woman to deposit her vote without having her finer sensibilities shocked by such disgraceful conduct, then there is an additional reason, as well as necessity, why she should be there to civilize, refine, and purify him, even at the ballot-box. Yes, in addition to the principle of right, this is one of the reasons, drawn from expediency, why woman should participate in all the important duties of life; for, with all due respect to the other sex, she is the true civilizer of man. With all my heart do I pity the man who has grown up and lives without the benign influence of woman. Even now, in spite of being considered the inferior, she exerts a most beneficial influence on man. Look at your annual festivities where woman is excluded, and you will find more or less drunkenness, disorder, vulgarity, and excess, to be the order of the day. Compare them with festive scenes where woman is the equal participant with man, and there you will see rational, social enjoyment and general decorum prevailing. If this is the case now--and who can deny it?--how much more beneficial would be woman's influence, if, as the equal with man, she should take her stand by his side, to cheer, counsel, and aid him through the drama of life, in the Legislative halls, in the Senate chamber, in the Judge's chair, in the jury box, in the Forum, in the Laboratory of the arts and sciences, and wherever duty would call her for the benefit of herself, her country, her race. For at every step she would carry with her a humanizing influence.

Oh! blind and misguided man! you know not what you do in opposing this great reform. It is not a partial affair confined to class, sect, or party. Nations have ever struggled against nations, people against despotic governments; from the times of absolute despotism to the present hour of comparative freedom, the weak have had to struggle against the strong, and right against might. But a new sign has appeared in our social zodiac, prophetic of the most important changes, pregnant with the most beneficial results, that have ever taken place in the annals of human history. We have before us a novel spectacle, an hitherto unheard-of undertaking, in comparison to which all others fall into insignificance, the grandest step in the onward progress of humanity. *One half of the race* stands up against the injustice and oppression of the other, and demands the recognition of its existence, and of its rights. Most sincerely do I pity those who have not advanced far enough to aid in this noble undertaking; for the attainment of woman's coequality with man is in itself not the *end*, but the most efficient *means* ever at the command of mankind towards a higher state of human elevation, without which the race can never attain it. Why should one half of the race keep the other half in subjugation? In this country it is considered wrong for one nation to enact laws and force them upon another. Does the same wrong not hold good of the sexes? Is woman a being like man? Then she is entitled to the same rights, is she not? How can he legislate rightfully for a being whose nature he cannot understand, whose motives he cannot appreciate, and whose feelings he cannot realize? How can he sit in judgment and pronounce a verdict against a being so entirely different from himself?

No! there is no reason against woman's elevation, but there are deep-rooted, hoary-headed prejudices. The main cause of them is, a pernicious falsehood propagated against her being, namely, that she is inferior by her nature. Inferior in what? What has man ever done, that woman, under the same advantages, could not do? In morals, bad as she is, she is generally considered his superior. In the intellectual sphere, give her a fair chance before you pronounce a verdict against her. Cultivate the frontal portion of her brain as much as that of man is cultivated, and she will stand his equal at least. Even now, where her mind has been called out at all, her intellect is as bright, as capacious, and as powerful as his. Will you tell us, that women have no Newtons, Shakespeares, and Byrons? Greater natural powers than even these possessed may have been destroyed in woman for want of proper culture, a just appreciation, reward for merit as an incentive to exertion, and freedom of action, without which, mind becomes cramped and stifled, for it cannot expand under bolts and bars; and yet, amid all blighting, crushing circumstances--confined within the narrowest possible limits, trampled upon by prejudice and injustice, from her education and position forced to occupy herself almost exclusively with the most trivial affairs--in spite of all these difficulties, her intellect is as good as his. The few bright meteors in man's intellectual horizon could well be matched by woman, were she allowed to occupy the same elevated position. There is no need of naming the De Staëls,[4] the Rolands,[5] the Somervilles,[6] the Wollstonecrafts,[7] the Sigourneys,[8] the Wrights,[9] the Martineaus,[10] the Hemanses,[11]

---

[4] See p. 45, n 6.

[5] Jeanne Manon Philipon Roland de la Platière (1754-93), French revolutionary, made her house the intellectual center of the Girondists. Her husband rose to prominence largely as a result of her ambition and political connections. When her party fell, she was arrested and as she walked to the guillotine, she cried: "O Liberty, what crimes are committed in thy name!"

[6] See p. 46, n 8.

[7] Mary Wollstonecraft (1759-97), English author and feminist whose *A Vindication of the Rights of Woman* (1792) was the first great feminist document.

[8] Lydia Howard Huntley Sigourney (1791-1865), author. After publication of *Letters to Young Ladies* (1833), her most popular prose work, she abandoned anonymity, despite her husband's disapproval, and set out frankly to pursue literature as a trade.

[9] Frances Wright [d'Arusmont] (1795-1852), Scottish freethinker who came to the United States in 1818 and again in 1824. Converted to the socialism of Robert Dale Owen, she set up a colony, Nashoba, to facilitate gradual emancipation of slaves. After its failure in 1824, she devoted herself to lecturing, advocating universal education, equality of women, religious freedom, abolition of slavery and worker's rights. She is thought to have been the first women to speak in public in the United States to "promiscuous" audiences of men and women. Her liberal ideas, combined with her costume (the

the Fullers,[12] Jagellos [sic],[13] and many more of modern as well as ancient times, to prove her mental powers, her patriotism, her self-sacrificing devotion to the cause of humanity, and the eloquence that gushes from her pen, or from her tongue. These things are too well known to require repetition. And do you ask for fortitude, energy, and perseverance? Then look at woman under suffering, reverse of fortune, and affliction, when the

---

tunic and bloomers of New Harmony women) and her short curly hair, caused a great sensation (Lane 1972, 3). Women who afterward attempted to speak were attacked as "Fanny Wrightists."

[10] See p. 45, n 5.

[11] Felicia Browne Hemans (1793-1835), English poet whose works were frequently set to music and praised as "beautiful and chaste songs . . . everything that comes from her pen is pure, and bears the image and superscription of an elevated and chastened mind" (Tick 1983, 28).

[12] Margaret Fuller [Ossoli] (1810-1850), author, critic, teacher, and feminist, held conversations from 1839-40, in which the most prominent women of Boston participated, including Elizabeth Cady Stanton. With Ralph Waldo Emerson and other transcendentalists, she edited the *Dial*. Her most famous work is *Woman in the Nineteenth Century* (1845), a feminist classic.

[13] Appolonia Jagiello (1825-1866) fought for the liberation of Poland and Hungary. During the Cracow insurrection in 1846, she assumed male attire and went into the thick of the fight. After the Hungarian Insurrection failed, she came to the United States in 1849, and married Gaspard Tochman, who in 1861 formed a brigade that fought on the side of the Confederacy in the Civil War.

strength and power of man have sunk to the lowest ebb, when his mind is overwhelmed by the dark waters of despair. She, like the tender ivy plant, bent yet unbroken by the storms of life, not only upholds her own hopeful courage, but clings around the tempest-fallen oak, to speak hope to his faltering spirit, and shelter him from the returning blast of the storm.

Wherein then, again I ask, is man so much woman's superior, that he must for ever remain her master? In physical strength? Allow me to say, that therein the inmates of the forest are his superior. But even on this point, why is she the feeble, sickly, suffering being we behold her? Look to her most defective and irrational education, and you will find a solution of the problem. Is the girl allowed to expand her limbs and chest in healthful exercise in the fresh breezes of heaven? Is she allowed to inflate her lungs and make the welkin ring with her cheerful voice like the boy? Who ever heard of a girl committing such improprieties? A robust development in a girl is unfashionable, a healthy, sound voice is vulgar, a ruddy glow on the cheek is coarse; and when vitality is so strong within her as to show itself in spite of bolts and bars, then she has to undergo a bleaching process, eat lemons, drink vinegar, and keep in the shade.

And do you know why these irrationalities are practised? Because man wishes them to be delicate; for whatever he admires in woman will she possess. That is the influence man has over woman, for she has been made to believe that she was created for his benefit only. "It was not well for man to be alone" [Gen. 2:18], therefore she was made as a plaything to pass away an idle hour, or as a drudge to do his bidding; and until this falsehood is eradicated from her mind, until she feels that the necessities, services, and obligations of the sexes are mutual, that she is as independent of him as he is of her, that she is formed for the same aims and ends in life that he is--until, in fact, she has all rights equal with man, there will be no other object in her education, except to get married, and what will best promote that desirable end will be cultivated in her. Do you not yet understand what has made woman what she is? Then see what the sickly taste and perverted judgment of man now admires in woman. Not physical and mental vigor, but a pale, delicate face; hands too small to grasp a broom, for that were treason in a lady; a voice so sentimental and depressed, that what she says can be learned only by the moving of her half parted lips; and above all, that nervous sensibility which sees a ghost in every passing shadow, that beautiful diffidence which dares not take a step without the protecting arm of man to support her tender frame, and that shrinking mock-modesty that faints at the mention of a leg of a table. I know there are many noble exceptions, who see and deplore these irrationalities; but as a general thing, the facts are as I state, or else why that hue and cry of "mannish," "unfeminine," "out of her sphere," etc., whenever woman evinces any strength of body or mind, and takes interest in anything deserving of a rational being? Oh! the crying injustice towards woman. She is crushed at every step, and then insulted for being what a most pernicious education and corrupt public sentiment have made her. But there is no confidence in her powers, nor principles.

After last year's Woman's Convention, I saw an article in the *Christian Inquirer*, a Unitarian paper, edited by the Rev. Mr. Bellows of New York, where, in reply to a correspondent on the subject of woman's rights, in which he strenuously opposed her taking part in anything in public, he said: "Place woman unbonneted and unshawled before the public gaze, and what becomes of her modesty and her virtue?"[14] In his benighted mind, the modesty and virtue of woman is of so fragile a nature, that when it is in contact with the atmosphere, it evaporates like chloroform. But I refrain to comment on such a sentiment. It carries with it its own deep condemnation. When I read the article, I earnestly wished I had the ladies of the writer's congregation before me, to see whether they could realize the estimation their pastor held them in. Yet I hardly know which sentiment was strongest in me, contempt for such foolish opinions, or pity for a man that has so degrading an opinion of woman--of the being that gave him life, that sustained his helpless infancy with her ever watchful care, and laid the very foundation for the little mind he may possess--of the being he took to his bosom as the partner of his joys and sorrows--the one whom, when he strove to win her affection, he courted, as all such men court woman, like some divinity. Such a man deserves our pity; for I cannot realize that a man purposely and willfully degrades his Mother, Sister, Wife, and Daughter. No! my better nature, my best knowledge and conviction forbid me to believe it.

It is from ignorance, not malice, that man acts towards woman as he does. In ignorance of her nature, and the interest and happiness of both sexes, he conceived ideas, laid down rules, and enacted laws concerning her destiny and rights. The same ignorance, strengthened by age, sanctified by superstition, ingrafted into his being by habit, makes him carry these convictions out to the detriment of his own as well as her happiness; for is he not the loser by his injustice? Oh! how severely he suffers. Who can fathom the depth of misery and suffering to society from the subjugation and injury inflicted on woman?

---

[14] Henry Whitney Bellows (1814-82), from 1839 to his death pastor of the First Congregational Society, Unitarian, New York City.

The race is elevated in excellence and power, or kept back in progression, in accordance with the scale of woman's position in society. But so firmly has prejudice closed the eyes of man to the light of truth, that though he feels the evils, he knows not their cause. Those men who have their eyes already open to these facts, earnestly desire the restoration of woman's rights, as the means of enabling her to take her proper position in the scale of humanity. If all men could see the truth, all would desire to aid this reform, as they desire their own happiness; for the interest and happiness of the sexes cannot be divided. Nature has too closely united them to permit one to oppress the other with impunity. I cast no more blame or reproach on man, however, than on woman, for she, from habit based on the same errors, is as much opposed to her interest and happiness as he is. How long is it, indeed, since any of us have come out of the darkness into the light of day? how long since any of us have advocated this righteous cause? The longest period is but, as it were, yesterday. And why has this been? From the same reason that so many of both sexes are opposed to it yet--ignorance. Both men and women have to be roused from that deathly lethargy in which they slumber. That worse than Egyptian darkness must be dispelled from their minds before the pure rays of the sun can penetrate them. And therefore, while I feel it my duty, ay, a painful duty, to point out the wrong done to woman and its consequences, and would do all in my power to aid in her deliverance, I can have no more ill feelings towards man than, for the same error, I have towards her. Both are the victims of error and ignorance, both suffer. Hence the necessity for active, earnest endeavors to enlighten their minds; hence the necessity for this, and many more Conventions, to protest against the wrong and claim our rights. And in so acting, we must not heed the taunts, ridicule, and stigmas cast upon us. We must remember that we have a crusade before us, far holier and more righteous than led warriors to Palestine--a crusade, not to deprive any one of his rights, but to claim our own. And as our cause is a nobler one, so also should be the means to achieve it. We therefore must put on the armor of charity, carry before us the banner of truth, and defend ourselves with the shield of right against the invaders of our liberty. And yet, like the knight of old, we must enlist in this holy cause with a disinterested devotion, energy, and determination never to turn back until we have conquered, not, indeed, by driving the Turk from his possession, but by claiming our rightful inheritance, for his benefit as well as for our own. To achieve this glorious victory of right over might, woman has much to do. Man may remove her legal shackles, and recognize her as his equal, which will greatly aid in her elevation; but the law cannot compel her to cultivate her mind and take an independent stand as a free being. She must cast off that mountain weight, that intimidating cowardly question, which like a nightmare presses down all her energies, namely, "What will people say? what will Mrs. Grundy say?" Away with such slavish fears! Woman must think for herself, and use for herself that greatest of all prerogatives--judgment of right and wrong. And next she must act according to her best convictions, irrespective of any other voice than that of right and duty. The time, I trust, will come, though slowly, yet surely, when woman will occupy that high and lofty position, for which nature has so eminently fitted her, in the destinies of humanity.

9

Clarina Howard Nichols, "The Responsibilities of Woman," Second National Woman's Rights Convention, Worcester, MA, 1851

Clarina Howard was born in Vermont in 1810. In 1830 she married Justin Carpenter, a Baptist minister, moved to New York and taught at the Brockport Academy, later founding a woman's seminary at Herkimer. In 1839 she separated from her husband and returned to Vermont with their three children; in 1843 she was granted a divorce by the Vermont legislature (Christiansen 1987, 28). *From 1843 through 1853, she edited the* **Windham County Democrat** *in Brattleboro, Vermont, published by her second husband, George Nichols. Beginning in 1847, she wrote a series of editorials detailing the effects of married women's property disabilities, which laid the foundation for a state law securing to the wife property she inherited or acquired by gift. In 1852, she was invited to address the Vermont legislature, but no text of that speech still exists. That year she met Susan B. Anthony, who remained a close friend until Howard Nichols's death in 1885.*

Between 1850 and 1854, she spoke at eight temperance and woman's rights conventions. In 1854 she moved her family to Kansas as part of the effort to make it a free state, later becoming associate editor of a free-state newspaper, the **Quindaro Chindowan.** *Although unable to vote on proposals, she is credited with considerable influence at the 1859 Kansas* *constitutional convention* (Gambone 1973, 12-13). She was invited to address that convention at a special session, and for that reason, no text of her speech exists. *When Kansas entered the Union in 1861, it had the most liberal laws relating to women of any other state. Howard Nichols lectured extensively, but her role in the early woman's rights movement is less well known because she left the east coast where most national conventions were held and where most national leaders resided.*

This speech, delivered at the second national convention, is an apt reflection of woman's rights activists' early concerns. It also illustrates the early use of arguments based in expediency or benefits, their efforts to present modest proposals and to adapt to diverse convention audiences that included hostile as well as sympathetic listeners. And finally, it displays an extremely skilled use of vivid examples.

The text is taken from the pamphlet of the same name in the Series of Woman's Rights Tracts (Nichols 1853).

My friends, I have made no preparation to address you. I left home, feeling that, if I had anything to do here, I should have the grace given me to do it; or if there should be any branch of the subject not sufficiently presented, I would present it. And now, friends, in following so many speakers, who have so well occupied the ground, I will come as a gleaner, and be as a Ruth among my fellow-laborers.[1]

I commenced life with the most refined notions of woman's sphere. My pride of womanhood lay within this nice sphere. I know now how it was,--perhaps because I am of mountain growth,--but I could, even than, see over the barriers of that sphere, and see that, however easy it might be for *me* to keep

---

[1] Ruth 2:2-23.

within it, as a daughter, a great majority of women were outside its boundaries; driven thither by their own, or invited by the necessities and interests of those they loved. I saw our farmers' wives,--women esteemed for every womanly virtue,--impelled by emergencies, helping their husbands in labors excluded from the modern woman's sphere. I was witness, on one occasion, to a wife's helping her husband--who was ill and of feeble strength, and too poor to hire--to pile the logs, preparatory to clearing the ground that was to grow their daily bread; and my sympathies, which recognized in her act the self-sacrificing love of woman, forbade that I should judge her out of her sphere. For I felt in my heart that, if I were a wife and loved my husband, I, too, would help him when he needed help, even if it were to *roll logs*; and what true-hearted woman would not do the same?

But, friends, it is only since I have met the varied responsibilities of life, that I have comprehended woman's sphere; and I have come to regard it as lying within the whole circumference of humanity. If, as is claimed by the most ultra opponents of the wife's legal individuality, claimed as a conclusive argument in favor of her legal nonentity, the *interests of the parties are identical*, then I claim, as a legitimate conclusion, that their spheres are also identical. For interests determine duties, and duties are the landmarks of spheres. Wherever a man may *rightfully* go, it is proper that woman should go, and share his responsibilities. Wherever my husband goes, thither would I follow him, if to the battle-field. No, I would not follow him *there*; I would hold him back by his coat-skirts, and say, "Husband, this is wrong. What will you gain by war? It will cost as much money to fight for a bag of gold, or a lot of land, as it will to pay the difference; and if you fight, our harvests are wasted, our hearths made desolate, our homes filled with sorrow, and vice and immorality roll back upon us from the fields of human slaughter." This is the way I would follow my husband where he cannot rightfully go.

But I may not dwell longer on woman's *sphere*. I shall say very little of woman's *rights*; but I would lay the axe at the root of the tree. I would impress upon you woman's *responsibilities*, and the means fitly to discharge them before Heaven.

I stand before you, a wife, a mother, a sister, a daughter; filling every relation that it is given to woman to fill. And by the token that I have a husband, a father and brothers, whom I revere for their manliness, and love for their tenderness, I may speak to you with confidence, and say, I respect manhood. I love it when it aspires to the high destiny which God has opened to it. And it is because I have confidence in manhood, that I am here to press upon it the claims of womanhood. My first claim for woman is the means of education, that she may understand and be able to meet her responsibilities.

We are told very much of "Woman's *Mission*." Well, every mission supposes a missionary. Every missionary whom God sends out, every being who is called of God to labor in the vineyard of humanity, recognizes his call before the world does. Not the world--not even God's chosen people--recognized the mission of his Son, till he had proclaimed that mission, and sealed it with his dying testimony. And the world has not yet fully recognized the saving power of the mission of Jesus Christ. Now, if woman has a mission, she must first feel the struggle of the missionary in her own soul, and reveal it to her brother man, before the world will comprehend her claims, and accept her mission. Let her, then, say to man "Here, God has committed to *me* the little tender infant to be developed in *body* and *mind* to the maturity of manhood, womanhood, and I am ignorant of the means for accomplishing either. Give me knowledge, instruction, that I may develop its powers, prevent disease, and teach it the laws of its mental and physical organism." It is you, fathers, husbands, who are responsible for this instruction; your happiness is equally involved with ours. Yourselves must reap the harvest of our ignorance or knowledge. If we suffer, you suffer also; both must suffer or rejoice in our mutual offspring.

I have introduced this subject of woman's responsibilities, that I might, if possible, impress upon you a conviction of the expediency and duty of yielding our right to the means that will enable us to be the helpers of men, in the true sense of helpers. A gentleman said to me, not long since, "I like your woman's rights, since I find it is the right of women to be good for something and help their husbands." Now, I do not understand the term helpmeet, as applied to woman, to imply all that has come to be regarded as within its signification.[2] I do not understand that we are at liberty to help men to the devil. (*Loud cheering*.) I believe it is our mission to help them heavenward, to the full development and right enjoyment of their being.

I would say, in reference to the rights of woman, it has come to be forgotten that, as the mother of the race, her rights are the rights of men also, the rights of her *sons*. As a mother, I may speak to you, freeman, *fathers*, of the rights of my sons--of every mother's sons--to the most perfect and vigorous development of their energies which the mother can secure to them by the application and through the use of *all* her God-given powers of body or of mind. It is in behalf of our sons, the future men of the republic, as well as for our daughters, its future mothers, that we claim the full development of our energies by education, and legal protection in the control of all the issues and profits of ourselves, called *property*.

As a parent, I have educated myself with

---

[2] Gen. 2:20.

reference to the wants of my children, that if, by the bereavements of life, I am left their sole parent, I can train them to be good and useful citizens. Such bereavement *has* left me the sole parent of sons by a first marriage. And how do the laws of the state protect the right of these sons to their mother's fostering care? The laws say that, having married again, I am a *legal nonentity*, and cannot "*give bonds*" for the faithful discharge of my maternal duties; therefore I shall not be their guardian. Having, in the first instance, robbed me of the property qualification for giving bonds, alienating my right to the control of my own earnings, the state makes its own injustice the ground for defrauding myself and children of the mutual benefits of our God-ordained relations; and others, destitute of every qualification and motive which my mother's love insures to them, may "give bonds" and become the legal guardians of my children!

I address myself to you, *fathers*, I appeal to every man who has lived a half-century, if the *mother* is not the most faithful guardian of her children's interests? If you were going on a long journey, to be absent for years, in the prosecution of business, or in the army or navy, would you exclude your wives from the care and guardianship of your children? Would you place them and the means for their support in any other hands than the mother's? If you would, *you have married beneath yourselves*. (*Cheers*.) Then I ask you how it happens that, when you die, your estates are cut up, and your children, and the means for their support, consigned to others' guardianship, by laws which yourselves have made or sworn to defend? Do you reply that women are not qualified by education for the business transactions involved in such guardianship? It is for this I ask that they may be educated. Yourselves must educate your wives in the conduct of your business. My friends, *love* is the best teacher in the world. Fathers, husbands, you do not know how fast you can teach, nor what apt scholars you will find in your wives and daughters, if, with loving confidence, you call them to your aid, and teach them those things in which they can aid you, and acquire the knowledge, which is "power," to benefit those they love. Would it not soothe your sick bed, would it not pluck thorns from your dying pillow, to confide in your wife that she could conduct the business on which your family relies for support, and, in case of your death, keep your children together, and educate them to go out into the world with habits of self-reliance and self-dependence? And do you know that, in withholding from your companions the knowledge and inducements which would fit them thus to share your cares, and relieve you in the emergencies of business, you deny them the richest rewards of affection? for "it *is* more blessed to give than to receive" [Acts 20:35]. Do you know that they would only cling the closer to you in the stern conflicts of life, if they were thus taught that you do not undervalue their devotion and despise their ability? Call woman to your side in the loving confidence of equal interests and equal responsibilities, and she will never fail you.

But I would return to woman's responsibilities, and the laws that alienate her means to discharge them. And here let me call your attention to my position, that *the law which alienates the wife's right to the control of her own property, her own earnings lies at the foundation of all her social and legal wrongs*. I have already shown you how the alienation of this right defrauds her of the legal guardianship of her children, in case of the father's death. I need not tell you, who see it every day in the wretched family of the drunkard, that it defrauds her of the means of discharging her responsibilities to her children and to society during the husband's life, when he proves recreant to his obligations, and consumes her earnings in the indulgence of idle and sinful habits. I know it is claimed by many, as a reason why this law should not be disturbed, that it is only the wives of reckless and improvident husbands who suffer under it operation. But, friends, I stand here prepared to show that, as an unjust law of general application, it is even more fruitful of suffering to the wives of what are called *good* husbands,--husbands who love and honor their wives while living, but, dying, leave them and their maternal sympathies to the dissecting-knife of the law. I refer you to the legal provision for the widow. The law gives her the *use* only of one-third of the estate which they have accumulated by their joint industry. I speak of the real estate; for, in the majority of estates, the personal property is expended in paying the debts and meeting the expenses of settlement. Now, I appeal to any man here, whose estate is sufficient to support either or both in comfort, and give them Christian burial, and yet is so limited that the *use* of one-third of it will support neither, whether his wife's interests are equally protected with his own, by the laws which "settle" his estate in the event of his dying first. Let me tell you a story to illustrate the "support" which, it is claimed, compensates the wife for the alienation of her earnings to the control of the husband. In my native town lived a single sister, of middle age. She had accumulated something, for she was capable in all the handicrafts pursued by women of her class. She married a worthy man, poor in this world's goods, and whose children were all settled in homes of their own. She applied her means, and, by the persevering use of her faculties, they secured a snug home, valued at some five hundred dollars, he doing what his feeble health permitted towards the common interest. In the course of years he died, and two-thirds of that estate was divided among *his* grown children; one-third remaining to her. No, she could only have the *use* of one-third, and must keep it in good repair,--the *law* said so! The *use* of less than two hundred dollars in a homestead, on condition of "*keeping it in good repair*," was the *legal* pittance of this poor woman, to whom, with the infirmities of age, had come the desolation of utter bereavement! The old lady patched and toiled, beautiful in her scrupulous cleanliness. The neighbors remembered her, and many a choice bit found its way to her table. At length she was found in her bed paralyzed; and never, to the day of her death,--three years,--could she lift her hand or make known the simplest want of her nature; and yet her countenance was agonized with the appeals of a clear and sound intellect. And now, friends, how did the laws support and protect this poor widow? I will tell you. *They set her up at auction, and struck her off to the man who had a heart to keep her at the cheapest rate!* Three years she enjoyed the pauper's support, then died; and when the decent forms of a pauper's burial were over, *that third* was divided--as had been the other two-thirds--among her husband's "well-to-do" children. (*Great sensation*.) And is it for *such* protection that the love of fathers, brothers, husbands, "represents" woman in the legislative halls of the freest people on earth? O, release to us our own, that we may protect ourselves, and we will bless you! If this old lady had died first, the laws would have protected her husband in appropriating the entire estate to his comfort or his *pleasure*! I asked a man, learned and experienced in jurisprudence by a half-century's discharge of the duties of legislator, administrator, guardian and probate judge, why the widow is denied absolute control of her third, there being no danger of creating "separate interests" when the husband is in his grave. He replied that it was to prevent a second husband from obtaining possession of the property of a first, to the defrauding of his children, which would be the result if the widow married again. Here, the law giving the control of the wife's earnings to the husband is made legal reason for cutting her off at his death with a pittance, so paltry, that, if too infirm to eke out a support by labor, she becomes a *pauper*! For if the law did not give the wife's earnings to the control and possession of a *first* husband, it would have no such excuse for excluding the second husband, or for defrauding herself, and her children by a subsequent marriage, of her earnings in the estate of the first husband. But having legalized the husband's claim to the wife's earnings, by a law of universal application, our legislators have come to legislate for widows on the ground that they have *no property rights in the estates which have swallowed up their entire earnings!* They have come to give the preference of rights to the children of the husband; and *sons*, as well as daughters, are defrauded, legislated out of their interests in their mother's property. For, the estate not being divided, when the *wife* dies, the earnings of a first wife are divided among the children of a second wife, to the prejudice of the children of the first wife. We ask for *equal* property rights, by the repeal of the laws which divert the earnings of the wife from *herself and her heirs*.

O men! in the enjoyment of well-secured property rights, you beautify your snug homesteads, and say within your hearts, "Here I may sit under my own vine and fig-tree; here have I made the home of my old age."[3] And it never occurs to you that no such blissful feeling of security finds rest in the bosom of your wives. The wife of a small householder reflects that if her husband should be taken from her by death, that home must be divided, and a corner in the kitchen, a corner in the garret, and a "*privilege*" in the cellar, be set off to her *use*, and she called, in legal phrase, an "*incumbrance*!" (*Great sensation*.) Or if she chooses the alternative of renting her fractional accommodations, and removing to other quarters, her sweet home-associations--

---

[3] Micah 4:4.

all that is left of her wedded love--are riven. The fireside that had been hallowed by family endearments, the chair vacant to other eyes, but to hers occupied by the loved husband still, all are desecrated by the law that drives her from the home which she had toiled and sacrificed to win for herself and loved ones, and she goes out to die under a vine and a fig-tree strange to her affections; and, it may be, as in the case before mentioned, to find them wither away like Jonah's gourd, in absolute pauperism![4]

But I will tell you a story illustrating how women view these things. It is not long since a gentleman of my acquaintance, who had often been heard to give his wife credit for having contributed equally to his success in laying up a property, was admonished by disease of the propriety of making a "will." He called his wife to him, and addressed her thus: "My dear, I have been thinking that the care of a third of my estate will be a burden to you, and that it will be better for you to have an annuity equal to your personal wants, and divide the rest among the children. The boys will supply you, if you should, from any unforeseen circumstance, need more. You can trust our boys to do what is right." "O yes, my dear," replied the wife, "we have excellent boys. You intrust to them the care of *your* business; and I could let them act as *my* agents in the care of my thirds. And I think, husband, that will be better. For there is this to be considered: We have other children, and differences obtain in their circumstances. You have seen these things, and, when one and another needed, you have opened your purse and given them help. When you are gone, there may still occur these opportunities for aiding them, and I should be glad to have it in my power to do as you have done. Besides, I have sometimes thought you had not done so well by the *girls*; and it would be

---

[4] Jonah 4:6-11.

very grateful to my feelings to make up the difference from my share of what our mutual efforts have accumulated."

Now, brothers, I appeal to you, whether you do not as much enjoy conferring benefits as receiving them? You have a wife whom you love. You present her with a dress, perhaps. And how rich you feel, that your love can give gifts! Women like to receive presents of dresses; I enjoy to have my husband give me dresses. (*Laughter.*) And women like to give presents to their husbands--a pair of slippers, or something of that sort. But they have no money of their own, and their thought is, "If I give my husband this, he will say to himself, It's of no account; it all comes out of my pocket in the end!" That is the feeling which rankles in the hearts of wives, whose provident husbands do not dream that they are not better content with gifts than their rights. We like, all of us, to give good gifts to those we love; but we do not want our husbands to *give* us something to give back to them. We wish to feel, and have *them* feel, that our own good right hands have won for them the gift prompted by our affection; and that we are conferring, from our own resources, the same pleasure and happiness which they confer on us by benefits given. (*Great cheering.*)

But I had not exhausted the wrongs growing out of this alienation of the wife's right to her earnings. There is a law in Vermont--and I think it obtains in its leading features in most, of not all, the states of the Union--giving to the widow, whose husband dies childless (she may or may not be the mother of children by a former marriage), a certain portion of the estate, and the remaining portion to his heirs. Till the autumn of 1850, a Vermont widow, in such cases, had only one-half the estate, however small; the other half was set off to her husband's heirs, if he had any; but, if he had none, the *state put it in its own treasury*, leaving the widow to a pauper's fate, unless her own energies could eke out a living by economy and hard toil! A worthy woman in the circle of my acquaintance, whose property at marriage paid for a homestead worth five hundred dollars, saw this law divide a half of it to the brothers and sisters of her husband at his death, and herself is left, in her old age, to subsist on the remaining half! In 1850, this law was so amended that the widow can have the whole property, if it be not more than one thousand dollars, and the half of any sum over than amount; the other half going to the husband's family; or, if he happen not to leave any fiftieth cousin Tom, Dick or Harry, in the Old World or the New, she may have it *all*! Our legislators tell us it is right to give the legal control of our earnings to the husband, because "in law" he is held responsible for our support, and is obliged to pay our debts (?), and *must have our earnings to do it with*! Ah, I answer, but why don't the state give us some security, then, for support during *our* life; or if it looses the husband from all obligation to see that we are supported after he is in his grave, why, like a just and shrewd business agent, does it not release to us the "*consideration*" of that support--our earnings in the property which he leaves at his death?

The law taking from the wife the control of her earnings is a fruitful source of divorces. To regain control of her earnings for the support of her children, many a woman feels compelled to sue for a *divorce*.

I am here in the hope that I can say something for the benefit of those who must suffer, because they cannot speak and show that they have wrongs to be redressed. It would ill become us, who are protected by love, or shielded by circumstances, to hold our peace while our sisters and their dependent children are mutilated in their hopes and their entire powers of existence, by wrongs against which we can protest till the legislators of the land shall hear and heed.

I was speaking of woman's self-created

resources as necessary means for the discharge of her duties. Created free agents that we might render to God an acceptable and voluntary service, our Maker holds each human being accountable for the discharge of individual, personal responsibilities. Man, under his present disabilities, cannot come up to the full measure of his own responsibilities; much less can he discharge his own and woman's too. Hence, in taking from woman any of the means which God has given her ability to acquire, he takes from her the means which God has given her for the discharge of her own duties, and thereby adds to the burthen of his own undischarged responsibilities. In taking from us our means of self-development, men expect us to discharge our duties, even as the Jews were expected to make brick without straw.[5] If we are not fitted to be capable wives and mothers,--as contended by a gentleman on the stand yesterday,--if we make poor brick, it is because our brother man has stolen our straw. Give us back our straw, brothers,--there is plenty of it,--and we will make you *good* brick. Brick we must make--men say so; then *give* us our straw,--we cannot *take* it. We are suffering; the race is suffering from the ill-performance of our duties. We claim that man has proved himself incompetent to be the judge of our needs. His laws concerning our interests show that his intelligence fails to prescribe means and conditions for the discharge of our duties. We are the best judges of the duties, as well as the qualifications, appropriate to our own department of labor; and should hold in our own hands, in our own right, means for acquiring the one and comprehending the other.

I have spoken of woman's legal disabilities as wife and mother; and adverted to the law which diverts from the wife the control of her own earnings, as a fruitful source of divorces. Increasing facilities for divorce

---

[5] Exod. 5:7.

are regarded by a majority of Christian men as significant of increasing immorality, and tending to weaken the sanctity of the marriage relation. But an examination of legislative proceedings will show that sympathy for suffering woman is the real source of these increasing facilities; and I am frank to say, that I consider man's growing consciousness of the wrongs to which wives and their helpless children are subject, by the laws which put it in the power of the husband and father to wrest from them the very necessaries of life, consuming their sole means of support--the earnings of the mother,--as heralding a good time coming, when every woman, as well as every man, "may sit under her own vine" [Micah 4:4]. Let me illustrate by relating one, among many incidents of the kind, which have fallen under my observation.

In travelling, some eighteen years ago, across the Green Mountains from Albany, a gentleman requested my interest in behalf of a young woman, whose history he gave me before placing her under my care, as a fellow-passenger. Said he, She was born here; is an orphan, and the mother of two young children, with no means of support but her earnings. She was a capable girl, and has been an irreproachable wife. From a love of the social glass, her husband in a few years became a drunkard and a brute; neglected his business, and expended their entire living. She struggled bravely, but in vain. At length, just before the birth of her youngest child, he pawned the clothing which she had provided for herself and babes, sold her only bed, and drove her into the streets to seek from charity aid in her hour of trial. After her recovery, she went to service, keeping her children with her. But he pursued her from place to place annoying her employers, collecting her wages by process of law, and taking possession of every garment not on her own or children's persons. Under these circumstances, and by the help of friends who pitied her sorrows, she, with her hatless and shoeless children, was flying from their "*legal protector*," half clothed, to New Hampshire, where friends were waiting to give her employment in a factory, till a year's residence should enable her to procure a divorce! Now, friends, if under New York laws this poor woman had enjoyed legal control of her own earnings, she might have retained her first home, supported her children, and, happy as a mother, endured hopefully the burden of unrequited affection, instead of flying to New Hampshire to regain possession of her alienated property rights, by the aid of "divorce facilities."

But, alas! not yet have I exhausted that fountain of wrongs growing out of the alienation of the wife's property rights. It gives to children *criminals* for guardians, at the same time that it severs what God hath joined together--the mother and her child! By the laws of all these United States, the father is in all cases the legal guardian of the child, in preference to the mother; hence, in cases of divorce for the criminal conduct of the father, the children are confided, by the natural operation of the laws, to the guardianship of the criminal party. I have a friend who, not long since, procured a divorce from her husband,--a libertine and a drunkard,--and by the power of *law* he wrested from her their only child, a son of tender age. Think of this, fathers, mothers! It is a sad thing to sever the marriage relation when it has become a curse--a demoralizing (?) thing; but what is it to sever the relation between mother and child, when that relation is a blessing to both, and to society? What is it to commit the tender boy to the training of a drunken and licentious father? The state appoints guardians for children physically orphaned; and much more should it appoint guardians for children morally orphaned. When it uses its power to imprison and hang the *man*, it is surely responsible for the moral training of the *boy*! But to return. I have asked learned judges why the state decrees that the father should retain the children, thus throwing upon the innocent mother the penalty which should fall upon the guilty party only? Say they, "It is because the father *has the property*; it would not be *just* (?) to burden the mother with the support of *his* children." O justice, how art thou perverted! Here again, is the unrighteous alienation of the wife's earnings made the reason for robbing the suffering mother of all that is left to her of a miserable marriage--her children! I appeal to Christian men and women, who would preserve the marriage relation inviolate, by discouraging increased divorce facilities, if prevention of the necessity be not the better and more hopeful course,--prevention by releasing to the wife means for the independent discharge of her duties as a mother. And I appeal to all present, whether, sacred as they hold the marriage relation, Christian men have not proved to the world that there is a something regarded by them as even more sacred--the *loaf*! The most scrupulous piety cites Bible authority for severing the marriage tie; but when has piety or benevolence put forth its hand to divide to helpless and dependent woman an equal share of the estate which she has toiled for, suffered for, in behalf of her babes, as she would never have done for herself--only to be robbed of both? If the ground of the divorce be the *husband's infidelity*, the law allows him to retain the children and whole estate; it being left with the court to divide to the wife (in answer to her prayer to that effect) a pittance called alimony, to keep starvation at bay. If the babe at her breast is decreed to her from its helplessness, it is, at her request, formally laid before the court; and the court has no power even to decree a corresponding pittance for its support. The law leaves her one hope of bread for her old age which should not be forgotten--if *he dies first*, she is entitled to dower! But let the wife's infidelity be the ground of divorce, and the laws send her out into the world, childless, without alimony, and cut off from her right of dower; *and property which came by her remains his forever*! What a contrast! He, the brutal husband, sits in the criminal's bench to draw a premium, be rid of an incumbrance; for what cares he for the severing of a tie that had ceased to bind him to his wife, that perhaps divided between him and a more coveted companion! If we *are* the *weaker* sex, O, give us, we pray you, equal protection with the stronger sex!

Now, my friends, you will bear me witness that I have said nothing about woman's right to vote or make laws. I have great respect for manhood. I wish to be able to continue to respect it. And when I listen to Fourth-of-July orations and the loud cannon, and reflect that these are tributes of admiration paid to our fathers because they compelled freedom for themselves and sons from the hand of oppression and power, I look forward with greater admiration on their sons who, in the good time coming will have won for themselves the unappropriated glory of having given justice to the physically weak; to those who could not, if they would, and would not, if they could, *compel* it from the hands of fathers, brothers, husbands and sons! I labor in hope; for I have faith that when men come to value their own rights, as means of human happiness, rather than of paltry gain, they will feel themselves more honored in releasing than in retaining the *"inalienable rights" of woman*.

Brothers, you ask us to accept the protection of your LOVE, and the law says that is sufficient for us, whether it feeds or robs us of our bread. You admit that woman exceeds man in self-sacrificing love; her devotion to you has passed into a proverb. Yet, for all this, you refuse to intrust *your interests to her love*. You do not feel safe in *your* interests without the protection of equal laws. You refuse to trust even the mother's love with the interests of her children! How, then, do you ask of us--you, who will not trust your interests to the love of a mother, wife, daughter, or sister--why do you ask of us to dispense with the protection of equal laws, and accept instead the protection of man's affection?

I would offer, in conclusion, a few thoughts on education. I would say to my sisters, lest they be discouraged under existing disabilities from attempting it,--we can educate ourselves. It may be that you hesitate, from a supposed inferiority of intellect. Now, I have never troubled myself to establish woman's intellectual equality. The inequality of educational facilities forbids us to sustain such a position by facts. But I have long since disposed of this question to my own satisfaction, and perhaps my conclusion will inspire you with confidence to attempt equal--I would hope *superior*--attainments, for man falls short of the intelligence within reach of his powers. We all believe that the Creator is both omniscient and omnipotent, wise and able to adapt means to the ends he had in view. We hold ourselves created to sustain certain relations as intelligent beings, and that God has endowed us with capabilities equal to the discharge of the duties involved in these relations. Now, let us survey woman's responsibilities within the narrowest sphere to which any common-sense man would limit her offices. As a mother, her powers mould and develop humanity, intellectual, moral and physical. Next to God woman is the creator of the race as it is and as it shall be. I ask, then, Has God created woman man's inferior? If so, he has been false to his wisdom, false to his power, in creating an inferior being for superior work! But if it be true, as all admit, that woman's *responsibilities* are equal to man's, I claim that God has endowed her with *equal powers* for their discharge.

And how shall we develop these powers? My sisters, for your encouragement, I will refer to my own experience in this matter. I claim to be self-educated. Beyond a single year's instruction in a high school for young men and women, I have enjoyed no public educational facilities but the common school which our Green Mountain state opens to all her sons and daughters. Prevented by circumstances from availing myself of the discipline of a classical school of the highest order, and nerved by faith in my ability to achieve equal attainments with my brother man, I resorted to books and the study of human nature, with direct reference to the practical application of my influence and my acquirements to my woman's work,--the development of the immortal spirit for the accomplishment of human destiny. And my own experience is, that the world in which we live and act, and by which we are impressed, is the best school for woman as well as man. Practical life furnishes the best discipline for our powers. It qualifies us to take life as we find it, and leave it better than we found it. I have been accustomed to look within my own heart to learn the springs of human action. By it I have read woman, read man; and the result has been a fixed resolution, an indomitable courage to do with my might what my hands find to do for God and humanity. And in *doing*, I have best learned my ability to accomplish, my capacity to enjoy. In the light of experience, I would say to you, my sisters, the first thing is to apply ourselves to the intelligent discharge of present duties, diligently searching out and applying all knowledge that will qualify us for higher and extended usefulness. Be always *learners*, and don't forget to teach. As individuals, as mothers, we must first achieve a knowledge of the laws of our physical and mental organisms; for these are the material which we work upon and the instruments by which we work; and, to do our work well, we must understand and be able to apply both. Then we need to understand the tenure of our domestic and social relations,--the laws by which we are linked to our kind. But I cannot leave this subject without briefly calling your attention to another phase of education.

Early in life, my attention was called to examine the value of beauty and accomplishments as permanent grounds of affection. I could not believe that God had created so many homely women, and suffered all to lose their beauty in the very maturity of their powers, and yet made it our duty to spend our best efforts in trying to look pretty. We all desire to be loved; and can it be that we have no more lasting claims to admiration than that beauty and those accomplishments which serve us only in the spring-time of life? Surely our days of dancing and musical performance are soon over, when musical instruments of sweeter tone cry "*Mother.*" (*Loud cheers.*) What, then, shall we do for admiration when stricken in years? Has not God endowed us with some lasting hold upon the affections? My sister, I can only find lasting charms in that thorough culture of the mind and heart which will enable us to win upon man's higher and better nature. If you have beauty and accomplishments, these address themselves to man's lower nature--his passions; and when age has robbed you of the one, and him of the other, you are left unloved and unlovely! Cultivate, then, your powers of mind and heart, that you may become necessary to his better and undying sympathies. Aid him in all the earnest work of life; and secure his aid in your self-development for noble purposes, by impressing upon him that you are in earnest. Sell your jewelry, if need be, abate your expenditures for show; and appropriate your means, and time spent in idle visiting, to the culture of your souls. Then will his *soul* respond to your worth, and the ties that bind you endure through time, and make your companions in eternity!

Let the daughters be trained for their responsibilities; and though you may say, "We do not know whom they will marry, whether a lawyer, a doctor, or farmer," if you educate them for practical life, by giving them general useful knowledge, their husbands can teach them the details of their mutual business interests, as easily as the new responsibilities of maternity will teach them the ways and means of being qualified to discharge *its* duties.

Educate your daughters for practical life, and you have endowed them better than if you had given them fortunes. When a young girl of fourteen, I said to my father, Give me education, instead of a "setting out in the world," if you can give me but one. If I marry, and am poor in this world's goods, I can educate my children myself. If my husband should be unfortunate, the sheriff can take his goods; but no creditor can attach the capital invested here. (*Touching her forehead.*) (*Loud cheers.*) And, friends, my education has not been only *bread*, but an inexhaustible fund of enjoyment, in all the past of my life.

10

Elizabeth Cady Stanton, Address to the Legislature of New York, 1854

In the years following the Seneca Falls convention, Cady Stanton remained a small-town housewife caring for five small children while her husband was absent from home for up to six months each year. She attended no national woman's rights conventions until 1860, but she delivered the keynote address at the Woman's State Temperance Society meeting in Rochester, New York, in 1852, while four months pregnant and dressed in a bloomer costume. By 1854, due to the ridicule it occasioned, she had abandoned that attire in public, and she appeared before members of the New York Legislature wearing a black silk dress with a white lace collar (Griffith 1984, 76, 82-83).

None of her family was in the audience, only her friend Susan B. Anthony, who had had fifty thousand copies of the speech printed, putting one on every legislator's desk and distributing the remainder as tracts. Ten weeks of petitioning by sixty women had gathered 5,931 signatures in support of amending the 1848 New York Married Woman's Property Act to increase married women's legal rights, as well as 4,164 signatures in support of woman suffrage. These petitions were the basis on which Cady Stanton was permitted to speak. Her address had been presented a few days earlier at a woman's rights convention in

Albany, which adopted it by only a slim majority; in a letter to her, Sarah Grimké said it was "too caustic" (Wagner 1978, p. 320). The speech is a complex mixture of high style, carefully supported arguments adapted to her male audience, and confrontational, satiric comments that reflect her frustration at the barriers women faced. *Cady Stanton herself considered it one of her finest addresses* (Banner 1980, 79).

The text was published as a pamphlet, **Address to the Legislature of New York, adopted by the State Woman's Rights Convention, held at Albany, Tuesday and Wednesday, February 14 & 15, 1854** (Albany: Weed, Parsons, 1854), *from which this text is taken, and is found in* **HWS** 1: 595-605.

To the Legislature of the State of New York:

"The thinking minds of all nations call for change. There is a deep-lying struggle in the whole fabric of society; a boundless, grinding collision of the New with the Old."

The tyrant, Custom, has been summoned before the bar of Common Sense. His Majesty no longer awes the multitude--his sceptre is broken--his crown is trampled in the dust--the sentence of death is pronounced upon him. All nations, ranks and classes have, in turn, questioned and repudiated his authority; and now, that the monster is chained and caged, timid woman, on tiptoe, comes to look him in the face, and to demand of her brave sires and sons, who have struck stout blows for liberty, if, in this change of dynasty, she, too, shall find relief.

Yes, gentlemen, in republican America, in the 19th century, we, the daughters of the revolutionary heroes of '76, demand at your hands the redress of our grievances--a revision of your state constitution--a new code of laws. Permit us then, as briefly as possible, to call your attention to the legal disabilities under which we labor.

1st. Look at the position of woman as woman. It is not enough for us that by your laws we are permitted to live and breathe, to claim the necessaries of life from our legal protectors--to pay the penalty of our crimes; we demand the full recognition of all our rights as citizens of the Empire State. We are persons; native, free-born citizens; property-holders, tax-payers; yet are we denied the exercise of our right to the elective franchise. We support ourselves, and, in part, your schools, colleges, churches, your poor-houses, jails, prisons, the army, the navy, the whole machinery of government, and yet we have no voice in your councils. We have every qualification required by the constitution, necessary to the legal voter, but the one of sex. We are moral, virtuous and intelligent, and in all respects quite equal to the proud white man himself, and yet by your laws we are classed with idiots, lunatics, and negroes; and though we do not feel honored by the place assigned us, yet, in fact, our legal position is lower than that of either; for the negro can be raised to the dignity of a voter if he possess himself of $250; the lunatic can vote in his moments of sanity, and the idiot, too, if he be a male one, and not more than nine-tenths a fool; but we, who have guided great movements of charity, established missions, edited journals, published works on history, economy, and statistics; who have governed nations, led armies, filled the professor's chair, taught philosophy and mathematics to the *savants* of our age, discovered planets, piloted ships across the sea, are denied the most sacred rights of citizens, because, forsooth, we came not into this republic crowned with the dignity of manhood! Woman is theoretically absolved from all allegiance to the laws of the State. Sec. 1, Bill of Rights, 2 R.S., 301, says that no authority can, on any pretense whatever, be exercised over the citizens of this state but such as is or shall be derived from, and *granted by, the people of this state*.

Now, gentlemen, we would fain know by what authority you have disfranchised one-half the people of this state? You who have so boldly taken possession of the bulwarks of this republic, show us your credentials, and thus prove your exclusive right to govern, not only yourselves, but us. Judge Hurlbut, who has long occupied a high place at the bar in this state, and who recently retired with honor from the bench of the Supreme Court, in his profound work on human rights, has pronounced your present position rank usurpation.[1] Can it be that here, where are acknowledged no royal blood, no apostolic descent, that you, who have declared that all men were created equal--that governments derive their just powers from the consent of the governed, would willingly build up an aristocracy that places the ignorant and vulgar above the educated and refined--the alien and the ditch-digger above the authors and poets of the day --an aristocracy that would raise the sons above the mothers that bore them? Would that the men who can sanction a constitution so opposed to the genius of this government, who can enact and execute laws so degrading to womankind, had sprung, Minerva-like, from the brains of their fathers, that the matrons of this republic need not blush to own their sons!

Woman's position, under our free institutions, is much lower than under the monarchy of England. "In England the idea of woman holding official station is not so strange as in the United States. The Countess of Pembroke, Dorset, and Montgomery held the office of hereditary sheriff of Westmoreland, and exercised it in person. At the assizes at Appleby, she sat with the judges on the bench.

---

[1] See p. 92, n 19.

In a reported case, it is stated by counsel, and substantially assented to by the court, that a woman is capable of serving in almost all the offices of the kingdom, such as those of queen, marshal, great chamberlain and constable of England, the champion of England, commissioner of sewers, governor of work-house, sexton, keeper of the prison, of the gatehouse of the dean and chapter of Westminster, returning officer for members of parliament, and constable, the latter of which is in some respects judicial. The office of jailor is frequently exercised by a woman. In the United States a woman may administer on the effects of her deceased husband, and she has occasionally held a subordinate place in the post office department. She has therefore a sort of post mortem, post mistress notoriety; but with the exception of handling letters of administration and letters mailed, she is the submissive creature of the old common law." True, the unmarried woman has a right to the property she inherits and the money she earns, but she is taxed without representation. And here again you place the negro, so unjustly degraded by you, in a superior position to your own wives and mothers; for colored males, if possessed of a certain amount of property and certain other qualifications, can vote, but if they do not have these qualifications *they are not subject to direct taxation*; wherein they have the advantage of woman, she being subject to taxation for whatever amount she may possess (Constitution of N. Y., Article 2, Sec. 2). But, say you, are not all women sufficiently represented by their fathers, husbands and brothers? Let your statute books answer the question.

Again we demand, in criminal cases, that most sacred of all rights, trial by a jury of our own peers. The establishment of trial by jury is of so early a date that its beginning is lost in antiquity; but the right of trial by a jury of one's own peers is a great, progressive step of advanced civilization. No rank of men have ever been satisfied with being tried by jurors higher or lower in the civil or political scale than themselves; for jealousy on the one hand, and contempt on the other, has ever effectually blinded the eyes of justice. Hence, all along the pages of history, we find the king, the noble, the peasant, the cardinal, the priest, the layman, each in turn protesting against the authority of the tribunal before which they were summoned to appear. Charles the First refused to recognize the competency of the tribunal which condemned him: For how, said he, can subjects judge a king?[2] The stern descendants of our Pilgrim Fathers refused to answer for their crimes before an English Parliament. For how, said they, can a king judge rebels? And shall woman here consent to be tried by her liege lord, who has dubbed himself law-maker, judge, juror, and sheriff, too?--whose power, though sanctioned by Church and State, has no foundation in justice and equity, and is a bold assumption of our inalienable rights. In England a parliament-lord could challenge a jury where a knight was not empannelled [sic]; an alien could demand a jury composed half of his own countrymen; or, in some special cases, juries were even constituted entirely of women. Having seen that man fails to do justice to woman in her best estate, to the virtuous, the noble, the true of our sex, should we trust to his tender

---

[2] Charles I (1600-49), king of England, Scotland, and Ireland (1625-49), offended his subjects by marrying the Catholic Henrietta Maria, sister of Louis XIII of France. The bitter struggle for supremacy between king and Parliament produced the English Civil War. A special high court of justice tried Charles and convicted him of treason for levying war against Parliament, and he was beheaded January 30, 1649.

mercies, the weak, the ignorant, the morally insane? It is not to be denied that the interests of man and woman in the present undeveloped state of the race, and under the existing social arrangements, are and must be antagonistic. The nobleman cannot make just laws for the peasant; the slaveholder for the slave; neither can man make and execute just laws for woman; because in each case, the one in power fails to apply the immutable principles of right to any grade but his own. Shall an erring woman be dragged before a bar of grim-visaged judges, lawyers, and jurors, there to be grossly questioned in public on subjects which women scarce breathe in secret to one another? Shall the most sacred relations of life be called up and rudely scanned by men who, by their own admission, are so coarse that women could not meet them even at the polls without contamination? and yet shall she find there no woman's face or voice to pity and defend? Shall the frenzied mother who, to save herself and child from exposure and disgrace, ended the life that had but just begun, be dragged before such a tribunal to answer for her crime? How can man enter into the feelings of that mother? How can he judge of the mighty agonies of soul that impelled her to such an outrage of maternal instincts? How can he weigh the mountain of sorrow that crushed that mother's heart when she wildly tossed her helpless babe into the cold waters of the midnight sea? Where is he who by false vows thus blasted this trusting woman? Had that helpless child no claims on his protection? Ah, he is freely abroad in the dignity of manhood, in the pulpit, on the bench, in the professor's chair. The imprisonment of his victim and the death of his child, detract not a tithe from his standing and complacency. His peers made the law, and shall law-makers lay nets for those of their own rank? Shall laws which come from the logical brain of man take cognizance of violence done to the moral and affectional nature which predominates, as is said, in woman? Statesmen of New York, whose daughters, guarded by your affection, and lapped amidst luxuries which your indulgence spreads, care more for their nodding plumes and velvet trains than for the statute laws by which their persons and properties are held--who, blinded by custom and prejudice to the degraded position which they and their sisters occupy in the civil scale, haughtily claim that they already have all rights they want, how, think ye, you would feel to see a daughter summoned for such a crime--and remember these daughters are but human--before such a tribunal? Would it not, in that hour, be some consolation to see that she was surrounded by the wise and virtuous of her own sex; by those who had known the depth of a mother's love and the misery of a lover's falsehood; to know that to these she could make her confession, and from them receive her sentence? If so, then listen to our just demands and make such a change in your laws as will secure to every woman tried in your courts, an impartial jury. At this moment among the hundreds of women who are shut up in prisons in this state, not one has enjoyed that most sacred of all rights--that right which you would die to defend for yourselves--trial by a jury of one's peers.

2d. Look at the position of woman as wife. Your laws relating to marriage--founded as they are on the old common law of England, a compound of barbarous usages, but partially modified by progressive civilization--are in open violation of our enlightened ideas of justice, and of the holiest feelings of our nature. If you take the highest view of marriage, as a Divine relation, which love alone can constitute and sanctify, then of course human legislation can only recognize it. Man can neither bind nor loose its ties, for that prerogative belongs to God alone, who makes man and woman, and the laws of attraction by which they are united. But if you regard marriage as a civil contract, then let it be subject to the same laws which control all other contracts. Do not make it a kind of half-human, half-divine institution, which you may build up but cannot regulate. Do not, by your special legislation for this one kind of contract, involve yourselves in the grossest absurdities and contradictions.

So long as by your laws no man can make a contract for a horse or piece of land until he is twenty-one years of age, and by which contract he is not bound if any deception has been practiced, or if the party contracting has not fulfilled his part of the agreement--so long as the parties in all mere civil contracts retain their identity and all the power and independence they had before contracting, with the full right to dissolve all partnerships and contracts for any reason, at the will and option of the parties themselves, upon what principle of civil jurisprudence do you permit the boy of fourteen and the girl of twelve, in violation of every natural law, to make a contract more momentous in importance than any other, and then hold them to it, come what may, the whole of their natural lives, in spite of disappointment, deception and misery? Then, too, the signing of this contract is instant civil death to one of the parties. The woman who but yesterday was sued on bended knee, who stood so high in the scale of being as to make an agreement on equal terms with a proud Saxon man, to-day has no civil existence, no social freedom. The wife who inherits no property holds about the same legal position that does the slave on the southern plantation. She can own nothing, sell nothing. She has no right even to the wages she earns; her person, her time, her services are the property of another. She cannot testify, in many cases, against her husband. She can get no redress for wrongs in her own name in any court of justice. She can neither sue nor be sued. She is not held morally responsible for any crime committed in the presence of her husband, so completely is her very existence supposed by the law to be merged in that of another. Think of it; your wives may be thieves, libelers, burglars, incendiaries, and for crimes like these they are not held amenable to the laws of the land, if they but commit them in your dread presence. For them, alas! there is no higher law than the will of man. Herein behold the bloated conceit of these Petruchios of the law, who seem to say:

> Nay, look not big, nor stamp, nor stare, nor fret,
> I will be master of what is mine own;
> She is my goods, my chattels; she is my house,
> My household stuff, my field, my barn,
> My horse, my ox, my ass, my any-thing;
> And here she stands, touch her whoever dare;
> I'll bring my action on the proudest he,
> That stops my way, in Padua.[3]

How could man ever look thus on woman? She, at whose feet Socrates learned wisdom[4]-- she, who gave to the world a Saviour [sic], and witnessed alike the adoration of the Magi and the agonies of the cross. How could such a being, so blessed and honored, ever become the ignoble, servile, cringing slave, with whom the fear of man could be paramount to the sacred dictates of conscience and the holy love of Heaven? By the common law of England,

---

[3] Shakespeare, *Taming of the Shrew*, 3.2.

[4] The reference is to Diotima. See Plato, *Symposium*, 201d-212c.

the spirit of which has been but too faithfully incorporated into our statute law, a husband has a right to whip his wife with a rod not larger than his thumb, to shut her up in a room, and administer whatever moderate chastisement he may deem necessary to insure obedience to his wishes, and for her healthful moral development! He can forbid all persons harboring or trusting her on his account. He can deprive her of all social intercourse with her nearest and dearest friends. If by great economy she accumulates a small sum, which for future need she deposit, little by little, in a savings bank, the husband has a right to draw it out, at his option, to use it as he may see fit.

"Husband is entitled to wife's credit or business talents (whenever their intermarriage may have occurred); and goods purchased by her on her own credit, with his consent, while cohabiting with him, can be seized and sold in execution against him for his own debts, and this, though she carry on business in her own name."--7 *Howard's Practice Reports*, 105, *Lovett agt. Robinson and Whitbeck, sheriff, &c.*

"No letters of administration shall be granted to a person convicted of infamous crime; nor to any one incapable by law of making a contract; nor to a person not a citizen of the United States, unless such person reside within this State; nor to any one who is under twenty-one years of age; nor to any person who shall be adjudged incompetent by the surrogate to execute duties of such trust, by reason of drunkenness, improvidence, or want of understanding, nor any married woman; but where a married woman is entitled to administration, the same may be granted to her husband in her right and behalf."

There is nothing that an unruly wife might do against which the husband has not sufficient protection in the law. But not so with the wife. If she have a worthless husband, a confirmed drunkard, a villain, or a vagrant, he has still all the rights of a man, a husband and a father. Though the whole support of the family be thrown upon the wife, if the wages she earns be paid to her by her employer, the husband can receive them again. If, by unwearied industry and perseverance, she can earn for herself and children a patch of ground and a shed to cover them, the husband can strip her of all her hard earnings, turn her and her little ones out in the cold northern blast, take the clothes from their backs, the bread from their mouths; all this by your laws may he do, and has he done, oft and again, to satisfy the rapacity of that monster in human form, the rumseller.

But the wife who is so fortunate as to have inherited property, has, by the new law in this state, been redeemed from her lost condition. She is no longer a legal nonentity. This property law, if fairly construed, will overturn the whole code relating to woman and property. The right to property implies the right to buy and sell, to will and bequeath, and herein is the dawning of a civil existence for woman, for now the "femme covert" must have the right to make contracts. So, get ready, gentlemen; the "little justice" will be coming to you one day, deed in hand, for your acknowledgment. When he asks you "if you sign without fear or compulsion," say yes, boldly, as we do. Then, too, the right to will is ours. Now what becomes of the "tenant for life?" Shall he, the happy husband of a millionaire, who has lived in yonder princely mansion in the midst of plenty and elegance, be cut down in a day to the use of one-third of this estate and a few hundred a year, as long as he remains her widower? And should he, in spite of this bounty on celibacy, impelled by his affections, marry again, choosing for a wife a woman as poor as himself, shall he be thrown penniless on the cold world--this child of fortune, enervated by ease and luxury, henceforth to be dependent wholly on his own resources? Poor man! He would be rich, though, in the *sympathies* of many women who have passed through just such an ordeal. But what is property without the right to protect that property by law? It is mockery to say a certain estate is mine, if, without my consent, you have the right to tax me when and how you please, while I have no voice in making the tax-gatherer, the legislator or the law. The right to property will, of necessity, compel us in due time to the exercise of our right to the elective franchise, and then naturally follows the right to hold office.

3d. Look at the position of woman as widow. Whenever we attempt to point out the wrongs of the wife, those who would have us believe that the laws cannot be improved, point us to the privileges, powers and claims of the widow. Let us look into these a little. Behold in yonder humble house a married pair, who, for long years, have lived together, childless and alone. Those few acres of well-tilled land, with the small white house that looks so cheerful through its vines and flowers, attest the honest thrift and simple taste of its owners. This man and woman, by their hard days labor, have made this home their own. Here they live in peace and plenty, happy in the hope that they may dwell together securely under their own vine and fig tree for the few years that remain to them,[5] and that under the shadow of these trees, planted by their own hands, and in the midst of their household gods, so loved and familiar, here may take their last farewell of earth. But, alas for human hopes! the husband dies, and without will, and the stricken widow, at one fell blow, loses the companion of her youth, her house and home, and half the little sum she had in bank. For the law, which takes no cognizance of widows left with

---

[5] Micah 4:4.

twelve children and not one cent, instantly spies out this widow, takes account of her effects, and announces to her the startling intelligence that but one-third of the house and lot, and one-half the personal property, are hers. The law has other favorites with whom she must share the hard-earned savings of years. In this dark hour of grief, the coarse minions of the law gather round the widow's hearth-stone, and, in the name of justice, outrage all natural sense of right; mock at the sacredness of human love, and with cold familiarity proceed to place a moneyed value on the old arm chair, in which, but a few brief hours since, she closed the eyes that had ever beamed on her with kindness and affection; on the solemn clock in the corner, that told the hour he passed away; on every garment with which his form and presence were associated, and on every article of comfort and convenience that the house contained, even down to the knives and forks and spoons--and the widow saw it all--and when the work was done, she gathered up what the law allowed her and went forth to seek her another home! This is the much talked of widow's dower. Behold the magnanimity of the law in allowing the widow to retain a life interest in one-third the landed estate, and one-half the personal property of her husband, and taking the lion's share to itself! Had she died first, the house and land would all have been the husband's still. No one would have dared to intrude upon the privacy of his home or to molest him in his sacred retreat of sorrow.

How, I ask you, can that be called justice, which makes such a distinction as this between man and woman?

By management, economy and industry, our widow is able, in a few years, to redeem her house and home. But the law never loses sight of the purse, no matter how low in the scale of being its owner may be. It sends its officers round every year to gather in the harvest for the public crib, and no widow who owns a piece of land two feet square ever escapes this reckoning. Our widow, too, who has now twice earned her home, has her annual tax to pay also--a tribute of gratitude that she is permitted to breathe the free air of this republic, where "taxation without representation," by such worthies as John Hancock and Samuel Adams, has been declared "intolerable tyranny."[6] Having glanced at the magnanimity of the law in its dealings with the widow, let us see how the individual man, under the influence of such laws, doles out justice to his helpmate. The husband has the absolute right to will away his property as he may see fit. If he has children, he can divide his property among them, leaving his wife her third only of the landed estate, thus making her a dependent on the bounty of her own children. A man with thirty thousand dollars in personal property, may leave his wife but a few hundred a year, as long as she remains his widow.

The cases are without number where women, who have lived in ease and elegance, at the death of their husbands have, by will, been reduced to the bare necessaries of life. The man who leaves his wife the sole guardian of his property and children is an exception to the general rule. Man has ever manifested a wish that the world should indeed be a blank to the companion whom he leaves behind him. The Hindoo [sic] makes that wish a law, and burns the widow on the funeral pile of her husband;[7] but the civilized man, impressed with a different view of the sacredness of

---

[6] John Hancock (1737-93) and Samuel Adams (1722-1803), leaders of the American Revolution and signers of the Declaration of Independence.

[7] This practice is called *suttee*. For a contemporary feminist analysis, see Daly 1978, 113-33.

life, takes a less summary mode of drawing his beloved partner after him; he does it by the deprivation and starvation of the flesh, and the humiliation and mortification of the spirit. In bequeathing to the wife just enough to keep soul and body together, man seems to lose sight of the fact that woman, like himself, takes great pleasure in acts of benevolence and charity. It is but just, therefore, that she should have it in her power to give during her life, and to will away at her death, as her benevolence or obligations might prompt her to do.

4th. Look at the position of woman as *mother*. There is no human love so generous, strong and steadfast as that of the mother for her child; yet behold how cruel and ruthless are your laws touching this most sacred relation.

Nature has clearly made the mother the guardian of the child; but man, in his inordinate love of power, does continually set nature and nature's laws at open defiance. The father may apprentice his child, bind him out to a trade or labor, without the mother's consent--yea, in direct opposition to her most earnest entreaties, her prayers and tears.

He may apprentice his son to a gamester or rumseller, and thus cancel his debts of *honor*. By the abuse of this absolute power, he may bind his daughter to the owner of a brothel, and, by the degradation of his child, supply his daily wants; and such things, gentlemen, have been done in our very midst. Moreover, the father, about to die, may bind out all his children wherever and to whomsoever he may see fit, and thus, in fact, will away the guardianship of all his children from the mother. The Revised Statutes of New York provide that "every father, whether of full age or a minor, of a child to be born, or of any living child under the age of twenty-one years, and unmarried, may by his *deed or last will*, duly executed, dispose of the custody and tuition of such child during its minority, or for any less time, to any person or persons, in possession or remainder." 2 R. S., page 150, sec. 1.

Thus, by your laws, the child is the absolute property of the father, wholly at his disposal in life or at death.

In case of separation, the law gives the children to the father; no matter what his character or condition. At this very time we can point you to noble, virtuous, well educated mothers in this state, who have abandoned their husbands for their profligacy and confirmed drunkenness. All these have been robbed of their children, who are in the custody of the husband, under the care of his relatives, whilst the mothers are permitted to see them but at stated intervals. But, said one of these mothers, with a grandeur of attitude and manner worthy the noble Roman matron in the palmiest days of that republic, I would rather never see my child again, than be the medium to hand down the low, animal nature of its father, to stamp degradation on the brow of another innocent being. It is enough that one child of his shall call me mother. If you are far sighted statesmen, and do wisely judge of the interests of this commonwealth, you will so shape your future laws as to encourage woman to take the high moral ground that the father of her children must be great and good.

Instead of your present laws, which make the mother and her children the victims of vice and license, you might rather pass laws prohibiting to all drunkards, libertines and fools, the rights of husbands and fathers. Do not the hundreds of laughing idiots that are crowding into our asylums, appeal to the wisdom of our statesmen for some new laws on marriage--to the mothers of this day for a higher, purer morality?

Again, as the condition of the child always follows that of the mother, and as by the abuse of your laws the father may beat the mother, so may he the child. What mother cannot bear me witness to untold sufferings which cruel, vindictive fathers have visited upon their helpless children? Who ever saw a human being that would not abuse unlimited power? Base and ignoble must that man be, who, let the provocation be what it may, would strike a woman; but he who would lacerate a trembling child is unworthy the name of man. A mother's love can be no protection to a child; she cannot appeal to you to save it from a father's cruelty, for the laws take no cognizance of the mother's most grievous wrongs. Neither at home nor abroad can a mother protect her son. Look at the temptations that surround the paths of our youth at every step; look at the gambling and drinking saloons, the club rooms, the dens of infamy and abomination that infest all our villages and cities--slowly but surely sapping the very foundations of all virtue and strength.

By your laws, all these abominable resorts are permitted. It is folly to talk of a mother moulding the character of her son, when all mankind, backed up by law and public sentiment, conspire to destroy her influence. But when woman's moral power shall speak through the ballot-box, then shall her influence be seen and felt; then, in our legislative debates, such questions as the canal tolls on salt, the improvement of rivers and harbors, and the claims of Mr. Smith for damages against the state, would be secondary to the consideration of the legal existence of all these public resorts, which lure our youth on to excessive indulgence and destruction.

Many times and oft it has been asked us, with unaffected seriousness, "what do you women want? What are you aiming at?" Many have manifested a laudable curiosity to know what the wives and daughters could complain of in republican America, where their sires and sons have so bravely fought for freedom and gloriously secured their independence, trampling all tyranny, bigotry and caste in the dust, and declaring to a waiting world the divine truth that all men are created equal. What can *woman* want under such a government? Admit a radical difference in sex and you demand different spheres--water for fish, and air for birds.

It is impossible to make the southern planter believe that his slave feels and reasons just as he does--that injustice and subjection are as galling as to him--that the degradation of living by the will of another, the mere dependent on his caprice, at the mercy of his passions, is as keenly felt by him as his master. If you can force on his unwilling vision a vivid picture of the negro's wrongs and for a moment touch his soul, his logic brings him instant consolation. He says, the slave does not feel this as I would. Here, gentlemen, is our difficulty: When we plead our cause before the law makers and *savants* of the republic, they cannot take in the idea that men and women are alike; and so long as the mass rest in this delusion, the public mind will not be so much startled by the revelations made of the injustice and degradation of woman's position as by the fact that she should at length wake up to a sense of it.

If you, too, are thus deluded, what avails it that we show by your statute books that your laws are unjust--that woman is the victim of avarice and power? What avails it that we point out the wrongs of woman in social life; the victim of passion and lust? You scorn the thought that she has any natural love of freedom burning in her breast, any clear perception of justice urging her on to demand her rights.

Would to God you could know the burning indignation that fills woman's soul when she turns over the pages of your statute books, and sees there how like feudal barons you freemen hold your women. Would that you could know the humiliation she feels for her sex, when she thinks of all the beardless boys in your law offices, learning these ideas of one-sided justice--taking their first lessons in contempt for all womankind--being indoctrinated into the incapacities of their mothers, and the lordly, absolute rights of man over all women, children and property, and to know that these are to be our future Presidents, Judges, Husbands and Fathers; in sorrow we exclaim, alas! for that nation whose sons bow not in loyalty to woman. The mother is the first object of the child's veneration and love, and they who root out this holy sentiment, dream not of the blighting effect it has on the boy and the man. The impression left on law students, fresh from your statute books, is most unfavorable to woman's influence; hence you see but few lawyers chivalrous and high-toned in their sentiments toward woman. They cannot escape the legal view which, by constant reading, has become familiarized to their minds: "*Femme covert*," "dower," "widow's claims," "protection," "incapacities," "incumbrance," is written on the brow of every woman they meet.

But if, gentlemen, you take the ground that the sexes are alike, and, therefore, you are our faithful representatives--then why all these special laws for woman? Would not one code answer for all of like needs and wants? Christ's golden rule is better than all the special legislation that the ingenuity of man can devise: "Do unto others as you would have others do unto you" [Matt. 7:12]. This, men and brethren, is all we ask at your hands. We *ask* no better laws than those you have made for yourselves. We need no other protection than that which your present laws secure to you.

In conclusion, then, let us say, in behalf of the women of this state, we ask for all that you have asked for yourselves in the progress of your development, since the *May Flower* cast anchor side [sic] Plymouth rock; and simply on the ground that the rights of every human being are the same and identical. You may say that the mass of the women of this

State do not make the demand; it comes from a few sour, disappointed old maids and childless women.

You are mistaken; the mass speak through us. A very large majority of the women of this state support themselves and their children, and many their husbands too. Go into any village you please, of three or four thousand inhabitants, and you will find as many as fifty men or more, whose only business is to discuss religion and politics, as they watch the trains come and go at the depot, or the passage of a canal boat through a lock; to laugh at the vagaries of some drunken brother, or the capers of a monkey dancing to the music of his master's organ. All these are supported by their mothers, wives or sisters.

Now, do you *candidly* think these wives do not wish to control the wages they earn--to own the land they buy--the houses they build? to have at their disposal their own children, without being subject to the constant interference and tyranny of an idle, worthless profligate? Do you suppose that any woman is such a pattern of devotion and submission that she willingly stitches all day for the small sum of fifty cents, that she may enjoy the unspeakable privilege, in obedience to your laws, of paying for her husband's tobacco and rum? Think you the wife of the confirmed, beastly drunkard would consent to share with him her home and bed, if law and public sentiment would release her from such gross companionship? Verily, no! Think you the wife, with whom endurance has ceased to be a virtue, who, through much suffering has lost all faith in the justice of both Heaven and earth, takes the law in her own hand, severs the unholy bond and turns her back forever upon him whom she once called husband, consents to the law that in such an hour tears her child from her--all that she has left on earth to love and cherish? The drunkards' wives speak through us, and they number 50,000. Think you that the woman who has worked hard all her days, in helping her husband to accumulate a large property, consents to the law that places this wholly at his disposal? Would not the mother, whose only child is bound out for a term of years, against her expressed wishes, deprive the father of this absolute power if she could?

For all these, then, we speak. If to this long list you add all the laboring women who are loudly demanding remuneration for their unending toil--those women who teach in our seminaries, academies and common schools for a miserable pittance; the widows, who are taxed without mercy; the unfortunate ones in our work houses, poor houses, and prisons; who are they that we do not now represent? But a small class of fashionable butterflies, who, through the short summer days, seek the sunshine and the flowers; but the cool breezes of autumn and the hoary frosts of winter will soon chase all these away; then, they too will need and seek protection, and through other lips demand, in their turn, justice and equity at your hands.

11

Elizabeth Cady Stanton, "A Slave's Appeal," Speech to the Judiciary Committee, New York State Legislature, 1860

After a pause of six years, in 1860 Cady Stanton made three major addresses in three months. In March she made the speech reprinted here on behalf of married women's property rights; in May she demanded suffrage for white and Afro-American women from the American Anti-Slavery Society in New York City; and two days later, she spoke in support of liberalizing divorce laws at the National Woman's Rights Convention in Cooper Union in New York City. She called this speech "A Slave's Appeal," and subsequent to its delivery, amendments passed the New York Assembly giving married women the right to their earnings, the right to contract and sue, and the right to joint guardianship of their children. An excerpted version of the speech may be found in **HWS** *1:679-85; this text is from the* **Proceedings** *of the national woman's rights convention of 1860, at which she repeated the speech. Her introductory remarks were greeted with much amusement: "As by particular request, I repeat to you the address I delivered at Albany last winter, you will please resolve yourselves into the 'Gentlemen of the Judiciary.'" No other complete text of the speech exists.*

GENTLEMEN OF THE JUDICIARY:--There are certain natural rights as inalienable to civilization as are the rights of air and motion to the savage in the wilderness. The natural rights of the civilized man and woman are government, property, the harmonious development of all their powers, and the gratification of their desires. There are a few people we now and then meet, who, like Jeremy Bentham, scout the idea of natural rights in civilization, and pronounce them mere metaphors, declaring there are no rights aside from those the law confers.[1] If the law made man too, that might do, for then he could be made to order, to fit the particular niche he was designed to fill. But inasmuch as God made man in his own image, with capacities and powers as boundless as the universe, whose exigencies no mere human law can meet, it is evident that the man must ever stand first--the law but the creature of his wants--the law-giver but the mouthpiece of humanity. If, then, the nature of a being decides its rights, every individual comes into this world with rights that are not transferable. He does not bring them like a pack on his back, that may be stolen from him, but they are a component part of himself--the laws which insure his growth and development. The individual may be put in the stocks, body and soul, he may be dwarfed, crippled, killed outright, but his rights can no man get--they live and die with him.

Though the atmosphere be forty miles deep all round the globe, no man can do more than fill his own lungs. No man can see, or hear, or smell, but just so far; and though hundreds are deprived of these senses, his are not the more acute. Though rights have been abundantly supplied by the good Father, no man can

---

[1] Jeremy Bentham (1748-1832), English philosopher, jurist, political theorist, and founder of utilitarianism, whose greatest work was the *Introduction to the Principles of Morals and Legislation* (1789).

appropriate to himself those that belong to another. A citizen can have but one vote, fill but one office, though thousands are not permitted to do either. These axioms prove that woman's poverty does not add to man's wealth, and if, in the plenitude of his power, he should secure to her the exercise of all her God-given rights, her wealth could not bring poverty to him. There is a kind of nervous unrest always manifested by those in power, whenever new claims are started by those out of their own immediate class. The philosophy of this is very plain. They imagine that if the rights of this new class be granted, they must, of necessity, sacrifice something of what they already possess. They cannot divest themselves of the idea that rights are very much like lands, stocks, bonds and mortgages, and that if every new claimant be satisfied, the supply of human rights must in time run low. You might as well carp at the birth of every child, lest there should not be enough air left to inflate your lungs; at the success of every scholar, for fear that your draughts at the fountain of knowledge, could not be so long and deep; at the glory of every hero, lest there be no glory left for you.

"If the citizens of the United States should not be free and happy, the fault," says Washington, "will be entirely their own." Yes, gentlemen, the basis of our government is broad enough and strong enough to securely hold the rights of all its citizens, and should we pile up rights ever so high, and crown the pinnacle with those of the weakest woman, there is no danger that it will totter to the ground. Yes, it is woman's own fault that she is where she is. Why has she not claimed all those rights, long ago guaranteed by our own declaration to all the citizens of this Republic? Why does she not this day stand in our Senate Chamber and House of Representatives, to look after her own interests? A citizen is defined to be a person, native or naturalized, who has the privilege of exercising the elective franchise, or the qualifications which enable him to vote for rulers, and to purchase and hold real estate. With this definition, a woman can hardly be called a citizen of this State, and if not, her position is a singularly anomalous one. She is a native and naturalized, yet has not the privilege of exercising the elective franchise. She has all the necessary qualifications to vote for rulers, and to govern herself,--yet she is denied the right. She may hold real estate, but cannot protect her property by law. She is taxed to support government, pays the penalty of her own crimes, and suffers the consequences of all man's false legislation, but she is not permitted to say what her taxes shall be, what civil acts shall be criminal, and she has no appeal from man's administration of law. She is, in fine, honored with all the duties and responsibilities of a citizen, and at the same time is denied all his rights and privileges. It is declared that every citizen has a right to life, liberty, and the pursuit of happiness. Can woman be said to have a right to life, if all means of self-protection are denied her,--if, in case of life and death, she is not only denied the right of trial by a jury of her own peers, but has no voice in the choice of judge or juror, her consent has never been given to the criminal code by which she is judged? Can she be said to have a right to liberty, when another citizen may have the legal custody of her person; the right to shut her up and administer moderate chastisement; to decide when and how she shall live, and what are the necessary means for her support? Can any citizen be said to have a right to the pursuit of happiness, whose inalienable rights are denied; who is disfranchised from all the privileges of citizenship; whose person is subject to the control and absolute will of another? Now, why is it, gentlemen, that woman stands at this day wholly unrepresented in this government? Why is it that the mass of laws affecting her special interests remain in their original barbarism at this hour, whilst all others have been undergoing change, and improvement? Simply because she has never exercised her right to the elective franchise. The grant of this right would secure all others, but the grant of every other, whilst this is denied, is a mockery! What is the right to property without the right to protect it? The enjoyment of that right to-day is no security it will be continued to-morrow, so long as it is granted to her as a favor by a privileged class, and not secured as a sacred right. It is folly to urge woman's claims on the broad platform of human rights, or from the grand basis of republicanism, upon which this government rests, for by your laws you deny her humanity, her citizenship, her identity with yourself. Justice, common sense, sound logic, all point to equality, to a full and perfect recognition of all her God-given rights. But as you are not yet prepared for any thing more than a partial legislation, believing, as you do, that womanhood is such a subtle essence of frivolities and contradictions that it needs some special code of laws to meet its exigencies, on the low ground of expediency and precedent must we plead our cause. Man having denied woman's identity with himself, has no data to go upon in judging of her interests. If the sexes are alike in their mental structure, then there is no reason why woman should not have a voice in making the laws which govern her? But if they are not alike, most certainly woman must make laws for herself, for who else can understand her wants and needs? If it be admitted in this government, that all men and women are free and equal, then must women claim a place in our Senate Chambers and Houses of Representatives. But if it be found that even here, we have classes and castes, not Lord and Commons, but Lords and Ladies, then must woman claim a lower house, where her representatives may watch the passage of all bills affecting her own welfare, and the good of the country.

Surely you should have as much respect for the rights of different classes as monarchical England. Experience taught her that the nobility could not legislate for the peasantry, and experience teaches us that man cannot legislate for woman. If the object of government is to protect the weak against the strong, how unwise to place the power wholly in the hands of the strong? Yet that is the history of all governments, even the model republic of these United States. You who have read the history of nations, from Moses down to our last election, where have you ever seen one class looking after the interests of another? Any of you can readily see the defects in other governments, and pronounce sentence against those who have sacrificed the masses to themselves; but when we come to our own case, we are blinded by custom and self-interest. Some of you who have no capital can see the injustice which the laborer suffers; some of you who have no slaves, can see the cruelty of his oppression; but who of you appreciate the galling humiliation, the refinements of degradation, to which women (the mothers, wives, sisters and daughters of freemen) are subject, in this the last half of the nineteenth century? How many of you have ever read even the laws concerning her that now disgrace your statute-books? In cruelty and tyranny, they are not surpassed by any slaveholding code in the Southern States; in fact they are worse, by just so far as woman, from her social position, refinement and education, is on a more equal ground with the oppressor. Allow me just here to call the attention of that party now so much interested in the slave of the Carolinas, to the similarity in his condition and that of the mothers, wives and daughters of the Empire State. The negro has no name. He is Cuffy Douglas or Cuffy Brooks, just whose Cuffy he may chance to be. The woman has no name. She is Mrs. Richard Roe or Mrs. John Doe, just whose Mrs. she may chance to be. Cuffy has no right to his earnings; he cannot buy or sell, or lay up anything that he can call his own. *Mrs. Roe has no right to her earnings; she can neither buy nor sell, make contracts, nor lay up anything that she can call her own. Cuffy has no right to his children; they can be sold from him at any time. *Mrs. Roe has no right to her children; they may be bound out to cancel a father's debts of honor. The unborn child, even by the last will of the father, may be placed under the guardianship of a stranger and a foreigner.[2] Cuffy has no legal existence; he is subject to restraint and moderate chastisement. Mrs. Roe has no legal existence; she has not the best right to her own person. The husband has the power to restrain, and administer moderate chastisement.

Blackstone declares that the husband and wife are one, and learned commentators have decided that that one is the husband.[3] In all civil codes, you will find them classified as one. Certain rights and immunities, such and such privileges are to be secured to white male citizens. What have women and negroes to do with rights? What know they of government, war or glory?

The prejudice against color, of which we hear so much, is no stronger than that against sex. It is produced by the same cause, and manifested very much in the same way. The negro's skin and the woman's sex are both *prima facie* evidence that they were intended to be in subjection to the white Saxon man. The few social privileges which the man gives

---

[2] She preceded each sentence with an asterisk with the words "But yesterday" and shifted the verbs in them and in this sentence to the past tense. She added here, "You see one republican legislature has spoiled our old similies [sic] already," reflecting the fact that these laws had been changed by the state legislature.

[3] See p. 37, n 1.

the woman, he makes up to the negro in civil rights. The woman may sit at the same table and eat with the white man; the free negro may hold property and vote. The woman may sit in the same pew with the white man, in church; the free negro may enter the pulpit and preach. Now, with the right to suffrage, the right unquestioned, even by Paul, to minister at the altar, it is evident that the prejudice against sex is more deeply rooted and more unreasonably maintained than that against color. As citizens of a republic, which should we most highly prize, social privileges or civil rights? The latter, most certainly.

To those who do not feel the injustice and degradation of the condition, there is something inexpressibly comical in man's "citizen woman." It reminds me of those monsters I used to see in the old world, head and shoulders woman, and the rest of the body sometimes fish, and sometimes beast. I used to think, What a strange conceit! but now I see how perfectly it represents man's idea! Look over all his laws concerning us, and you will see just enough of woman to tell of her existence; all the rest is submerged, or made to crawl upon the earth. Just imagine an inhabitant of another planet entertaining himself some pleasant evening in searching over our great national compact, our Declaration of Independence, our Constitutions, or some of our Statute-books; what would he think of those "*women and negroes*" that must be so fenced in, so guarded against? Why, he would certainly suppose we were monsters, like those fabulous giants or Brobdignagians of olden times, so dangerous to civilized man, from our size, ferocity and power.[4] Then let him take

---

[4] In Jonathan Swift's *Gulliver's Travels* (1726), Brobdignagians were giants twelve times the size of humans. Told by Gulliver of European customs and institutions, their King observed: "I cannot but conclude the bulk of your natives to be the most pernicious vermin

up our poets, from Pope[5] down to Dana;[6] let him listen to our Fourth of July toasts, and some of the sentimental adulations of social life, and no logic could convince him that this creature of the law, and this angel of the family altar, could be one and the same being. Man is in such a labyrinth of contradictions with his marital and property rights; he is so befogged on the whole question of maidens, wives and mothers, that from pure benevolence we should relieve him from this troublesome branch of legislation. We should vote, and make laws for ourselves. Do not be alarmed, dear ladies! You need spend no time reading Grotius,[7] Coke,[8] Puffendorf [sic],[9] Blackstone, Bentham, Kent[10]

---

that nature ever suffered to crawl upon the earth."

[5] Alexander Pope (1688-1744), English poet, author of *The Rape of the Lock* (1714), translations of Homer's *Iliad* (1720) and *Odyssey* (1725-26) in heroic couplets, and *The Dunciad* (1728-43).

[6] Richard Henry Dana (1787-1879), critic and poet, founder and editor of the *North American Review*, to whose lecture Lucretia Coffin Mott's "Discourse on Woman," 1849, was a response.

[7] Hugo Grotius (1583-1645), Dutch jurist and humanist, who published the first definitive text on international law, *Concerning the Law of War and Peace* (1625;1631).

[8] Sir Edward Coke (1552-1634), one of the most eminent jurists in the history of English law; author of *Reports*, a series of commentaries on cases in common law.

[9] Samuel, Baron von Pufendorf (1632-94), German jurist and historian, noted as an early theorist in international law.

and Story[11] to find out what you need. We may safely trust the shrewd selfishness of the white man, and consent to live under the same broad code where he has so comfortably ensconced himself. Any legislation that will do for man, we may abide by most cheerfully.

"Governments derive their just powers from the consent of the governed." "Taxation and representation are inseparable." These glorious truths were uttered for some higher purpose than to decorate holiday flags, or furnish texts for Fourth of July orations. If they mean any thing, by what right do you try woman by your civil code, or tax her to support this government? Do you claim that she is represented by her father, husband, brother, son? Your statute-books testify against you. They show but too well how faithless you have been to the high and holy trust you have assumed. A proper self-respect forbids such an admission. If those to whom woman is bound, by all the ties of blood and affection, have made, and do now sanction, such laws as disgrace your whole code, may Heaven save her from her friends! But if man claims to be her representative, let him pay her taxes. Instead of sending his tax-gatherer round to poor widows, let him look up their fathers, brothers, sons, or some negro that they have helped to emancipate, or some clergyman they have helped to educate. Get it out of some one crowned with the glory of manhood. But for consistency's sake; for

---

[10] James Kent (1763-1847), American jurist, first professor of law at Columbia College, judge and later chief judge of the New York State supreme court, whose written opinions as chancellor were instrumental in reviving equity law.

[11] Joseph Story (1779-1845), associate justice of the Supreme Court (1811-45), who, with James Kent, helped to found American equity jurisprudence.

the respect you bear to republican principles; as you honor the memory of those who settled this question for you, by the veneration we all feel for the sufferings and glory of those who sent forth that grand declaration of rights which made every crowned head in Europe tremble on his throne; for the memory of all those mighty words and deeds of the past, do not hold one half of the people of this State beyond the limits of justice. Our State Treasury reports show thousands of dollars collected every year from the one-house and lot of poor widows and maidens. Taxation without representation was the theme for many a hot debate in the parliaments of the old world, and for many an eloquent oration in the forests of the new. We but re-echo those undying truths uttered by the heroes of American liberty, scarce one century ago. It must strike every mind as just, that if man is not willing to have woman represented in this government, then she should not be subject to taxation. Your Constitution regards the negro, so unjustly degraded, with far more consideration than your wives and mothers. If he is possessed of a certain amount of property, then is he permitted to vote, and pay taxes, too. If he has not that amount, then he is not permitted to vote, neither is he taxed. But woman--no matter how rich, how noble, how virtuous, she shall have no voice in the government; and no matter how weak or ignorant, how wretched or worn out with life's struggles, if, by unwearied industry, she has made a home for herself and children, she must be subject to taxation. Talk not of chivalry, men of New York, so long as feeble women, who own but one house and lot, are legal subjects of taxation! Talk not of justice, so long as sex is made a badge of oppression! I am better educated than the Irishman who saws my wood. I read and write his letters for him to the Emerald Isle, and in conversation, I find myself better posted that he is on law and politics, and with a far higher appreciation of the blessings of a republican form of government. Yet he suffers none of the injustice I do, but is in the full possession of all his civil and political rights, equally with any member of your honorable body. In standing before grave and reverend senators, full of years, experience and wisdom, I might find in their vast superiority sufficient ground for their superior rights. But when I contrast myself with the ignorant alien, the gambler, the drunkard, the prize-fighter, the licentious profligate, the silly stripling of twenty-one, the fool, the villain, I see no ground for these broad distinctions.

But, say you, we would not have woman exposed to the grossness and vulgarity of public life, or encounter what she must at the polls. When you talk, gentlemen, of sheltering woman from the rough winds and revolting scenes of real life, you must be either talking for effect, or wholly ignorant of what the facts of life are. The man, whatever he is, is known to the woman. She is the companion, not only of the accomplished statesman, the orator and the scholar, but the vile, vulgar, brutal man has his mother, his wife, his sister, his daughter. Yes, delicate, refined, educated women are in daily life with the drunkard, the gambler, the licentious man, the rogue and the villain; and if man shows out what he is any where, it is at his own hearthstone. There are over forty thousand drunkards in this State. All these are bound by the ties of family to some woman. Allow but a mother and a wife to each, and you have over eighty thousand women. All these have seen their fathers, brothers, husbands, sons, in the lowest and most debased stages of obscenity and degradation. In your own circle of friends, do you not know refined women, whose whole lives are darkened and saddened by gross and brutal associations? Now, gentlemen, do you talk to woman of a rude jest or jostle at the polls, where noble, virtuous men stand ready to protect her person and her rights, when, alone in the darkness and solitude and gloom of night, they have trembled on their own thresholds, awaiting the return of husbands from their midnight revels?--when, stepping from her chamber, she has beheld her royal monarch, her lord and master,--her legal representative,--the protector of her property, her home, her children and her person, down on his hands and knees slowly crawling up the stairs? Behold him in her chamber--*in her bed*! The fairy tale of Beauty and the Beast is far too often realized in life. Gentlemen, such scenes as woman has witnessed at her own fireside, where no eye save Omnipotence could pity, no strong arm could help, can never be realized at the polls, never equalled elsewhere, this side the bottomless pit. No, woman has not hitherto lived in the clouds, surrounded by an atmosphere of holiness and divinity, ignorant of vice and impurity,--but she has been the companion of man in health, in sickness and in death, in his highest and in his lowest moments. She has worshipped him as a saint and an orator, and pitied him as madman and a fool. In Paradise, man and woman were placed together, and so they must ever be. They must sink or rise together. If man is low and wretched and vile, woman cannot escape the contagion, and any atmosphere that is unfit for woman to breathe, is not fit for man. Verily, the sins of the fathers shall be visited upon the children to the third and fourth generation.[12] You, by your unwise legislation, have crippled and dwarfed womanhood, by closing to her all honorable and lucrative means of employment, have driven her into the garrets and dens of our cities, where she now revenges herself on your innocent sons, sapping the very foundations of national virtue and strength. Alas! for the young men just coming on the stage of action, who soon shall fill your vacant places--our future Senators, our Presidents, the expounders of our constitutional law! Terrible are the

---

[12] Exod. 20:5; Num. 14: 18.

penalties we are now suffering for the ages of injustice done to woman.

But, say you, God has appointed woman's sphere; it is His will that she is as she is. Well, if that be so, then woman will be kept in her sphere by God's laws. It is folly, said Daniel Webster, to rënact God's laws.[13] Wherever God has placed woman, there must she ever be. You might as well pass laws to keep Venus, the beautiful morning star, from refreshing herself by an occasional promenade on the broad belt of Saturn. Nature's laws are immutable; no planet or immortal being can ever get out of its prescribed orbit. Again, the condition of woman, in all ages, has differed materially, and differs at this moment, among the various nations of the earth. Now, which of all these conditions, think you, is in accordance with the will of God? Enervated and voluptuous by confinement, as she is in the Turkish harem, or exhausted by toil and out-door labor, as she is in Switzerland and Germany,--with her feet compressed in iron boots to the smallest possible dimensions, depending on man to carry her about, as she is in China, or standing all day in the intense heat of a summer's sun in the cotton field and rice plantation, as she is in Christian America,--with the crown and sceptre ruling the mightiest nation on the globe, or burning on the funeral pile of her husband, a useless relic of her lordly dead, as she is in India,--who can decide which of all these is the woman's true sphere?

Ever and anon, through the long ages, great emergencies have called forth the true, the individual woman, and multitudes have always greeted her with joy, and proudly welcomed her success. On the war-horse, bearing the flag of conquest, she has led the armies of mighty nations. With telescopic vision, she has prescribed the orbit of planetary worlds. In the midst of peril,

---

[13] See p. 54, n 12.

mutiny and death, she has seized the command of the lonely ship, and brought it safely to its destined port. With the mild gospel of Jesus, she has passed, unscathed, through all earthly dangers. What depths of pollution and vice have been unwatched and unpitied by the eye of woman? An angel of mercy, she has walked up and down the solitary places, by-lanes and dark prison-houses of our modern Babylons, ministering to the children of suffering and want, cheering the trembling criminal, the depraved and the profligate with bright hopes of the future! Amid all the horrors of the French Revolution, in the gloomy Bastile [sic], at the guillotine, through all the tragic scenes of the Crimea,[14] amid all the dangers and sudden emergencies of every-day life, self-poised and self-sustained, tell me,

> Can she be too great, too grand,
> To fill the place where she can
> stand,
> To do and dare what she has done
> Before all Israel and the sun?

Again, it is said that the majority of women do not ask for any change in the laws, that it is time enough to give them the elective franchise when they, as a class, demand it.

Wise statesmen legislate for the best interests of the nation; the State, for the highest good of its citizens; the Christian, for the conversion of the world. Where would have been our railroads, our telegraphs, our ocean steamers, our canals and harbors, our arts and sciences, if government had withheld the means from the far-seeing minority? This

---

[14] A reference to Florence Nightingale (1820-1910), the founder of modern nursing, who in 1854 organized a unit of 38 women nurses for service in the Crimean War; by the end of the war, she had become a legend.

State established our present system of common schools, fully believing that educated men and women would make better citizens than ignorant ones. In making this provision for the education of its children, had they waited for a majority of the urchins of this State to petition for schools, how many, think you, would have asked to be transplanted from the street to the school-house? Does the State wait for the criminal to ask for his prison-house? the insane, the idiot, the deaf and dumb for his asylum? Does the Christian, in his love to all mankind, wait for the majority of the benighted heathen to ask him for the gospel? No; unasked and unwelcomed, he crosses the trackless ocean, rolls off the mountain of superstition that oppresses the human mind, proclaims the immortality of the soul, the dignity of manhood, the right of all to be free and happy. No, gentlemen, if there is but one woman in this State who feels the injustice of her position, she should not be denied her inalienable rights, because the common household drudge and the silly butterflies of fashion are ignorant of all laws, both human and Divine. Because they know nothing of governments, or rights, and therefore ask nothing, shall my petitions be unheard? I stand before you the rightful representative of woman, claiming a share in the halo of glory that has gathered round her in the ages, and by the wisdom of her past words and works, her peerless heroism and self-sacrifice, I challenge your admiration, and, moreover, claiming, as I do, a share in all her outrages and sufferings, in the cruel injustice, contempt and ridicule now heaped upon her, in her deep degradation, hopeless wretchedness, by all that is helpless in her present condition, that is false in law and public sentiment, I urge your generous consideration; for as my heart swells with pride to behold woman in the highest walks of literature and art, it grows big enough to take in those who are bleeding in the dust.

Now do not think, gentlemen, we wish you

to do a great many troublesome things for us, that you need spend a whole session in fixing up a code of laws to satisfy a class of most unreasonable women. We ask no more than the poor devils in the Scripture asked, "Let us alone" [Mark 1:24]. In mercy, let us take care of ourselves, our property, our children and our homes. True, we are not so strong, so wise, so crafty as you are, but if any kind friend leaves us a little money, or we can by great industry earn fifty cents a day, we would rather buy bread and clothes for our children, than cigars and champagne for our legal protectors. There has been a great deal written and said about protection. We, as a class, are tired of one kind of protection, that which leaves us everything to do, to dare and to suffer, and strips us of all means for its accomplishment. We would not tax man to take care of us. No, the Great Father has endowed all his creatures with the necessary powers for self-support, self-defence and protection. We do not ask man to represent us, it is hard enough in times like these for man to carry back-bone enough to represent himself. So long as the mass of men spend most of their time on the fence, not knowing which way to jump, they are surely in no condition to tell us where we had better stand. In pity for man, we would no longer hang like a millstone round his neck. Undo what man did for us in the dark ages, and strike out all special legislation for us; strike out the name, *woman*, from all your constitutions, and then, with fair sailing, let us sink or swim, live or die, survive or perish together.

At Athens, an ancient apologue tells us, on the completion of the temple of Minerva, a statue of the goddess was wanted to occupy the crowning point of the edifice.[15] Two of the

---

[15] Minerva was the widely worshipped Roman goddess of handicrafts with whom the Greek Athena was regularly identified.

greatest artists produced what each deemed his master-piece. One of these figures was the size of life, admirably designed, exquisitely finished, softly rounded, and beautifully refined. The other was of Amazonian stature, and so boldly chiselled that it looked more like masonry than sculpture. The eyes of all were attracted by the first, and turned away in contempt from the second. That, therefore, was adopted, and the other rejected, almost with resentment, as though an insult had been offered to a discerning public. The favored statue was accordingly borne in triumph to the place for which it was designed, in the presence of applauding thousands, but as it receded from their up-turned eyes, all, all at once agaze upon it, the thunders of applause unaccountably died away,--a general misgiving ran through every bosom,--the mob themselves stood like statues, as silent and as petrified, for as it slowly went up, and up, the soft expression of those chiselled features, the delicate curves and outlines of the limbs and figure, became gradually fainter and fainter, and when at last it reached the place for which it was intended, it was a shapeless ball, enveloped in mist. Of course, the idol of the hour was now clamored down as rationally as it had been cried up, and its dishonored rival, with no good will and no good looks on the part of the chagrined populace, was reared in its stead. As it ascended, the sharp angles faded away, the rough points became smooth, the features full of expression, the whole figure radiant with majesty and beauty. The rude hewn mass, that before scarcely appeared to bear even the human form, assumed at once the divinity which it represented, being so perfectly proportioned to the dimensions of the building, and to the elevation on which it stood, that it seemed as though Pallas herself had alighted upon the pinnacle of the temple in person, to receive the homage of her worshippers.

The woman of the nineteenth century is the shapeless ball in the lofty position which she was designed fully and nobly to fill. The place is not too high, too large, too sacred for woman, but the type that you have chosen is far too small for it. The woman we declare unto you is the rude, misshapen, unpolished object of the successful artist. From your stand-point, you are absorbed with the defects alone. The true artist sees the harmony between the object and its destination. Man, the sculptor, has carved out his ideal, and applauding thousands welcome his success. He has made a woman that from his low stand-point looks fair and beautiful, a being without rights, or hopes, or fears but in him--neither noble, virtuous nor independent. Where do we see, in Church or State, in school-house or at the fireside, the much talked-of moral power of woman? Like those Athenians, we have bowed down and worshiped in woman, beauty, grace, the exquisite proportions, the soft and beautifully rounded outline, her delicacy, refinement, and silent helplessness--all well when she is viewed simply as an object of sight, never to rise one foot above the dust from which she sprung. But if she is to be raised up to adorn a temple, or represent a divinity--if she is to fill the niche of wife and counsellor to true and noble men, if she is to be the mother, the educator of a race of heroes or martyrs, of a Napoleon, or a Jesus--then must the type of womanhood be on a larger scale than that yet carved by man.

In vain would the rejected artist have reasoned with the Athenians as to the superiority of his production; nothing short of the experiment they made could have satisfied them. And what of your experiment, what of your wives, your homes? Alas! for the folly and vacancy that meet you there! But for your club-houses and newspapers, what would social life be to you? Where are your beautiful women? your frail ones, taught to lean lovingly and confidingly on man? Where are the crowds of educated dependents--where the long line of pensioners on man's bounty? Where all the young girls, taught to believe that marriage is the only legitimate object of a woman's pursuit--they who stand listlessly on life's shores, waiting, year after year, like the sick man at the pool of Bethesda, for some one to come and put them in?[16] These are they who by their ignorance and folly curse almost every fireside with some human specimen of deformity or imbecility. These are they who fill the gloomy abodes of poverty and vice in our vast metropolis. These are they who patrol the streets of our cities, to give our sons their first lessons in infamy. These are they who fill our asylums, and make night hideous with their cries and groans.

The women who are called masculine, who are brave, courageous, self-reliant and independent, are they who, in the face of adverse winds, have kept one steady course upward and onward in the paths of virtue and peace--they who have taken their gauge of womanhood from their own native strength and dignity--they who have learned for themselves the will of God concerning them. This is our type of womanhood. Will you help us raise it up, that you too may see its beautiful proportions--that you may behold the outline of the goddess who is yet to adorn your temple of Freedom? We are building a model republic; our edifice will one day need a crowning glory. Let the artists be wisely chosen. Let them begin their work. Here is a temple to Liberty, to human rights, on whose portals behold the glorious declaration, "All men are created equal." The sun has never yet shone upon any of man's creations that can compare with this. The artist who can mould a statue worthy to crown magnificence like this, must be godlike in his conceptions, grand in his comprehensions, sublimely beautiful in his power of execution. The woman--the crowning glory of the model republic among the nations of the earth--what must she not be? (*Loud applause.*)

---

[16] John 5:2-7.

12

National Woman's Rights Convention Debate, New York City, 1860

Controversial claims routinely were put forward as resolutions at woman's rights conventions. These were then supported in a speech by their proposers, followed by lively and sometimes contentious discussion, usually in the form of speeches. Finally, there was a vote to determine whether the resolutions expressed the opinions of those assembled. Elizabeth Cady Stanton had urged permitting divorce on the grounds of habitual drunkenness at the New York State Woman's Temperance Convention of 1852 (**HWS** 1:482, 485). *The issue of liberalizing New York laws on divorce had been publicly argued in newspapers, first between November 1852 and February 1853 and then in March and April of 1860* (James et al. 1853; Greeley and Owen 1860). *Current law permitted divorce only on grounds of adultery; legal separations were permitted for cruel and inhuman treatment, for conduct threatening a wife's safety, and for abandonment or refusal by the husband to provide for her.*

Two separate issues emerged in the 1860 convention debate. In the initial speeches and resolutions of Cady Stanton, Antoinette Brown [Blackwell], and Ernestine Potowski Rose, the issue concerned liberalizing New York laws on divorce. With Wendell Phillips's speech, the issue shifted from marriage and divorce to movement strategy. The division in views, reflected also in the discussion that followed, was an early indicator of differences that would split the movement into two rival organizations, the American and the National Woman Suffrage Associations, in 1869.

Cady Stanton and Potowski Rose have been discussed in previous headnotes. Antoinette Brown [Blackwell] became a Congregational minister in 1853, and was thus the first woman ordained in a recognized denomination in the United States; one year later, however, she severed that affiliation to become a Unitarian. After her marriage to Samuel Blackwell, she rarely spoke in public, but she published **Studies in General Science** (1869) *and* **The Sexes Throughout Nature** (1875), *the latter a refutation of Charles Darwin's views of the females of the species. In 1879 she returned to lecturing and preaching. She also encouraged young women to pursue scientific studies and was an inspiration to female aspirants to the ministry.*

Wendell Phillips (1811-84), abolitionist and orator, followed William Lloyd Garrison (1805-79), editor of the **Liberator** *and founder of the American Anti-Slavery Society (1833), into the woman's rights movement. He was a trustee of the Charles F. Hovey fund established to support work for anti-slavery and woman's rights, a fund that provided some support for the work of Susan B. Anthony. Phillips was one of those who, following the Civil War, argued that woman suffrage should be deferred to avoid controversy over extending suffrage to freed male slaves. He allied himself with the more conservative Boston-based American Woman Suffrage Association.*

The text of the debate is taken from the convention **Proceedings** (1860).

Mrs. Elizabeth Cady Stanton then presented the following resolutions, in support of which she purposed to address the Convention:

1. Resolved, That, in the language (slightly varied) of John Milton, "Those who

marry intend as little to conspire their own ruin, as those who swear allegiance, and as a whole people is to *an ill government*, so is one man or woman *to an ill marriage*. If a whole people, against any authority, covenant or statute, may, by the sovereign edict of charity, save not only their lives, but honest liberties, from unworthy bondage, as well may a married party, against any private covenant, which he or she never entered, *to his or her mischief*, be redeemed from unsupportable disturbances, to honest peace, and just contentment."[1]

2. Resolved, That all men are created equal, and all women, in their natural rights, are the equals of men; and endowed by their Creator with the same inalienable right to the pursuit of happiness.

3. Resolved, That any constitution, compact or covenant between human beings, that failed to produce or promote human happiness, could not, in the nature of things, be of any force or authority;--and it would be not only a right, but a duty, to abolish it.

4. Resolved, That though marriage be in itself divinely founded, and is fortified as an institution by innumerable analogies in the whole kingdom of universal nature, still, a true marriage is only known by its results; and, like the fountain, if pure, will reveal only pure manifestations. Nor need it ever be said, "What God hath joined together, let not man put asunder" [Matt. 19:6; Mark 10:9], for man could not put it asunder; nor can he any more unite what God and nature have not joined together.

---

[1] John Milton (1608-74), English poet and prose writer best known for *Paradise Lost* (1667) and *Paradise Regained* (1671). This quotation is from *The Doctrine and Discipline of Divorce* (*Works* 1931, Vol. III, Part II, 374, lines 19-27). Cady Stanton has altered the pronouns to render the statement in non-sexist language that includes women.

5. Resolved, That of all insulting mockeries of heavenly truth and holy law, none can be greater than that physical *impotency* is cause sufficient for divorce, while no amount of mental or moral or spiritual *imbecility* is ever to be pleaded in support of such a demand.

6. Resolved, That such a law was worthy those dark periods when marriage was held by the greatest doctors and priests of the Church to be a *work of the flesh only*, and almost, if not altogether, a defilement; denied wholly to the clergy, and a second time, forbidden to all.

7. Resolved, That an unfortunate or ill-assorted marriage is ever a calamity, but not ever, perhaps never, a crime;--and when society or government, by its laws or customs, compels its continuance, always to the grief of one of the parties, and the actual loss and damage of both, it usurps an authority never delegated to man, nor exercised by God himself.

8. Resolved, That observation and experience daily show how incompetent are men, as individuals, or as governments, to select partners in business, teachers for their children, ministers of their religion, or makers, adjudicators or administrators of their laws; and as the same weakness and blindness must attend in the selection of matrimonial partners, the dictates of humanity and common sense alike show that the latter and most important contract should no more be perpetual than either or all of the former.

9. Resolved, That children born in these unhappy and unhallowed connections are, in the most solemn sense, of *unlawful birth*,--the fruit of lust, but not of love;--and so not of God, divinely descended, but from beneath, whence proceed all manner of evil and uncleanness.

10. Resolved, That next to the calamity of such a birth to the child, is the misfortune of being trained in the atmosphere of a household where love is not the law, but where

discord and bitterness abound; stamping their demoniac features on the moral nature, with all their odious peculiarities;--thus continuing the race in a weakness and depravity that must be a sure precursor of its ruin, as a just penalty of long-violated law.

ADDRESS OF MRS. E. C. STANTON.

Mrs. President,--In our common law, in our whole system of jurisprudence, we find man's highest idea of right. The object of law is to secure justice. But inasmuch as fallible man is the maker and administrator of law, we must look for many and gross blunders in the application of its general principles to individual cases.

The science of theology, of civil, political, moral and social life, all teach the common idea, that man ever has been, and ever must be, sacrificed to the highest good of society; the one to the many--the poor to the rich--the weak to the powerful--and all to the institutions of his own creation. Look, what thunderbolts of power man has forged in the ages for his own destruction!--at the organizations to enslave himself! And through those times of darkness, those generations of superstition, behold all along the relics of his power and skill, that stand like milestones, here and there, to show how far back man was great and glorious! Who can stand in those vast cathedrals of the old world, as the deep-toned organ reverberates from arch to arch, and not feel the grandeur of immortality? Here is the incarnated thought of man, beneath whose stately dome the man himself now bows in fear and doubt, knows not himself, and knows not God,--a mere slave to symbols,--and with holy water signs the Cross, whilst he who died thereon declared man God.

I repudiate this popular idea. I place man above all governments, all institutions--ecclesiastical and civil--all constitutions and laws. (*Applause.*) It is a mistaken idea, that the same law that oppresses the individidual, can promote the highest good of society. The best interests of a community never can require the sacrifice of one innocent being--of one sacred right. In the settlement, then, of any question, we must simply consider the highest good of the individual. It is the inalienable right of all to be happy. It is the highest duty of all to seek those conditions in life, those surroundings, which may develop what is noblest and best, remembering that the lessons of these passing hours are not for time alone, but for the ages of eternity. They tell us, in that future home--the heavenly paradise--that the human family shall be sifted out, and the good and pure shall dwell together in peace. If that be the heavenly order, is it not our duty to render earth as near like heaven as we may?

For years, there has been before the Legislature of this State a variety of bills, asking for divorce in cases of drunkenness, insanity, desertion, cruel and brutal treatment, endangering life. My attention was called to this question very early in life, by the sufferings of a friend of my girlhood, a victim of one of those unfortunate unions, called marriage. What my great love for that young girl, and my holy intuitions, then decided to be right, has not been changed by years of experience, observation and reason. I have pondered well these things in my heart,[2] and ever felt the deepest interest in all that has been written and said upon the subject, and the most profound respect and loving sympathy for those heroic women, who, in the face of law and public sentiment, have dared to sunder the unholy ties of a joyless, loveless union.

If marriage is a human institution, about which man may legislate, it seems but just that he should treat this branch of his legislation with the same common sense that he

---

2 "And Mary kept all these things, and pondered them in her heart" [Luke 2: 19].

applies to all others. If it is a mere legal contract, then should it be subject to the restraints and privileges of all other contracts. A contract, to be valid in law, must be formed between parties of mature age, with an honest intention in said parties to do what they agree. The least concealment, fraud, or intention to deceive, if proved, annuls the contract. A boy cannot contract for an acre of land, or a horse, until he is twenty-one, but he may contract for a wife at fourteen. If a man sell a horse, and the purchaser find in him great incompatibility of temper--a disposition to stand still, when the owner is in haste to go--the sale is null and void, the man and his horse part company. But in marriage, no matter how much fraud and deception are practiced, nor how cruelly one or both parties have been misled; no matter how young, inexperienced or thoughtless the parties, nor how unequal their condition and position in life, the contract cannot be annulled. Think of a husband telling a young and trusting girl, but one short month his wife, that he married her for her money; that those letters, so precious to her, that she had read and re-read, and kissed and cherished, were written by another; that their splendid home, of which, on their wedding day, her father gave to him the deed, is already in the hands of his creditors; that she must give up the elegance and luxury that now surround her, unless she can draw fresh supplies of money to meet their wants! When she told the story of her wrongs to me,--the abuse to which she was subject, and the dread in which she lived,--I impulsively urged her to fly from such a monster and villain, as she would before the hot breath of a ferocious beast of the wilderness. (*Applause.*) And she did fly; and it was well with her. Many times since, as I have felt her throbbing heart against my own, she has said, "Oh, but for your love and sympathy, your encouragement, I should never have escaped from that bondage. Before I could, of myself, have found courage to break those chains, my heart would have broken in the effort."

Marriage, as it now exists, must seem to all of you a mere human institution. Look through the universe of matter and mind,--all God's arrangements are perfect, harmonious and complete! There is no discord, friction, or failure in his eternal plans. Immutability, perfection, beauty, are stamped on all his laws. Love is the vital essence that pervades and permeates, from the centre to the circumference, the graduating circles of all thought and action. Love is the talisman of human weal and woe,--the *open sesame* to every human soul. Where two beings are drawn together, by the natural laws of likeness and affinity, union and happiness are the result. Such marriages might be Divine. But how is it now? You all know our marriage is, in many cases, a mere outward tie, impelled by custom, policy, interest, necessity; founded not even in friendship, to say nothing of love; with every possible inequality of condition and development. In these heterogeneous unions, we find youth and old age, beauty and deformity, refinement and vulgarity, virtue and vice, the educated and the ignorant, angels of grace and goodness, with devils of malice and malignity: and the sum of all this is human wretchedness and despair; cold fathers, sad mothers, and hapless children, who shiver at the hearthstone, where the fires of love have all gone out. The wide world, and the stranger's unsympathizing gaze, are not more to be dreaded for young hearts than homes like these. Now, who shall say that it is right to take two beings, so unlike, and anchor them right side by side fast bound--to stay all time, until God shall summon one away?

Do wise, Christian legislators need any arguments to convince them that the sacredness of the family relation should be protected at all hazards? The family, that great conservator of national virtue and strength, how can you hope to build it up in the midst of violence, debauchery and excess? Can there be any thing sacred at that family altar, where the chief priest who ministers makes sacrifice of human beings, of the weak and the innocent? where the incense offered up is not to the God of justice and mercy, but to those heathen divinities, who best may represent the lost man in all his grossness and deformity? Call that sacred, where woman, the mother of the race,--of a Jesus of Nazareth,--unconscious of the true dignity of her nature, of her high and holy destiny, consents to live in legalized prostitution!--her whole soul revolting at such gross association!--her flesh shivering at the cold contamination of that embrace, --held there by no tie but the iron chain of the law, and a false and most unnatural public sentiment? Call that sacred, where innocent children, trembling with fear, fly to the corners and dark places of the house, to hide themselves from the wrath of drunken, brutal fathers, but, forgetting their past sufferings, rush out again at their mother's frantic screams, "Help, oh help"? Behold the agonies of those young hearts, as they see the only being on earth they love, dragged about the room by the hair of the head, kicked and pounded, and left half dead and bleeding on the floor! Call that sacred, where fathers like these have the power and legal right to hand down their natures to other beings,--to curse other generations with such moral deformity and death?

Men and brethren, look into your asylums for the blind, the deaf and dumb, the idiot, the imbecile, the deformed, the insane; go out into the by-lanes and dens of this vast metropolis, and contemplate that reeking mass of depravity; pause before the terrible revelations made by statistics of the rapid increase of all this moral and physical impotency, and learn how fearful a thing it is to violate the immutable laws of the beneficent Ruler of the universe; and there behold the terrible retributions of your violence on woman! Learn how false and cruel are those institutions, which, with a coarse materialism, set aside those holy instincts of the woman to bear no children but those of love! In the best condition of marriage, as we now have it, to woman comes all the penalties and sacrifices. A man, in the full tide of business or pleasure, can marry and not change his life one iota; he can be husband, father, and every thing beside: but in marriage, woman gives up all. Home is her sphere, her realm. Well, be it so. If here you will make us all supreme, take to yourselves the universe beside; explore the North Pole; and, in your airy car, all space; in your Northern homes and cloud-capt towers, go feast on walrus flesh and air, and lay you down to sleep your six months' night away, and leave us to make these laws that govern the inner sanctuary of our own homes, and faithful satellites we will ever be to the dinner-pot, the cradle, and the old arm-chair. (*Applause.*)

Fathers, do you say, let your daughters pay a life-long penalty for one unfortunate step? How could they, on the threshold of life, full of joy and hope, believing all things to be as they seemed on the surface, judge of the dark windings of the human soul? How could they foresee that the young man, to-day so noble, so generous, would in a few short years be transformed into a cowardly, mean tyrant, or a foul-mouthed, bloated drunkard? What father could rest at his home by night, knowing that his lovely daughter was at the mercy of a strong man drunk with wine and passion, and that, do what he might, he was backed up by law and public sentiment? The best interests of the individual, the family, the State, the nation, cry out against these legalized marriages of force and endurance. There can be no heaven without love, and nothing is sacred in the family and home, but just so far as it is built up and anchored in love. Our newspapers teem with startling accounts of husbands and wives having shot or poisoned each other, or committed suicide, choosing death rather than the indissoluble tie; and, still worse, the living death of faithless wives and daughters, from the first families in this State, dragged from the privacy of home into the public prints and courts, with all the painful details of sad, false lives. What say you to facts like these? Now, do you believe, men and women, that all these wretched matches are made in heaven? that all these sad, miserable people are bound together by God? I know Horace Greeley has been most eloquent, for weeks past, on the holy sacrament of ill-assorted marriages; but let us hope that all wisdom does not live, and will not die, with Horace Greeley.[3] I think, if he had been married to the *New York Herald*,[4] instead of the Republican party, he would have found out some Scriptural arguments against life-long unions, where great incompatibility of temper existed between the parties. (*Laughter and applause*.) Our law-makers have dug a pit, and the innocent have fallen into it; and now will you coolly cover them over with statute laws,

---

[3] Horace Greeley (1811-72), founder (1841) and editor of the *New York Tribune*, created to provide a paper for the laboring classes that would be as cheap as but less sensational and more informative than those of his rivals, it grew to a circulation of 200,000 by 1860. Greeley was strongly anti-slavery and supported early woman's rights efforts, although he opposed liberalization of New York's divorce laws.

[4] Founded in 1835 by James Gordon Bennett (1795-1872), the *Herald* was the chief rival of Greeley's *Tribune*. Initially a sensational penny paper, by the time of the Civil War it had achieved a credible journalistic reputation. Bennett, however, opposed many causes that Greeley espoused, such as woman's rights.

Tribunes, and Weeds,[5] and tell them to stay there, and pay the life-long penalty of having fallen in? Nero was thought the chief of tyrants, because he made laws and hung them up so high that his subjects could not read them, and then punished them for every act of disobedience.[6] What better are our Republican legislators? The mass of the women of this nation know nothing about the laws, yet all their specially barbarous legislation is for woman. Where have they made any provision for her to learn the laws? Where is the Law School for our daughters?--where the law office, the bar, or the bench, now urging them to take part in the jurisprudence of the nation?[7] But, say you, does not separation cover all these difficulties? No one objects to separation when the parties are so disposed. Now, to separation there are two very serious objections. First, so long as you insist on marriage as a Divine institution, as an indissoluble tie, so long as you maintain your present laws against divorce, you make

---

[5] Thurlow Weed (1797-1882), American journalist and Republican political leader, who after 1830 exerted influence as editor of the Albany *Evening Journal*.

[6] Nero Claudius Caesar (37-68 C.E.), Roman emperor (54-68 C.E.).

[7] Woman's exclusion was a carryover from English common law, which explicitly prohibited women from being called to the bar. The first woman regularly admitted to the practice of law was Mrs. Arabella Mansfield of Iowa in 1869. Myra Colby Bradwell of Illinois appealed her denial to the Supreme Court under the Fourteenth Amendment, but in 1873 it ruled that such denial was constitutional. In 1880 there were only 200 women lawyers in the nation. By 1920 all states had admitted women to be bar, but the total number of women lawyers was 1,171 (Chester 1984, 8).

separation, even, so odious, that the most noble, virtuous and sensitive men and women choose a life of concealed misery, rather than a partial, disgraceful release. Secondly, those who, in their impetuosity and despair, do, in spite of public sentiment, separate, find themselves in their new position beset with many temptations to lead a false, unreal life. This isolation bears especially hard on woman. Marriage is not all of life to man. His resources for amusement and occupation are boundless. He has the whole world for his home. His business, his politics, his club, his friendships with either sex, can help to fill up the void made by an unfortunate union or separation. But to woman, marriage is all and every thing; her sole object in life,--that for which she is educated,--the subject of all her sleeping and her waking dreams. Now, if a noble, generous girl of eighteen marries, and is unfortunate, because the cruelty of her husband compels separation, in her dreary isolation, would you drive her to a nunnery; and shall she be a nun indeed? Her solitude is nothing less, as, in the present undeveloped condition of woman, it is only through our fathers, brothers, husbands, sons, that we feel the pulsations of the great outer world.

One unhappy, discordant man or woman in a neighborhood, may mar the happiness of all the rest. You cannot shut up discord, any more than you can small-pox. There can be no morality, where there is a settled discontent. A very wise father once remarked, that in the government of his children, he forbid [sic] as few things as possible; a wise legislation would do the same. It is folly to make laws on subjects beyond human prerogative, knowing that in the very nature of things they must be set aside. To make laws that man cannot and will not obey, serves to bring all law into contempt. It is very important in a republic, that the people should respect the laws, for if we throw them to the winds, what becomes of civil government? What do our present divorce laws amount to? Those who wish to evade them have only to go into another State to accomplish what they desire. If any of our citizens cannot secure their inalienable rights in New York State, they may in Connecticut and Indiana. Why is it that all agreements, covenants, partnerships, are left wholly at the discretion of the parties, except the contract, which of all others is considered most holy and important, both for the individual and the race? This question of divorce, they tell us, is hedged about with difficulties; that it cannot be approached with the ordinary rules of logic and common sense. It is too holy, too sacred to be discussed, and few seem disposed to touch it. From man's stand-point, this may be all true,--as to him they say belong reason, and the power to retiocinate [sic]. Fortunately, I belong to that class endowed with mere intuitions,--a kind of moral instinct, by which we feel out right and wrong. In presenting to you, therefore, my views of divorce, you will of course give to them the weight only of the woman's intuitions. But inasmuch as that is all God saw fit to give us, it is evident we need nothing more. Hence, what we do perceive of truth must be as reliable as what man grinds out by the longer process of reason, authority, and speculation.

Horace Greeley (1860), in his recent discussion with Robert Dale Owen,[8] said, this whole question has been tried, in all its varieties and conditions, from indissoluble monogamic marriage down to free love; that the

---

[8] Robert Dale Owen (1801-77), who, with his father Robert Owen, English industrialist and socialist, founded (1825) the utopian community of New Harmony, Indiana; established (1829) the *Free Enquirer* in New York City with Frances Wright; in *Moral Physiology* (1830) first publicly advocated birth control in the United States; member of Congress (1843-47); U.S. Minister to Naples (1853-58).

ground has been all gone over and explored. Let me assure him that but just one-half of the ground has been surveyed, and that half but by one of the parties, and that party certainly *not* the most interested in the matter. Moreover, there is one kind of marriage that has not been tried, and that is, a contract made by equal parties to live an equal life, with equal restraints and privileges on either side. Thus far, we have had the man marriage, and nothing more. From the beginning, man has had the sole and whole regulation of the matter. He has spoken in Scripture, he has spoken in law. As an individual, he has decided the time and cause for putting away a wife, and as a judge and legislator, he still holds the entire control. In all history, sacred and profane, the woman is regarded and spoken of simply as the toy of man,--made for his special use,--to meet his most gross and sensuous desires. She is taken or put away, given or received, bought or sold, just as the interest of the parties might dictate. But the woman has been no more recognized in all these transactions, through all the different periods and conditions of the race, than if she had had no part nor lot in the whole matter. The right of woman to put away a husband, be he ever so impure, is never hinted at in sacred history. Even Jesus himself failed to recognize the sacred rights of the holy mothers of the race. We cannot take our gauge of womanhood from the past, but from the solemn convictions of our own souls, in the higher development of the race. No parchments, however venerable with the mould of ages, no human institutions, can bound the immortal wants of the royal sons and daughters of the great I Am,--rightful heirs of the joys of time, and joint heirs of the glories of eternity.

If in marriage either party claims the right to stand supreme, to woman, the mother of the race, belongs the sceptre and the crown. Her life is one long sacrifice for man. You tell us that among all womankind there are no Moses, Christs, or Pauls,--no Michael Angelos [sic],[9] Beethovens, or Shakespeares,--no Columbuses or Galileos,--no Lockes[10] or Bacons.[11] Behold those mighty minds attuned to music and the arts, so great, so grand, so comprehensive,--these are our great works of which we boast! Which, think you, stands first, the man, or what he does? By just so far as Galileo is greater than his thought, is the mother far above the man. Into you, oh sons of earth, go all of us that is great and grand. In you centre our very life-thoughts, our hopes, our intensest love. For you we gladly pour out our heart's blood and die. Willingly do we drink the cup in the holy sacrament of marriage, in the same faith that the Son of Mary died on Calvary,--knowing that from our suffering comes forth a new and more glorious resurrection of thought and life. (*Loud applause.*)

SPEECH OF REV. ANTOINETTE BROWN [BLACKWELL]

Mrs. President,--Ours has always been a free platform. We have believed in the fullest freedom of thought and in the free expression of individual opinion. I propose to speak upon the subject discussed by our friend, Mrs.

---

[9] Michelangelo Buonarroti (1475-1564), Italian sculptor, painter, architect, and poet.

[10] John Locke (1632-1704), English philosopher, founder of British empiricism, best known for *Essay Concerning Human Understanding* (1690).

[11] Francis Bacon (1561-1626), English philosopher, essayist, and statesman, best known for *The Advancement of Learning* (1605), expanded in Latin as *De augmentis scientiarum* (1623) and the *Novum Organum* (1620), which began the application of the inductive method of modern science.

Stanton. It is often said that there are two sides to every question; but there are three sides, many sides, to every question. Let Mrs. Stanton take hers; let Horace Greeley take his; I only ask the privilege of stating mine. (*Applause*.) I have embodied my thought, hastily, in a series of resolutions, and my remarks following them will be very brief.

1. Resolved, That marriage is the voluntary alliance of two persons of opposite sexes into one family, and that such an alliance, with its possible incidents of children, its common interests, &c., must be, from the nature of things, as permanent as the life of the parties.

2. Resolved, That if human law attempts to regulate marriage at all, it should aim to regulate it according to the fundamental principles of marriage; and that as the institution is inherently as continuous as the life of the parties, so all laws should look to its control and preservation as such.

3. Resolved, That as a parent can never annul his obligations towards even a profligate child, because of the inseparable relationship of the parties, so the married partner cannot annul his obligations towards the other, while both live, no matter how profligate that other's conduct may be, because of their still closer and alike permanent relationship; and, therefore, that all divorce is naturally and morally impossible, even though we should succeed in annulling all legalities.

4. Resolved, That gross fraud and want of good faith in one of the parties contracting this alliance, such as would invalidate any other voluntary relation, are the only causes which can invalidate this, and this, too, solely upon the ground that the relation never virtually existed, and that there are, therefore, no resulting moral obligations.

5. Resolved, however, That both men and women have a first and inviolable right to

themselves, physically, mentally and morally, and that it can never be the duty of either to surrender his personal freedom in any direction to his own hurt.

6. Resolved, That the great duty of every human being is to secure his own highest moral development, and that he cannot owe to society, or to an individual, any obligation which shall be degrading to himself.

7. Resolved, That self-devotion to the good of another, and especially to the good of the sinful and guilty, like all disinterestedness, must redound to the highest good of its author, and that the husband or wife who thus seeks the best interest of the other, is obedient to the highest law of benevolence.

8. Resolved, That this is a very different thing from the culpable weakness which allows itself to be immolated by the selfishness of another, to the hurt of both; and that the miserable practice, now so common among wives, of allowing themselves, their children and family interests, to be sacrificed to a degraded husband and father, is most reprehensible.

9. Resolved, That human law is imperatively obligated to give either party ample protection to himself, to their offspring, and to all other family interests, against wrong, injustice, and usurpation on the part of the other; and that, if it be necessary to this, it should grant a legal separation; and yet, that even such separation cannot invalidate any real marriage obligation.

10. Resolved, That every married person is imperatively obligated to do his utmost thus to protect himself and all family interests against injustice and wrong, let it arise from what source it may.

11. Resolved, That every woman is morally obligated to maintain her equality in human rights in all her relations in life, and that if she consents to her own subjugation, either in the family, Church or State, she is as guilty as the slave is in consenting to be a slave.

12. Resolved, That a perfect union cannot be expected to exist until we first have perfect units, and that every marriage of finite beings must be gradually perfected through the growth and assimilation of the parties.

13. Resolved, That the permanence and indissolubility of marriage tend more directly than any thing else towards this result.

I believe that all the laws which God has established are sacred and inviolable; that his laws are the best which exist; that they are all founded on the natures or relation of things, and that he has no laws which are not as eternal as the natures and relations to which he has given existence. (*Applause.*) I believe, therefore, that the highest laws of our being are those which we find written within our being; that the first moral laws which we are to obey are the laws which God's own finger has traced upon our own souls. Therefore, our first duty is to ourselves, and we may never, under any circumstances, yield this to any other. I say, we are first responsible for ourselves to ourselves, and to the God who has laid the obligation upon us to make ourselves the best, the grandest we may. Marriage grows out of the relations of parties. The law of our development comes wholly from within; but the relation of marriage supposes two persons as being united to each other, and from this relation originates the law. Mrs. Stanton calls marriage a "tie." No, marriage is a *relation*; and, once formed, that relation continues as long as the parties continue with the natures which they now essentially have. Let, then, the two parties deliberately, voluntarily consent to enter into this relation. It is one which, from its very nature, must be permanent. Its interests are permanent. Can the mother ever destroy the relation which exists between herself and her child? Can the father annul the relation which exists between himself and his child? Then, can the father and mother annul the relation which exists between themselves, the parents of the child? It cannot be. The interests of marriage are such that they cannot be destroyed, and the only question must be, "Has there been a marriage in this case or not?" If there has, then the social law, the obligations out-growing from the relation, must be life-long.

But I assert that every woman, in the present state of society, is bound to maintain her own independence and her own integrity of character; to assert herself, earnestly and firmly, as the equal of man, who is only her peer. This is her first right, her first duty; and if she lives in a country where the law supposes that she is to be subjected to her husband, and she consents to this subjection, I do insist that she consents to degradation; that this is sin, and it is impossible to make it other than sin. True, in this State, and in nearly all the States, the idea of marriage is that of subjection, in all respects, of the wife to the husband--personal subjection, subjection in the rights over their children, and over their property; but this is a false relation. Marriage is a union of equals--equal interests being involved, equal duties at stake; and if any woman has been married to a man who chooses to take advantage of the laws as they now stand, who chooses to subject her, ignobly, to his will, against her own, to take from her the earnings which belong to the family, and to take from her the children which belong to the family, I hold that that woman, if she cannot, by her influence, change this state of things, is solemnly obligated to go to some State where she can be legally divorced; and then she would be as solemnly bound to return again, and, standing for herself and her children, regard herself, in the sight of God, as being bound still to the father of those children, to work for his best interests, while she still maintains her own sovereignty. Of course, she must be governed by the circumstances of the case. She may be obliged, for the protection of the family, to live on one continent while her husband is on the other; but she is never to forget that in the sight of God and her own soul, she is his wife, and that she owes to him the wife's loyalty; that to work for his redemption is her highest social obligation, and that to teach her children to do the same is her first motherly duty. Legal divorce may be necessary for personal and family protection; if so, let every woman obtain it. This, God helping me, is what I would certainly do; for under no circumstances will I ever give my consent to be subjected to the will of another, in any relation, for God has bidden me not to do it. But the idea of most women is, that they must be timid, weak, helpless, and full of ignoble submission. Only last week, a lady who has just been divorced from her husband said to me--"I used to be required to go into the field and do the hardest laborer's work, when I was not able to do it, and my husband would declare, that if I would not thus labor, I should not be allowed to eat, and I was obliged to submit." I say, the fault was as much with the woman as with the man; she should *never* have submitted.

Our trouble is not with marriage as a relation between two; it is all individual. We have few men or women fit to be married. They neither fully respect themselves and their own rights and duties, nor yet those of another. They have no idea how noble, how godlike is the relation which ought to exist between the husband and wife.

Tell me, is marriage to be merely a contract--something entered into for a time, and then broken again--or is the true marriage permanent? One resolution read by Mrs. Stanton said that, as men are incompetent to select partners in business, teachers for their children, ministers of their religion, or makers, adjudicators or administrators of their laws, and as the same weakness and blindness must attend in the selection of matrimonial partners, the latter and most important contract should no more be perpetual than either or all of the former. I do not believe that, rightly understood, she quite holds to that position herself. Marriage must be either permanent, or capable of being any time dissolved. Which ground shall we take? I insist, that from the nature of things, marriage must be as permanent and indissoluble as the relation of parent and child. If so, let us legislate towards the right. Though evils must sometimes result, we are still to seek the highest law of the relation.

Self-devotion is always sublimely beautiful, but the law has no right to require either a woman to be sacrificed to any man, or a man to be sacrificed to any woman, or either to the good of society; but if either chooses to devote himself to the good of the other, no matter how low that other may have fallen, no matter how degraded he may be, let the willing partner strive to lift him up, not by going down and sitting side by side with him--that is wrong--but by steadily trying to win him back to the right; keeping his own sovereignty, but trying to redeem the fallen as long as life shall endure. I do not wish to go to the other state of being, and state what shall be our duty there, but I do say, that where there is sin and suffering in this universe of ours, we may none of us sit still until we have overcome that sin and suffering. Then, if my husband were wretched and degraded in this life, I believe God would give me strength to work for him while life lasted. I would do that for the lowest drunkard in the street, and certainly I would do as much for my husband. I believe that the greatest boon of existence is the privilege of working for those who are oppressed and fallen; and those who have oppressed their own natures are those who need the most help. My great hope is, that I may be able to lift them upwards. The great responsibility that has been laid upon me is the responsibility never to sit down and sing to myself psalms of happiness and content while any body suffers. (*Applause.*) Then, if

I find a wretched man in the gutter, and feel that as a human sister, I must go and lift him up, and that I can never enjoy peace or rest until I have thus redeemed him and brought him out of his sins, shall I, if the man whom I solemnly swore to love, to associate with in all the interests of home and its holiest relations--shall I, if he falls into sin, turn him off, and go on enjoying life, while he is sunk in wretchedness and sin? I will not do it. To me, there is a higher idea of life. If, as an intelligent human being, I promised to co-work with him in all the higher interests of life, and if he prove false, I will not turn from him, but I must seek first to regenerate him, the nearest and dearest to me, as I would work, secondly, to save my children, who are next, and then my brothers, my sisters, and the whole human family. (*Applause*.)

Mrs. Stanton asks, "Would you send a young girl into a nunnery, when she has made a mistake?" Does Mrs. Stanton not know that nunneries belong to a past age, that people who had nothing to do might go there, and try to expiate their own sins? I would teach the young girl a higher way. I do not say to her, "If you have foolishly united yourself to another"--(not "if you have been tied by law;" for, remember, it was not the law that tied her; she said, "I will do it," and the law said, "So let it be!")--"sunder the bond;" but I say to her, that her duty is to reflect, "Now that I see my mistake, I will commence being true to myself; I will become a true unit, strong and noble in myself; and if I can never make our union a true one, I will work toward that good result, I will live for this great work--for truth and all its interests." Let me tell you, if she is not great enough to do this, she is not great enough to enter into any union!

Look at those who believe in thus easily dissolving the marriage obligation! In very many cases, they cannot be truly married, or truly happy in this relation, because there is something incompatible with it in their own natures. It is not always so; but when one feels that it is a relation easily to be dissolved, of course, incompatibility at once seems to arise in the other, and every difficulty that occurs, instead of being overlooked, as it ought to be, in a spirit of forgiveness, is magnified, and the evil naturally increased. We purchase a house, the deed is put into our hands, and we take possession. We feel at once that it is really very convenient. It suits us, and we are surprised that we like it so much better than we supposed. The secret is, that it is our house, and until we are ready to part with it, we make ourselves content with it as it is. We go to live in some country town. At first, we do not like it; it is not like the home we came from; but soon we begin to be reconciled, and feel that, as Dr. Holmes said of Boston, our town is the hub of the universe.[12] So, when we are content to allow our relations to remain as they are, we adapt ourselves to them, and they adapt themselves to us, and we constantly, unconsciously (because God made us so) work towards the perfecting of all the interest arising from those relations. But the moment we wish to sell a house, or remove from a town, how many defects we discover! The place has not the same appearance to us at all; we wish we could get out of it; we feel all the time more and more dissatisfied. So, let any married person take the idea that he may dissolve this relation, and enter into a new one, and how many faults he may discover that otherwise never would have been noticed! The marriage will become intolerable. The theory will work that result; it is in the nature of things, and that to me is every thing. Of course, I would not have man or

---

[12] Oliver Wendell Holmes (1809-94), American author and physician, father of Oliver Wendell Holmes, Jr., American jurist and Associate Justice of the Supreme Court.

woman sacrificed--by no means. First of all, let every human being maintain his own position as a self-protecting human being. At all hazards, let him never sin, or consent to be sacrificed to the hurt of himself or of another; and when he has taken this stand, let him act in harmony with it. Would I say to any woman, "You are bound, because you are legally married to one who is debased to the level of the brute, to be the mother of his children?" I say to her, "No! while the law of God continues, you are bound never to make one whom you do not honor and respect, as well as love, the father of any child of yours. It is your first and highest duty to be true to yourself, true to posterity, and true to society." (*Applause.*) Thus, let each decide for himself and for herself what is right. But, I repeat, either marriage is in its very nature a relation which, once formed, never can be dissolved, and either the essential obligations growing out of it exist for ever, or the relation may at any time be dissolved, and at any time those obligations be annulled. And what are those obligations? Two persons, if I understand marriage, covenant to work together, to uphold each other in all excellence, and to mutually blend their lives and interests into a common harmony. I believe that God has so made man and woman, that it is not good for them to be alone, that they each need a co-worker.[13] There is no work on God's footstool which man can do alone and do well, and there is no work which woman can do alone and do well. (*Applause.*) We need that the two should stand side by side every where. All over the world, we need this coöperation of the two classes,--not because they are alike, but because they are unlike,--in trying to make the whole world better. Then we need something more than these class workers. Two persons need to stand side by side, to stay up each other's hands, to take an interest in

---

[13] Gen. 2: 18.

each other's welfare, to build up a family, to cluster about it all the beauties and excellencies of home life; in short, to be to each other what only one man and one woman can be to each other in all God's earth. No grown up human being ought to rush blindly into this most intimate, most important, most enduring of human relations; and will you let a young man, at the age of fourteen, contract marriage, or a young maiden either? If the law undertakes to regulate the matter at all, let it regulate it upon principles of common sense. But this is a matter which must be very much regulated by public opinion, by our teachers. What do you, the guides of our youth, say? You say to the young girl, "You ought to expect to be married before you are twenty, or about that time; you should intend to be; and from the time you are fifteen, it should be made your one life purpose; and in all human probability, you may expect to spend the next ten or twenty years in the nursery, and at forty or fifty, you will be an old woman, your life will be well-nigh worn out." I stand here to say that this is all false. Let the young girl be instructed that, above her personal interests, her home, and social life, she is to have a great life purpose, as broad as the rights and interests of humanity. I say, let every young girl feel this, as much as every young man does. We have no right, we, who expect to live for ever, to play about here as if we were mere flies, enjoying ourselves in the sunshine. We ought to have an earnest purpose outside of home, outside of our family relations. Then let the young girl fit herself for this. Let her be taught that she ought not to be married in her teens. Let her wait, as a young man does, if he is sensible, until she is twenty-five or thirty. (*Applause.*) She will then know how to choose properly, and probably she will not be deceived in her estimate of character; she will have had a certain life-discipline, which will enable her to control her household matters with wise judgment, so that, while she is looking after her family, she may still keep her great life purpose, for which she was educated, and to which she has given her best energies, steadily in view. She need not absorb herself in her home, and God never intended that she should; and then, if she has lived according to the laws of physiology, and according to the laws of common sense, she ought to be, at the age of fifty years, just where man is, just where our great men are, in the very prime of life! When her young children have gone out of her home, then let her enter in earnest upon the great work of life outside of home and its relations. (*Applause.*) It is a shame for our women to have no steady purpose or pursuit, and to make the mere fact of womanhood a valid plea for indolence; it is a greater shame that they should be instructed thus to throw all the responsibility of working for the general good upon the other sex. God has not intended it. But as long as you make women helpless, inefficient beings, who never expect to earn a farthing in their lives, who never expect to do any thing outside of the family, but to be cared for and protected by others throughout life, you cannot have true marriages; and if you try to break up the old ones, you will do it against the woman and in favor of the man. Last week, I went back to a town where I used to live, and was told that a woman, whose husband was notoriously the most miserable man in the town, had in despair taken her own life. I asked what had become of the husband, and the answer was, "Married again." And yet, every body there knows that he is the vilest and most contemptible man in the whole neighborhood. Any man, no matter how wretched he may be, will find plenty of women to accept him, while they are rendered so helpless and weak by their whole education that they must be supported or starve. The advantage, if this theory of marriage is adopted, will not be on the side of woman, but altogether on the side of man. The cure for the evils that now exist is not in dissolving marriage, but it is in giving to the married woman her own natural independence and self-sovereignty, by which she can maintain herself. Yes, our women and our men are both degenerate; they are weak and ignoble. "Dear me!" said a pretty, indolent young lady, "I had a great deal rather my husband would take care of me, than to be obliged to do it for myself." "Of course you would," said a blunt old lady who was present; "and your brother would a great deal rather marry an heiress, and lie upon a sofa eating lollypops [sic], bought by her money, than to do any thing manly or noble. The only difference is, that as heiresses are not very plenty, he may probably have to marry a poor girl, and then society will insist that he shall exert himself to earn a living for the family; but you, poor thing, will only have to open your mouth, all your life long, like a clam, and eat." (*Applause and laughter.*)

So long as society is constituted in such a way that woman is expected to do nothing if she have a father, brother, or husband, able to support her, there is no salvation for her, in or out of marriage. When you tie up your arm, it will become weak and feeble; and when you tie up woman, she will become weak and helpless. Give her, then, some earnest purpose in life, hold up to her the true ideal of marriage, and it is enough--I am content! (*Loud applause.*)

SPEECH OF MRS. E. I. ROSE

Mrs. President,--The question of a Divorce law seems to me one of the greatest importance to all parties, but I presume that the very advocacy of divorce will be called "Free Love." For my part, (and I wish distinctly to define my position,) I do not know what others understand by that term; to me, in its truest significance, love must be free, or it ceases to be love. In its low and degrading sense, it is not love at all, and I have as little to do with its name as its reality.

The Rev. Mrs. Blackwell gave us quite a

sermon on what woman ought to be, what she ought to do, and what marriage ought to be; an excellent sermon in its proper place, but not when the important question of a Divorce law is under consideration. She treats woman as some etherial [sic] being. It is very well to be etherial to some extent, but I tell you, my friends, it is quite requisite to be a little material, also. At all events, we are so, and being so, it proves a law of our nature. (*Applause*.)

It were indeed well if woman could be what *she* ought to be, man what *he* ought to be, and marriage what it ought to be; and it is to be hoped that through the Woman's Rights movement--the equalizing of the laws, making them more just, and making woman more independent--we will hasten the coming of the millennium, when marriage shall indeed be a bond of union and affection. But, alas! it is not yet; and I fear that sermons, however well meant, will not produce that desirable end, and as long as the evil is here, we must look it in the face without shrinking, grapple with it manfully, and, the more complicated it is, the more courageously must it be analyzed, combatted, and destroyed. (*Applause*.)

Mrs. Blackwell told us that, marriage being based on the perfect equality of husband and wife, it cannot be destroyed. But is it so? Where? Where and when have the sexes yet been equal in physical or mental education, in position, or in law? When and where have they yet been recognized by society, or by themselves, as equals? "Equal in rights," says Mrs. B. But are they equal in rights? If they were, we would need no conventions to claim our rights. "She can assert her equality," says she. Yes, she can assert it, but does that assertion constitute a true marriage? And when the husband holds the iron heel of legal oppression on the subjugated neck of the wife until every spark of womanhood is crushed out, will it heal the wounded heart, the lacerated spirit, the destroyed hope, to assert her equality? And shall she still continue the wife? Is that a marriage which must not be dissolved? (*Applause.*)

According to Mr. Greeley's definition, *viz.*, that there is no marriage unless the ceremony is performed by a minister and in a church, the tens of thousands married according to the laws of this and most of the other States, by a lawyer or justice of the peace, a Mayor or an Alderman, are not married at all. According to the definition of our Rev. sister, *no one has ever yet been married*, as woman has never yet been perfectly equal with man. I say to both, Take your position, and abide by the consequences. If the few only, or no one, is really married, why do you object to a law that shall acknowledge the fact? You certainly ought not to force people to live together who are not married. (*Applause.*)

Mr. Greeley tells us that marriage, being a Divine institution, nothing but death should ever separate the parties; but when he was asked, "Would you have a being who, innocent and inexperienced, in the youth and ardor of affection, in the fond hope that the sentiment was reciprocated, united herself to one she loved and cherished, and then found (no matter from what cause) that his profession was false, his heart hollow, his acts cruel, that she was degraded by his vice, despised for his crimes, cursed by his very presence, and treated with every conceivable ignominy,--would you have her drag out a miserable existence as his wife?" "No, no," says he; "in that case, they ought to separate." Separate? But what becomes of the union divinely instituted, which death only should part? (*Applause.*)

The papers have of late been full with the heart-sickening accounts of wife poisoning. Whence come these terrible crimes? From the want of a Divorce law. Could the *Hardings* be legally separated, they would not be driven to the commission of murder to be free from each other; and which is preferable, a Divorce law, to dissolve an unholy union, which all parties agree is no true marriage, or a murder of one, and an execution (legal murder) of the other party? But had the unfortunate woman, just before the poisoned cup was presented to her lips, pleaded for a divorce, Mrs. Blackwell would have read her sermon equal to St. Paul's "Wives, be obedient to your husbands," only she would have added, "You must assert your equality," but "you must keep with your husband and work for his redemption, *as I would do for my husband;*" and Mr. Greeley would say, "As you chose to marry him, it is your own fault; you must abide the consequences, for it is a 'divine institution, a union for life, which nothing but death can end.'" (*Applause.*)

The *Tribune* had recently a long sermon, almost equal to the one we had this morning from our Rev. sister, on "Fast Women." The evils it spoke of were terrible indeed, but like all other sermons, it was one-sided. Not one single word was said about fast men, except that the "poor victim had to spend so much money." The writer forgot that it is the demand which calls the supply into existence. But what was the primary cause of that tragic end? Echo answers, "what?" Ask the lifeless form of the murdered woman, and she may disclose the terrible secret, and show you that, could she have been legally divorced, she might not have been driven to the watery grave of a "fast woman." (*Applause.*)

But what is marriage? A human institution, called out by the needs of social, affectional human nature, for human purposes, its objects are, first, the happiness of the parties immediately concerned, and, secondly, the welfare of society. Define it as you please, these only are its objects; and therefore if, from well ascertained facts, it is demonstrated that the real objects are frustrated, that instead of union and happiness, there are only discord and misery to themselves, and vice and crime to society, I ask, in the name of individual happiness and social morality and well-being, why such a marriage should be binding for life?--why one human being should be chained for life to the dead body of another? "But they may separate and still remain married." What a perversion of the very term! Is that the union which "death only should part"? It may be according to the definition of the Rev. Mrs. Blackwell's Theology and Mr. Greeley's Dictionary, but it certainly is not according to common sense or the dictates of morality. No, no! "it is not well for man to be alone," *before* nor *after* marriage. (*Applause*.)

I therefore ask for a Divorce law. Divorce is now granted for some crimes, I ask it for others also. It is granted for a State's Prison offence, I ask that personal cruelty to a wife, whom he swore to "love, cherish and protect," may be made a heinous crime--a perjury and a State's Prison offence,for which divorce shall be granted. Wilful desertion for one year should be a sufficient cause for divorce, for the wilful deserter forfeits the sacred title of husband or wife. Habitual intemperance, or any other vice which makes the husband or wife intolerable and abhorrent to the other, ought to be sufficient cause for divorce. I ask for a law of Divorce, so as to secure the real objects and blessings of married life, to prevent the crimes and immoralities now practiced, to prevent "Free Love," in its most hideous form, such as is now carried on but too often under the very name of marriage, where hypocrisy is added to the crime of legalized prostitution. "Free Love," in its degraded sense, asks for no Divorce law. It acknowledges no marriage, and therefore requires no divorce. I believe in true marriages, and therefore I ask for a law to free men and women from false ones. (*Applause*.)

But it is said that if divorce were easily granted, "men and women would marry to-day and unmarry to-morrow." Those who say that only prove that they have no confidence in themselves, and therefore can have no confidence in others. But the assertion is false; it is a libel on human nature. It is the indissoluble chain that corrodes the flesh. Remove the indissolubility, and there would be less separation than now, for it would place the parties on their good behavior, the same as during courtship. Human nature is not quite so changeable; give it more freedom, and it will be less so. We are a good deal the creatures of habit, but we will not be forced. We live (I speak from experience) in uncomfortable houses for years, rather than move, though we have the privilege to do so every year; but force any one to live for life in one house, and he would run away from it, though it were a palace.

But Mr. Greeley asks, "How could the mother look the child in the face, if she married a second time?" With infinitely better grace and better conscience than to live as some do now, and show their children the degrading example, how utterly father and mother despise and hate each other, and still live together as husband and wife. She could say to her child, "As, unfortunately, your father proved himself unworthy, your mother could not be so unworthy as to continue to live with him. As he failed to be a true father to you, I have endeavored to supply his place with one, who, though not entitled to the name, will, I hope, prove himself one in the performance of a father's duties. (*Applause*.)

Finally, educate woman, to enable her to promote her independence, and she will not be obliged to marry for a home and a subsistence. Give the wife an equal right with the husband in the property acquired after marriage, and it will be a bond of union between them. Diamond cement, applied on both sides of a fractured vase, reünites the parts, and prevents them from falling asunder. A gold band is more efficacious than an iron grace and better conscience than to live as some do now, and show their children the degrading example, how utterly father and mother despise and hate each other, and still live together as husband and wife. She could say to her child, "As, unfortunately, your father proved himself unworthy, your mother could not be so unworthy as to continue to live with him. As he failed to be a true father to you, I have endeavored to supply his place with one, who, though not entitled to the name, will, I hope, prove himself one in the performance of a father's duties. (*Applause.*)

Finally, educate woman, to enable her to promote her independence, and she will not be obliged to marry for a home and a subsistence. Give the wife an equal right with the husband in the property acquired after marriage, and it will be a bond of union between them. Diamond cement, applied on both sides of a fractured vase, reünites the parts, and prevents them from falling asunder. A gold band is more efficacious than an iron law. Until now, the gold has all been on one side, and the iron law on the other. Remove it; place the golden band of justice and mutual interest around both husband and wife, and it will hide the little fractures which may have occurred, even from their own perception, and allow them effectually to reünite. A union of interest helps to preserve a union of hearts. (*Loud applause.*)

SPEECH OF WENDELL PHILLIPS, ESQ.

I object to entering these resolutions upon the journal of this Convention. (*Applause.*) I would move to lay them on the table; but my conviction that they are out of order is so emphatic, that I wish to go further than that, and move that they do not appear on the journals of this Convention. If the resolutions were merely the expressions of individual sentiments, then they ought not to appear in the form of resolutions, but as speeches, because a resolution has a certain emphasis and authority. It is assumed to give the voice of an assembly, and is not taken as an individual expression, which a speech is.

Of course, every person must be interested in the question of Marriage, and the branch that grows out of it, the question of Divorce; and no one could deny, who has listened for an hour, that we have been favored with an exceedingly able discussion of those questions. But here we have nothing to do with them, any more than with the question of Intemperance, or Kansas, in my opinion. This Convention is no Marriage Convention,--if it were, the subject would be in order; but this Convention, if I understand it, assembles to discuss the laws that rest unequally upon women, not those that rest equally upon men and women. It is the laws that make distinctions between the sexes. Now, whether a man and a woman are married for a year or a life is a question which affects the man just as much as the woman. At the end of a month, the man is without a wife exactly as much as the woman is without a husband. The question whether, having entered into a contract, you shall be bound to an unworthy partner, affects the man as much as the woman. Certainly, there are cases where men are bound to women carcasses as well as where women are bound to men carcasses. (*Laughter and applause.*) We have nothing to do with a question which affects both sexes equally. Therefore, it seems to me we have nothing to do with the theory of Marriage, which is the basis, as Mrs. Rose has very clearly shown, of Divorce. One question grows out of the other; and therefore the question of the permanence of marriage, and the laws relating to marriage, in the essential meaning of that word, are not for our consideration. Of course I know, as every body else does, that the results of marriage, in the present condition of society, are often more disastrous to woman than to man. Intemperance, for instance, burdens a wife worse than a husband, owing to the present state of society. It is not the fault of the statute-book, and no change in the duration of marriage would alter that inequality.

The reason why I object so emphatically

to the introduction of the question here is because it is a question which admits of so many theories, physiological and religious, and what is technically called "free-love," that it is large enough for a movement of its own. Our question is only unnecessarily burdened with it. It cannot be kept within the convenient limits of this enterprise; for this Woman's Rights Convention is not Man's Convention, and I hold that I, as a man, have an exactly equal interest in the essential question of marriage as woman has. I move, then, that these series of resolutions do not appear at all upon the journal of the Convention. If the speeches are reported, of course the resolutions will go with them. Most journals will report them as adopted. But I say to those who use this platform to make speeches on this question, that they do far worse than take more than their fair share of the time; they open a gulf into which our distinctive movement will be plunged, and its success postponed two years for every one that it need necessarily be.

Of course, in these remarks, I intend no reflection upon those whose views differ from mine in regard to introducing this subject before the Convention; but we had an experience two years ago on this point, and it seems to me that we might have learned by that lesson. No question--Anti-Slavery, Temperance, Woman's Rights--can move forward efficiently, unless it keeps its platform separate and unmixed with extraneous issues, unmixed with discussions which carry us into endless realms of debate. We have now, under our present civilization, to deal with the simple question which we propose--how to make that statute-book look upon woman exactly as it does upon man. Under the law of Divorce, one stands exactly like the other. All we have asked in regard to the law of property has been, that the statute-book of New York shall make the wife exactly like the husband; we do not go another step, and state what that right shall be. We do not ask law-makers whether there shall be rights of dower and courtesy--rights to equal shares--rights to this or that interest in property. That is not our business. All we say is, "Gentlemen law-makers, we represent woman; make what laws you please about marriage and property, but let woman stand under them exactly as man does; let sex deprive her of no right, let sex confer no special right; and that is all we claim." (*Applause.*) Society has done that as to Marriage and Divorce, and we have nothing more to ask of it on this question, as a Woman's Rights body.

I do not know that there is any occasion, at this late hour, longer to detain this assembly. Certainly, I have nothing to add to the exceedingly interesting and able discussions to which we have listened in the course of our sessions. It seems to me that these arguments come always more fitly and more emphatically from the lips of women. They know better how to describe their own position than you or I can, fellow-citizens. One of my friends used to say that she did not believe a man ever could make a decent Woman's Rights speech! (*Laughter.*) I agree with her entirely. It needs a personal experience; it needs to be on the other side--outside of the law. Our sympathy is not equal to your experience. All we can do is to listen and to obey.

I congratulate you, as friends of this cause, on the progress of the last twelve months. You know that, when you look at a barometer on a common sunshiny day, you must furnish yourself with an infinitesimal point of brass, and a machinery of delicate wheels to move it a small atom of space, sufficient to measure the changes of the quicksilver. But when you are in the East India seas, and the monsoon is about to blow, or the tempest is about to sweep the surface of the waters, the barometer will jump an inch, or fall down an inch, according as the change is to be. You need no machinery then, when a storm is coming that will lift your ship out of the very sea itself. I think, that in the twenty years that have gone by, we have had the little, infinitesimally minute changes of the barometer; but the New York Legislature has risen a full inch in the moral barometer the last twelve months.[14] (*Applause.*) It is a proof that the monsoon is coming that will lift the old conservative ship, carrying the idea that woman is a drudge and a slave, out of the waters, and dash her into fragments on the surface of our Democratic sea. In a few years more, I do not know but we shall disband, and watch these women to the ballot-box, to see that they do their duty. (*Applause.*) You will have your State Constitution to change in five or six years. Use such meetings as these, and perhaps the Empire State will earn its title, by inaugurating the great movement becoming Democratic and Saxon civilization, by throwing open civil life to woman. I hope it may be so. Let us go out and labor that it shall be so. Men say, "You will introduce all sorts of family quarrels." Yes, they told Luther that, three hundred years ago; but he introduced the principle that a woman might be a Calvinist, even if her husband was an Episcopalian, or that she might be an unbeliever, even, if her husband was Orthodox. It has not led to any great domestic dissension. I do not believe there has been one divorce founded on it since Luther's day. So, when a woman may be a thoroughgoing Republican, even if her husband is a Democrat--I shall not make the alternative; I shall not suppose that a fresh hand ever can be a Democrat (*laughter and applause*) --I do not think there will be any more difficulty than if she went to Beecher's, and her husband went--where could he go?--perhaps to Dr. Spring's! (*Laughter and applause.*)

Mrs. Abby H. Gibbons, of New York city, seconded the motion of Mr. Phillips, and said

---

[14] A reference to 1860 amendments to the New York Married Woman's Property Act.

that she wished the whole subject of Marriage and Divorce might be swept from that platform, as it was manifestly not the place for it.

Mr. Garrison said he fully concurred in opinion with his friend, Mr. Phillips, that they had not come together to settle definitely the question of Marriage, as such, on that platform; still, he should be sorry to have the motion adopted, as against the resolutions of Mrs. Stanton, because they were a part of her speech, and her speech was an elucidation of her resolutions, which were offered on her own responsibility, not on behalf of the Business Committee, and which did not, therefore, make the Convention responsible for them. It seemed to him that, in the liberty usually taken on that platform, both by way of argument and illustration, to show the various methods by which woman was unjustly, yet legally, subjected to the absolute control of man, she ought to be permitted to present her own sentiments. It was not the specific object of Anti-Slavery Convention--for example--to discuss the conduct of Rev. Nehemiah Adams, or the position of Stephen A. Douglas,[15] or the course of the *New York Herald*; yet they did, incidentally, discuss all these, and many other matters closely related to the great struggle for the freedom of the slave. So this question of Marriage came in as at least incidental to the main question of the equal rights of woman.

Mr. G. said that if there had been time, he should like to have spoken directly in support of the following resolution:

Resolved, That the rights of woman are coëqual and coëternal with the rights of man, being

---

[15] Stephen A. Douglas (1813-61), U.S. Representative from Illinois (1843), U.S. Senator (1847-61) who developed the doctrine of popular sovereignty as the means to settle the extension of slavery to the territories, which led to the Kansas-Nebraska Act of 1854.

based upon human nature; and, therefore, are not to be determined nor circumscribed by an appeal to any book in the world, however excellent that book may be.

It was his conviction that, until the true origin of all rights was perceived and acknowledged, very slow progress would be made towards their obtainment. No matter what any book might say to the contrary, human rights were equal, inalienable, indestructible, without reference to sex or complexion. They belonged to the constitution of every human being.

It seemed to him, in a government like this, that they had nothing more to do than to put the ballot into the hand of woman, as it was in the hand of man. If, after she had a fair share of political power and representation, any of her rights were cloven down, then the fault would be her own. Let her say what shall be the laws, in coöperation with man, and the work would be done. He trusted the day was not far distant when woman would fully enjoy the benefit of the democratic theory of government. That theory we must carry out, or go backward to despotism, repudiating the revolutionary struggle, and spitting upon Bunker Hill and Lexington. We must give to all the same rights under a free government; and then we should be a consistent and glorious republic.

Mrs. Blackwell. I should like to say a few words in explanation. I do not understand whether our friend *Wendell Phillips* objects to both series of resolutions on the subject of divorce, or merely to mine.

Mr. Phillips. To both.

Mrs. Blackwell. I wish simply to say, that I did not come to the Convention proposing to speak on this subject, but on another; but, finding that these resolutions were to be introduced, and believing the subject legitimate, I said, "I will take my own position." So I prepared the resolutions, as they enabled me at the moment better to express my thought, than I could do by merely extemporising.

Now, does this question grow legitimately out of the great question of woman's equality? The world says, marriage is not an alliance between equals in human rights. My whole argument was based on the position that it is. If this question is not legitimate, what is? Then do we not ask for laws which are not equal between man and woman? What have we been doing here in New York State? I spent three months asking the State to allow the drunkard's wife her own earnings. Do I believe that the wife ought to take her own earnings, as her own earnings? No; I do not believe it. I believe that in a true marriage, the husband and wife earn for the family, and that the property is the family's --belongs jointly to the husband and wife. But if the law says that the property is the husband's, if it says that he may take the wages of his wife, just as the master does those of the slave, and she has no right to them, we must seek a temporary redress. We must take the first step, by compelling legislators, who will not look at great principles, to protect the wife of the drunkard, by giving her her own earnings to expend upon herself and her children, and not allow them to be wasted by the husband. I say that it is legitimate for us to ask for a law which we believe is merely a temporary expedient, not based upon the great principle of human and marriage equality. Just so with this question of marriage. It *must* come upon this platform, for at present it is a relation which legally and socially bears unequally upon woman. We must have temporary redress for the wife. The whole subject must be incidentally opened for discussion. The only question is one of present fitness. Was it best, under all the circumstances, to introduce it now? I have not taken the responsibility of answering in the affirmative. But it must come here and be settled, sooner or later, because its interests are every where, and all human relations centre in this one marriage relation. (*Applause.*)

Miss Anthony. I wish to say, in the first place, that I hope Mr. Phillips will withdraw his motion that these resolutions shall not appear on the records of the Convention. I am very sure that it would be contrary to all parliamentary usages in Conventions of this kind to say, that when the speech which enforced and advocated the resolutions is reported and published in the proceedings, the resolutions shall not be placed there. And as to the point that this question does not belong to this platform,--from that I totally dissent. Marriage has ever and always been a one-sided matter, resting most unequally upon the sexes. By it, man gains all--woman loses all; tyrant law and lust reign supreme with him--meek submission, and cheerful, ready obedience, alone befit her. Woman has never been consulted; her wish has never at all been taken into consideration as regards the terms of the marriage compact. By law, public sentiment, and religion, from the time of Moses down to the present day, woman has never been thought of other than as a piece of property, to be disposed of at the will and pleasure of man. And this very hour, by our statute-books, by our (so called) enlightened Christian civilization, woman has no voice whatever in saying what shall be the terms of the marriage compact. She must accept marriage as man proffers it, or accept it not at all. Therefore, in my opinion, this discussion of the marriage question is perfectly in order on this Woman's Rights platform. I hope, at any rate, that the resolutions, which embody the ideas of the persons, at least, who presented them, will be allowed to go out to the public, that there may be a fair understanding and a fair report of the ideas which have actually been presented here upon these subjects, and that they shall not be left to the mercy of the secular press. I therefore hope that the Convention will not vote to forbid the appearance of these resolutions with the proceedings.

Rev. Wm H. Hoisington, ("the blind preacher"). Publish all you have done and said here, and let the public know it.

The question was then put on the motion of Mr. Phillips, and it was lost. The resolutions presented by the Business Committee were then adopted, without dissent.

To the Editor of the N.Y. Tribune:

Sir,--At our recent National Woman's Rights Convention, many were surprised to hear *Wendell Phillips* object to the question of Marriage and Divorce, as irrelevant to our platform. He said, "We had no right to discuss there any laws or customs but those where inequality existed in the sexes; that the laws on Marriage and Divorce rested equally on man and woman; that he suffered, as much as she possibly could, the wrongs and abuses of an ill-assorted marriage."

Now, it must strike every careful thinker, that an immense difference rests in the fact, that man has made the laws, cunningly and selfishly, for his own purpose. From Coke[16] down to Kent[17], who can cite one clause of the marriage contract where woman has the advantage? When man suffers from false legislation, he has his remedy in his own hands. Shall woman be denied the right of protest against laws in which she has had no voice--laws which outrage the holiest affections of her nature--laws which transcend the limits of human legislation--in a Convention called for the express purpose of considering her wrongs? He might as well object to a protest against the injustice of hanging a woman, because Capital Punishment bears equally on man and woman.

The contract of marriage is by no means

---

[16] See p. 175, n 8.

[17] See p. 176, n 10.

equal. The law permits the girl to marry at twelve years of age, while it requires several years more of experience on the part of the boy. In entering this compact, the man gives up nothing that he before possessed--he is a man still; while the legal existence of the woman is suspended during marriage, and henceforth she is known but in and through the husband. She is nameless, purseless, childless,--though a woman, an heiress, and a mother.

Blackstone says, "The husband and wife are one, and that one is the husband."[18] Kent says, "The legal effects of marriage are generally deducible from the principle of the Common Law, by which the husband and wife are regarded as one person, and her legal existence and authority lost or suspended during the continuance of the matrimonial union." Vol. 2, p. 109. Kent refers to Coke on Littleton, 112, at 187.B. Litt. sec. 168, 291.[19]

The wife is regarded by all legal authorities as a "*feme-covert*," placed wholly "*sub potestate viri*." Her moral responsibility, even, is merged in the husband. The law takes it for granted that the wife lives in fear of her husband; that his command is her highest law: hence a wife is not punishable for theft committed in presence of her husband. Kent, vol. 2, p. 127. An unmarried woman can make contracts, sue and be sued, enjoy the rights of property, to her inheritance--to her wages--to her person--to her children; but, in marriage, she is robbed by law of all and every natural and civil right. "The disability of the wife to contract, so as

---

18 See p. 37, n 1.

19 Sir Thomas Littleton (1422?-81), English jurist, best known for *Tenures*, which, in the much-expanded edition of Sir Edward Coke, was the standard text on property law until the 19th century.

to bind herself, arises not from want of discretion, but because she has entered into an indissoluble connexion, by which she is placed under the power and protection of her husband." Kent, vol. 2, p. 127. She is possessed of certain rights until she is married; then all are suspended, to revive again the moment the breath goes out of the husband's body. See "Cowen's Treatise," vol. 2, p. 709.[20]

If the contract be equal, whence come the terms "*marital power*"--"MARITAL RIGHTS"--"obedience and restraint"--"dominion and control," "power and protection," &c. &c.? Many cases are stated, showing the exercise of a most questionable power over the wife, sustained by the courts. See Bishop on Divorce, p. 489.[21]

The laws on Divorce are quite as unequal as those on Marriage; yes, far more so. The advantages seem to be all on one side, and the penalties on the other. In case of divorce, if the husband be the guilty party, he still retains the greater part of the property. If the wife be the guilty party, she goes out of the partnership pennyless. Kent, vol. 2, p. 33; Bishop on Divorce, p. 492.

In New York and some other States, the wife of the guilty husband can now sue for a divorce in her own name, and the costs come out of the husband's estate; but, in a majority of the States, she is still compelled to sue in the name of another, as she has no means of paying costs, even though she may have brought her thousands into the partnership. "The allowance to the innocent wife of

---

[20] Esek Cowen (1787-1844), *Treatise on the Civil Jurisdiction of Justices of the Peace in the State of New York* 2d ed. (Albany, NY: Wm. A. Gould, 1841).

[21] Joel Prentiss Bishop (1814-1901), *Commentaries on the Law of Marriage an Divorce* (Boston: Little, Brown, 1852).

ad interim alimony and money to sustain the suit, is not regarded as strict right in her, but of sound discretion in the court." Bishop on Divorce, p. 581.

"Many jurists," says Kent, vol. 2, p. 88, "are of opinion that the adultery of the husband ought not to be noticed or made subject to the same animadversions as that of the wife, because it is not evidence of such entire depravity, nor equally injurious in its effects upon the morals, good order and happiness of domestic life. Montesquieu,[22] Pothier,[23] and Dr. Taylor,[24] all insist that the cases of husband and wife ought to be distinguished, and that the violation of the marriage vow, on the part of the wife, is the most mischievous, and the prosecution ought to be confined to the offence on her part. *Esprit des Loix*, tome 3, 186; *Traité du Contrat de Marriage*, No. 516; *Elements of Civil Law*, p. 254."

Say you, "These are but the opinions of men"? On what else, I ask, are the hundreds of women depending, who this hour demand in our courts a release from burdensome con-

---

[22] Charles Louis de Secondat, baron de la Brède et de Montesquieu (1689-1755), French jurist and political philosopher, whose greatest work, *The Spirit of Laws* (1748) is a comparative study of three types of government--republic, monarchy, and despotism.

[23] Robert Joseph Pothier (1699-1772), *Traité du contrat de marriage, par l'auteur du traité des obligations* (Paris, 1772); trans. as *A Treatise on the Law of Obligations or Contracts* by William David Evans, 2 vols., 3d Am. ed. (Philadelphia: Robert H. Small, 1853).

[24] Probably Alfred Swaine Taylor, M.D., F.R.S. (1806-80), lecturer in medical jurisprudence at Guy's Hospital Medical School, London, and author of *Principles and Practice of Medical Jurisprudence* (1865).

tracts? Are not these delicate matters left wholly to the discretion of courts? Are not young women from the first families dragged into the public courts--into assemblies of men exclusively--the Judges all men, the Jurors all men?--no true woman there to shield them by her presence from gross and impertinent questionings, to pity their misfortunes, or to protest against their wrongs?

The administration of justice depends far more on the opinions of eminent jurists than on law alone, for law is powerless when at variance with public sentiment.

Do not the above citations clearly prove inequality? Are not the very letter and spirit of the marriage contract based on the idea of the supremacy of man as the keeper of woman's virtue--her sole protector and support? Out of marriage, woman asks nothing at this hour but the elective franchise. It is only in marriage that she must demand her rights to person, children, property, wages, life, liberty and the pursuit of happiness. How can we discuss all the laws and conditions of marriage, without perceiving its essential essence, end and aim? Now, whether the institution of marriage be human or divine, whether regarded as indissoluble by Ecclesiastical Courts, or dissoluble by Civil Courts, Woman, finding herself equally degraded in each and every phase of it, always the victim of the institution, it is her right and her duty to sift the relation and the compact through and through, until she finds out the true cause of her false position. How can we go before the Legislatures of our respective States, and demand new laws, or no laws, on Divorce, until we have some idea of what the true relation is?

We decide the whole question of Slavery by settling the sacred rights of the individual. We assert that man cannot hold property in man, and reject the whole code of laws that conflicts with the self-evident truth of that assertion.

Again I ask, is it possible to discuss all the laws of a relation, and not touch the relation itself?

Elizabeth Cady Stanton

New York Tribune, May 30, 1860

13

Elizabeth Cady Stanton, "On Divorce," Speech before the Judiciary Committee of the New York Senate, 1861

This speech was delivered some nine months after the 1860 convention debate on marriage and divorce, and it illustrates the consistency of Cady Stanton's stance on these issues. However, the speech also reflects the delicacy of her position as a woman speaker discussing topics not considered fitting for a woman to address. Her plea was unsuccessful; New York did not extend the grounds for divorce to include matters other than adultery for more than a century.

Her speech was published as **Address of Elizabeth Cady Stanton on the Divorce Bill Before the Judiciary Committee of the New York Senate, in the Assembly Chamber, February 8, 1861** (Albany, NY: Weed, Parsons and Co., 1861), *from which this text is taken.*

Gentlemen of the Judiciary--In speaking to you, gentlemen, on such delicate subjects as marriage and divorce, in the revision of laws which are found in your statute books, I must use the language I find there.

May I not, without the charge of indelicacy, speak in a mixed assembly of Christian men and women, of wrongs which my daughter may to-morrow suffer in your courts, where there is no woman's heart to pity, and no woman's presence to protect?

I come not before you, gentlemen, at this

time, to plead simply the importance of divorce in cases specified in your bill, but the justice of an entire revision of your whole code of laws on marriage and divorce. We claim that here, at least, woman's equality should be recognized. If civilly and politically man must stand supreme, let us at least be equals in our nearest and most sacred relations.

As a distinguished Massachusetts lawyer [Wendell Phillips], not long ago, declared in a public meeting, that our laws on marriage and divorce, bore, equally, on man and woman, it may be that some, even among you, are ignorant of what your code really is on these questions. Permit me, as briefly as possible, to state some of the inequalities, not only in the contract itself, but in all its privileges and penalties. It must strike every careful thinker that an immense difference rests in the fact, that man has made the laws. Inasmuch as all history shows that one class never did legislate for another with justice and equality, those who lack time to look up authorities and facts, might safely decide by pure reason, that man had made the laws cunningly and selfishly for his own purpose.

When man suffers from false legislation, he has the remedy in his own hands; but an [sic] humble petition, protest or prayer, is all that woman can claim.

The contract of marriage, is by no means equal. From Coke[1] down to Kent,[2] who can cite one law under the marriage contract, where woman has the advantage? The law permits the girl to marry at twelve years of age, while it requires several years more of experience on the part of the boy. In entering this compact, the *man* gives up nothing that he before possessed; he is a *man* still: while the legal existence of the woman is suspended

---

[1] See p. 175, n 8.

[2] See p. 176, n 10.

during marriage, and is known but in and through the husband. She is nameless, purseless, childless; though a woman, an heiress, and a mother.

Blackstone says, "the husband and wife are one, and that one is the husband."[3] Kent says, "the legal effects of marriage are generally deducible from the principle of common law, by which the husband and wife are regarded as one person, and her legal existence and authority lost or suspended during the continuance of the matrimonial union." Vol. 2, p. 109. Kent refers to *Coke on Littleton*[4], 112 A., 187 B.; *Litt.*, sec. 168, 291.

The wife is regarded by all legal authorities as a "*feme covert*," placed wholly "*sub potestate viri*." Her moral responsibility, even, is merged in the husband. The law takes it for granted that the wife lives in fear of her husband; that his command is her highest law; hence a wife is not punishable for theft committed in presence of her husband. *Kent*, vol. 2, p. 127. An unmarried woman can make contracts, sue and be sued, enjoy the rights of property, to her inheritance, her wages, her person, her children; but in marriage she is robbed by law of her natural and civil rights. "The disability of the wife to contract, so as to bind herself, arises not from want of discretion, but because she has entered into an indissoluble connection by which she is placed under the power and protection of her husband." *Kent*, vol. 2, p. 127. "She is possessed of certain rights until she is married; then all are suspended, to revive again the moment the breath goes out of the husband's body." See *Cowen's Treatise*, vol. 2, p. 709.[5] If the

---

[3] See p. 37, n 1.

[4] See p. 230, n 19.

[5] See p. 231, n 20.

contract be equal, whence come the terms, "marital power," "marital rights," "obedience and restraint," "dominion and control?" Many cases are stated showing a most questionable power over the wife sustained by the courts. See *Bishop on Divorce*, p. 489.[6]

Woman, as woman, has nothing to ask of our legislators but the right of suffrage. It is only in marriage, that she must demand her rights to person, children, property, wages, life, liberty and the pursuit of happiness. All the special statutes of which we complain --all the barbarities of the law--fall on her as wife and mother. We have not yet outlived the old feudal idea, the right of property in woman.

The term marriage expresses the nature of the relation in which man alone is recognized. It comes from the Latin "*maris*," husband; hence, as you look through the statutes and old common law, you find constant mention of "marital rights." Here and there, through the endless labyrinth of authorities, you will be refreshed with a bit of benevolence for the wife in the form of "protection." You never hear of "uxorial rights"; but the "widow's dower," the "widow's incumbrance," "the wife's alimony."

The laws on divorce are quite as unequal as those on marriage; yes, far more so. The advantages seem to be all on one side, and the penalties on the other. In case of divorce, if the husband be the guilty party, he still retains a greater part of the property! If the wife be the guilty party, she goes out of the partnership penniless. *Kent*, vol. 2, p. 33. *Bishop on Divorce*, p. 489. In New York, and some other states, the wife of the guilty husband can now sue for a divorce in her own name, and the costs come out of the husband's estate; but in a majority of the states she is still compelled to sue in the name of another, as she has no means of paying costs, even

---

[6] See p. 231, n 21.

though she may have brought her thousands into the partnership. "The allowance to the innocent wife, of '*ad interim*,' alimony, and money to sustain the suit, is not regarded as strict right in her, but of sound discretion in the court." *Bishop on Divorce*, p. 581. "Many jurists," says *Kent* (vol. 2, p. 88), "are of opinion that the adultery of the husband ought not to be noticed or made subject to the same animadversions as that of the wife, because it is not evidence of such entire depravity, nor equally injurious in its effects upon the morals and good order, and happiness of domestic life." Montesquieu,[7] Pothier,[8] and Dr. Taylor,[9] all insist, that the cases of husband and wife ought to be distinguished, and that the violation of the marriage vow, on the part of the wife, is the most mischievous, and the prosecution ought to be confined to the offense on her part." *Esprit des Loix*, tome 3, 186. *Traité du Contrat de Marriage*, No. 516. *Elements of Civil Law*, p. 254.

Say you, these are but the opinions of men? On what else, I ask, are the hundreds of women depending, who this hour demand in our courts a release from burdensome contracts? Are not these delicate matters left wholly to the discretion of the courts? Are not young women, from our first families, dragged into your public courts--into assemblies of men exclusively? The judges all men, the jurors all men? No true woman there to shield them, by her presence, from gross and impertinent questionings, to pity their misfortunes, or to protest against their wrongs! The administration of justice depends far more on the opinions of eminent jurists, than on law alone, for law is powerless, when at variance

---

[7] See p. 232, n 22.

[8] See p. 232, n 23.

[9] See p. 232, n 24.

with public sentiment.

For years there has been before the legislature of this state, a variety of bills asking for divorce in cases of drunkenness, insanity, desertion, and cruel and brutal treatment, endangering life. My attention was called to this question very early in life, by the sufferings of a friend of my girlhood--a victim of one of those unfortunate unions, called marriage. What my great love for that young girl, and my holy intuitions, then decided to be right, has not been changed by years of experience, observation and reason. I have pondered well these things in my heart, and ever felt the deepest interest in all that has been written and said on this subject; and the most profound respect and loving sympathy for those heroic women, who, in the face of law and public sentiment, have dared to sunder the unholy ties of a joyless, loveless union.

If marriage is a human institution, about which man may legislate, it seems but just that he should treat this branch of his legislation with the same common sense that he applies to all others. If it is a mere legal contract, then should it be subject to the restraints and privileges of all other contracts. A contract, to be valid in law, must be formed between parties of mature age, with an honest intention in said parties to do what they agree. The least concealment, fraud or intention to deceive, if proved, annuls the contract. A boy cannot contract for an acre of land, or a horse, until he is twenty-one, but he may contract for a wife, at fourteen. If a man sell a horse, and the purchaser find in him "great incompatibility of temper"--a disposition to stand still, when the owner is in haste to go--the sale is null and void; the man and his horse part company. But in marriage, no matter how much fraud and deception are practised, nor how cruelly one or both parties have been misled; no matter how young or inexperienced or thoughtless the parties, nor how unequal their condition and position in life, the contract cannot be annulled. Think of a husband telling a young and trusting girl, but one short month his wife, that he married her for her money; that those letters, so precious to her, that she had read and re-read, and kissed and cherished, were written by another; that their splendid home, of which, on their wedding day, her father gave to him the deed, is already in the hands of his creditors; that she must give up the elegance and luxury that now surround her, unless she can draw fresh supplies of money to meet their wants. When she told the story of her wrongs to me--the abuse to which she was subject, and the dread in which she lived, I impulsively urged her to fly from such a monster and villain, as she would before the hot breath of a ferocious beast of the wilderness; and she did fly, and it was well with her. Many times since, as I have felt her throbbing heart against my own, she has said: "Oh, but for your love and sympathy, your words of encouragement, I should never have escaped from that bondage; before I could, of myself, have found courage to break those chains, my heart would have broken in the effort."

Marriage, as it now exists, must seem to all of you a mere human institution. Look through the universe of matter and mind--all God's arrangements are perfect, harmonious and complete; there is no discord, friction or failure in His eternal plans. Immutability, perfection, beauty, are stamped on all His laws. Love is the vital essence that pervades and permeates from center to circumference--the graduating circle of all thought and action; Love is the talisman of human weal and woe--the "open sesame" to every human soul. Where two human beings are drawn together by the natural laws of likeness and affinity, union and happiness are the result. Such marriages, might be divine. But how is it now? You all know our marriage is, in many cases, a mere outward tie, impelled by custom, policy, interest, necessity; founded not even in friendship, to say nothing of love; with every possible inequality of condition and development. In these heterogeneous unions, we find youth and old age, beauty and deformity, refinement and vulgarity, virtue and vice, the educated and the ignorant, angels of grace and goodness with devils of malice and malignity; and the sum of all this is human wretchedness and despair--cold fathers, sad mothers and hapless children, who shiver at the hearthstone, where the fires of love have all gone out. The wide world and the stranger's unsympathizing gaze are not more to be dreaded for young hearts than homes like these. Now, who shall say that it is right to take two beings so unlike, and anchor them right side by side--fast bound--to stay all time, until God, in mercy, shall summon one away?

Do wise Christian legislators need any arguments to convince them that the sacredness of the family relation should be protected at all hazards? The family--that great conservator of national virtue and strength--how can you hope to build it up in the midst of violence, debauchery and excess? Can there be anything sacred, at that family altar, where the chief priest who ministers makes sacrifice of human beings--of the weak and the innocent? where the incense offered up is not to a God of justice and mercy, but those heathen divinities who best may represent the lost man, in all his grossness and deformity? Call that sacred, where woman, the mother of the race--of a Jesus of Nazareth--unconscious of the true dignity of her nature, of her high and holy destiny, consents to live in legalized prostitution! her whole soul revolting at such gross association! her flesh shivering at the cold contamination of that embrace! held there by no tie but the iron chain of the law, and a false and most unnatural public sentiment? Call that sacred, where innocent children, trembling with fear, fly to the corners and dark places of the house, to hide from the wrath of drunken, brutal fathers, but forgetting their past sufferings, rush out again at their mother's frantic screams, "Help! oh, help!" Behold the agonies of those young hearts, as they see the only being on earth they love, dragged about the room by the hair of her head, kicked and pounded, and left half dead and bleeding on the floor! Call that sacred, where fathers like these have the power and legal right to hand down their natures to other beings, to curse other generations with such moral deformity and death!

Men and brethren! look into your asylums for the blind, the deaf and dumb, the idiot, the imbecile, the deformed, the insane; go out into the by-lanes and dens of your cities, and contemplate the reeking mass of depravity; pause before the terrible revelations, made by statistics, of the rapid increase of all this moral and physical impotency, and learn how fearful a thing it is, to violate the immutable laws of the beneficent Ruler of the Universe; and there behold the sorrowful retributions of your violence on woman. Learn how false and cruel are those institutions, which, with a coarse materialism, set aside the holy instincts of the woman, to seek no union but one of love.

Fathers! do you say, let your daughters pay a lifelong penalty for one unfortunate step? How could they, on the threshold of life, full of joy and hope, believing all things to be as they seemed on the surface, judge of the dark windings of the human soul? How could they foresee that the young man, to-day, so noble, so generous, would, in a few short years, be transformed into a cowardly, mean tyrant, or a foul-mouthed, bloated drunkard? What father could rest at his home by night, knowing that his lovely daughter was at the mercy of a strong man, drunk with wine and passion, and that, do what he might, he was backed up by law and public sentiment? The best interests of the individual, the family, the state, the nation, cry out against these legalized marriages of force and endurance.

There can be no heaven without love; and nothing is sacred in the family and home, but just so far, as it is built up and anchored in purity and peace. Our newspapers teem with startling accounts of husbands and wives having shot or poisoned each other, or committed suicide, choosing death rather than the indissoluble tie, and still worse, the living death of faithless men and women, from the first families in the land, dragged from the privacy of home into the public prints and courts, with all the painful details of sad, false lives.

Now, do you believe, honorable gentlemen, that all these wretched matches were made in heaven? that all these sad, miserable people are bound together by God? But, say you, does not separation cover all these difficulties? No one objects to separation, when the parties are so disposed. To separation, there are two serious objections: first, so long as you insist on marriage as a divine institution, as an indissoluble tie, so long as you maintain your present laws against divorce, you make separation, even, so odious, that the most noble, virtuous and sensitive men and women, choose a life of concealed misery, rather than a partial, disgraceful release. Secondly, those who, in their impetuosity and despair, do, in spite of public sentiment, separate, find themselves, in their new position, beset with many temptations to lead a false, unreal life. This isolation bears especially hard on woman. Marriage is not all of life to man. His resources for amusement and occupation are boundless. He has the whole world for his home. His business, his politics, his club, his friendships, with either sex, can help to fill up the void, made by an unfortunate union, or separation. But to woman, as she is now educated, marriage is all and everything--her sole object in life--that for which she is taught to live--the all-engrossing subject of all her sleeping and her waking dreams. Now, if a noble girl of seventeen, marries, and is unfortunate in her choice, because the cruelty of her husband compels separation, in her dreary isolation, would you drive her to a nunnery, and shall she be a nun indeed? She, innocent child, perchance the victim of a father's pride, or a mother's ambition, betrayed into a worldly union for wealth, or family, or fame, shall the penalty be all visited on the heart of the only guiltless one in the transaction? If henceforth do you doom this fair young being, just on the threshold of womanhood, to a joyless, loveless solitude? By your present laws, you say, although separated she is married still; unbreakably bound to him who never loved, by whom she was never wooed or won; but by false guardians sold. And now, no matter though in the coming time her soul should, for the first time, wake to love, and one of God's own noblemen, should echo back her choice, the gushing fountains of her young affections must all be stayed. Because some man still lives, who once called her wife, no other man may give to her his love: and if she love not the tyrant to whom she is legally bound, she shall not love at all.

Think you that human law can set bounds to love? Alas! like faith, it comes upon us unawares. It is not by an act of will, we believe new doctrines, nor love what is true and noble in mankind. If you think it wise to legislate on human affections, pray make your laws with reference to what our natures are; let them harmonize in some measure with the immutable laws of god. A very wise father once remarked, that in the government of his children he forbid [sic] as few things as possible; a wise legislation would do the same. It is folly to make laws on subjects beyond human prerogative, knowing that in the very nature of things they must be set aside. To make laws that man cannot, and will not obey, serves to bring all law into contempt. It is all important in a republican government that the people should respect the laws; for if we throw law to the winds, what becomes of civil government?

What do our present divorce laws amount to? Those who wish to evade them have only to go into another state to accomplish what they desire. If any of our citizens cannot secure their inalienable rights in New York state, they may in Connecticut and Indiana.

Why is it that all contracts, covenants, agreements and partnerships are left wholly at the discretion of the parties, except that which, of all others, is considered most holy and important, both for the individual and the race?

But, say you, what a condition we should soon have in social life, with no restrictive laws. I ask you, what have we now? Separation and divorce cases in all your courts; men disposing of their wives in every possible way; by neglect, cruelty, tyranny, excess, poison, and imprisonment in insane asylums. We would give the parties greater latitude, rather than drive either to extreme measures, or crime. If you would make laws for our protection, give us the power to release from legal conjugal obligations, all husbands who are unfit for that relation. Woman loses infinitely more than she gains, by the kind of protection you now impose; for, much as we love and honor true and noble men, life and liberty are dearer far to us, than even the legalized slavery of an indissoluble tie. In this state, are over forty thousand drunkards' wives, earnestly imploring you to grant them deliverance from their fearful bondage. Thousands of sad mothers, too, with helpless children, deserted by faithless husbands, some in California, some in insane asylums, and some in the gutter, all pleading to be released. They ask nothing, but a quit-claim deed to themselves.

Thus far, we have had the man-marriage, and nothing more. From the beginning, man has had the whole and sole regulation of the matter. He has spoken in Scripture, and he has spoken in law. As an individual, he has decided the time and cause for putting away a wife; and as a judge and legislator, he still holds the entire control. In all history, sacred and profane, woman is regarded and spoken of, simply, as the toy of man. She is taken or put away, given or received, bought or sold, just as the interests of the parties might dictate. But the woman has been no more recognized in all these transactions, through all the different periods and conditions of the race, than if she had no part or lot in the whole matter. The right of woman to put away a husband, be he ever so impure, is never hinted at in sacred history.

We cannot take our gauge of womanhood from the past, but from the solemn convictions of our own souls, in the higher development of the race. No parchments, however venerable with the mould of ages, no human institutions, can bound the immortal wants of the royal sons and daughters of the great I Am.

I place man above all governments, all institutions, ecclesiastical and civil, all constitutions and laws. It is a mistaken idea that the same law that oppresses the individual can promote the highest good of society. The best interests of a community never can require the sacrifice of one innocent being, of one sacred right.

In the settlement, then, of any question, we must simply consider the highest good of the individual. It is the inalienable right of all to be happy. It is the highest duty of all to seek those conditions in life, those surroundings, which may develop what is noblest and best, remembering that the lessons of these passing hours, are not for time alone, but for the ages of eternity. They tell us, in that future home, the heavenly paradise, that the human family shall be sifted out, and the good and pure shall dwell together in peace. If that be the heavenly order, is it not our duty to render earth as near like heaven as we may? Inasmuch as the greater includes the less, let me repeat that I come not before you to plead simply the importance of divorce in cases proposed in your bill, but the justice of an entire revision of your whole code of laws on marriage and divorce. In our common law in our whole system of jurisprudence, we find man's highest idea of right. The object of law is to secure justice. But inasmuch as fallible man is the maker, administrator and adjudicator of law, we must look for many and gross blunders in the application of its general principles to individual cases. The science of theology, of civil, political, moral and social life, all teach the common idea that man ever has been and ever must be, sacrificed to the highest good of society--the one to the many--the poor to the rich--the weak to the powerful--and all to the institutions of his own creation. Look, what thunderbolts of power man has forged in the ages for his own destruction! at the organizations to enslave himself! And through these times of darkness, those generations of superstition, behold, all along, the relics of his power and skill, that stand like milestones, here and there, to show how far back man was great and glorious. Who can stand in those vast cathedrals of the old world, as the deep-toned organ reverberates from arch to arch, and not feel the grandeur of immortality. Here is the incarnated thought of man, beneath whose stately dome, the man himself, now bows in fear and doubt--knows not himself --and knows not God, a mere slave to symbols --and with holy water signs the cross while he who died thereon, declared man, God.

In closing, let me submit for your consideration the following propositions:

1st. In the language (slightly varied) of John Milton, "Those who marry intend as little to conspire their own ruin, as those who swear allegiance, and as a whole people is *to an ill government*, so is one man or woman *to an ill marriage*. If a whole people against any authority, covenant or statute, may, by the sovereign edict of charity, save not only their lives, but honest liberties, from unworthy bondage, as well may a married party, against any private covenant, which he or she never entered *to his or her mischief*, be redeemed from unsupportable disturbances to honest peace and just contentment."[10]

2nd. Any constitution, compact or covenant between human beings that failed to produce or promote human happiness, could not, in the nature of things, be of any force or authority; and it would be not only a right, but a duty to abolish it.

3rd. Though marriage be in itself divinely founded and is fortified as an institution by innumerable analogies to the whole kingdom of universal nature, still, a true marriage is only known by its results, and like the fountain, if pure, will reveal only pure manifestations. Never let it ever be said, "What God hath joined together, let no man put asunder" [Matt. 19:6; Mark 10:9], for man could not put it asunder; nor can he any more unite what God and nature have not joined together.

4th. Of all insulting mockeries of heavenly truth and holy law, none can be greater than that *physical impotency* is cause sufficient for divorce, while no amount of mental or moral or spiritual imbecility is ever to be pleaded in support of such a demand.

5th. Such a law was worthy those dark periods when marriage was held by the greatest doctors and priests of the Church to be a *work of the flesh only*, and almost, if not altogether, a defilement; denied wholly to the clergy, and a second time, forbidden to all.

6th. An unfortunate or ill-assorted marriage is ever a calamity but not ever, perhaps never, a crime; and when society or government, by its laws or customs, compels its continuance, always to the grief of one of the parties, and the actual loss and damage of both, it usurps an authority never delegated to man, nor exercised by God himself.

---

[10] See p. 189, n 1.

7th. Observation and experience daily show how incompetent are men, as individuals, or as governments, to select partners in business, teachers for their children, ministers of their religion, or makers, adjudicators or administrators of their laws; and as the same weakness and blindness must attend in the selection of matrimonial partners, the dictates of humanity and common sense alike show that the latter and most important contract should no more be perpetual than either or all of the former.

8th. Children born in these unhappy and unhallowed connections are in the most solemn sense, of *unlawful birth*--the fruit of lust but not of love; and so not of God, divinely descended, but from beneath, whence proceed all manner of evil and uncleanness.

9th. Next to the calamity of such a birth to the child, is the misfortune of being trained in the atmosphere of a household where love is not the law but where discord and bitterness abound, stamping their demoniac features on the moral nature, with all their odious peculiarities, thus continuing the race in a weakness and depravity that must be a sure precursor of its ruin, as a just penalty of long violated law.

14

Sojourner Truth, Two Speeches at the American Equal Rights Association Convention, 1867

The post-Civil War period created conflicts between those primarily concerned to obtain suffrage for freed male slaves and those committed to equal or universal suffrage--for white women and for all Afro-Americans. The American Equal Rights Association was formed in 1866 to promote universal suffrage. The extemporaneous speeches Sojourner Truth delivered at its first annual convention are the only complete texts of her speeches that still exist, but they illustrate her style, including a link between speech and singing,[1] and the interrelationship between rights for Afro-Americans and for women. The views she expressed were in contrast with those of another former slave, Frederick Douglass, who argued that suffrage for freed Afro-American males had to take precedence. Republicans saw great political opportunities for influence in the South if Afro-American males were enfranchised, and they feared that neither Afro-American males nor women would

---

[1] *This link persists in the rhetoric of more contemporary Afro-American women, for example, in the rhetoric of Fannie Lou Townsend Hamer (1917-1977), a founder of the Mississippi Freedom Democratic party (1964) and of the National Women's Political Caucus (1972).*

be enfranchised if the issues were linked. As a result, the Fourteenth and Fifteenth Amendments omitted women.

The texts are from the **National Anti-Slavery Standard,** *June 1, 1867, p. 3. Paragraphing has been added.*

SPEECH OF MAY 9, 1867

My friends, I am rejoiced that you are glad, but I don't know how you will feel when I get through. I come from another field--the country of the slave. They have got their rights--so much good luck: now what is to be done about it? I feel that I have got as much responsibility as anybody else. I have got as good rights as anybody.

There is a great stir about colored men getting their rights, but not a word about the colored women; and if colored men get their rights, and not colored women get theirs, there will be a bad time about it. So I am for keeping the thing going while things are stirring; because if we wait till it is still, it will take a great while to get it going again.

White women are a great deal smarter, and know more than colored women, while colored women do not know scarcely anything. They go out washing, which is about as high as a colored woman gets, and their men go about idle, strutting up and down; and when the women come home, they ask for their money and take it all, and then scold because there is no food. I want you to consider on that, chil'n [sic].

I want women to have their rights. In the Courts women have no right, no voice; nobody speaks for them. I wish woman to have her voice there among the pettifoggers. If it is not a fit place for women, it is unfit for men to be there.

I am above 80 years old; it is about time for me to be going. But I suppose I am kept here because something remains for me to do; I suppose I am yet to help break the chain.

I have done a great deal of work; as much as a man, but did not get so much pay. I used to work in the field and bind grain, keeping up with the cradler; but men never doing no more, got twice as much pay.[2] So with the German women. They work in the field and do as much work, but do not get the pay. We do as much, we eat as much, we want as much.

I suppose I am about the only colored woman that goes about to speak for the rights of the colored woman. I want to keep the thing stirring, now that the ice is broken. What we want is a little money. You men know that you get as much again as women when you write, or for what you do. When we get our rights, we shall not have to come to you for money, for then we shall have money enough of our own. It is a good consolation to know that when we have got this we shall not be coming to you any more.

You have been having our right so long, that you think, like a slaveholder, that you own us. I know that it is hard for one who has held the reins for so long to give up; it cuts like a knife. It will feel all the better when it closes up again. I have been in Washington about five years, seeing about these colored people. Now colored men have a right to vote; and what I want is to have colored women have the right to vote. There ought to be equal rights more then ever, since colored people have got their freedom.

I am going to talk several times while I am here; so now I will do a little singing. I have not heard any singing since I came here.

(Accordingly, suiting the action to the word, Sojourner sang, "We are going home.")

There, children, we shall rest from all our labors; first do all we have to do here.

---

[2] A cradle was a frame projecting above a scythe used to catch grain as it was cut so that it could be laid flat. Cradlers were workers who used a scythe so equipped.

There I am determined to go, not to stop till I get there to that beautiful place, and I do not mean to stop till I get there.

SPEECH OF MAY 10, 1867

Well, children--I know it is hard for men to give up entirely. They must run in the old track. (*Laughter.*) I was amused how men speaks up for one another. They cannot bear that a woman should say anything about the man, but they will stand here and take up the time in man's cause. But we are going, tremble or no tremble. (*Laughter.*)

Men is trying to help us. I know that all--the spirit they have got; and they cannot help us much until some of the spirit is taken out of them that belongs among the women. (*Laughter.*) Men have got their rights, and women has not got their rights. That is the trouble. When woman gets her rights man will be right. How beautiful that will be. Then it will be peace on earth and good will to men. (*Laughter and applause.*) But it cannot be that until it be right.

I am glad that men get here. They have to do it. I know why they edge off, for there is a power they cannot gainsay or resist. It will come. A woman said to me, "Do you think it will come in ten or twenty years?" Yes, it will come quickly. (*Applause.*) It must come. (*Applause.*) And now then the waters is troubled, and now is the time to step into the pool. There is a great deal now with the minds, and now is the time to start forth.

I was going to say that it was said to me some time ago that "a woman was not fit to have any rule. Do you want women to rule? They ain't fit. Don't you know that a woman had seven devils in her, and do you suppose that a man should put her to rule in the government?"

"Seven devils is of no account"--(*laughter*)--said I, "just behold, the man had a legion." (Loud laughter.) They never thought about that. A man had a legion--(*laughter*)--and the devils didn't know where to go. That was the trouble. (*Laughter and applause.*) They asked if they might get among the swine; they thought it was about as good a place as where they came from.[3] (*Laughter.*) Why didn't the devils ask to go among the sheep? (*Laughter.*) But no. But that may have been selfish of the devils--(*laughter*)--and certainly a man has a little touch of that selfishness that don't want to give the women their right. I have been twitted many times about this, and I thought how queer it is that men don't think of that. Never mind.

Look at the woman after all, the woman when they were cast out, and see how much she loved Jesus, and how she followed, and stood and waited for him.[4] That was the faithfulness of a woman. You cannot find any faith of man like that, go where you will.

After those devils had gone out of the man he wanted to follow Jesus. But what did Jesus say? He said: "Better go back and tell what had been done for you!" (*Laughter.*) He didn't seem as he wanted him to come along right away. (*Laughter.*) He was to be clean after that.

Look at that and look at the woman; what a mighty courage. When Mary stood and looked for Jesus, the man looked and didn't stop long enough to find out whether He was there or not; but when the woman stood there (blessed be God, I think I can see her!) she staid [sic] until she knew where He was, and said: "I will carry Him away!" Was woman true? She guarded it. The truth will reign triumphant.

---

[3] This story is found in Mark 5:1-20.

[4] Mary Magdalene, "out of whom went seven devils" (Luke 8:2); on her faithfulness, see Matt. 27: 56, 61; Mark 15: 40, 47; 16: 9-11; John 20: 1-2, 11-18.

I want to see, before I leave here--I want to see equality. I want to see women have their rights, and then there will be no more war. All the fighting has been for selfishness. They wanted something more than their own, or to hold something that was not their own; but when we have woman's rights, there is nothing to fight for. I have got all I want, and you have got all you want, and what do you fight for? All the battles that have even been was for selfishness--for a right that belonged to some one else, or fighting for his own right. The great fight was to keep the rights of the poor colored people. That made a great battle. And now I hope that this will be the last battle that will be in the world. Fighting for rights.

And we ought to have it all finished up now. Let us finish it up so that there be no more fighting. I have faith in God, and there is truth in humanity. Be strong women! blush not! tremble not! I know men will get up and brat, brat, brat, brat (*laughter*) about something which does not amount to anything except talk. We want to carry the point to one particular thing, and that is woman's rights, for nobody has any business with a right that belongs to her. I can make use of my own right. I want the same use of the same right. Do you want it? Then get it. If men had not taken something that did not belong to them they would not fear. But they tremble! They dodge! (*Laughter.*)

We will have nothing owned by anybody. That is the time you will be a man, if you don't get scared before it goes to parties. (*Laughter.*) I want you to look at it and be men and women. Men speak great lies, and it has made a great sore, but it will soon heal up. For I know when men, good men, discuss sometimes, that they say something or other and then take it half back. You must make a little allowance. I hear them say good enough at first, but then there was a going back a little more like the old times. It is hard for them to get out of it. Now we will help you out, if you want to get out. I want you to keep a good faith and good courage. And I am going round after I get my business settled and get more equality.

People in the North, I am going round to lecture on human rights. I will shake every place I go to. (*Loud laughter and applause.*)

15

Elizabeth Cady Stanton, Kansas State Referendum Campaign Speech at Lawrence, Kansas, 1867

In Kansas the legislature approved the submission of two referenda to voters--one removing the word "white" and the other removing the word "male" from the state constitution. Suffragists saw the campaign as highly significant because this was the first time the question of woman suffrage had come before the male voters of any state. Moreover, they were reasonably confident of success: Kansas had not only a strong abolitionist tradition, but also an excellent record on woman's rights. Lucy Stone and Henry Blackwell, Universalist minister Olympia Brown, Susan B. Anthony, and Elizabeth Cady Stanton all traveled to the state to seek support for woman suffrage. However, most abolitionists and Republicans, former allies of the movement, declined to support woman's enfranchisement with money or endorsements in their newspapers, the **New York Tribune**, *edited by Horace Greeley, and the* **Independent**, *edited by abolitionist Theodore Tilton. Encouraged by the decision in the New York state constitutional convention to reject woman suffrage, anti-suffragists in the Kansas*

Republican party ousted their leader Sam Wood,[1] who was sympathetic to woman suffrage, and the local equal rights organization disintegrated. Abandoned by their traditional allies, Anthony and Cady Stanton made the controversial decision to join forces with George Francis Train, a Democrat, Copperhead, dandy, and railroad speculator, who combined appeals for woman suffrage with scathing attacks on Afro-Americans. Train financed a joint lecture tour and provided Anthony and Cady Stanton with the funds to begin publishing their own journal, the **Revolution.** *Their decision outraged abolitionists, and contributed to a split in the woman's movement in 1869.*

Despite the efforts of equal suffrage advocates, both Afro-American and woman suffrage referenda failed. Suffrage for Afro-American men was voted down 19,421 to 10,483; woman suffrage 19,857 to 9,070. Elizabeth Cady Stanton's first speech in the 1867 Kansas referendum campaign was delivered at Lawrence, and she donated her handwritten copy of the speech to the Kansas State Historical Society in Topeka, from which this text is taken (Stanton 1867). *Some paragraphing has been added.*

How shall I find fitting words to express all I would say as I stand for the first time before an audience in Kansas?[2] As the pious Catholic on entering his Cathedral kneels and with holy water makes the sign of the cross upon his brow before lifting his eyes to the Holy of Holies, so would I reverently tread

---

[1] Samuel Newitt Wood (1825-91), elected to the Kansas Senate in 1859, speaker of the Kansas House of Representatives in 1877, and leader of the state Republican party.

[2] Arthur Schlesinger, Jr., has briefly described the symbolism of Kansas in U.S. history (Stratton 1981, 11-15).

this soil as the vestabule [sic] to our Temple of Liberty, the opening vista to the future grandeur of the new republic. Here the youngest civilization in the world is about to establish a government on that divine idea of equality uttered on the cross 1800 years ago, echoed by the Pilgrim Fathers in '76, and already twice baptized in American blood within one century. Here scanting kings, thrones, principalities and powers, it is proposed to make all your citizens equal before the law! Here at last is the idea to be realized, fortold [sic] by prophets and seers from the beginning and struggled for by the nations of the earth throughout the centuries. Here the mother of the race, the most important character in the drama of life is for the first time in the history of the world to stand the peer of man. It is fitting that the corner stone of the new republic should be laid here, where the first battles of liberty were fought and won over the monster slavery: that most deadly enemy of free institutions.

For forty years the monster slavery has ruled this country with a high hand. It gave us in quick succession the annexation of Texas,[3] the Fugitive Slave law,[4] the denial of the right of petition in Congress[5] and of free

---

[3] Texas was admitted to the Union in 1845 as the 28th state.

[4] See p. 109, n 2.

[5] In response to thousands of antislavery petitions, most of which requested abolition of slavery in the District of Columbia, "gag rules" were passed by the House of Representatives (1836-44) that prevented the discussion of antislavery proposals. The fight to secure the right to petition, waged almost singly by former President John Quincy Adams, aroused the North, repealed the rules, and strengthened the abolitionists' cause.

speech in all the northern states, the repeal of the Missouri Compromise[6] and mob law throughout the Union, culminating here in the Lecompton Constitution,[7] the dynasty of Atchison and the enrolling of voters from the Cincinnati directory, inaugurating a long and bloody political struggle in Kansas where southern tyrants were taught for the first time at the feet of the brave men and women of this state that freedom was stronger than slavery.

When the telegraphic wires brought us the news last winter of a proposition before your Legislature to take the words white male from your Constitution, we were holding meetings all through New York preparatory to our Constitutional Convention, patiently laboring in the faith that the efforts of our lives, if never realized to ourselves, would descend in

---

[6] The Missouri Compromise refers to measures passed (1820-21) to end a crisis over the extension of slavery in the territories that balanced the number of slave and free states and that prohibited slavery in the Louisiana Purchase north of the southern boundary of Missouri. The Kansas-Nebraska Act of 1854 repealed this compromise.

[7] The pro-slavery Lecompton Constitution was formulated September 1857 and ratified after an election in which voters were given a choice only between limited or unlimited slavery and in which free staters refused to cast their ballots. President Buchanan urged Congress to admit Kansas as a slave state under this document, but Stephen A. Douglas and his followers broke with the pro-slavery Democrats and the bill did not have enough support to pass. At a subsequent election (1858) this constitution was decisively defeated; in 1861 Kansas was admitted as a free state.

blessing to our children's children.[8] But the action of Kansas seemed to bring the prize at once within our grasp; it gave us new hope, new courage and an assurance that we should ourselves see a speedy and complete success. With a feeling of independence such as I had never known before, I said to my friends, Now if we fail to secure our political rights in N.Y. we will shake the dust of the Empire State from our feet[9] and go out towards the setting sun, where Kansas, the young and beautiful hero of the West, is already beconing [sic] us to her rich fields and rolling prairies, that we may at least lay our bones beneath a soil sacred to freedom and equality. Yes we will leave those white male fossils, with their odious statutes and that second Art[icle] of their Constitution to find a common grave while that state becomes one vast scene of desolation and not with my consent shall the ghost of a woman go back to shed one tear over their downfall.

White male. Old Bridget.[10]

---

[8] Cady Stanton spoke to the Judiciary Committee and Members of the New York state legislature on January 23, 1867 asking not only that the word "male" be stricken from Sec. 1, Art. 2, but that women be permitted to vote for members to that Convention (Stanton 1867; excerpted HWS 2:271-82). This speech includes some of the arguments made in Kansas.

[9] "And whosoever shall not receive you, nor hear your words, when ye depart out of that house of city, shake off the dust of your feet" (Matt. 10:14; see also Mark 6:11; Luke 9:5).

[10] According to a handwritten addition to the manuscript by Cady Stanton's daughter, "*This was a note to throw in one of her favorite stories, if the occasion seemed to permit the telling.*" *Signed: H[arriot] S[tanton] B[latch].*

It is better for many reasons, that this new experiment should be tried in a young state, rather than in older civilizations with the multiplied vices and crimes, of dense population in luxurious and indolent conditions of life.

The precious seeds of equality garnered from the sufferings of our forefathers under a British yoke, brought in the May Flower [sic] to these western shores, are to find here for the first time, a rich soil and genial atmosphere and with woman to help in the planting you may look for a full fruition and harvests of plenty.

On the rock bound coast of New England where they export nothing but ice and codfish, there was no soil for seed like this. Fresh from the corrupting influences of Kings and Courts it was a great thing for our Fathers to get the idea of equality on paper, to send forth a declaration of rights that made every crowned head in Europe tremble on his throne; but it is a greater thing for you to day to make it a fact in the government of a mighty state and show the world the possibility of its realization, the beneficence of its growth and protection, and the immortality of a nation founded on the Gibraltar rock of justice and equality. I say "nation," for what you now do in this state is the inauguration of the future policy of the nation. Wherever you lead, other states will follow. In deciding last winter to extend [the] right of suffrage to all the citizens of this state you struck the key note of reconstruction. Your far reaching wisdom embraced more than state institutions, and if you realize what you propose, to you will belong the honor of solving the national problem that has so long perplexed our political leaders, for as in the war freedom was the key note of victory, so now is universal suffrage the key note of reconstruction.

The partial demand of negro suffrage has been the one weak point in the republican battlements at which the enemy have kept up a continual fire, while friends have been able to make no defence.

For the same exhaustive arguments by which the rights of black men have been maintained, have been arguments against all class and caste legislation. The inconsistency of our position has been remarked alike by friends and foes. The President of the United States [Andrew Johnson] in his veto on [sic] the District of Columbia suffrage bill says, "It hardly seems consistent with the principles of justice and right that representatives of states where suffrage is denied the colored man or granted to him on qualifications requiring intelligence or property should compel the people of the District to try an experiment which their own constituents have thus far shown an unwillingness to try for themselves." In the debate on Nebraska Senator Sumner expresses the same opinion. He said, "When we demand equal rights of the southern states, we must not be so inconsistent as to admit any new state with a constitution disfranchising citizens on account of color. Congress must be itself just if it would recommend it to others. Reconstruction must begin at home."[11] When men from such opposite points of view express the same opinion, it is well for us to consider what they say.

Every thoughtful person must see that northern representatives are in no condition to reconstruct the southern states until their constitutions are purged of all invidious distinctions among the citizens of their own states. As the fountain rises no higher than

---

[11] Charles Sumner (1811-74), U.S. Senator from Massachusetts (1851-74). An aggressive abolitionist, he delivered his notable antislavery speech, "The Crime Against Kansas," on May 19-20, 1856, and after the war was a leader of the radical Republicans in their reconstruction program for the South.

its source, how can New York press on South Carolina a civilization she has never tried herself? But say you we can coerce the South to do what we have no right to force on a loyal state. Has not each state a right to amend her own constitution and establish a genuine republic within her own boundaries? Let each man mend one, says the old proverb, and the world is mended. Let each state bring its constitution into harmony with the Federal Constitution, and the Union will be a republic. Would you press impartial suffrage on the South recognize it first at home. Would you have Congress do its duty in the coming session, let the action of every State Legislature teach their representatives what that duty is. Does the North think it absurd for its women to vote and hold office; the South thinks the same of its negroes. Does the North consider its women a part of the family, to be represented by the "white male citizen"? So views the South her negroes. Is there anything more rasping to a proud spirit than to be rebuked for short comings by those who are themselves guilty of the grossest violations of law and justice. How different would our attitude be to day towards the South, were all the Northern States so amending their constitutions as to meet the requisitions they press on them. Example is better than precept. Would New York now take the lead in making herself a genuine republic, with what a new and added power our representatives could press universal suffrage on the Southern States. The work of this hour is a broader one than the reconstruction of the rebellious states, it is the lifting of the entire nation into higher ideas of justice and equality. It is the realization of what the world has never yet seen--a genuine republic. "Universal suffrage," says Lamartine, "is the first truth and only basis of every genuine republic."[12] "The ballot," says Senator Sumner, "is the Columbiad of our political life, and every citizen who has it is a full armed Monitor."[13] It is in no narrow captious or selfish spirit that at this hour we press woman's claim to the ballot, but that we may end all class and caste legislation, vindicate the republican idea, and set a spotless example to the nations of the world.

In this prolonged unsettlement of the country, I see a wise Providence, that the people may thus have time to debate the great fundamental principles of government, that when we do again crystallize into any form it will be on a foundation that will stand forever and ever.

As in the war freedom was the key note of victory, so now is universal suffrage the key note of reconstruction. John Stuart Mill in a late letter to Hon. S.N. Wood has well said: "If your citizens next November give effect to the enlightened views of your Legislature history will remember that one of the youngest states in the civilized world, has been the first to adopt a measure of liberation, destined to extend all over the earth and to be looked back to as is my fixed conviction as one of the most fertile in beneficial consequences, of all the improvements yet effected

---

[12] Alphonse Marie Louis de Lamartine (1790-1869), French poet, novelist, and statesman, an idealist who held aloof from parties while embracing the principles of democracy, social justice, and international peace, he briefly headed the provisional government after the revolution of 1848 but subsequently lost the election for the presidency to Louis Napoleon Bonaparte (Napoleon III).

[13] With the *Merrimack*, one of two American warships that fought the first engagement between two ironclads on March 9, 1862 and battled to a draw.

in human affairs."[14]

And in saying thus much Mr. Mill does not overestimate the importance of the enfranchisement of women. When you come to appreciate the fact that there is sex in mind, that ideas as well as beings need the mother soul for their growth and development, you will appreciate how much has been lost in the world of morals and intellect, through the ignorance and degradation of woman, in thus blotting out one half the race.

As there is just that physical difference in man and woman necessary to the preservation of the race so there is just that spiritual difference necessary to the vitalizing of thought. Hence in the education and elevation of woman I see the growth and full development of the grand ideas enunciated by man in ages hitherto cold, barren and speculative because not met by the faith, hope and enthusiasm of a true womanhood. But when she awakes to the poetry of real life and sees the beauty of science, philosophy and government, then will the first note of harmony be struck, then will the great organ of humanity be played on all its keys with every stop rightly adjusted and with louder, loftier string the march of civilization will be immeasurably quickened. The distinguished historian Henry Thomas Buckle says, "The turn of thought of women, their habits of mind, their conversation invariably extending over the whole surface of society and frequently penetrating its intimate structure, have more than all other things put together tended to raise us into an ideal world and lift us from the dust into

---

[14] John Stuart Mill (1806-73), British philosopher and economist, who, strongly influenced by his wife Harriet Taylor, delivered a speech in Parliament that was subsequently published as *On the Subjection of Women* (1869).

which we are too prone to grovel."[15] And this will be her influence in exalting and purifying the world of politics.

When woman understands the momentous interests that depend on the ballot, she will make it her first duty to educate every American boy and girl into the idea that to vote is the most sacred act of citizenship:--a religious duty not to be discharged thoughtlessly, selfishly or corruptly but conscientiously remembering that in a republican government to each citizen is entrusted the interests of a nation. Would you fully estimate the responsibility of the ballot, think of it as the great regulating power of a continent of all our interests political, commercial, religious, educational, social and sanitary. To many minds this claim for the ballot suggests nothing more than a rough polling booth where coarse drunken men elbowing each other wade knee deep in mud to drop a little piece of paper two inches long into a box--simply this and nothing more. The poet Wordsworth showing the blank materialism of those who see only with their outward eyes says of his Peter Bell:

> A primrose on the river's brim
> A yellow primrose was to him
> And it was nothing more.[16]

So our political Peter Bells see the rough polling booth in this great act of citizenship as nothing. But in this act so lightly esteemed by the mere materialist behold the realization of that great idea struggled for in the ages and proclaimed by the Fathers the right of self government. That little piece

---

[15] Henry Thomas Buckle (1821-62), English historian, author of *History of Civilization in England*, 2 vols. (1857-61).

[16] William Wordsworth (1770-1850), English romantic poet.

of paper dropped into a box is the symbol of citizenship: of equality, wealth, virtue, education, self-protection, dignity, independence and power, the mightiest engine yet placed in the hand of man for the uprooting of ignorance, tyranny and superstition, the overthrowing of Kings, Popes, Thrones, Altars, despotisms, monarchies and Empires.

What phantom can the sons of the Pilgrims be chasing when they make merchandise of a power like this. Judas Iscariot selling his Master for thirty pieces of silver is a fit type of these American citizens who sell their votes and thus betray the right of self-government.[17] Talk not of the muddy pool of politics as if such things must need be. Behold with the coming of woman into this higher sphere of influence the dawn of the new day when politics so called are to be lifted up into the world of morals and religion, when the polling booth shall be a beautiful Temple, surrounded by fountains and flowers and triumphal arches through which young men and maidens shall go up in joyful procession to ballot for justice and mercy and when our elections shall be like the holy feasts of the Jews at Jerusalem. When you say, gentlemen, it would degrade woman to go to the polls, you make a sad confession of your irreligious mode of observing that most sacred right of citizenship. The ballot box in a republican government should be guarded with as much love and care as was the Ark of the Lord among the children of Israel. Here where we have no Heaven-anointed Kings or Priests, law must be to us a holy thing and the ballot box the Holies of Holies, for on it depends the safety and stability of our institutions!!

Do you shrink from having woman exposed to the grossness and vulgarity of public life, or encounter what she must at the polls? When you talk, gentlemen, of sheltering woman from the rough winds and revolting scenes of real

---

[17] Matt. 26:15.

life, you must be either talking for effect or wholly ignorant of what the facts of life are. The man whatever he is is known to woman. She is the companion not only of the accomplished gentleman, the statesman, the scholar, the orator, but the ignorant, vile, brutal, obscene man has his mother, wife, daughter, sister. Delicate, refined, educated women are in daily life with the drunkard, the gambler, the licentious and the criminal. And if man shows out what he is anywhere it is at his own hearthstone. There are over 40,000 drunkards in the state of New York. All these are bound by the ties of family to some woman. Allow but a mother and wife to each and you [have] 80,000 women. All these have seen their fathers, brothers, husbands, sons in the lowest stages of degradation. In your own circle of friends do you not know refined women whose whole lives are darkened and saddened by gross and brutal associations? Now, gentlemen, do you talk to woman of a rude jest or jostle at the polls, where noble, virtuous men stand ready to protect her person and her rights when alone in the darkness and solitude and gloom she has trembled at her own fireside waiting the return of a husband from his midnight revels? When stepping from her chamber door in bridal veil and orange blossoms she has beheld her royal monarch, her lord and master, her legal representative, the protector of her person and property, down on his hands and knees slowly crawling up the stairs with drunken curses on the lips that one short month before vowed love eternal. Behold him in her chamber in her bed! Is there a degradation more damning into which woman can sink in the muddiest pool of politics? Ah! the fairy tale of Beauty and the Beast is far too often realized in life. Gentlemen such scenes as woman has witnessed at her own fireside where no eye save Omnipotence could pity, no strong arm could help can never be realized at the polls, never equalled elsewhere this side the bottomless pit. Woman has not hitherto lived in the clouds surrounded by an atmosphere of purity and peace but she has been the companion of man, in health, in sickness and in death, alike in his triumphs and degradation. She has worshiped him as a hero and saint and pitied him as a madman and a fool. In Paradise they were placed together and so they must ever be to rise or sink as one. If man is low, wretched and vile, woman cannot escape the contagion. An atmosphere that is unfit for one is unfit for the other. The customs of a darker age have already placed woman by the side of man in all his crimes, vices and amusements, oft sinking him to the lowest depths of degradation and despair. In the full blaze of civilization let us then demand that she be with him in his highest moments in all his profitable and honorable employments.

If the facts of life were not so truly humiliating it would be amusing to hear men talk of woman's "coming dawn." Do you not know, women of Kansas, that in your constitution you are ranked with minors, criminals, rebels, the lowest classes of your population? In none of the nations of modern Europe are women politically degraded as in this Republic. In the old world where the government is the aristocracy, where it is considered a mark of nobility to share its offices and powers--there women of rank have certain hereditary rights,--which raise them above a majority of the men--certain honors and privileges not granted to serfs or peasants. In England woman may be Queen, hold some offices, vote on some questions. In the southern states before the war women were not degraded in seeing their ditch diggers, gardeners, coachmen and waiters go to the polls to legislate on their interests. But in these northern states where the aristocracy is "male," washed or unwashed, lettered or unlettered, rich or poor, black or white, women of wealth and education who pay taxes on half the property in the country, your peers in art, science and literature, are thrust outside the pale of political consideration with the most degraded classes in the state. Your creeds and codes and customs harmonize with this position. Our lawyers see "femme covert," "widows claims," "dower," "protection," "incapacities," "incumbrance," "ad interim alimony" written on the brow of every woman they meet. And our clergy always think of the "weaker vessel," "wives obey your husband" whenever they hear of woman's equality. Now from such a position in the public mind where is the degradation in being crowned with all the rights of citizenship, in being ranked with such men as Gov. Robinson,[18] Senator Pomeroy or Ross,[19] instead of the inmates of your state's prison? Taking the word "male" out of the constitution is lifting us at once to the level of our best and truest men, from all our degrading associations with our present political compeers, minors, criminals, paupers, rebels and idiots, for a man can vote if he is not more than nine-tenths a fool. But you are afraid this right to vote would take woman out of her sphere.

The North Pole and the passage round it, the nature of woman and her sphere, have troubled explorers and philosophers from the beginning, and will to the end because God never designed man to find out either. If it would not be audacious to dictate to the Lord of Creation, I would suggest, that the field of his labours is already so vast and varied that he might safely leave the discovery of these new regions to walruses and women. Man in unbounded freedom has discovered that the universe is not too large to feed his thought. Woman with the same latitude might not stay within four walls, but the world is large enough for both. Now it seems to me it is not a great mark of presumption on our part when

---

[18] Charles Robinson (1818-94), first governor of the state of Kansas (1861-63).

[19] Samuel Clarke Pomeroy (1816-91) and Edmund Gibson Ross (1826-1907), U.S. Senators from Kansas, 1861-73 and 1866-71, respectively.

we claim that woman is the best judge of her own sphere and that, if left to herself she will find it out. Man has marked it out for her, made laws for her, educated her and governed her for six thousand years and by their own telling they have made a failure. They say we cannot reason. There is no reasoning with a woman.

"Frailty thy name is woman."[20] History describes us a wicked, weak and sensuous. Our poets and novelists make these men grand, heroic, capable of great deeds, but their women weak, helpless and vacillating, while our lawmakers have legislated us into a nutshell, technically saying that as we have not souls large enough to claim justice and equality,it makes but little difference how we are classed politically. Yes, my brothers, you have undoubtedly failed in the type of woman developed under your ministrations. Now if you will let us alone 6,000 years, we will show you an order of women worthy [of] your love, admiration and worship.

Take care of yourselves. The "masculine element" needs a little looking after. You have generously devoted so much time to "woman's sphere" and "the feminine element" that you have quite forgotten that one of the greatest needs of the republic is high-toned, manly men.

We ask you literally to do nothing for us. Take our names out of your constitutions and statute books and have no more special legislation for us. Let your codes be for persons, for citizens, throw all the Negroes and women overboard. If they cannot live under the broad codes and constitutions which the best legal minds from Coke[21] and Blackstone[22] down to our Story[23] [and] Kent,[24] have

---

[20] Shakespeare, *Hamlet*, 1.2.

[21] See p. 175, n 8.

[22] See p. 37, n 1.

been perfecting for years for "white men," let them perish. Let us try it. Let us rough it with you for a few centuries and see what will come [of] it. I have an idea that self made black men and women will be of a better stamp, than the anomalous beings now extant, the dwarfed and crippled creations of your fancies.

But I pray you, men of Kansas, do not lay the blame of your failure on Providence. Do not say that woman's condition in the world has always been in harmony with the will of God. For such an assertion invokes the immutable and eternal in the administration of a changing, shortsighted policy. For the condition of woman in all ages has differed materially, and differs at this moment among the various nations of the earth, and which of all these conditions is in accordance with the will of God, enervated and voluptuous by confinement, as she is in Turkish harem or exhausted by excessive toil and outdoor labour as she is in Switzerland and Germany, with her feet compressed in iron boots to the smallest dimensions, depending on man to carry her about as she is in China, or standing all day in the intense heat of a summer's sun as she is in Christian America, with the crown and sceptre ruling the mightiest nation on the globe, as she is in England; or burning on the funeral pile of her husband, a useless relic of her lordly dead as she is in India? Who can decide which of all these is woman's true sphere?

I met a gentleman last winter who had just been to hear Anna Dickinson.[25] I said

---

[23] See p. 176, n 11.

[24] See p. 176, n 10.

[25] Anna E. Dickinson (1842-1932), orator and lecturer, made her first speech in 1860 before the Pennsylvania Anti-Slavery Society and achieved her first major success in 1861

how did you like her? Oh! very much, but I could not help feeling she was out of her sphere. Ah! said I have you heard Ristori?[26] Yes. Did you feel she was out of her sphere? No! What's the difference? He could give no satisfactory reason. So I explained his feelings to him to his satisfaction.

It has always been considered legitimate for women to amuse men but not to reprove them or teach them. But there was a time when women were not permitted to play in our public theatres. As late as Shakspeare [sic] day, all his tragedies were represented by men alone. Juliet, Ophelia, Rosalind, Portia, Cate [sic], Desdemona were all represented by men.[27]

We find gentlemen with the most latitudinarian views on the question of morals the most concerned just now lest this movement for the enfranchisement of woman should make her an individual and in so doing that the home and conjugal relations should be disturbed.

---

when she addressed a packed audience at Philadelphia's Concern Hall on "The Rights and Wrongs of Women." She campaigned for the Republicans in 1863, and on January 16, 1864, she spoke by invitation in the House of Representatives before a distinguished audience of political, diplomatic, and military figures that included President Lincoln. After the war she became a popular lyceum speaker whose most frequently delivered lecture was in praise of Joan of Arc.

[26] Adelaide Ristori, an actor, Italy's first international star, in later years compared most favorably to Sarah Bernhardt. Her acting troupe made four visits to the United States between 1853 and 1855.

[27] Characters, respectively, in Shakespeare's *Romeo and Juliet, Hamlet, As You Like It, The Merchant of Venice, Taming of the Shrew,* and *Othello*.

With the education and elevation of woman we shall have most radical changes in the marriage relation. When woman is self-supporting and independent, she will not desecrate that holy relation by marrying for bread and a home. Drunkards, gamblers, licentious men and criminals will be at a discount. If the Bible, that best of books, teaches one thing, it is a pure and holy marriage. Be ye not unequally yoked with unbelievers, for vice and virtue, beauty and deformity, purity and corruption can never harmonize together.[28] When woman understands the immutable laws of her being, the science of social life, she will see the wisdom of that warning in the second commandment uttered mid the thunders of Sinai. The sins of the fathers shall be visited upon the children unto the third and fourth generation.[29]

When woman holds the lofty position God meant she should as mother of the race, base men will find no women base enough willingly to hand down their vices, diseases, crimes, their morbid appetites, their low desires, their tainted blood, that fire in the veins that consumes the workers of unrighteousness. The family, that great conservator of national strength and morals, how can you cement its ties, but in the independence and virtue of both man and woman. Man has hitherto educated woman according to his idea and marked out her sphere. Woman has now to find out her own sphere and educate herself according to her own highest idea and in another generation you will see the glory of the new experiment.

---

[28] 2 Cor. 6:14.

[29] Exod. 20:5; Num. 14:18.

16

Susan B. Anthony, "Is it a Crime for a U.S. Citizen to Vote?" 1872-73

Anthony delivered this speech some forty times to defend her act of voting in the 1872 election, an act for which she was arrested and indicted. Because of the impact of this speech, delivered in every postal district of Monroe County, the prosecutor requested and was granted a change of venue from Rochester to Canandaigua, New York. With the help of Matilda Joslyn Gage, though, Anthony also made her case throughout Ontario County prior to her trial.

The speech addresses the audience as jurors: it urges them to make law through finding in her favor, arguing that such a conclusion is the only judgment consistent with the nation's founding documents, its state constitutions, court decisions, the understanding of great statesmen of the past and present, and the meaning of the Fourteenth and Fifteenth Amendments. Anthony's powerful speech not only struck fear in the prosecutor, it also convinced the judge that he had to direct the jury to find her guilty (they did not have an opportunity to withdraw and vote). Yet the judge outraged the prosecutor by fining her only one hundred dollars, and by refusing to jail her when she publicly stated in court that she would never pay it. The effort to gain suffrage through the courts finally failed when, in Minor v. Happersett *(1875), the Supreme Court ruled that citizenship, defined in the Fourteenth Amendment, did not confer the franchise on women. The text is from Anthony* (1874)*; capitalization has been made consistent.*

Friends and Fellow-citizens: I stand before you to-night, under indictment for the alleged crime of having voted at the last Presidential election, without having a lawful right to vote. It shall be my work this evening to prove to you that in thus voting, I not only committed no crime, but, instead, simply exercised my *citizen's right*, guaranteed to me and all United States citizens by the National Constitution, beyond the power of any State to deny.

Our democratic-republican government is based on the idea of the natural right of every individual member thereof to a voice and a vote in making and executing the laws. We assert the province of government to be to secure the people in the enjoyment of their unalienable rights. We throw to the winds the old dogma that governments can give rights. Before governments were organized, no one denies that each individual possessed the right to protect his own life, liberty and property. And when 100 or 1,000,000 people enter into a free government, they do not barter away their natural rights; they simply pledge themselves to protect each other in the enjoyment of them, through prescribed judicial and legislative tribunals. They agree to abandon the methods of brute force in the adjustment of their differences, and adopt those of civilization.

Nor can you find a word in any of the grand documents left us by the fathers that assumes for government the power to create or to confer rights. The Declaration of Independence, the United States Constitution, the constitutions of the several States and the organic laws of the territories, all alike propose to protect the people in the exercise of their God-given rights. Not one of them pretends to bestow rights.

> All men are created equal, and endowed by their Creator with certain unalienable rights. Among these are life, liberty and the pursuit of happiness. That to secure these, governments are instituted among men, deriving their just powers from the consent of the governed.

Here is no shadow of government authority over rights, nor exclusion of any class from their full and equal enjoyment. Here is pronounced the right of all men, and "consequently," as the Quaker preacher said, "of all women," to a voice in the government. And here, in this very first paragraph of the Declaration, is the assertion of the natural right of all to the ballot; for, how can "the consent of the governed" be given, if the right to vote be denied. Again:

> That whenever any form of government becomes destructive of these ends, it is the right of the people to alter or abolish it, and to institute a new government, laying its foundation on such principles, and organizing its powers in such forms as to them shall seem most likely to effect their safety and happiness.

Surely, the right of the whole people to vote is here clearly implied. For however destructive to their happiness this government might become, a disfranchised class could neither alter nor abolish it, nor institute a new one, except by the old brute force method of insurrection and rebellion. One-half of the people of this nation to-day are utterly powerless to blot from the statute books an unjust law, or to write there a new and a just one. The women, dissatisfied as they are with this form of government, that enforces taxation without representation,--that compels them to obey laws to which they have never given their consent,--that imprisons and hangs them without a trial by a jury of their peers, that robs them, in marriage, of the custody of their own persons, wages and children,--are this half of the people left wholly at the mercy of the other half, in direct violation of the spirit and letter of the declarations of the framers of this government, every one of which was based on the immutable principle of equal rights to all. By those declarations, kings, priests, popes, aristocrats, were all alike dethroned, and placed on a common level, politically, with the lowliest born subject or serf. By them, too, men, as such, were deprived of their divine right to rule, and placed on a political level with women. By the practice of those declarations all class and caste distinction will be abolished; and slave, serf, plebian, wife, woman, all alike, bound from their subject position to the proud platform of equality.

The preamble of the Federal Constitution says:

> We, the people of the United States, in order to form a more perfect union, establish justice, insure *domestic* tranquility, provide for the common defence, promote the general welfare and secure the blessings of liberty to ourselves and our posterity, do ordain and establish this constitution for the United States of America.

It was we, the people, not we, the white male citizens, nor yet we, the male citizens; but we, the whole people, who formed this Union. And we formed it, not to give the blessings of liberty, but to secure them; not to the half of ourselves and the half of our posterity, but to the whole people--women as well as men. And it is downright mockery to talk to women of their enjoyment of the blessings of liberty while they are denied the use of the only means of securing them provided by this democratic-republican government--the ballot.

The early journals of Congress show that when the committee reported to that body the original Articles of Confederation, the very first article which became the subject of discussion was that respecting equality of suffrage. Article 4th said: "The better to secure and perpetuate mutual friendship and intercourse between the people of the different States of this Union, the free inhabitants of each of the States, (paupers, vagabonds and fugitives from justice excepted,) shall be entitled to all the privileges and immunities of the free citizens of the several States."

Thus, at the very beginning, did the fathers see the necessity of the universal application of the great principle of equal rights to all--in order to produce the desired result--a harmonious union and a homogeneous people.

Luther Martin, attorney-general of Maryland, in his report to the Legislature of that State to the convention that framed the United States Constitution, said:

> Those who advocated the equality of suffrage took the matter up on the original principles of government: that the reason why each individual man in forming a State government should have an equal vote, is because each individual, before he enters into government, is equally free and equally independent.[1]

---

[1] Luther Martin (c. 1748-1826), first attorney-general of Maryland. As a delegate to the Federal Constitutional Convention, he refused to sign the Constitution because he felt that it violated states' rights. He was a bitter opponent of Thomas Jefferson.

James Madison said: "Under every view of the subject, it seems indispensable that the mass of the citizens should not be without a voice in making the laws which they are to obey, and in choosing the magistrates who are to administer them." Also, "Let it be remembered, finally, that it has ever been the pride and the boast of America that the rights for which she contended were the rights of human nature."[2]

And these assertions of the framers of the United States Constitution of the equal and natural rights of all the people to a voice in the government, have been affirmed and reaffirmed by the leading statesmen of the nation, throughout the entire history of our government.

Thaddeus Stevens, of Pennsylvania, said in 1866: "I have made up my mind that the elective franchise is one of the inalienable rights meant to be secured by the Declaration of Independence."[3]

B. Gratz Brown, of Missouri, in the three days' discussion in the United States Senate in 1866, on Senator Cowan's motion to strike "male" from the District of Columbia suffrage bill, said:[4]

---

[2] James Madison (1751-1836), 4th President of the United States. He served in the Continental Congress, with John Jay and Alexander Hamilton was author of the *Federalist Papers*, was a delegate to the Federal Constitutional Convention, and led the fight for constitutional ratification in Virginia.

[3] Thaddeus Stevens (1792-1868), U.S. Representative from Pennsylvania (1849-53, 1859-68), radical reconstructionist who led the fight for Andrew Johnson's impeachment.

[4] Benjamin Gratz Brown (1826-85), U.S. Senator (1863-67) and governor of Missouri (1871-73).

> Mr. President, I say here on the floor of the American Senate, I stand for universal suffrage; and as a matter of fundamental principle, do not recognize the right of society to limit it on any ground of race or sex. I will go farther and say, that I recognize the right of franchise as being intrinsically a natural right. I do not believe that society is authorized to impose any limitations upon it that do not spring out of the necessities of the social state itself. Sir, I have been shocked, in the course of this debate, to hear Senators declare this right only a conventional and political arrangement, a privilege yielded to you and me and others; not a right in any sense, only a concession! Mr. President, I do not hold my liberties by any such tenure. On the contrary, I believe that whenever you establish that doctrine, whenever you crystalize that idea in the public mind of this country, you ring the death-knell of American liberties.

Charles Sumner, in his brave protests against the fourteenth and fifteenth amendments, insisted that, so soon as by the thirteenth amendment the slaves became free men, the original powers of the United States Constitution guaranteed to them equal rights--the right to vote and to be voted for. In closing one of his great speeches he said:

> I do not hesitate to say that when the slaves of our country became 'citizens' they took their place in the body politic as a component part of the 'people,' entitled to equal rights, and under the protection of these two guardian principles: First--That all just governments

> stand on the consent of the governed; and second, that taxation without representation is tyranny; and these rights it is the duty of Congress to guarantee as essential to the idea of a Republic.[5]

The preamble of the Constitution of the State of New York declares the same purpose. It says: "We, the people of the State of New York, grateful to Almighty God for our freedom, in order to secure its blessings, do establish this Constitution."

Here is not the slightest intimation, either of receiving freedom from the United States Constitution, or of the State conferring the blessings of liberty upon the people; and the same is true of every one of the thirty-six state constitutions. Each and all, alike declare rights God-given, and that to secure the people in the enjoyment of their inalienable rights, is their one and only object in ordaining and establishing government. And all of the state constitutions are equally emphatic in their recognition of the ballot as the means of securing the people in the enjoyment of these rights.

Article 1 of the New York State Constitution says: "No member of this State shall be disfranchised or deprived of the rights or privileges secured to any citizen thereof, unless by the law of the land, or the judgment of his peers."

And so carefully guarded is the citizen's right to vote, that the Constitution makes special mention of all who may be excluded. It says: "Laws may be passed excluding from the right of suffrage all persons who have been or may be convicted of bribery, larceny or any infamous crime."

In naming the various employments that shall not affect the residence of voters--the 3d section of Article 2d says "that being kept

---

[5] See p. 265, n 11.

at any alms house, or other asylum, at public expense, nor being confined at any public prison, shall deprive a person of his residence," and hence his vote. Thus is the right of voting most sacredly hedged about. The only seeming permission in the New York State Constitution for the disfranchisement of women is in section 1st of Article 2d, which says: "Every male citizen of the age of twenty-one years, &c., shall be entitled to vote."

But I submit that in view of the explicit assertions of the equal right of the whole people, both in the preamble and previous article of the constitution, this omission of the adjective "female" in the second, should not be construed into a denial; but, instead, counted as of no effect. Mark the direct prohibition: "No member of this State shall be disfranchised, unless by the 'law of the land,' or the judgment of his peers." "The law of the land," is the United States Constitution: and there is no provision in that document that can be fairly construed into a permission to the States to deprive any class of their citizens of their right to vote. Hence New York can get no power from that source to disfranchise one entire half of her members. Nor has "the judgment of their peers" been pronounced against women exercising their right to vote; no disfranchised person is allowed to be judge or juror--and none but disfranchised persons can be women's peers; nor has the legislature passed laws excluding them on account of idiocy or lunacy; nor yet the courts convicted them of bribery, larceny, or any infamous crime. Clearly, then, there is no constitutional ground for the exclusion of women from the ballot-box in the State of New York. No barriers whatever stand to-day between women and the exercise of their right to vote save those of precedent and prejudice.

The clauses of the United States Constitution, cited by our opponents as giving power to the States to disfranchise any classes of citizens they shall please, are contained in

Sections 2d and 4th of Article 1st. The second says:

> The House of Representatives shall be composed of members chosen every second year by the people of the several States; and the electors in each State shall have the qualifications requisite for electors of the most numerous branch of the State Legislature.

This cannot be construed into a concession to the States of the power to destroy the right to become an elector, but simply to prescribe what shall be the qualifications, such as competency of intellect, maturity of age, length of residence, that shall be deemed necessary to enable them to make an intelligent choice of candidates. If, as our opponents assert, the last clause of this section makes it the duty of the United States to protect citizens in the several States against higher or different qualifications for electors for representatives in Congress, than for members of Assembly, then must the first clause make it equally imperative for the national government to interfere with the States, and forbid them from arbitrarily cutting off the right of one-half of the people to become electors altogether.

Section 4th says: "The times, places and manner of holding elections for Senators and Representatives shall be prescribed in each State by the Legislature thereof; but Congress may at any time, by law, make or alter such regulations, except as to the places of choosing Senators."

Here is conceded the power only to prescribe times, places and manner of holding the elections; and even with these Congress may interfere, with all excepting the mere place of choosing Senators. Thus you see, there is not the slightest permission in either section for the States to discriminate against the right of any class of citizens to vote. Surely, to regulate cannot be to annihilate! nor to qualify to wholly deprive. And to this principle every true Democrat and Republic said amen, when applied to black men by Senator Sumner in his great speeches for EQUAL RIGHTS TO ALL from 1865 to 1869; and when, in 1871, I asked that Senator to declare the power of the United States Constitution to protect women in their right to vote--as he had done for black men--he handed me a copy of all his speeches during that reconstruction period, and said:

> Miss Anthony, put "sex" where I have "race" or "color," and you have here the best and strongest argument I can make for woman. There is not a doubt but women have the constitutional right to vote, and I will never vote for a sixteenth amendment to guarantee it to them. I voted for both the fourteenth and fifteenth under protest; would never have done it but for the pressing emergency of that hour; would have insisted that the power of the original Constitution to protect all citizens in the equal enjoyment of their rights should have been vindicated through the courts. But the newly made freedmen had neither the intelligence, wealth nor time to wait that slow process. Women possess all these in an eminent degree, and I insist that they shall appeal to the courts, and through them establish the powers of our American *magna charta*, to protect every citizen of the Republic.

But, friends, when in accordance with Senator Sumner's counsel, I went to the ballot-box, last November, and exercised my citizen's right to vote, the courts did not wait for me to appeal to them--they appealed to me, and indicted me on the charge of having voted illegally.

Senator Sumner, putting sex where he did color, said:

> Qualifications cannot be in their nature permanent or insurmountable. Sex cannot be a qualification any more than size, race, color, or previous condition of servitude. A permanent or insurmountable qualification is equivalent to a deprivation of the suffrage. In other words, it is the tyranny of taxation without representation, against which our revolutionary mothers, as well as fathers, rebelled.

For any State to make sex a qualification that must ever result in the disfranchisement of one entire half of the people, is to pass a bill of attainder, or an *ex post facto* law, and is therefore a violation of the supreme law of the land. By it, the blessings of liberty are forever withheld from women and their female posterity. To them, this government has no just powers derived from the consent of the governed. To them this government is not a democracy. It is not a republic. It is an odious aristocracy; a hateful oligarchy of sex. The most hateful aristocracy ever established on the face of the globe. An oligarchy of wealth, where the rich govern the poor; an oligarchy of learning, where the educated govern the ignorant; or even an oligarchy of race, where the Saxon rules the African, might be endured; but this oligarchy of sex, which makes father, brothers, husband, sons, the oligarchs over the mother and sisters, the wife and daughters of every household; which ordains all men sovereigns, all women subjects, carries dissension, discord and rebellion into every home of the nation. And this most odious aristocracy exists, too, in the face of Section 4, of Article 4, which says: "The United States shall guarantee to every State in the Union a Republican form of government."

What, I ask you, is the distinctive difference between the inhabitants of a monarchical and those of a republican form of government, save that in the monarchical the people are subjects, helpless, powerless, bound to obey laws made by superiors--while in the republican, the people are citizens, individual sovereigns, all clothed with equal power, to make and unmake both their laws and law makers, and the moment you deprive a person of his right to voice in the government, you degrade him from the status of a citizen of the republic, to that of a subject, and it matters very little to him whether his monarch be an individual tyrant, as is the Czar of Russia, or a 15,000,000 headed monster, as here in the United States; he is a powerless subject, serf or slave; not a free and independent citizen in any sense.

But, it is urged, the use of the masculine pronouns *he, his*, and *him*, in all the constitutions and laws, is proof that only men were meant to be included in their provisions. If you insist on this version of the letter of the law, we shall insist that you be consistent, and accept the other horn of the dilemma, which would compel you to exempt women from taxation for the support of the government, and from penalties for the violation of laws.

A year and a half ago I was at Walla Walla, Washington Territory. I saw there a theatrical company, called the "Pixley Sisters," playing before crowded houses, every night of the whole week of the territorial fair. The eldest of those three fatherless girls was scarce eighteen. Yet every night a United States officer stretched out his long fingers, and clutched six dollars of the proceeds of the exhibitions of those orphan girls, who, but a few years before, were half starvelings in the streets of Olympia, the capital of that far-off northwest territory. So the poor widow, who keeps a boarding house, manufactures shirts, or sells apples and peanuts on the street corners of our cities, is compelled to pay taxes from her scanty pittance. I would that the women of this republic, at once, resolve, never again to submit to taxation, until their right to vote be recognized.

Miss Sarah E. Wall, of Worcester, Mass., twenty years ago, took this position. For several years, the officers of the law distrained her property, and sold it to meet the necessary amount; still she persisted, and would not yield an iota, though every foot of her lands should be struck off under the hammer. And now, for several years, the assessor has left her name off the tax list, and the collector passed her by without a call.

Mrs. J.S. Weeden, of Viroqua, Wis., for the past six years, has refused to pay her taxes, though the annual assessment is $75.

Mrs. Ellen Van Valkenburg, of Santa Cruz, Cal., who sued the County Clerk for refusing to register her name, declares she will never pay another dollar of tax until allowed to vote; and all over the country, women property holders are waking up to the injustice of taxation without representation, and ere long will refuse, *en masse*, to submit to the imposition.[6]

There is no *she*, or *her*, or *hers*, in the tax laws.

The statute of New York reads: "Every person shall be assessed in the town or ward where *he* resides when the assessment is made, for the lands owned by *him*, &c." "Every collector shall call at least once on the person taxed, or at *his* usual place of residence, and shall demand payment of the taxes charged on *him*. If any one shall refuse to pay the tax imposed on *him*, the collector shall levy the same by distress and sale of *his* property."

---

[6] Women's tax protests are briefly described in Wagner 1987, 27-34.

The same is true of all the criminal laws: "No person shall be compelled to be a witness against *himself*, &c."

The same with the law of May 31st, 1870, the 19th section of which I am charged with having violated; not only are all the pronouns in it masculine, but everybody knows that that particular section was intended expressly to hinder the rebels from voting. It reads: "If any person shall knowingly vote without *his* having a lawful right," &c. Precisely so with all the papers served on me--the U.S. Marshal's warrant, the bail-bond, the petition for habeas corpus, the bill of indictment--not one of them had a feminine pronoun printed in it; but, to make them applicable to me, the Clerk of Court made a little carat [sic] at the left of "he" and placed an "s" over it, thus making *she* out of *he*. Then the letters "is" were scratched out, the little carat under an "er" over, to make *her* out of *his*, and I insist if government officials may thus manipulate the pronouns to tax, fine, imprison and hang women, women may take the same liberty with them to secure to themselves their right to a voice in the government.

So long as any classes of men were denied their right to vote, the government made a show of consistency, by exempting them from taxation. When a property qualification of $250 was required of black men in New York, they were not compelled to pay taxes, so long as they were content to report themselves worth less than that sum; but the moment the black man died, and his property fell to his widow or daughter, the black woman's name would be put on the assessor's list, and she be compelled to pay taxes on the same property exempted to her husband. The same is true of ministers in New York. So long as the minister lives, he is exempted from taxation on $1,500 of property, but the moment the breath goes out of his body, his widow's name will go down on the assessor's list, and she will have to pay taxes on the $1,500. So much for the special legislation in favor of women.

In all the penalties and burdens of the government, (except the military,) women are reckoned as citizens, equally with men. Also, in all the privileges and immunities, save those of the jury box and ballot box, the two fundamental privileges on which rest all the others. The United States government not only taxes, fines, imprisons and hangs women, but it allows them to pre-empt lands, register ships, and take out passport and naturalization papers. Not only does the law permit single women and widows to the right of naturalization, but Section 2 says: "A married woman may be naturalized without the concurrence of her husband." (I wonder the fathers were not afraid of creating discord in the families of foreigners); and again:

"When an alien, having complied with the law, and declared his intention to become a citizen, dies before he is actually naturalized, his widow and children shall be considered citizens, entitled to all rights and privileges as such, on taking the required oath." If a foreign born woman by becoming a naturalized citizen, is entitled to all the rights and privileges of citizenship, is not a native born woman, by her national citizenship, possessed of equal rights and privileges?

The question of the masculine pronouns, yes and nouns, too, has been settled by the United States Supreme Court, in the Case of *Silver versus Ladd*, December, 1868, in a decision as to whether a woman was entitled to lands, under the Oregon donation law of 1850.[7] Elizabeth Cruthers, a widow, settled upon a claim and received patents. She died, and her son was heir. He died. Then Messrs. Ladd & Nott took possession, under the general

---

[7] The Supreme Court treated the words generically, although the fifth section of the act passed by Congress on September 27, 1850, used the words "white male citizens of the United States" (Wallace 1887, 219-28).

pre-emption law, December, 1861. The administrator, E.P. Silver, applied for a writ of ejectment at the land office in Oregon City. Both the Register and Receiver decided that an unmarried woman could not hold land under that law. The Commissioner of the General Land Office, at Washington, and the Secretary of the Interior, also gave adverse opinions. Here patents were issued to Ladd & Nott, and duly recorded. Then a suit was brought to set aside Ladd's patent, and it was carried through all the State Courts and the Supreme Court of Oregon, each, in turn, giving adverse decisions. At last, in the United States Supreme Court, Associate Justice Miller reversed the decisions of all the lower tribunals, and ordered the land back to the heirs of Mrs. Cruthers. The Court said:

> In construing a benevolent statute of the government, made for the benefit of its own citizens, inviting and encouraging them to settle on its distant public lands, the words 'single man,' and 'unmarried man' may, especially if aided by the context and other parts of the statute, be taken in a generic sense. Held, accordingly, that the Fourth Section of the Act of Congress, of September 27th, 1850, granting by way of donation, lands in Oregon Territory, to every white settler or occupant, American half-breed Indians included, embraced within the term *single man* an *unmarried woman*.

And the attorney, who carried this question to its final success, is now the United States Senator elect from Oregon, Hon. J.H. Mitchell, in whom the cause of equal rights to women has an added power on the floor of the United States Senate.

Though the words persons, people, inhabitants, electors, citizens, are all used indiscriminately in the national and state constitutions, there was always a conflict of opinion, prior to the war, as to whether they were synonymous terms, as for instance: "No *person* shall be a *representative* who shall not have been seven years a *citizen*, and who shall not, when elected, be an *inhabitant* of that State in which he is chosen. No *person* shall be a senator who shall not have been a *citizen* of the United States, and an *inhabitant* of that State in which he is chosen."

But, whatever room there was for a doubt, under the old regime, the adoption of the fourteenth amendment settled that question forever, in its first sentence: "All persons born or naturalized in the United States and subject to the jurisdiction thereof, are citizens of the United States and of the State wherein they reside."

And the second settles the equal status of all persons--all citizens: "No State shall make or enforce any law which shall abridge the privileges or immunities of citizens; nor shall any State deprive any person of life, liberty or property, without due process of law, nor deny to any person within its jurisdiction the equal protection of the laws."

The only question left to be settled, now, is: Are women persons? And I hardly believe any of our opponents will have the hardihood to say they are not. Being persons, then, women are citizens, and no State has a right to make any new law, or to enforce any old law, that shall abridge their privileges or immunities. Hence, every discrimination against women in the constitutions and laws of the several States, is to-day null and void, precisely as is every one against negroes.

Is the right to vote one of the privileges or immunities of citizens? I think the disfranchised ex-rebels, and the ex-state prisoners will all agree with me, that it is not only one of them, but the one without which all the others are nothing. Seek first the kingdom of the ballot, and all things else shall be given thee, is the political injunction.[8]

Webster,[9] Worcester[10] and Bouvier[11] all define citizen to be a person, in the United States, entitled to vote and hold office.

Prior to the adoption of the thirteenth amendment, by which slavery was forever abolished, and black men transformed from property to persons, the judicial opinions of the country had always been in harmony with these definitions. To be a person was to be a citizen, and to be a citizen was to be a voter.

Associate Justice Washington, in defining the privileges and immunities of the citizen, more than fifty years ago, said: "they included all such privileges as were fundamental in their nature. And among them is the right to exercise the elective franchise, and to hold office."[12]

---

8 A paraphrase of Matt. 6:33 and Luke 12:31.

9 Noah Webster (1758-1843) published the *American Dictionary of the English Language* (1828).

10 Joseph Emerson Worcester, lexicographer, who issued three reputable dictionaries of American usage in 1830, 1846, and 1860.

11 John Bouvier (1787-51), whose *Law Dictionary* (1839) was a reference work for U.S. law students and practitioners.

12 Bushrod Washington (1762-1829), nephew of George Washington, served in the American Revolution, was a member of the Virginia house of delegates and of the Virginia convention that adopted the Constitution, and was appointed Associate Justice of the Supreme Court in 1798.

Even the "Dred Scott" decision,[13] pronounced by the abolitionists and Republicans infamous, because it virtually declared "black men had no rights white men were bound to respect," gave this true and logical conclusion, that to be one of the people was to be a citizen and a voter.

Chief Judge Daniels [sic] said: "There is not, it is believed, to be found in the theories of writers on government, or in any actual experiment heretofore tried, an exposition of the term citizen, which has not been considered as conferring the actual possession and enjoyment of the perfect right of acquisition and enjoyment of an entire equality of privileges, civil and political."[14]

Associate Justice Taney said: "The words 'people of the United States,' and 'citizens,' are synonymous terms, and mean the same thing. They both describe the political body, who, according to our republican institutions, form the sovereignty, and who hold the power and conduct the government, through their representatives. They are what we familiarly call the sovereign people, and every citizen is one of this people, and a constituent member of this sovereignty."[15]

---

[13] Supreme Court Decision of 1857, *Scott v. Sandford*, that held that Congress had no power to prohibit slavery in the territories and that the Missouri Compromise was unconstitutional, a decision that inflamed the sectional controversy leading to the Civil War.

[14] Peter Vivian Daniel (1784-1860), U.S. Supreme Court Justice (1841-60).

[15] Roger Brooke Taney (1777-1864), fifth Chief Justice of the Supreme Court (1836-64), whose support of slavery laws was most clearly expressed in the Dred Scott Case, in which the Court held that slaves and even the free descendants of slaves were not citizens and

Thus does Judge Taney's decision, which was such a terrible ban to the black man, while he was a slave, now, that he is a person, no longer property, pronounce him a citizen, possessed of an entire equality of privileges, civil and political. And not only the black man, but the black woman, and all women as well.

And it was not until after the abolition of slavery, by which the negroes became free men, hence citizens, that the United States Attorney General Bates, rendered a contrary opinion.[16] He said:

> The Constitution uses the word 'citizen' only to express the political quality, (not equality mark,) of the individual in his relation to the nation; to declare that he is a member of the body politic, and bound to it by reciprocal obligations of allegiance on the one side, and protection on the other. The phrase, 'a citizen of the United States,' without addition or qualification, means neither more nor less than a member of the nation.

Then, to be a citizen of this republic, is no more than to be a subject of an empire. You and I, and all true and patriotic citizens must repudiate this base conclusion. We all know that American citizenship, without addition or qualification, means the possession of equal rights, civil and political. We all know that the crowning glory of every citizen of the United States is, that he can

---

might not sue in the Federal courts.

[16] Edward Bates (1793-1869), Missouri lawyer and Lincoln's opponent for presidential nomination in 1860; later attorney-general in his cabinet.

either give or withhold his vote from every law and every legislator under the government.

Did "I am a Roman citizen," mean nothing more than that I am a "member" of the body politic of the republic of Rome, bound to it by the reciprocal obligations of allegiance on the one side, and protection on the other?[17] Ridiculously absurd question, you say. When you, young man, shall travel abroad, among the monarchies of the old world, and there proudly boast yourself an "American citizen," will you thereby declare yourself neither more nor less than a "member" of the American nation?

And this opinion of Attorney General Bates, that a black citizen was not a voter, made merely to suit the political exigency of the Republican party, in that transition hour between emancipation and enfranchisement, was no less infamous, in spirit or purpose, than was the decision of Judge Taney, that a black man was not one of the people, rendered in the interest and at the behest of the old Democratic party, in its darkest hour of subjection to the slave power. Nevertheless, all of the adverse arguments, adverse congressional reports and judicial opinions, thus far, have been based on this purely partisan, time-serving opinion of General Bates, that the normal condition of the citizen of the United States is that of disfranchisement. That only such classes of citizens as have had special legislative guarantee have a legal right to vote.

And if this decision of Attorney General Bates was infamous, as against black men, but yesterday plantation slaves, what shall we pronounce upon Judge Bingham, in the House of

---

[17] The power of Roman citizenship is illustrated by Paul's appeal to Caesar, recounted in Acts 25.

Representatives,[18] and Carpenter, in the Senate of the United States,[19] for citing it against the women of the entire nation, vast numbers of whom are the peers of those honorable gentlemen, themselves, in morals!! intellect, culture, wealth, family--paying taxes on large estates, and contributing equally with them and their sex, in every direction, to the growth, prosperity and well-being of the republic? And what shall be said of the judicial opinions of Judges Carter, Jameson,[20] McKay and Sharswood,[21] all based upon this aristocratic, monarchial [sic] idea, of the right of one class to govern another?

I am proud to mention the names of the two United States Judges who have given opinions honorable to our republican idea, and honorable to themselves--Judge Howe, of Wyoming Territory, and Judge Underwood, of Virginia.[22]

---

[18] John Armor Bingham (1815-1900), a representative from Ohio (1855-63; 1865-73), was one of the managers appointed by the House of Representatives in 1868 for the impeachment trial of President Andrew Johnson.

[19] Matthew Hale Carpenter (1824-81), Senator from Wisconsin (1869-75, 1879-81).

[20] John Alexander Jameson (1824-90), eminent Chicago jurist, best known for *The Constitutional Convention: Its History, Powers, and Modes of Proceeding* (1867).

[21] George Sharswood (1810-83), associate judge of the district court of Philadelphia (1845-67), associate, later chief justice, of the Pennsylvania supreme court (1868-82).

[22] John Curtiss Underwood (1809-73), appointed judge of the district court of Virginia in 1864, presided over the treason trial of Jefferson Davis; in 1867 he was

The former gave it as his opinion a year ago, when the Legislature seemed likely to revoke the law enfranchising the women of that Territory, that, in case they succeeded, the women would still possess the right to vote under the fourteenth amendment.

Judge Underwood, of Virginia, in noticing the recent decision of Judge Carter, of the Supreme Court of the District of Columbia, denying to women the right to vote, under the fourteenth and fifteenth Amendment, says: "If the people of the United States, by amendment of their Constitution, could expunge, without any explanatory or assisting legislation, an adjective of five letters from all state and local constitutions, and thereby raise millions of our most ignorant fellow-citizens to all of the rights and privileges of electors, why should not the same people, by the same amendment, expunge an adjective of four letters from the same state and local constitutions, and thereby raise other millions of more educated and better informed citizens to equal rights and privileges, without explanatory or assisting legislation?"

If the fourteenth amendment does not secure to all citizens the right to vote, for what purpose was that grand old charter of the fathers lumbered with its unwieldy proportions? The Republican party, and Judges Howard and Bingham, who drafted the document, pretended it was to do something for black men; and if that something was not to secure them in their right to vote and hold office, what could it have been? For, by the thirteenth amendment, black men had become people, and hence were entitled to all the privileges and immunities of the government, precisely as were the women of the country, and foreign men not naturalized. According to Associate

---

president of the Richmond convention that, as part of Reconstruction, drew up the so-called "Underwood Constitution" that, as amended, remains the Virginia State Constitution.

Justice Washington, they already had the "Protection of the government, the enjoyment of life and liberty, with the right to acquire and possess property of every kind, and to pursue and obtain happiness and safety, subject to such restraints as the government may justly prescribe for the general welfare of the whole; the right of a citizen of one State to pass through or to reside in any other State for the purpose of trade, agriculture, professional pursuit, or otherwise; to claim the benefit of the writ of habeas corpus, to institute and maintain actions of any kind in the courts of the State; to take, hold, and dispose of property, either real or personal, and an exemption from higher taxes or impositions than are paid by the other citizens of the State."

Thus, you see, those newly freed men were in possession of every possible right, privilege and immunity of the government, except that of suffrage, and hence, needed no constitutional amendment for any other purpose. What right, I ask you, has the Irishman the day after he receives his naturalization papers that he did not possess the day before, save the right to vote and hold office? And the Chinamen [sic], now crowding our Pacific coast, are in precisely the same position. What privilege or immunity has California or Oregon the constitutional right to deny them, save that of the ballot? Clearly, then, if the fourteenth amendment was not to secure to black men their right to vote, it did nothing for them, since they possessed everything else before. But, if it was meant to be a prohibition of the States, to deny or abridge their right to vote--which I fully believe--then it did the same for all persons, white women included, born or naturalized in the United States; for the amendment does not say all male persons of African descent, but all persons are citizens.

The second section is simply a threat to punish the States, by reducing their representation on the floor of Congress, should they disfranchise any of their male citizens, on account of color, and does not allow of the inference that the States may disfranchise from any, or all other causes; nor in any wise weaken or invalidate the universal guarantee of the first section. What rule of law or logic would allow the conclusion, that the prohibition of a crime to one person, on severe pains and penalties, was a sanction of that crime to any and all other persons save that one?

But, however much the doctors of the law may disagree, as to whether people and citizens, in the original Constitution, were one and the same, or whether the privileges and immunities in the fourteenth amendment include the right of suffrage, the question of the citizen's right to vote is settled forever by the fifteenth amendment. "The citizen's right to vote shall not be denied by the United States, nor any State thereof; on account of race, color, or previous condition of servitude." How can the State deny or abridge the right of the citizen, if the citizen does not possess it? There is no escape from the conclusion, that to vote is the citizen's right, and the specifications of race, color, or previous condition of servitude can, in no way, impair the force of the emphatic assertion, that the citizen's right to vote shall not be denied or abridged.

The political strategy of the second section of the fourteenth amendment, failing to coerce the rebel States into enfranchising their negroes, and the necessities of the Republican party demanding their votes throughout the South, to ensure the re-election of Grant in 1872, that party was compelled to place this positive prohibition of the fifteenth amendment upon the United States and all the States thereof.[23]

If we once establish the false principle,

---

[23] Ulysses S. Grant (1822-85), 18th President of the United States (1869-77).

that United States citizenship does not carry with it the right to vote in every State in this Union, there is no end to the petty freaks and cunning devices, that will be resorted to, to exclude one and another class of citizens from the right of suffrage.

It will not always be men combining to disfranchise all women; native born men combining to abridge the rights of all naturalized citizens, as in Rhode Island. It will not always be the rich and educated who may combine to cut off the poor and ignorant; but we may live to see the poor, hard-working, uncultivated day laborers, foreign and native born, learning the power of the ballot and their vast majority of numbers, combine and amend state constitutions so as to disfranchise the Vanderbilts[24] and A.T. Stewarts,[25] the Conklings[26] and Fentons.[27] It is a poor rule that won't work more ways than one. Establish this precedent, admit the right to deny suffrage to the States, and there is no power to foresee the confusion, discord and disruption that may await us. There is, and can be, but one safe principle of government--equal rights to all. And any and every

---

24 The family of Cornelius Vanderbilt (1794-1877), American railroad magnate.

25 Alexander Turney Stewart (1803-76), American merchant, whose store, opened in 1862, was the largest retail store in the world.

26 Roscoe Conkling (1829-88), U.S. Representative (1859-63, 1865-67), Senator (1867-81), and undisputed leader of the Republican party in New York.

27 Reuben Eaton Fenton (1819-85), governor of New York (1864-68), later U.S. Senator (1869-74), who lost his seat in a dispute with Sen. Conkling over control of the distribution of patronage.

discrimination against any class, whether on account of color, race, nativity, sex, property, culture, can but imbitter [sic] and disaffect that class, and thereby endanger the safety of the whole people.

Clearly, then, the national government must not only define the rights of citizens, but it must stretch out its powerful hand and protect them in every State in this Union.

But if you will insist that the fifteenth amendment's emphatic interdiction against robbing United States citizens of their right to vote, "on account of race, color, or previous condition of servitude," is a recognition of the right, either of the United States, or any State, to rob citizens of that right, for any or all other reasons, I will prove to you that the class of citizens for which I now plead, and to which I belong, may be, and are, by all the principles of our government, and many of the laws of the States, included under the term "previous condition of servitude."

First.--The married women and their legal status. What is servitude? "The condition of a slave." What is a slave? "A person who is robbed of the proceeds of his labor; a person who is subject to the will of another."

By the law of Georgia, South Carolina, and all the States of the South, the negro had no right to the custody and control of his person. He belonged to his master. If he was disobedient, the master had the right to use correction. If the negro didn't like the correction, and attempted to run away, the master had a right to use coercion to bring him back.

By the law of every State in this Union to-day, North as well as South, the married woman has no right to the custody and control of her person.[28] The wife belongs to her

---

[28] Friedman (1985), Grossberg (1985), and Rabkin (1980) provide histories of laws as they affected married women.

husband; and if she refuses obedience to his will, he may use moderate correction, and if she doesn't like his moderate correction, and attempts to leave his "bed and board," the husband may use moderate coercion to bring her back. The little word "moderate," you see, is the saving clause for the wife, and would doubtless be overstepped should her offended husband administer his correction with the "cat-o'-nine-tails," or accomplish his coercion with blood-hounds.

Again, the slave had no right to the earnings of his hands, they belonged to his master; no right to the custody of his children, they belonged to his master; no right to sue or be sued, or testify in the courts. If he committed a crime, it was the master who must sue or be sued.

In many of the States there has been special legislation, giving to married women the right to property inherited, or received by bequest, or earned by the pursuit of any avocation outside of the home; also, giving her the right to sue and be sued in matters pertaining to such separate property; but not a single State of this Union has ever secured the wife in the enjoyment of her right to the joint ownership of the joint earnings of the marriage copartnership. And since, in the nature of things, the vast majority of married women never earn a dollar, by work outside of their families, nor inherit a dollar from their fathers, it follows that from the day of their marriage to the day of the death of their husbands, not one of them ever has a dollar, except it shall please her husband to *let* her have it.

In some of the States, also, there have been laws passed giving to the mother a joint right with the father in the guardianship of the children. But twenty years ago, when our woman's rights movement commenced, by the laws of the State of New York, and all the States, the father had the sole custody and control of the children. No matter if he were a brutal, drunken libertine, he had the legal right, without the mother's consent, to apprentice her sons to rumsellers, or her daughters to brothel keepers. He could even will away an unborn child, to some other person than the mother. And in many of the States the law still prevails, and the mothers are still utterly powerless under the common law.

I doubt if there is, to-day, a State in this Union where a married woman can sue or be sued for slander of character, and until quite recently there was not one in which she could sue or be sued for injury of person. However damaging to the wife's reputation any slander may be, she is wholly powerless to institute legal proceedings against her accuser, unless her husband shall join with her; and how often have we heard of the husband conspiring with some outside barbarian to blast the good name of his wife? A married woman cannot testify in courts in cases of joint interest with her husband. A good farmer's wife near Earlville, Ill., who had all the rights she wanted, went to a dentist of the village and had a full set of false teeth, both upper and under. The dentist pronounced them an admirable fit, and the wife declared they gave her fits to wear them; that she could neither chew nor talk with them in her mouth. The dentist sued the husband; his counsel brought the wife as witness; the judge ruled her off the stand, saying "a married woman cannot be a witness in matters of joint interest between herself and her husband." Think of it, ye good wives, the false teeth in your mouths are joint interest with your husbands, about which you are legally incompetent to speak!! If in our frequent and shocking railroad accidents a married woman is injured in her person, in nearly all of the States, it is her husband who must sue the company, and it is to her husband that the damages, if there are any, will be awarded. In Ashfield, Mass., supposed to be the most advanced of any State in the Union in all things, humanitarian as well as intellectual, a married woman was severely injured by a defective sidewalk. Her husband sued the corporation and recovered $13,000 damages. And those $13,000 belong to him *bona fide;* and whenever that unfortunate wife wishes a dollar of it to supply her needs she must ask her husband for it; and if the man be of a narrow, selfish, niggardly nature, she will have to hear him say, every time, "What have you done, my dear, with the twenty-five cents I gave you yesterday?" Isn't such a position, I ask you, humiliating enough to be called "servitude?" That husband, as would any other husband, in nearly every State of this Union, sued and obtained damages for the loss of the services of his wife, precisely as the master, under the old slave regime, would have done, had his slave been thus injured, and precisely as he himself would have done had it been his ox, cow or horse instead of his wife.

There is an old saying that "a rose by any other name would smell as sweet,"[29] and I submit if the deprivation by law of the ownership of one's own person, wages, property, children, the denial of the right as an individual, to sue and be sued, and to testify in the courts, is not a condition of servitude most bitter and absolute, though under the sacred name of marriage?

Does any lawyer doubt my statement of the legal status of married women? I will remind him of the fact that the old common law of England prevails in every State in this Union, except where the Legislature has enacted special laws annulling it. And I am ashamed that not one State has yet blotted from its statute books the old common law of marriage, by which Blackstone, summed up in the fewest words possible, is made to say, "husband and wife are one, and that one is the husband."[30]

Thus may all married women, wives and widows, by the laws of the several States, be

---

29 Shakespeare, *Romeo and Juliet*, 2.2.

30 See p. 37, n 1.

technically included in the fifteenth amendment's specification of "condition of servitude," present or previous. And not only married women, but I will also prove to you that by all the great fundamental principles of our free government, the entire womanhood of the nation is in a "condition of servitude" as surely as were our revolutionary fathers, when they rebelled against old King George.[31] Women are taxed without representation, governed without their consent, tried, convicted and punished without a jury of their peers. And is all this tyranny any less humiliating and degrading to women under our democratic-republican government to-day than it was to men under their aristocratic, monarchical government one hundred years ago? There is not an utterance of old John Adams, John Hancock or Patrick Henry, but finds a living response in the soul of every intelligent, patriotic woman of the nation.[32] Bring to me a common-sense woman property holder, and I will show you one whose soul is fired with all the indignation of 1776 every time the tax-gatherer presents himself at her door. You will not find one such but feels her condition of servitude as galling as did James Otis when he said:[33]

> The very act of taxing exercised over those who are not represented

---

[31] George III (1738-1820), king of Great Britain and Ireland (1760-1820).

[32] Patrick Henry (1736-99), political leader in the American Revolution, whose phrases, "If this be treason, make the most of it," and "Give me liberty or give me death," are symbols of that period.

[33] James Otis (1725-83) led the radical political wing of the colonial opposition to British measures and was head of the Massachusetts committee of correspondence.

> appears to me to be depriving them of one of their most essential rights, and if continued, seems to be in effect an entire disfranchisement of every civil right. For, what one civil right is worth a rush after a man's property is subject to be taken from him at pleasure without his consent? If a man is not his own assessor in person, or by deputy, his liberty is gone, or he is wholly at the mercy of others.

What was the three-penny tax on tea, or the paltry tax on paper and sugar to which our revolutionary fathers were subjected, when compared with the taxation of the women of this republic? The orphaned Pixley sisters, six dollars a day, and even the women, who are proclaiming the tyranny of our taxation without representation, from city to city throughout the country, are often compelled to pay a tax for the poor privilege of defending our rights. And again, to show that disfranchisement was precisely the slavery of which the fathers complained, allow me to cite to you old Ben. Franklin, who in those olden times was admitted to be good authority, not merely in domestic economy, but in political as well; he said:

> Every man of the commonalty [sic], except infants, insane persons and criminals, is, of common right and the law of God, a freeman and entitled to the free enjoyment of liberty. That liberty or freedom consists in having an actual share in the appointment of those who are to frame the laws, and who are to be the guardians of every man's life, property and peace. For the all of one man is as dear to him as the all of another; and the poor man has an equal right, but more need to have representatives in the Legislature

> than the rich one. That they who have no voice or vote in the electing of representatives, do not enjoy liberty, but are absolutely enslaved to those who have votes and their representatives; for to be enslaved is to have governors whom other men have set over us, and to be subject to laws made by the representatives of others, without having had representatives of our own to give consent in our behalf.

Suppose I read it with the feminine gender:

> That women who have no voice nor vote in the electing of representatives, do not enjoy liberty, but are absolutely enslaved to men who have votes and their representatives; for to be enslaved is to have governors whom men have set over us, and to be subject to the laws made by the representatives of men, without having representatives of our own to give consent in our behalf.

And yet one more authority; that of Thomas Paine, than whom not one of the Revolutionary patriots more able vindicated the principles upon which our government is founded:

> The right of voting for representatives is the primary right by which other rights are protected. To take away this right is to reduce man to a state of slavery; for slavery consists in being subject to the will of another; and he that has not a vote in the election of representatives is in this case. The proposal, therefore, to disfranchise any class of men is as criminal as

> the proposal to take away property.[34]

Is anything further needed to prove woman's condition of servitude sufficiently orthodox to entitle her to the guarantees of the fifteenth amendment?

Is there a man who will not agree with me, that to talk of freedom without the ballot, is mockery--is slavery--to the women of this Republic, precisely as New England's orator Wendell Phillips, at the close of the late war, declared it to be to the newly emancipated black men?[35]

I admit that prior to the rebellion, by common consent, the right to enslave, as well as to disfranchise both native and foreign born citizens, was conceded to the States. But the one grand principle, settled by the war and the reconstruction legislation, is the supremacy of national power to protect the citizens of the United States in their right to freedom and the elective franchise, against any and every interference on the part of the several States. And again and again, have the American people asserted the triumph of this principle, by their overwhelming majorities for Lincoln and Grant.

The one issue of the last two Presidential elections was, whether the fourteenth and fifteenth amendments should be considered the irrevocable will of the people; and the decision was, they shall be--and that it is not only the right, but duty of the National Government to protect all United States citizens in the full enjoyment and free exercise of all their privileges and immunities against any attempt of any State to deny

---

34 Thomas Paine (1737-1809) author of the pamphlet *Common Sense* (1776), which sparked the movement for independence from Britain in Philadelphia.

35 See headnote p. 188.

or abridge.

And in this conclusion Republicans and Democrats alike agree. Senator Frelinghuysen said: "The heresy of State rights has been completely buried in these amendments, that as amended, the Constitution confers not only national but State citizenship upon all persons born or naturalized within our limits."[36]

The Call for the National Republican Convention said: "Equal suffrage has been engrafted on the National Constitution; the privileges and immunities of American citizenship have become a part of the organic law."

The National Republican platform said: "Complete liberty and exact equality in the enjoyment of all civil, political and public rights, should be established and maintained throughout the Union by efficient and appropriate State and federal legislation."

If that means anything, it is that Congress should pass a law to require the States to protect women in their equal political rights, and that the States should enact laws making it the duty of inspectors of elections to receive women's votes on precisely the same conditions they do those of men.

Judge Stanley Mathews--a substantial Ohio Democrat--in his preliminary speech at the Cincinnati convention, said most emphatically: "The constitutional amendments have established the political equality of all citizens before the law."

President Grant, in his message to Congress March 30th, 1870, on the adoption of the fifteenth amendment, said: "A measure which makes at once four millions of people voters, is indeed a measure of greater importance than any act of the kind from the

---

[36] Frederick Theodore Frelinghuysen (1817-85), U.S. Senator from New Jersey (1866-69, 1871-77), U.S. Secretary of State (1881-85) under President Chester Alan Arthur.

foundation of the Government to the present time."

How could *four* millions [sic] negroes be made voters if *two* millions were not included?

The California State Republican Convention said: "Among the many practical and substantial triumphs of the principles achieved by the Republican party during the past twelve years, it enumerated with pride and pleasure, the prohibiting of any State from abridging the privileges of any citizen of the Republic, the declaring the civil and political equality of every citizen, and the establishing all these principles in the Federal Constitution by amendments thereto, as the permanent law."

Benjamin F. Butler, in a recent letter to me, said: "I do not believe anybody in Congress doubts that the Constitution authorizes the right of women to vote, precisely as it authorizes trial by jury and many other like rights guaranteed to citizens."[37]

And again, General Butler said:

> It is not laws we want; there are plenty of laws--good enough, too. Administrative ability to enforce law is the great want of the age, in this country especially. Everybody talks of law, law. If everybody would insist on the enforcement of law, the government would stand on a firmer basis, and questions would settle themselves.

And it is upon this just interpretation of the United States Constitution that our National Woman Suffrage Association which

---

[37] Benjamin F. Butler (1818-93), military governor of New Orleans (1862), radical Republican member of the House of Representatives (1867-75), one of the House managers who conducted the impeachment proceedings against President Andrew Johnson.

celebrates the twenty-fifth anniversary of the woman's rights movement in New York on the 6th of May next, has based all its arguments and action the past five years.

We no longer petition Legislature or Congress to give us the right to vote. We appeal to the women everywhere to exercise their too long neglected "citizen's right to vote." We appeal to the inspectors of election everywhere to receive the votes of all United States citizens as it is their duty to do. We appeal to United States commissioners and marshals to arrest the inspectors who reject the names and votes of United States citizens, as it is their duty to do, and leave those alone who, like our eighth ward inspectors, perform their duties faithfully and well.

We ask the juries to fail to return verdicts of "guilty" against honest, law-abiding, tax-paying United States citizens for offering their votes at our elections. Or against intelligent, worthy young men, inspectors of elections, for receiving and counting such citizens' votes.

We ask the judges to render true and unprejudiced opinions of the law, and wherever there is room for a doubt to give its benefit on the side of liberty and equal rights to women, remembering that "the true rule of interpretation under our national Constitution, especially since its amendments, is that anything for human rights is constitutional, everything against human rights is unconstitutional."

And it is on this line that we propose to fight our battle for the ballot--all peaceably, but nevertheless persistently through to complete triumph, when all United States citizens shall be recognized as equals before the law.

17

Frances E. Willard, A White Life for Two, *1890*

Frances E. Willard (1839-1898) was a founder of the Woman's Christian Temperance Union (WCTU) in 1874 and became its president in 1879, a position she held for the rest of her life. Under her leadership the WCTU grew to be the largest women's organization in the United States. The group led a movement dedicated not only to urging total abstinence from and legal prohibition of liquor but also to a broad range of other causes. Between national conventions, Willard became the Union's mouthpiece on long speaking tours, traveling more than 15,000 miles annually for over ten years, introducing the WCTU and its reforms to all areas of the country. Each summer she was a popular speaker at the Lake Chautauqua, NY, summer assembly. In 1880 the national convention endorsed "the ballot for woman as a weapon for the protection of her home."

Probably the most controversial aspect of Willard's career was her persistent attempt to use the WCTU to influence U.S. party politics. In 1880, she endorsed Republican presidential candidate James A. Garfield, who reneged on what she took to be his pledge to support prohibition and woman suffrage after election. In 1882 she persuaded the Prohibition party to endorse woman suffrage, a position reversed in 1884. In 1892, she hoped to secure a Populist commitment to prohibition and woman suffrage and to bring the Prohibition party into the Populist fold, but this plan ultimately failed.

Under Willard's able leadership the WCTU grew to a membership of 250,000 and succeeded in obtaining laws raising the age of consent to age sixteen for women in twenty states in which it had been lower, permitting local option, and requiring education about liquor in the public schools in most states. After her death, the WCTU narrowed its focus to advocacy of total abstinence from and prohibition of the manufacture and sale of liquor.

This speech reflects Willard's broad program of reform. It also illustrates the character of arguments from benefits or expediency and a highly romantic style adapted to the more traditional men and women in her audiences. Sections of it appeared in her speeches to annual WCTU conventions and in her other writings of this period. This version was published as a pamphlet in 1890, from which this text is taken (Willard 1890).

America may well be called "God's Country," a gracious Mother-land that women well might live to serve or die to save. For in America, home questions have become the living issues of the time, and "Home Protection" is the battle cry of preachers, publicists and politicians. The mighty war of words that culminated in the Presidential election of 1888, was waged on both sides in the interest of the home, but only on a materialistic money basis.[1] The three questions that alone

---

[1] The candidates in the election were incumbent Democrat Grover Cleveland, Republican Benjamin Harrison, Prohibitionist Clinton B. Fisk, and Alson J. Streeter of the Union Labor party. The issue was the tariff. With the support of businessmen who had grown rich from protectionism, Harrison won, but he received fewer popular votes than Cleveland,

engross our people are the Temperance, the Labor, and the Woman Questions, and these three agree in one. Only by convincing Labor that a high tariff meant material protection for the home, was that election won; only by convincing wage-workers and women that the outlawing of the saloon means protection for those who dwell within the home, will Prohibition ever gain the day; only by convincing wage-workers and temperance voters that through equal suffrage women will help to protect both the external and the internal interests of the home, will the Woman Question ever be wrought out in government. But beneath this trinity of issues is the fount from which they flow and that is Home itself, and back of Home is the one relationship that makes it possible. In view of this, I dare affirm that the reciprocal attraction of two natures, out of a thousand million, for each other, is the strongest, though one of the most unnoted proofs of a beneficent Creator. It is the fairest, sweetest Rose of Time, whose petals and whose perfume expand so far that we are all inclosed and sheltered in their tenderness and beauty. For, folded in its heart, we find the germ of every home; of those beatitudes, fatherhood and motherhood; the brotherly and sisterly affection, the passion of the patriot, the calm and steadfast love of the philanthropist. For the faithfulness of two, each to the other, alone makes possible the true home, the pure church, the righteous Nation, the great, kind brotherhood of man.

The inmost instincts of each human spirit must cry out to God,

> Comfort our souls with Love,
> Love of all human kind,
> Love special, close, in which like
> sheltered dove

---

and the outcome was influenced by bribery, intrigue, and fraud (Lorant 1953, 405).

Each heart its own safe nest may
find;
And Love that turns above adoringly,
contented to resign
All loves if need be, for the love
divine.

Marriage is not, as some surface-thinkers have endeavored to make out, an episode in man's life and an event in woman's. Sup your fill of horrors on the daily record of suicides by young men who are lovers, of sweethearts shot, and murdered wives, if you have ever fancied marriage to be the unequal thing that such phrasing indicates. Nay, it is the sum of earthly weal or woe to *both*. Doubtless there are in this modern land and age, almost as many noble men unmated because they had to be, as there are women. Because of a memory cherished, an estrangement unexplained, an ideal unrealized, a duty bravely met, many of the best men living go their way through life alone. Sometimes I think that of the two it is man who loves home best; for while woman is hedged into it by a thousand considerations of expediency and prejudice, he, "With all the world before him where to choose," still chooses home freely and royally for her sake who is to him the world's supreme attraction.

The Past has bequeathed us no records more sublime than the heart-histories of Dante,[2] of Petrarch,[3] of Michael Angelo,[4] and,

---

[2] Dante Alighieri (1265-1321), author of the *Divine Comedy (Inferno, Purgatorio, Paradiso)*, whose source of spiritual inspiration was a woman named Beatrice.

[3] Francesco Petrarca (1307-74), whose great vernacular love lyrics were inspired by a woman named Laura.

[4] See p. 202, n 9. Michelangelo dedicated many religious sonnets to Vitorria Colonna.

in our own time, of Washington Irving,[5] Henry Martyn[6] and others whom we dare not name. It was a chief among our own poets who said:--

> I look upon the stormy wild,
> I have no wife, I have no child;
> For me there gleams no household
> hearth
> I've none to love me on the earth.[7]

We know that "he who wrote home's sweetest song ne'er had one of his own,"[8] and our gracious Will Carleton sang concerning

---

[5] Washington Irving (1783-1859), American author of "Rip Van Winkle" and "The Legend of Sleepy Hollow." After the death of his fiancée, he sailed for Europe and remained there for 17 years.

[6] Henry Martyn (1781-1812), English missionary who from 1805 labored in India and Persia, superintending and partly preparing translations of the New Testament into Persian and Hindustani, and translated the Psalms into Persian. In his *Journal and Letters* (1851, 104), he wrote of the struggle between his love for Lydia Grenfell and his devotion to God. Ironically, Martyn was also author of a pamphlet entitled "Deceitfulness of the Heart" (1846).

[7] Bayard Taylor (1825-78), American poet and journalist best known for the poem *Bedouin Song*, is identified as the author of these lines in Willard's autobiography (1889, 605).

[8] Howard Payne (1791-1852), wrote the lyrics for the song "Home, Sweet Home" (music by Sir Henry Bishop) that appeared in his play, *Clari, the Maid of Milan* (1823). He unsuccessfully courted Mary Wollstonecraft Shelley, author of *Frankenstein*, daughter of Mary Wollstonecraft and William Godwin, and widow of the poet Percy Bysshe Shelley.

John Howard Payne--

> Sure, when thy gentle spirit fled
> To lands beyond the azure dome,
> With arms out-stretched God's angels said,
> "Welcome to Heaven's home, sweet home."[9]

There are men and women--some of them famous, some unknown--the explanation of whose uncompanioned lives may be found in the principle that underlies those memorable words applied to [George] Washington: "Heaven left him childless that a Nation might call him Father."

In such considerations as I have here urged, and in this noblest side of human nature, a constant factor always to be counted on, I found my faith in the response of the people to the work of promoting social purity. "Sweet bells jangled, out of tune," now fill the air with minor cadences, often, alas, with discords that are heart-breaks, but all the same they are "sweet bells," and shall chime the gladdest music heaven has heard, "Some sweet day, by and by." This gentle age into which we have happily been born, is attuning the twain whom God hath made for such great destiny, to higher harmonies than any other age has known, by a reform in the denaturalizing methods of a civilization largely based on force, by which the boy and girl have been sedulously trained apart. They are now being set side by side in school, in church, in government, even as God sets male and female everywhere side by side throughout His realm

---

[9] Will Carleton (1845-1912), American poet known for his sentimental poems of rural life, author of *Farm Ballads* (1873), *Farm Legends* (1875) and *City Ballads* (1885). Lines in praise of John Howard Payne are found in *City Ballads* (1885, 175-76) although not as Willard quoted them here.

of law, and has declared them one throughout His realm of grace. Meanwhile, the conquest, through invention, of matter by mind, lifts woman from the unnatural subjugation of the age of force. In the presence of a Corliss engine, which she could guide as well as he, but which is an equal mystery to them both, men and women learn that they are fast equalizing on the plane of matter, as a prediction of their confessed equalization upon the planes of mind and of morality.[10]

We are beginning to train those with each other who were formed for each other, and the American Home, with its Christian method of a two-fold headship, based on laws natural and divine, is steadily rooting out all that remains of the mediaeval continental and harem philosophies concerning this greatest problem of all time. The true relations of that complex being whom God created by uttering the mystic thought that had in it the potency of Paradise: "In our *own* image let *us* make man, and let *them* have dominion over all the earth" [Gen. 1:26], will ere long be ascertained by means of the new correlation and attuning, each to other, of a more complete humanity upon the Christ-like basis that "*there shall be no more curse*" [Rev. 22:3; Gal. 3:13]. The Temperance Reform is this correlation's necessary and true fore-runner, for while the race-brain is bewildered it can not be thought out. The Labor Reform is another part, for only under co-operation can material conditions be adjusted to a non-combatant state of society, and every yoke lifted from the laboring man lifts one still heavier from the woman at his side. The Equal Suffrage

---

[10] An engine using the valve gear invented in 1849 by G.H. Corliss of Providence, RI, a trip gear in which a central wrist plate, moved by an eccentric rod, operates four rocking valves, one steam valve, and one exhaust valve at each end of the cylinder.

Movement is another part, for a government organized and conducted by one half the human unit, a government of the minority, by the minority, for the minority, must always bear unequally upon the whole. The Social Purity Movement could only come after its heralds, the three other reforms I have mentioned, were well under way, because alcoholized brains would not tolerate its expression; women who had not learned to work would lack the individuality and intrepidity required to organize it, and women perpetually to be disfranchised, could not hope to see its final purposes wrought out in law.[11] But back of all were the father and mother of all reforms--Christianity and Education--to blaze the way for all these later comers.

The Woman's Christian Temperance Union is doing no work more important than that of reconstructing the ideal of womanhood. The sculptor Hart told me, when I visited his studio in Florence many years ago, that he was investing his life to work into marble a new feminine type which should "express, unblamed," the Twentieth Century's womanhood.[12] The Venus de [sic] Medici, with its small head and button-hole eyelids matched the Greek conception of woman well, he thought, but America was slowly evolving another and a loftier type. His statue, named by him, "Woman Triumphant," and purchased by patriotic ladies of his native state, Kentucky, adorns the city hall at Lexington, and shows

---

[11] In 1885, Willard became superintendent of the WCTU's controversial Department of Social Purity (also referred to as the White Shield-White Cross Program), which was concerned with age of consent laws, prostitution, and sex education (Dow 1987, 62; Bordin 1981, 110-11).

[12] Joel T. Hart (1810-77).

A perfect woman, nobly planned,
To warn, to comfort, and command;
A creature not too bright or good,
For human nature's daily food,
And yet a spirit pure and bright,
With something of an angel's
light.[13]

She is the embodiment of what shall be. In an age of force, woman's greatest grace was to cling; in this age of peace she doesn't cling much, but is every bit as tender and as sweet as if she did. She has strength and individuality, a gentle seriousness; there is more of the sisterly, less of the syren [sic] --more of the duchess and less of the doll. Woman is becoming what God meant her to be, and Christ's Gospel necessitates her being, the companion and counsellor not the incumbrance and toy of man.

To meet this new creation, how grandly men themselves are growing; how considerate and brotherly, how pure in word and deed! The world has never yet known half the aptitude of character and life to which men will attain when they and women live in the *same* world. It doth not yet appear what they shall be, or we either, for that matter, but in many a home presided over by a Temperance voter and a White Ribbon worker, I have thought the Heavenly Vision was really coming down to terra firma.

With all my heart I believe, as do the best men of the nation, that woman will bless and brighten every place she enters, and that she will enter every place on the round earth. Its welcome of her presence and her power will be the final test of any institution's fitness to survive.

---

[13] William Wordsworth, "She was a Phantom of Delight." "A perfect woman nobly planned/ To warn, to comfort, and command" was often quoted by feminist abolitionists to describe their ideal woman (Hersh 1978, 152 n 1).

Happily for us, every other genuine reform helps to push forward the white car of Social Purity. The great Peace Movement, seeking as its final outcome a Court of International Arbitration as a substitute for war, promises more momentum to our home cause than to almost any other. For as the chief corner-stone of the peaceful State is the hearthstone, so the chief pulverizer of that corner-stone is war.

An organized and systematic work for the promotion of Social Purity was undertaken in 1885 by the Woman's Christian Temperance Union. Under the three subdivisions of Preventive, Reformatory and Legal Work, this society has gone steadily forward until the White Cross Pledge, appealing to the chivalry of men, has grown familiar in thousands of homes, and the White Shield Pledge, appealing to the chivalry of women, is following fast after the first.

Its pledges are based on the belief that you can not in mature years get out of a character what was not built into it when the youthful nature was like "wax to receive and marble to retain"; that the *arrest of thought* must be secured by mother, minister and teacher, before the common talk of street and play-ground has wrenched that thought away from the white line of purity and truth. Innocence may be founded on ignorance, but virtue is ever more based upon knowledge. In the presence of temptation one is a rope of sand, the other, a keen Damascus blade. To be forewarned is the only way to be fore-armed. A precipice lies before every boy and girl when they emerge beyond the sheltering fortress of their home, but a safe, sure path leads around it; we must gently warn them of the one; we must tenderly lead them to the other.

The personal habits of men and women must reach the same high level. On a low plane and for selfish ends primeval and mediaeval man wrought out, with fiercest cruelty, virtue as the only tolerated estate of one-half the human race. On a high plane Christianity working through modern womanhood, shall yet make virtue the only tolerated estate of the other half of the human race, and may Heaven speed that day! A woman knows that she must walk the straight line of a true life or men will look upon her with disdain. A man needs, for his own best good, to find that in the eyes of women, just the same is true of him.

Evermore be it remembered, this earnest effort to bring in the day of "sweeter manners, purer laws" is as much in man's interest as our own.

Why are the laws so shamelessly unequal now? Why do they bear so heavily upon the weaker, making the punishment for stealing away a woman's honor no greater than that for stealing a silk gown; purloining her character at a smaller penalty than the picking of a pocket would incur? Why is the age of protection or consent but ten years in twenty States, and in one, only seven years? Who would have supposed, when man's great physical strength is considered, he would have fixed upon an age so tender, and declared that after a child had reached it, she should be held equally accountable with her doughty assailant for a crime in which he was the aggressor? And who would not suppose that the man who had been false to one woman would be socially ostracized by all the rest of womankind? What will explain the cruelty of men and the heartlessness of women in this overmastering issue of womanhood's protection and manhood's loyalty?

The answer is not far to seek. Women became, in barbarous ages, the subjects of the stronger. Besides, what suits one age becomes a hindrance to the next, and as Christianity went on individualizing woman, uplifting her to higher levels of education and hence of power, the very laws which good men in the past had meant for her protection, became to her a snare and danger.

But, while all this heritage of a less developed past has wrought such anguish and injustice upon woman as she is to-day, it has been even more harmful to man, for it is always worse for character to be sinning than to be sinned against. Our laws and social customs make it too easy for men to do wrong. They are not sufficiently protected by the strong hand of penalty, from themselves, from the sins that do most easily beset them, and from the mad temptations that clutch at them on every side. Suppose the outragers of women, whose unutterable abominations crowd the criminal columns of our newspapers each day, knew that life-long imprisonment might be the penalty, would not the list of their victims rapidly diminish? The Woman's Christian Temperance Union has taken up this sacred cause of protection for the home, and we shall never cease our efforts until women have all the help that law can furnish them throughout America. We ask for heavier penalties, and that the age of consent be raised to eighteen years; we ask for the total prohibition of the liquor traffic, which is leagued with every crime that is perpetrated against the physically weaker sex, and we ask for the ballot, that law and law-maker may be directly influenced by our instincts of self-protection and home protection.

We hear much of physical culture for boys, but it is girls that need this most. We hear much of manual training schools to furnish every boy at school with a bread-winning weapon; but in the interest of boys and girls alike, girls need this most. Hence it is in our plans to work for these. Mothers' Meetings are becoming one of the most familiar features of the W.C.T.U. For these we prepare programs, leaflets, and courses of reading at the Woman's Temperance Publishing House, Chicago, from which hundreds of thousands of pledges and pages of literature have gone, as pure and elevated in style and spirit as consecrated pens could render them.

REFORMATORY WORK is the most difficult of all and yet has been of all others most earnestly carried forward thus far by women.

Matrons have been placed in the police stations to look after arrested women, Reading Rooms, Lodging Houses and Industrial Homes for women are multiplying now on every hand. State care for moral as well as mental incapables is being urged and with some small beginnings of success. Statistics of such work are difficult to gain. A single fact vouched for by the women who have in charge one of these homes in Massachusetts, is fitted to encourage every worker in this trying field. They tell us that one woman who had been arrested forty-five times was taken to the home, lifted by kindness from the depths, put into self-supporting lines and for seven years has been an honorable, hard-working woman, happy in her rescued life.

The awful deeds done by white men in the great woods of Alaska, the brutal relations of our soldiery to the Indian women of the plains; the unspeakable atrocities of the lumber camps in Wisconsin and in Michigan; the daily calendar of crimes against women as set forth by the press, and the blood-curdling horrors of Whitechapel, London, have aroused the civilized world.[14] Womanhood's loyalty to woman has overleaped the silence and reserve of centuries and Christendom rings with her protest to-day. It is now the deliberate purpose of as capable and trusty women as live, that the *laissez-faire* method of dealing with these crimes against nature, shall cease; that the method of license, high or low, shall never be for one moment tolerated, and that the prohibitory method shall come and come to stay.

Within three years immense advances have been made in legislation. England has cleared the Blue Books of the "Contagious Diseases

---

[14] The reference is to Jack the Ripper, the psychopathic killer who, between August 31 and November 9, 1888, stabbed 5 prostitutes to death in the Whitechapel slums of East London.

Acts";[15] has repealed the atrocious army regulations of India, and raised the age of protection to sixteen years. America is moving forward rapidly, improved legislation having been obtained in almost every State and Territory. The following petition is being everywhere circulated and its plea, already partially responded to in several States, is now before the National Congress:

> The increasing and alarming frequency of assaults upon women, and the frightful indignities to which even little girls are subject, have become the shame of our boasted civilization. A study of the Statutes has revealed their utter failure to meet the demands of that newly awakened public sentiment which requires better legal protection for womanhood and girlhood. Therefore we do most earnestly appeal to you to enact such statutes as shall provide for the adequate punishment of crimes against women and girls.

But, as I have said, we are not working for ourselves alone in this great cause of Social Purity. As an impartial friend to the whole human race in both its fractions, man and woman, I, for one, am not more in earnest

---

[15] Parliament passed acts in 1864, 1866, and 1869 that made it obligatory for any woman merely suspected of being a prostitute in the ports and army towns where the laws applied to report to a police station to be inspected for venereal disease. The campaign against them was led by Josephine Butler, who had worked among prostitutes in Liverpool and who believed all women were debased by these acts because "in them the buying and selling of the female body was sanctified by statute law" (Forster 1985, 170).

for this great advance because of the good it brings to the gentler than because of the blessing that it prophesies for the stronger sex. I have long believed that when that greatest of all questions, the question of a life companionship, shall be decided on its merits, pure and simple, and not complicated with the other questions, "Did she get a good home?" "Is he a generous provider?" "Will she have plenty of money?" then will come the first fair chance ever enjoyed by young manhood for the building up of genuine character and conduct. For it is an immense temptation to the "sowing of wild oats," when the average youth knows that the smiles he covets most will be his all the same, no matter whether he smokes, swears, drinks beer and leads an impure life, or not. The knowledge on his part that the girls of his village or "set" have no way out of dependence, reproach or oddity except to say "yes" when he chooses to "propose"; that they dare not frown on his lower mode of life; that the world is indeed all before him where to choose; that not one girl in one hundred is endowed with the talent and pluck that make her independent of him and his ilk--all this gives him a sense of freedom to do wrong which, added to inherited appetite and outward temptation, is impelling to ruin the youth of our day with a force strong as gravitation and relentless as fate. Besides all this, the utterly false sense of his own value and importance which "Young America" acquires from seeing the sweetest and most attractive beings on earth thus virtually subject to him, often develops a lordliness of manner which is ridiculous to contemplate in boys who, otherwise would be modest, sensible and brotherly young fellows such as we are most of all likely to find in co-educational schools, where girls take their full share of prizes, and where many young women have in mind a European trip with some girl friend, or mayhap 'a career.'

Multiplied forces in law and gospel are

to-day conspiring for the deliverance of our young men from the snares of the present artificial environment and estimate of their own value; but the elevation of their sisters to the plane of perfect financial and legal independence, from which the girls can dictate the equitable terms, "You must be as pure and true as you require me to be, ere I give you my hand," is the brightest hope that gleams in the sky of modern civilization for our brothers; and the greater freedom of women to make of marriage an affair of the heart and not of the purse, is the supreme result of Christianity, up to this hour.

There is no man whom women honor so deeply and sincerely, as the man of chaste life; the man who breasts the buffetings of temptation's swelling waves, like some strong swimmer in his agony, and makes the port of perfect self-control. Women have a thousand guarantees and safeguards for their purity of life. "Abandon hope, all ye who enter here," is written in letters of flame for them above the haunt of infamy, while men may come and go and are yet smilingly received in the most elegant homes.[16] But in spite of all this accursed latitude, how many men are pure and true!

It is said, that when darkness settles on the Adriatic Sea, and fishermen are far from land, their wives and daughters, just before putting out the lights in their humble cottages, go down by the shore and in their clear, sweet voices sing the first lines of the Ave Maria. Then they listen eagerly, and across the sea are borne to them the deep tones of those they love, singing the strains that follow, "Ora pro nobis," and thus each knows that with the other all is well. I often think that from the home-life of the Nation, from its mothers and sisters, daughters and sweethearts, there sounds through the

---

[16] These words appear on the gates of hell in Dante's *Inferno*.

darkness of this transition age the tender notes of a dearer song, whose burden is being taken up and echoed back to us from those far out amid the billows of temptation, and its sacred words are, "Home, Sweet Home!" God grant that deeper and stronger may grow that heavenly chorus from men's and women's lips and lives! For with all its faults, and they are many, I believe the present marriage system to be the greatest triumph of past Christianity, and that it has created and conserves more happy homes than the world has ever before known. Any law that renders less binding the mutual, life-long loyalty of one man and woman to each other, which is the central idea of every home, is an unmitigated curse to that home and to humanity. Around this union, which alone renders possible a pure society, and a permanent state, the law should build its utmost safeguards, and upon this union the gospel should pronounce its most sacred benedictions. But while I hold these truths to be self-evident, I believe that a constant evolution is going forward in the home as in every other place, and that we may have but dimly dreamed the good in store for those whom God for holiest love hath made.

In the nature of the case, the most that even Christianity itself could do at first, though it is the strongest force ever let loose upon the planet, was to separate one man and one woman from the common herd, into each home, telling the woman to remain there in grateful quietness, while the man stood at the door to defend its sacred shrine with fist and spear, to insist upon its rights of property, and later on, to represent it in the State. Thus, under the conditions of a civilization crude and material, grew up that well-worn maxim of the common law, "Husband and wife are one, and that one is the husband." But such supreme power as this brought to the man supreme temptation. By the laws of mind he legislated first for himself and afterward for the physically weaker one within "his" home. The *femme couverte* is not a character appropriate to our peaceful, home-like communities, although she may have been and doubtless was a necessary figure in the days when women were safe only as they were shut up in castles and when they were the booty chiefly sought in war. To-day a woman may circumnavigate the world alone and yet be unmolested. Our marriage laws and customs are changing to meet these new conditions. It will not do to give the husband of the modern woman power to whip his wife, "provided the stick he uses is not larger than his finger"; to give him the right to will away her unborn child; to have control over her property; to make all the laws under which she is to live; adjudicate all her penalties; try her before juries of men; conduct her to prison under the care of men; cast the ballot for her; and in general, hold her in the estate of a perpetual minor. It will not do to let the modern man determine the age of "consent," settle the penalties that men should suffer whose indignities and outrages upon women are worse than death, and by his exclusive power to make all laws and choose all officers, judicial and executive, thus leaving his own case wholly in his own hands. To continue this method is to make it as hard as possible for men to do right, and as easy as possible for them to do wrong; the magnificent possibilities of manly character are best prophesied from the fact that under such a system so many men are good and gracious. My theory of marriage in its relation to society would give this postulate. Husband and wife are one, and that one is--husband and wife. I believe they will never come to the heights of purity, of power and peace, for which they were designed in heaven, until this better law prevails. One undivided half of the world for wife and husband equally; co-education to mate them on the plane of mind; equal property rights to make her God's own free woman, not coerced into marriage for the sake of support, nor a bond-slave after she is married, who asks her master for the price of a paper of pins, and gives him back the change; or, if she be a petted favorite, who owes the freedom of his purse wholly to his will and never to her right; woman left free to go her honored and self-respecting way as a maiden *in perpetuo*, rather than marry a man whose deterioration through the alcohol and nicotine habits is a deadly menace to herself and the descendants that such a marriage has invoked--these are the outlooks of the future that shall make the marriage system, never a failure since it became monogamous, an assured, a permanent, a paradisiacal [sic] success.

In that day the wife shall surrender at marriage no right not equally surrendered by the husband, not even her own name. Emile Ollivier, that keen-sighted writer of France, says that it is so much easier, for obvious reasons, to trace ancestry along the mother's line, that historic records have incalculably suffered by the arbitrary relinquishment of her name.[17] Probably the French have hit upon the best expedient--the union of the two. Thus I recall that in Paris my home was with an accomplished lady whose name was Farjon and whose husband's was Perrot; her visiting card always bore the inscription:

MADAME EGLANTINE PERROT-FARJON.

The growing custom, in this country at least, to give the mother's name to son or daughter indicates the increasing, though perhaps unconscious, recognition of woman as an equal partner in the marriage bond. But

---

[17] Emile Ollivier (1825-1913), a leading figure in the "Liberal Empire" of Napoleon III. He formed a new ministry in 1870 that instituted sweeping constitutional reforms, transforming the empire into a parliamentary regime. These gains were offset by the Franco-Prussian war into which the regime plunged France, in which she lost both Alsace and Lorraine.

the custom, even among men of intelligence, of signing themselves, "John Jones, wife, child and nurse," as we see it in the registers of fashionable hotels, is a frequent reminder of the pit from which wives are slowly being digged. The man who writes "Mr. John and Mrs. Jane Jones," may be regarded as well on the road to a successful evolution; though "Mr. and Mrs. John Jones" seems to most of us about the correct thing up to this date!

The time will come when the mother's custody of children will constructively be preferred in law to that of the father, on the ground that it is surer and more consonant with natural laws. Last of all, and chiefest, the *magnum opus* of Christianity, and Science, which is its handmaid, the wife will have undoubted custody of herself, and as in all the lower ranges of the animal creation, she will determine the frequency of the investiture of life with form. My library groans under accumulations of books written by men to teach women the immeasurable iniquity of arrested development in the genesis of a new life, but not one of these volumes contains the remotest suggestion that this responsibility should be equally divided between husband and wife. The untold horrors of this injustice dwarf all others out of sight, and the most hopeless feature of it is the utter unconsciousness with which it is perpetuated. But better days are dawning; the study of heredity and pre-natal influences is flooding with light the Via Dolorosa of the past; the White Cross army with its equal standard of purity for men and women is moving to its rightful place of leadership among the hosts of God's elect.

> Then reign the world's chaste bridals, chaste and calm,
> Then springs the crowning race of humankind.
> *May these things be*!

I believe in uniform national marriage laws; in divorce for one cause only; in legal separation on account of drunkenness; but I would guard the marriage tie by every guarantee that could make it at the top of society, the most coveted estate of the largest-natured and most endowed, rather than at the bottom, the necessary refuge of the smallest-natured and most dependent women. Besides all this, in the interest of men--i.e., that their incentives to the best life might be raised to the highest power--I would make women so independent of marriage that men who, by bad habits and niggardly estate, whether physical, mental or moral, were least adapted to help build a race of human angels, should find the facility with which they now enter its hallowed precincts reduced to the lowest minimum. Until God's laws are better understood and more reverently obeyed, marriage cannot reach its best. The present abnormal style of dress among women, heavily mortgages the future of their homes and more heavily discounts that of their children. Add to this the utter recklessness of immortal consequences that characterizes the mutual conduct of so many married pairs and only the everlasting tendency toward good that renders certain the existence and supremacy of a Goodness that is infinite, can explain so much health and happiness as our reeling old world persists in holding while it rolls onward toward some far-off perfection, bathed in the sunshine of our Father's Omnipotent Love. Our own Julia Ward Howe has given us our noblest motto for Social Purity:[18]

---

[18] Julia Ward Howe (1819-1910), woman's club and suffrage leader, who published "Battle Hymn of the Republic," from which the cited lines are quoted, in the *Atlantic Monthly*, February 1862. The poem was set to the tune of "John Brown's Body," and by 1864 had swept the North and made its author famous. In 1868 Ward Howe founded the New

In the beauty of the lilies Christ
was born across the sea;
With a glory in his bosom that
transfigures you and me;
As He died to make men holy, let us
die to make men free,
While God is marching on.

England Woman's Club and, with others, the New England Woman Suffrage Association; she later became a leader in the American Woman Suffrage Association, in 1870 founding, with others, the *Woman's Journal*.

18

Matilda Joslyn Gage, "The Dangers of the Hour," Women's National Liberal Convention, 1890

Matilda Joslyn Gage (1826-98) was the daughter of a physician who supervised her study of Greek, mathematics, and physiology, and who sent her to the Clinton, NY, Liberal Institute to complete her education. She entered public life at the National Woman's Rights Convention held in Syracuse, NY, in 1852. She joined the National Woman Suffrage Association at its inception in 1869 and was a contributor to the **Revolution.** *She assisted Susan B. Anthony in her defense of her vote in 1872 by speaking throughout Ontario County. In 1875, she became head of the National and New York State Woman Suffrage Associations; in 1876, she co-authored the "Declaration of Rights" presented at the centennial celebration of independence in Philadelphia; in 1879, she became president of the National Woman Suffrage Association. She edited the* **National Citizen and Ballot Box** (1878-81), *wrote pamphlets, and, with Elizabeth Cady Stanton and Anthony, edited the first three volumes of the* **History of Woman Suffrage** (1881-86).

Joslyn Gage believed that the teachings of the churches were the major obstacle to woman's emancipation. When, in 1890, the National Woman Suffrage Association merged with its still more conservative rival, the American Woman Suffrage Association, she left the organization to form a more radical organization, the Woman's National Liberal Union, which she led until her death. Her book, **Woman, Church, and State** (1891) *developed her anti-clerical views at length. The speech that follows was delivered at the first national convention of her new organization and subsequently was printed as a pamphlet. Its blunt tone contrasts sharply to that of Coffin Mott in 1849; the positions it espouses contrast sharply to those of Frances Willard. Its attitude toward organized religion was reflected in the* **Woman's Bible** (1895, 1898), *edited by Cady Stanton. It addresses issues regarding the separation of church and state that remain contemporary.*

The text is taken from a copy of the pamphlet found in the Matilda Joslyn Gage Papers at the Schlesinger Library of Radcliffe (Gage 1890). *Capitalization has been made consistent and, on rare occasions, punctuation has been added for clarity.*

For one hundred and fourteen years we have seen our country gradually advancing in recognition of broader freedom, fewer restrictions upon personal liberty, and the peoples of all nations looking towards us as the great exemplar of political and religious freedom. But of late a rapidly increasing tendency has been shown towards the destruction of our civil liberties. The work has been stealthily carried on for a number of years under names and purposes which have prevented a real recognition of the design in view. So strong has this movement now become that we are confronted by the fact that our form of government is undergoing a radical change, with a well organized body greedy for power pressing to that end so that centralization instead of diffused power has overcome the aim and intent of a large body of people, a fact that can be traced to the war of the sixties[1] and the condition of the country immediately

---

[1] The Civil War.

afterwards. Personal freedom is now threatened by two foes, alike in character although differing in name, centralization and clericalism, ever the great antagonists to liberty. The control of questions which should be entirely left with the respective States in being gradually assumed by the United States. It has been said that the war proved one thing--our nationality; it seems likely to prove much more--the destruction of local self-government, which is becoming gradually lost. This general tendency towards centralizing power in the nation is a vast help to those persons who wish to incorporate certain religious dogmas in the Federal Constitution. The Constitution is superior to all statutory enactments and for this reason the Christian party in politics is not content that laws favoring it should be enacted by Congress alone, but aim to secure a constitutional amendment of like character. Albion Tourgee[2] says our conservatism consists in doing nothing until it is absolutely necessary. Americans never move until the fifty-ninth minute of the eleventh hour. The fifty-ninth minute is now upon us. (*Applause*.) There is an impending struggle greater in its influence upon humanity than the one fought for freedom thirty years since. The government is undergoing changes which are signs of danger. The red signal is out, if you are color blind and cannot see it the more the pity for you. An unreasoning confidence is the chronic state of the people. To them it does not seem possible there is danger to their free inheritance. They forget that liberty must

---

[2] Albion Winegar Tourgee (1838-1905), judge of the North Carolina Supreme Court, and author of novels of the South during Reconstruction, of which the most popular was *A Fool's Errand* (1879). He was also U.S. consul in Bordeaux (1897-1903).

ever be guarded. They forget the hereditary enslavement, the bondage of the human will to the church, and thousands bound do not heed this enslavement--to them it seems liberty. In 1889, four new States were admitted to the union, not one possessing a republican form of government as required by the Federal Constitution, not one recognizing the rights of one-half their citizens to self-government.[3] The defeat of woman suffrage was remarkable because in each of these four States a battle was fought in its favor by women. The new state of Washington is especially noticeable as three times under territorial laws woman had gained and used the ballot. Eighteen hundred and eighty-nine will not soon be forgotten by the friends of woman suffrage. Forty-one years after the first convention making such demand, four new States which at that period were unknown portions of the world, their very names yet to be given, if at all on geography or atlas, noted as desert lands, but now possessing tens of thousands of inhabitants, have this year come into the union denying the first principles upon which this government purports to be founded, equality of rights and self-government. We are told the country is in a dangerous condition with tens of thousands uncultured emigrants yearly pouring onto its shores; we are told our flag is hissed by anarchists who have 25,000 drilled men at their command; we are told the experiment of free government in towns and cities is a failure, but what danger from ignorant emigrants so great, what peril from anarchists so near, what experiment of free government such an utter failure as the admission of four new States largely populated by native-born American citizens, men and women of eastern birth, the young, the cultured, wide-awake business men and business women, under denial of the first principles of

---

[3] Washington, Montana, North and South Dakota.

freedom?

The danger menacing our country does not lie with the foreigners, nor the Anarchists, nor in municipal mismanagement. Free institutions are jeopardized because the country is false to its principles in the case of one-half of its citizens. But back of this falsity away down to the depths of causes deep in the hidden darkness of men's minds, must we look for the source of this perennial wrong. To a person of thought this is easily found in early religious training. Men have not yet learned to regard woman as a being of equal creation with themselves; do not yet believe that she stands on a par with them in natural rights even to the air she breathes. In order to secure victory for woman we must unfetter the minds of men from religious bondage. We have petitioned legislatures and Congress, we have appeared before committees with the best arguments founded on justice, we have educated men politically, and yet the victory is not ours because the teachings of the church have stood in the way. Now our warfare must be upon another plan[e], now we must free men from that bondage of the will which is the most direful form of slavery, now we must show the falsity of that reed upon which men lean. In the old anti-slavery times men did not hesitate to call the American Church the bulwark of American slavery. In like manner to-day, we shall proclaim the Church--American, English, Greek, Protestant, Catholic--to be the bulwark of woman's slavery. Man trained by the church from infancy that woman is secondary and inferior to him, made for him, to be obedient to him, the same idea permeating the Jewish and all Christian churches, all social, industrial and educational life, all civil and religious institutions, it is no subject of astonishment, if one gives a moment's thought, that woman's political enfranchisement is so long delayed.

In the State of Washington where suffrage for woman had in its territorial days been so long and so happily tried there were never better laid plans to bring about its defeat in the new constitution. Miss [Matilda] Hindman, who spoke throughout the territory in its favor, says there were three political parties in the field all *as parties* opposed to woman suffrage, even its old friends among men refusing to speak for it lest it should delay statehood; the churches also refusing to take it up or advocate it on the specious ground that it was a political question, those ministers solitary and few who did favor it doing so not because of justice nor even because the basic principles of the nation demanded it, but "that woman might vote for temperance," or aid some plan of the church.

It has not been without bitter resistance by the clergy that woman's property and educational rights have advanced. Woman's anti-slavery work--her temperance work, her demand for personal rights, for political equality, for religious freedom and every step of kindred character has met with opposition from the church as a body and from the clergy as exponents of its views.

The St. Louis *Globe-Democrat* in an editorial of May 5, 1888, said:

> There is no more striking anomaly in the history of civilization than the fact that the churches have profited in the greatest degree by the devotion of women, and yet have been among the slowest of organized institutions to concede to the sex the rights and advantages which it has managed to obtain. Most of the work done for the improvement of woman's condition as a member of society has been accomplished, not without a certain measure of Church sympathy, but without distinct and aggressive Church support. We refer particularly to the removal of invidious legal restrictions, and the development of sentiments of justice and fairness with regard to

woman's political interests, and her relation to the philosophy of general progress.

Many insidious steps by both Catholic and Protestant prove the church now, as of old, the enemy of freedom. In 1884, a Plenary Council, preceded by an encyclical from the Pope laying out its line of work,[4] was held in Baltimore. The two points against which the effort of the church is now chiefly directed, are marriage and public schools. In its control of these two questions it has ever found its chief sources of power. The Pope's encyclical declared that "civil marriage must be resented by the whole Catholic world." The establishment of parochial schools in every parish was also commanded within two years unless excused therefrom by the bishop.

In compliance with papal demand the Plenary Council formulated decrees against marriage as a civil act, or as under civil authority; against marriage with a Protestant, and against evening marriages. The sacramental character of the rite was solemnly affirmed, the necessity of priestly benediction and nuptial mass enforced. But well knowing the immediate promulgation of its decrees would rouse public attention to its aim, these were held in abeyance until such times as the dignitaries of the church deemed best. Not until three years later were the canons upon marriage made known on the Pacific Coast, at which time the archbishop of San Francisco, the bishops of Monterey, Los Angeles, and Grass Valley, addressed a pastoral letter to the Catholics of that region condemning civil marriage as a sin and sacrilege, illegal, and a "horrible concubinage." Marriage with a Protestant was also

---

[4] Leo XIII's encyclical *Arcanum* (On Christian marriage), dated February 10, 1880, may be found in English in *American Catholic Quarterly Review*, 5 (April 1880): 346-61.

forbidden, and marriage unblessed by a priest it was declared, subjected the parties to excommunication.

When the territory about my own city of Syracuse was formed into a diocese, one of the first acts of its newly appointed bishop was a prohibition against evening marriages. Archbishop Ryan of Philadelphia has commanded the observance of these decrees in his diocese enjoining nuptial mass, &c. The bishop of Savannah, Ga., some time since issued an order prohibiting marriages after nightfall, and thus have these decrees been gradually brought to bear over different portions of the country.

It must be remembered that the Baltimore council was a body composed wholly of celibates governed by the chief celibate, the Pope of Rome, and that it decided upon a question of which it possessed no practical knowledge. It must also be recollected that no woman's voice was heard in this council in regard to a relation in which as wife, she takes an equal, and as mother a superior part. The judgment of these celibate men was alone to decide upon the form, obligation, validity and permanence of marriage, the church threatening penalties for their non-observance. In the decrees upon marriage of this council and the preceding encyclical, two points are especially to be borne in mind. First, that woman is the chief victim--not alone the question decided without her voice but its indissolubility pressing most heavily upon her. For it must be remembered that while the church asserts marriage to be an indissoluble sacrament, her past history shows it to have been in the power of man, of the husband, to secure that release from its bonds that has ever been denied to the wife.

The second point not to be forgotten, is that the power possessed by the church during the middle ages was largely due to the control it had secured over domestic relations, and that no more severe blow has ever been inflicted upon it than the institution of civil marriage. This fact is well known to the church and its persistent effort to again secure control of this relation is for the purpose of once more acquiring the power it has lost in those countries where civil marriage exists. Wherever established by the state it has met with determined opposition by the church. Historians agree as to the power the church acquired by its hold upon marriage. Lecky says that when religious marriages were alone recognized they were a potent instrument in securing the power of the priesthood who were able to compel men to submit to the conditions they imposed in the formation of the most important contract in life.[5]

Draper also declares the secret of much of the influence of the church in the middle ages lay in the control she has so skillfully gained over domestic life.[6] The authority of the church over marriage has always been especially prejudicial to woman; it is from teachings of the church, that in the family, power over the wife is given to the husband. It is the church and not the state, to which the teaching of woman's inferiority is due; it is the church which primally [sic] commanded the obedience of woman to man. It is the church which stamps with religious authority the political and domestic degradation of woman. It is the church which has placed

---

[5] William Edward Hartpole Lecky (1838-1903), British historian, author of *History of the Rise and Influence of the Spirit of Rationalism in Europe* (1865), *History of European Morals from Augustus to Charlemagne* (1869), and his masterpiece, *History of England in the Eighteenth Century* (8 vol., 1878-90).

[6] Lyman Copeland Draper (1815-91), founder and corresponding secretary of the State Historical Society of Wisconsin.

itself in opposition to all efforts looking towards her enfranchisement and it has done this under professed divine authority, and wherever we find laws of the state bearing with greater hardship upon woman than upon man, we shall ever find them due to the teachings of the church.

But while I have first referred to the encyclical of the Pope and the action of the plenary council, upon this question of marriage, Catholics are scarcely more greedy for power over this relation than are Protestants. The church has ever been a barrier to advancing civilization; when it was the strongest at the time spoken of, when it possessed the greatest control over marriage, civilization was at the lowest.

The Protestant pulpit is only less dangerous than the Catholic to the liberties of the people in that its organized strength is less. The old mediaeval control of the family under and through marriage is now as fully the aim of the Protestant church as of the Catholic. The General Episcopal convention has not convened of late years without canvassing the question of marriage and divorce. In 1886 a most stringent Canon upon this relation was proposed and although it failed of adoption, a similar effort was made at the recent triennial convention in New York the fall of 1889.

The Rev. George Z. Gray, dean of the Episcopal Theological School in Cambridge, Mass., is author of a book in which he asserts, referring to scripture as authority, that marriage is not a contract between equals, but an appropriation of the woman by the man, the wife becoming merged in him and owing him obedience, the right of divorce lying alone with the husband, the wife not an independent being possessing independent rights, but a veritable slave of the husband. Not alone the Episcopalians, but Congregationalists, Presbyterians and other sects oppose marriage as a civil contract declaring it a rite to be solemnized by the church alone, and using influence upon legislative bodies to have it legally declared a rite pertaining to the church alone. In 1888 a committee from the Presbyterian synod of New York, waited upon the legislature of that state for the purpose of influencing changes in the celebration of this rite, requesting the publication of banns, etc., and a bill to this effect passed both houses but fortunately met with a veto from the governor.

The clergy of Derby, England, have recently decided not to accept a marriage fee, in the hope of thus securing control of marriage by the church, and expect their example to be followed by their brethren throughout England. These are dangerous signs of the times as to the effort of the church to obtain increased power over the laity. It is also an attack of the church upon the state. The courts of this country have decided that marriage is a civil contract. As such a clergyman is no more fitted to take part in it than he would be to take acknowledgement of a deed, or part in the legalization of any other contract. In fact a marriage performed by a clergyman of any denomination should be regarded as invalid in the light of civil law.

It is an infringement of individual rights, that either state or church should possess absolute control over this important relation,--one that enters the inmost life of the individual persons contracting it. The parties themselves as chiefly interested, should hold power over its forms. When consummated it might be placed upon record for their own safety as is done in case of other contracts.

The Grand Jury of the General Sessions, New York City, 1887, in addition to its presentment in regard to court accommodations also advanced opinions that marriage should be taken from magistrates and the laws so amended as to require all marriages to be performed by a "duly authenticated and licensed minister," mayor or Judge of court record.

While still recognizing the right of the

higher state officials to perform marriages, the dangerous suggestion of the Grand Jury calls to memory a canon of the Baltimore council which directed Catholics to use constant influence upon legislation in line with church plans. The other important subject against which the powers of the Catholic church has ever been arrayed, and whose touch we are beginning to feel in this country, is that of secular schools. As an ecclesiastical body the church is opposed to general education and to systems of public instruction in any part of the world. In Belgium, in 1879, when the state established communal schools under its own control the opposition of the clerical party was strenuous and bitter. The sacrament was refused to those whose children or grandchildren attended public schools; masters of state schools were excommunicated and communion refused to the children in attendance. The sacrament of extreme unction was also refused to parents whose children were in the state communal schools.

A curious division of penalty upon parents whose children were in these schools is notable as showing the opinion of the church as to where her chief power in ignorance lies--with women. The parents of girls attending state schools were excommunicated, but not those of boys.

The stronghold of the church has ever been the ignorance and degradation of women. Its control over woman in the two questions of marriage and education have given it keys of power more potent than those of Peter. With her uneducated, without civil or political rights, the church is sure of its authority; but once arouse woman to a disbelief in church teachings regarding her having brought sin into the world; once open to her all avenues of education, so that her teaching of the young in her charge will be of a broader, more scientific character than in the past and the doom of the church is sealed.

Persecution of like character as that of

Belgium has taken place in Prussia and other countries where state schools exist. Even here within the past twenty-four hours the threat of excommunication by a Catholic bishop, against the parents of children not attending parochial schools, has appeared in your city papers. Instances of like character have come under my own observation in the city of Syracuse.

In order to maintain its authority over mankind it is necessary that the church should control human thought; freedom of the will has ever been its most dangerous foe. The theory of the superiority of the church over the state, the doctrine that teaching is a function of the church and not of the state presents itself in many forms, and during the present session of Congress, has been the ground of the bitter opposition to efforts for the establishment of a common school system for the education of all Indian children. It was the church that in the interests of Catholicism by the priesthood opposed the confirmation by Congress of General Morgan and Dr. Dorchester.[7] But let it not be thought that the Protestant clergy are less desirous of priestly control over education. While their efforts have not been as apparent to the general public, they no less exist, both in

---

[7] Gen. Thomas Jefferson Morgan (1839-1902), Baptist clergyman, in 1889 appointed commissioner of Indian Affairs by President Benjamin Harrison. He insisted, in spite of much political and ecclesiastical opposition, that the principle of separation of church and state must be recognized in the control of Indian schools. Dr. Daniel Dorchester (1827-1907), Methodist clergyman, also appointed by President Harrison superintendent of United States Indian schools (1889-93), was instrumental in having government appropriations for sectarian Indian schools withdrawn and increased emphasis placed on industrial education.

this country and abroad. Frances Lord,[8] an English literary woman and reformer, at one time member of the London School Board, says of England: "The Church still clings tenaciously to its authority over the teachers of the youth of both sexes. The head-masters of our great public schools, like Eton and Rugby, for instance, must be clergymen of the Church of England. Unless a candidate for such a post has taken orders, he has no chance of being accepted. No woman will be made head mistress of a girl's High School, if she be not a trinitarian."

She declares those great universities controlled by the church stand as bulwarks against the advance of new ideas, even though they are deeply tinctured with infidelity.

The school established by Harriet Martineau at Cheddar, among an ignorant, vicious, neglected population was ultimately broken up by the priesthood, although it was accomplishing an inconceivable amount of good.[9] The Catholic clergy of France in a similar way destroyed the schools of Madam Pepe-Carpentier, who was in reality the originator of the kindergarten system. When the statute providing for the admission of women to Oxford was passed in England a few years since, the Dean of Norwich characterized it as "an attempt to defeat Divine Providence and the Holy Scriptures." It is no less the Protestant than the Catholic clergy that show themselves opposed to woman's education, the church, whether Catholic or Protestant, possessing the same contemptuous opinion of

---

[8] Henrietta Frances Lord, author of *Christian Science Healing* (1888); translator of Henrik Ibsen's *The Doll's House* (1889) and other plays.

[9] See p. 45, n 5. Martineau's feminism pervaded her political philosophy (Yates 1985, 2). I can find no information about the school referred to here.

woman, the same fear of the results to follow her education, the same teaching that through her, sin and death were brought into the world.

In our own country most of the colleges and universities are presided over by clergymen; Harvard, Yale, Princeton, all closing their doors against the admission of girls.[10] Even Vassar, a university for women alone, has a clergyman at its head.[11]

Dr. M'Glynn asserts that the Roman church threatens the republic, especially referring to the efforts of its clergy against the

---

[10] Harvard was intended to be an institution for the education of Puritan ministers as was Yale. Princeton was established by the "New Light" evangelical Presbyterians, and was originally intended to train ministers. Its founder and first president was Jonathan Dickinson (1688-1747), a Presbyterian clergyman; another was John Witherspoon (1723-94), also a Presbyterian clergyman, who became president in 1768. None admitted women.

[11] Vassar's first president (1865-78) was John Howard Raymond, a graduate of the Baptist theological seminary of Madison, now Colgate, University in 1838, where he remained as a professor until 1850 when he and others left to organize what became the University of Rochester. In 1855 he became the first president of the Brooklyn Collegiate and Polytechnic Institute, after which he went to Vassar. Contrary to the speech, the *Dictionary of American Biography* describes him as "a man of strong convictions without a trace of bigotry" (p. 413). The second president (1878-85) was Samuel L. Caldwell, D.D., a clergyman who had been professor of ecclesiastical history at the Theological Institution at Newton, MA. A provisional president, J. Ryland Kendrick, D.D. was a clergyman, who was followed by the Reverend James M. Taylor of Providence, RI, who served 1886-1913.

common school system "things happening which but a generation ago would have stirred the country to a white heat of anger." But the efforts of the Protestant clergy are no less dangerous. It is the Protestant priesthood now inciting the bills before Congress to make religious teaching obligatory in common schools. Cardinal Gibbons thinks religious and secular education should not be divorced,[12] but no less does Protestant Rev. Dr. Hill, in the *Forum*, also warmly vindicate the right of the state to compel religious teaching in the public schools.[13] Dr. Hodge, of Princeton, a short time before his death published an article to which the press referred at [the] time of its publication as very similar to those presented by the Roman Catholic clergy.[14] Dr. Hodge declared Catholics had maintained a sounder and more consistent position as to education than Protestants had had the courage to assume. Bishop Littlejohn characterized Dr. Hodge's paper as an expression of the views entertained by many thoughtful men--"a deep and serious dissatisfaction with the drift of the public schools."[15] Prof. Seeley, a foremost

---

[12] James Gibbons (1834-1921), appointed the second American Cardinal by Pope Leo XIII in 1886.

[13] Thomas Hill (1818-1891), Unitarian clergyman and scientist, who in 1858 delivered the Phi Beta Kappa oration, *Liberal Education*, at Harvard; in 1859 he became president of Antioch College; from 1862-68 he was president of Harvard.

[14] Archibald Alexander Hodge (1823-1886), Presbyterian clergyman, professor of theology at Princeton (1877-86), best known for *Outlines of Theology* (1860, 1879).

[15] Abraham Newkirk Littlejohn (1824-1901), Episcopal Bishop of Long Island.

representative of New England Congregationalism, has expressed like opinions, while other Protestant bodies are showing increasing opposition to a form of purely secular education. And yet the history of the world shows that wherever ecclesiastical schools have been tried,--wherever the church as secured influence above that of the state, the standard of education has been universally lowered.

Governor Thomas, of Utah, only last fall speaking of the public schools of that territory under control of the Mormon Church, says they in no respect compare with the schools of Washington, Montana, or the Dakotas but are practically worthless.[16] The experience of centuries past and present prove the danger of allowing a church of any name, the control of secular education. This not alone because of the lowered grade of instruction, but also because of the greatly increased power of the church over human thought and human will gained by this means. In the light of past experience all bills, legislative or congressional, looking towards compulsory religious education of whatsoever character, should be most persistently and energetically opposed.

In November last a Catholic Congress in honor of the hundredth anniversary of the establishment of the Roman Catholic Hierarchy in this country assembled in Baltimore. Priests of every degree, cardinal[s], monseigneurs, arch-bishops, bishops, with hundreds of the laity took part. The whole tenor of this congress was an affirmation of the superiority of the church over the state. Among the notable points of its platform was

---

[16] Arthur Lloyd Thomas (1851-1924) appointed Utah Territory Secretary by President Hayes in 1869 and Utah Territory Governor (1889-93) by President Benjamin Harrison.

one declaring that as the state made no provision for teaching religion, Catholics must continue to support their own schools, colleges, universities already established, and multiply and perfect others so that a Catholic education might be brought within the reach of every Catholic child in the United States. That resolution points to the first danger,--that the state must teach religion.

The second notable point was shown in the tendency towards a prohibition of free thought and free action on questions of labor, and what is known in Russia as "The will of the People." It condemned nihilism, the one bright ray in that land of torture, Russia. Macaulay said of the French toilers what may be said of those of many another country, be that country Russia, England or the United States: "In their wretchedness and despair there they sat waiting any leader that might bid them follow."[17] "How far from that condition now are myriads of our working men to-day, aye, and working women, too?" queries that old anti-slavery apostle, Parker Pillsbury.[18]

The most brilliant leaders of the commune were women; and was it not just,--woman, the part of the humanity most debased by church and by state--woman, upon whom the heaviest weight of all oppression falls?

"We hear," remarks the Rev. Dr. Channing,

---

[17] Thomas Babington Macaulay (1800-59), English historian, essayist, and politician, best known for *History of England*, 4 vols. (1848, 1855).

[18] Parker Pillsbury (1809-98), Congregational minister who left his pulpit to devote himself to social reform; abolitionist who edited *Herald of Freedom* (1845-6) and the *National Anti-Slavery Standard* (1866); woman's rights advocate and editor, with Elizabeth Cady Stanton, of the *Revolution* (1868-69).

of the horrors of the Revolution; but in this, as in other things, we recollect the effect, without thinking of the guiltier cause. The Revolution was, indeed, a scene of horror; but when I look back on the reigns which preceded it, and which made Paris almost one great play and gambling-house, and when I see altar and throne desecrated by a licentiousness unsurpassed in any former age, I look on scenes as shocking to the calm and searching eye of reason and virtue as the 10th of August and the massacre of September. Bloodshed is indeed a terrible spectacle, but there are other things almost as fearful as blood.

There are crimes which do not make us shout and turn pale like the guillotine, but deadlier in their workings. God forbid that I should say a work to weaken the thrill of horror with which we contemplate the outrages of the French Revolution! But when I hear that Revolution quoted to frighten us from Reform, to show us the danger of lifting up the depressed and ignorant mass, I must ask whence it came? and the answer is, from the want of culture among the mass of the people, and from a corruption of the great, too deep to be purged away except by destruction. Even the Atheism and Infidelity of France were due chiefly to a licentious priesthood and a licentious court. It was Religion, so called, that dug her own grave. (*Works*, vol. vi., 175, 176.)[19]

A third notable recommendation of the

[19] See p. 51, n 10.

Catholic platform was union of work with non-Catholics, *i.e.*, Protestant, in order to bring about certain restrictive laws. It reads thus: "There are many christian issues in which Catholics could come together with non-Catholics and shape civil legislation for the public weal. We should seek alliance with non-Catholics for proper Sunday observance."

A paper read during the congress upon 'Sunday Observance' by Mark B. Tullo, of Cleveland, declared "what we should seek is an *en rapport* with the Protestant Christians who desire to keep the Sunday holy."

Cardinal Gibbons published a book as a contribution to the centennial anniversary, in which he also discusses this point of work in unison with Protestants. "So far from despising or rejecting their support," he says, "I would gladly hold out to them the right hand of fellowship so long as they unite with us in striking the common foe."

Thus the Catholic Church places itself in line with the National Reform Association, the American Sabbath Union, the Woman's Christian Temperance Union, and with those bills already before Congress which are conspiring against the freedom of the people at large. As politics is said to make strange bed-fellows, so does conspiracy against freedom unite strange forces.

A fourth notable suggestion of the platform was one looking to the formation of an exclusively Catholic associated press agency.

To those who realize the formidable power of the *Associated Press*,--its capability of creating public opinion,--its ability to report or suppress the truth--to color or to distort as it pleases--this recommendation was one of the most dangerous in the platform.[20]

---

[20] In 1856 the General News Association, comprising many New York City papers, was organized, out of which emerged in the 1870s the New York Associated Press (AP), a coopera-

Fifth: Divorces were declared to be the plague-spot on our civilization--a discredit to the government, a degradation of the female sex and a standing menace to the sanctity of the marriage bond. It should be noted that this was the only time that woman or her especial interests were mentioned during the congress. It should also be noted that it was under the offensive term of 'female,' a word solely applicable to the animal functions which the church regards as woman's single reason of existence. The subject of divorce thus far has been entirely under control of man, whether in church or state. It is now time that woman should be consulted, and her opinion obtained as to the "sanctity" of a relation that brings sufficient cause for her to seek divorce. Not alone the rights of woman as wife and mother but the rights of children demand a home where, if there is cause for divorce, either through cruelty, drunkenness, incompatibility of temper or breaking of marriage vows, it can be obtained. Believing that the wife is not the servant of the husband, but possesses equality of natural rights with him in the marriage relation, we look upon that portion of the Catholic platform as a renewed menace to the growing legal independence of women, and as such we call especial attention to this point.

Sixth: The key-note of the whole congress, its last public statement in line with its general tendency towards declaring the church to be superior to the state, lay in that portion of the platform which demanded that the temporal power of the Pope should be guaranteed; which declared that the absolute freedom of the Holy See was indispensible to the peace of the church and the welfare of mankind and which asserted that this freedom should be scrupulously maintained by all

---

tive news agency for the New York papers that sold copy to daily papers throughout the country.

secular governments.

Charles J. Bonaparte discussed this portion of the platform in a speech, "The Independence of the Holy See," suggesting that the more important provisions of the "law of guarantees" might be enforced in a treaty between all the great powers and thus obtain an international sanction. He counselled Catholics not to be passive, declaring that a real solution of the question must be the universal conviction among good men of all countries, that to violate it would be to wrong mankind. "Whether a captive or an exile, the Pope can never be a subject."

Thus the whole drift of this congress was shown to be the supremacy of the church and the restoration to the Pope of the power held by him in the middle ages when he excommunicated kings, released subjects from their national allegiance, held the priesthood of every country as above the control of civil law, and for the grossest crimes subject only to ecclesiastical rule:--a system which really destroyed the national form of every government, making them but dependencies upon the papal power. The same view was continued in a speech by the Right Rev. R. Gilmour, bishop of Cleveland, at the dedication of the Catholic University in Washington, immediately following the congress. He declared it to be a political and social heresy which assumes and asserts that the state is all temporal and religion all spiritual. He declared that no state can or should exist which does not recognize God as the supreme authority, that Catholics were willing to accept state schools as such on condition that the child should be taught religion and the laws of morality.

Early this year, some two months after the centenary, the Pope issued another encyclical, the most important since his accession to the throne of the Pontiff. Its chief points were the declaration of the supremacy of the church over the state; its order of resistance to the state if things prejudicial to the church, or hostile to the duties imposed by religion, or the authority of Jesus Christ in the person of the supreme pontiff are commanded. Directions were given to make politics serve the interests of Catholicism; that men who promised to merit well of Catholicism should be supported for office, the encyclical closing with an admonition not to criticize the actions of a superior, even when they appear to merit just censure.

No more thoroughly retrogressive middle-age document has appeared from papacy during the present century, none more antagonistic to the republican ideas of the equality of man with man, the equal right of each human being to self-government in all things.

The great danger of the papacy lies in that it places itself above all civil power; the real meaning of the word 'papacy,' is religion in place of civil power, and it is not confined in signification to the church of Rome. The papacy exists in the Greek Church of Russia, in the Anglican Church of England, and it is making an attempt to fasten itself upon this country through the efforts of "the Christian party in politics" to introduce an acknowledgement of the Christian religion and the Bible as the source of all governmental power in the United States. It is not the Pope of Rome alone who places himself above all civil power in the demand made by himself and his followers that he shall be acknowledged the source of civil and political power, but the various Protestant sects of this country are working to a similar end--that the form of religion known as Protestant shall be recognized in the Constitution as the source of all power, instead as now, the people.

The modern democratic-republican idea is the right of every individual to his own or her own judgment upon all matters. The centralized-clerical idea is that no person has a right to his or her own judgment upon either religious or political questions. In all that most deeply concerns the individual he or she is to bow to the church, embodied in the priesthood. The laity, unless acting under specific direction of the priesthood, are not recognized as possessing right to thought or the exercise of judgment.

But while in this country there is "less friction between Catholics and Protestants than elsewhere in the world," it is because here religious liberty is based upon civil liberty, and while, as shown by the Catholic Centenary, this body is better and more fully organized for aggressive work than ever before, it is necessary for us to examine the condition of Protestantism. In the statements with reference to Catholic intent doubtless all before me will agree. We have been taught to watch Catholic action, while blindly looking upon Protestants as to be fully trusted. Because of this blind faith in the purity of Protestant motives--a belief in their entire devotion to liberty--the present danger from Protestant effort towards the destruction of secular liberty in the United States, is much beyond that of Catholicism. The same spirit animates each body--the effort of each is the same--a union of the church and the state, with the church as controlling power. But Catholicism has not proceeded as far, has not taken as decided steps to bring this condition about, as Protestantism has.

Church aggression is the foremost danger of the day, and in saying church aggression I do not refer specifically to the Catholics, but more emphatically to the Protestants. The Church as a Church of whatever name is based on the one central idea, supreme control over the thought, will and action of mankind.

The National Reform Association is a body of Protestants, members of many different denominations, which declares that a written constitution ought to contain explicit evidence of the christian character and purpose of the nation which frames it. The silence of the Constitution of the United States in regard to christianity, causes this body to seek an amendment which shall incorporate in it a statement of such belief. As the preamble is everywhere recognized as the most important part of a constitution, stating the source of its authority and the objects for which it is framed, it is this part of the Constitution that "The Christian Party in Politics" has selected for its attack. As it now stands the preamble reads thus:

> We the people of the United States in order to form a more perfect union, establish justice, insure domestic tranquility, provide for the common defence, promote the general welfare and secure the blessings of liberty to ourselves and our posterity, do ordain and establish this constitution for the United States of America.

As amended, after "We the people of the United States," it would read: "*recognizing Almighty God as the source of all power and authority in civil government, our Lord Jesus Christ as the Ruler of nations, and the Bible as the standard to decide all moral issues in political life, in order to form a Christian government, etc.*"

At a convention of the National Reform Association, 1888, [the] Rev. W. J. Coleman, Professor of Political Science in Geneva College, Pennsylvania, spoke upon "The proposed Christian Amendment." As has many times been done at woman suffrage conventions, he critically defined the constitution as

First. "The Constitution of the United States is the supreme law of the land."

Second. "The Constitution is the only authoritative expression of the will of the people of the United States."

Third. "The Constitution is the exclusive basis of statute law, both in the national government and in the States."

Fourth. "The Constitution is a statement

of the principles by which the people have chosen to be governed."

These statements of the reverend gentleman will be admitted, and it is because a constitution is superior to all statutory enactments that the wary and jesuitical National Reform Association, and the entire "Christian Party in Politics," are not content with the enactment of laws by Congress in their interest, but demand a constitutional amendment, so that their plans may enter the very basis of statute laws. Moreover with the wisdom of the serpent it makes the preamble its point of attack, well knowing that in law, the preamble is held as the explanatory part--the dictionary I may say of the whole Constitution.

Chief Justice Jay regarded the preamble of the Constitution of the United States as an authoritative guide to a correct interpretation of that instrument (2 Dallas 419).[21] Coke says (Lit. 796), "The preamble of a statute is a good means to find out the meaning of the statute, and is, as it were, a key to the understanding thereof."[22]

Judge Story in commentaries on the Constitution (vol. 1, book 3, chap. 6) says, "The importance of examining the preamble for the purpose of expounding the language of a statute has always been felt and universally conceded in all judicial proceedings."[23]

---

[21] John Jay (1745-1829), U.S. statesman, diplomat, and jurist, and first chief justice of the Supreme Court (1789-95). He drafted *The Address to the People of Great Britain* (1774), stating the rights of colonists, as well as the first New York State Constitution.

[22] See p. 175, n 8.

[23] See p. 176, n 11.

Under this array of authority as to the importance of the preamble, we easily discover the reason that the National Reform Association desires 'to amend' the preamble of the Constitution of the United States. Once that is changed to read as it desires, this association will possess the power to interpret the whole instrument in unison with that change. As legal authorities maintain that the Constitution was not established by the United States in their sovereign capacity, but by 'the people' of the United States, in attacking the preamble, 'the Christian Party in Politics' works as astutely as any jesuitical body on earth. Subtilty [sic], finesse, intrigue could go no further than the effort to change the preamble to the Constitution.

At a convention of the Reformed Presbyterians in Newburgh, New York, 1887, the synod after discussion of "National Reform" and the question of acknowledgement of God in the Constitution, adopted this resolution:

> *Resolved*, That we will endeavor to teach more forcibly the duty of our nation to God and the Bible view of civil government, and will make our testimony more emphatic against the infidelity of the civil government, and will maintain our position of political dissent in refusing the election franchise to put into office men who are bound by their official oath to support the Constitution of the United States, and we will become responsible for suffrage only when they become responsible to Christ by their official oath.

At the convention of this sect in Pittsburgh, Pennsylvania, June 1888, resolutions were adopted disowning the nation as long as it refused to acknowledge Christ as its king, and the synod was directed to see that members of the congregation did not identify themselves with the nation by any act implying allegiance.

The Woman's Christian Temperance Union is firmly united with the National Reform Association; it is a component part of that body; its chief officers are officers of that association; its work is the same, as the speeches of its president [Frances E. Willard] and the resolutions of its conventions fully show. It not only endorses the aim and ends of that association, but that body depends more fully upon the work of the W.C.T.U. for ultimate success than it does upon its own specific efforts. As far back as 1886 the leaders of the W.C.T.U. were enrolled among the Vice-Presidents of the National Reform Association. At its annual convention, 1888, Dr. McAllister declared that "movement bound to succeed through the influence of the Woman's Christian Temperance Union," while district secretary Gault said, that "The Woman's Christian Temperance Union and the Prohibition Party had become so entirely National Reform organizations, that the regular National Reform organizers had ceased to organize local National Reform clubs as such, but worked through those bodies to spread its ideas."

When the purposes of the National Reform Association are accomplished the consent of the governed for *men* will stand where it does among women to-day--*nowhere*.

The first national convention of the American Sabbath Union was held in Washington, December, 1888. Just previous to this convention the state of Illinois held a convention of similar purport at which time two statements were especially emphasized.

1. That Christians do not keep Sunday as they ought.

2. That other people do not go to church as they ought.

Members of the Christian Party have not hesitated to declare that attendance upon church should be made compulsory. But as long as the sun shines, the wind blows, flowers blossom and all nature performs its usual functions on that day, man should be as free as nature. Sunshine and storm are out of such people's reach or they too would doubtless be held responsible. To be fully consistent the 'Christian Party' should place animals and insects on trial as was done in Christian lands only a few hundred years since. The light of advancing civilization has not yet touched the majority of Christians; the Christian party in politics is the fifteenth century living in the nineteenth--its members are the heathen of the world whom civilization has not yet touched.

This National Sunday Union, which is another branch of the Christian party in politics, was first suggested by Dr. H.F. Crafts in 1887. In May, 1888, he addressed a memorial to the Methodist General Conference assembled in New York,--that same General Conference, that in emulation of the world's anti-slavery conference in London, 1840, and the world's temperance convention in New York, 1854, refused to receive regularly appointed woman delegates.[24] The Methodist Conference of 1888, having denied to women the right of representation on the ground that laymen did not include women, entered "cordially" into the plan of a National Sabbath Union. The general assembly of the Presbyterian church north, the Presbyterian church south, the United Presbyterian church, the Baptist Union, the Congregationalists, the Methodist Protestant church and fifteen others entered heartily into this plan of organization. In addition the Woman's Christian Temperance Union, the National Reform Association, the various State and National Sunday Schools, the Knights of Labor, the body of Locomotive Engineers and the 9,000,000 of the Catholic church, priestly and lay, men, women, children and the babe in arms, are all counted as

---

[24] See HWS 1:506-10.

sustaining this union.

As Catholics and Protestants are united in this Sunday observance demand it has been pertinently asked which kind of Sunday keeping is expected? All the Catholic priesthood require is morning attendance upon mass; this is especially true in Europe, after which observance the day is spent as one of holiday enjoyment. Bull-fights in Catholic Spain, the opera in music-loving Italy, dances in merry France, drives, sails, drinks everywhere.

Is *this* to be the style, or are we to return to Puritan custom,

> Hanging of his cat on Monday
> For killing of a mouse on Sunday,

and no one allowed to drive or walk for pleasure, or for rest. Which Sunday is it to be?

The purpose of Sunday observance, as directly stated by Dr. Crafts himself, is not that people should enjoy the day as one of rest from usual labor, it is not for the benefit of man, but in order to commemorate the work of creation. The grounds for its demand are purely religious.

Every law of this character is dangerous because of the fact that law and right soon grow to be synonymous in the minds of men. Hon. Sheldon Amos, former Professor of Jurisprudence in Oxford University, speaking in regard to certain evil legislation in England, said: "Whatever law recognizes and provides for is regarded as morally right, comes to be so regarded by the hereditary instincts of the human mind."

It has been clearly proven that the enforcement of rest at any time, is the enforcement of idleness, and not only tends to the destruction of self-reliance but to the increase of crime. In some branches of business enforced Sunday rest means overwork the remaining six days, or as Chauncey Depew says of railroading, "somebody must work harder during the rest of the week than has hitherto been the case."[25]

While France, Mexico, Brazil and other countries are getting rid of clericalism and centralized power, it is one of the mysteries of the age that the United States seems striving to incorporate these two systems in her form of government. This tendency strikes every observant person, as does also its pretext, 'protection of the people.' This theory of 'protection' has been the assumption through past ages, governing every attempt for the destruction of liberty. There are now before Congress several bills and amendments of this dangerous 'protective' character. Forty-four amendments to the Constitution were introduced during the fiftieth Congress, ranging from the control of marriage and divorce to a six years term for the Presidency.

The chief danger of the present situation lies in the fact that the majority of the people do not see that there is danger. One friend wrote, "To me it does not mean that so alarming a state of things exists, to me it is daybreak everywhere."

Yes, it *is* daybreak everywhere; we see its radiance in Europe, in South America, in Africa. Peaceful revolutions are rapidly taking place on two hemispheres, yet just as a dark cloud shadows some parts of the earth even at break of day, heralding a coming storm, so while it is breaking day in many countries, yet over our own beloved land the fell shadow sweeps,--over it falls the pall of a coming storm. Amid so much liberty, people fail to see the gradual encroachments of organized power either in the church or in the state. But so sure am I of the coming storm that I cannot believe it will pass over us without the possible shedding of blood. The

---

[25] Chauncey Depew (1834-1928), American orator, politician, president and chairman of the board of the New York Central Railroad, and U.S. Senator (1899-1911).

struggle will be fierce and bitter; a man's enemies will be of his own household, for this storm will not be, as some surmise, a warfare between Catholic and Protestant; it will be a battle of the liberal element against the church and its dogmas of whatever name or nature. After a time liberty will triumph, and then and not until then shall we see a true Republic upon this soil. As the battle for political liberty began here so will that for full religious liberty end here. The conflict we were sure had gone by will again arise; the decisive battle has yet to be fought. It seems to me when that hour has passed there will be no more church forever, for science and the spirit of free thought will have destroyed its very foundations.

19

Elizabeth Cady Stanton, "The Solitude of Self," 1892

There is disagreement about whether Cady Stanton delivered this speech before both the House Committee on the Judiciary on January 18 and the Senate Committee on Woman Suffrage on January 20. According to her diary, she delivered it herself on both occasions, as well as at the annual convention of the National American Woman Suffrage Association on January 18, 1892. Although she spoke occasionally afterward, "The Solitude of Self" was the climax of Cady Stanton's career as a speaker. It stands as a rhetorical masterpiece because it explores the values underlying natural rights philosophy, because it responds creatively to the problems faced by social movements as their arguments become familiar to audiences, and because it still has the capacity to speak to contemporary audiences. It is also the most finished statement of the humanistic ideology underlying feminism.

At age 76 Cady Stanton had great presence; a year earlier she had been described in the press as "looking as if she should be the Lord Chief Justice with her white hair puffed all over her head, and her amiable and intellectual face marked with lines of wisdom" (Hersh 1978, 103). *The speech was a success with her immediate audiences. The Senate committee made a favorable majority report;*

the House committee had 10,000 copies reprinted from the **Congressional Record** *and sent throughout the country* (Lutz 1940, 290). *Two texts exist. As delivered before congressional committees, the speech began: "Mr. Chairman and gentlemen of the Committee: We have been speaking before Committees of the Judiciary for the last twenty years, and we have gone over all the arguments in favor of the sixteenth [ultimately, the nineteenth] amendment which are familiar to all you gentlemen; therefore, it will not be necessary that I should repeat them again."*

That sentence was omitted when she delivered the speech to the NAWSA convention. The text is from the **Woman's Journal**, *January 23, 1892* (Stanton 1892a).

The point I wish plainly to bring before you on this occasion is the individuality of each human soul; our Protestant idea, the right of individual conscience and judgment; our republican idea, individual citizenship. In discussing the rights of woman, we are to consider, first, what belongs to her as an individual, in a world of her own, the arbiter of her own destiny, an imaginary Robinson Crusoe, with her woman Friday on a solitary island. Her rights under such circumstances are to use all her faculties for her own safety and happiness.

Secondly, if we consider her as a citizen, as a member of a great nation, she must have the same rights as all other members, according to the fundamental principles of our government.

Thirdly, viewed as a woman, an equal factor in civilization, her rights and duties are still the same; individual happiness and development.

Fourthly, it is only the incidental relations of life, such as mother, wife, sister, daughter, that may involve some special duties and training. In the usual discussion in regard to woman's sphere, such men as Herbert Spencer, Frederic Harrison and

Grant Allen,[1] uniformly subordinate her rights and duties as an individual, as a citizen, as a woman, to the necessities of these incidental relations, neither of which a large class of women may ever assume. In discussing the sphere of man, we do not decided his rights as an individual, as a citizen, as a man, by his duties as a father, a husband, a brother or a son, relations he may never fill. Moreover, he would be better fitted for these very relations, and whatever special work he might choose to do to earn his bread, by the complete development of all his faculties as an individual.

Just so with woman. The education that will fit her to discharge the duties in the largest sphere of human usefulness will best fit her for whatever special work she may be compelled to do.

The isolation of every human soul, and the necessity of self-dependence, must give each individual the right to choose his own surroundings.

The strongest reason for giving woman all the opportunities for higher education, for the full development of her faculties, forces of mind and body; for giving her the most enlarged freedom of thought and action; a complete emancipation from all forms of bondage, of custom, dependence, superstition; from all the crippling influences of fear--is the solitude and personal responsibility of her own individual life. The strongest reason why we ask for woman a voice in the government under which she lives; in the religion she is

---

[1] Herbert Spencer (1920-1903), English philosopher who applied the theory of evolution to all life; Frederic Harrison (1931-99), jurist, historian, sociologist, and leader of English positivism; Grant Allen (1848-99), English author, who wrote on popular science, known for his novel *The Woman Who Did* (1895), an attack on the moral double standard.

asked to believe; equality in social life, where she is the chief factor; a place in the trades and professions, where she may earn her bread, is because of her birthright to self-sovereignty; because, as an individual, she must rely on herself. No matter how much women prefer to lean, to be protected and supported, nor how much men desire to have them to do so, they must make the voyage of life alone, and for safety in an emergency, they must know something of the laws of navigation. To guide our own craft, we must be captain, pilot, engineer; with chart and compass to stand at the wheel; to watch the winds and waves, and know when to take in the sail, and to read the signs in the firmament over all. It matters not whether the solitary voyager is man or woman; nature, having endowed them equally, leaves them to their own skill and judgment in the hour of danger, and, if not equal to the occasion, alike they perish.

To appreciate the importance of fitting every human soul for independent action, think for a moment of the immeasurable solitude of self. We come into the world alone, unlike all who have gone before us; we leave it alone, under circumstances peculiar to ourselves. No mortal ever has been, no mortal ever will be like the soul just launched on the sea of life. There can never again be just such a combination of prenatal influences; never again just such environments as make up the infancy, youth and manhood of this one. Nature never repeats herself, and the possibilities of one human soul will never be found in another. No one has ever found two blades of ribbon grass alike, and no one will ever find two human beings alike. Seeing, then, what must be the infinite diversity in human character, we can in a measure appreciate the loss to a nation when any large class of the people is uneducated and unrepresented in the government.

We ask for the complete development of every individual, first, for his own benefit and happiness. In fitting out an army, we give each soldier his own knapsack, arms, powder, his blanket, cup, knife, fork and spoon. We provide alike for all their individual necessities; then each man bears his own burden.

Again, we ask complete individual development for the general good; for the consensus of the competent on the whole round of human interests, on all questions of national life; and here each man must bear his share of the general burden. It is sad to see how soon friendless children are left to bear their own burdens, before they can analyze their feelings; before they can even tell their joys and sorrows, they are thrown on their own resources. The great lesson that nature seems to teach us at all ages is self-dependence, self-protection, self-support. What a touching instance of a child's solitude, of that hunger of the heart for love and recognition, in the case of the little girl who helped to dress a Christmas tree for the children of the family in which she served. On finding there was no present for herself, she slipped away in the darkness and spent the night in an open field sitting on a stone, and when found in the morning was weeping as if her heart would break. No mortal will ever know the thoughts that passed through the mind of that friendless child in the long hours of that cold night, with only the silent stars to keep her company. The mention of her case in the daily papers moved many generous hearts to send her presents, but in the hours of her keenest suffering she was thrown wholly on herself for consolation.

In youth our most bitter disappointments, our brightest hopes and ambitions, are known only to ourselves. Even our friendship and love we never fully share with another; there is something of every passion, in every situation, we conceal. Even so in our triumphs and our defeats. The successful candidate for the presidency, and his opponent, each has a solitude peculiarly his own, and good form forbids either to speak of his pleasure or regret. The solitude of the king on his throne and the prisoner in his cell differs in character and degree, but it is solitude, nevertheless.

We ask no sympathy from others in the anxiety and agony of a broken friendship or shattered love. When death sunders our nearest ties, alone we sit in the shadow of our affliction. Alike amid the greatest triumphs and darkest tragedies of life, we walk alone. On the divine heights of human attainment, eulogized and worshipped as a hero or saint, we stand alone. In ignorance, poverty and vice, as a pauper or criminal, alone we starve or steal; alone we suffer the sneers and rebuffs of our fellows; alone we are hunted and hounded through dark courts and alleys, in by-ways and highways; alone we stand in the judgment seat; alone in the prison cell we lament our crimes and misfortunes; alone we expiate them on the gallows. In hours like these we realize the awful solitude of individual life, its pains, its penalties, its responsibilities; hours in which the youngest and most helpless are thrown on their own resources for guidance and consolation. Seeing, then, that life must ever be a march and a battle, that each soldier must be equipped for his own protection, it is the height of cruelty to rob the individual of a single natural right.

To throw obstacles in the way of a complete education is like putting out the eyes; to deny the rights of property, like cutting off the hands. To deny political equality is to rob the ostracised of all self-respect; of credit in the market place; of recompense in the world of work; of a voice in those who make and administer the law; a choice in the jury before whom they are tried, and in the judge who decides their punishment. Shakespeare's play of "Titus Andronicus" contains a terrible satire on woman's position in the 19th century. Rude men (the play tells us) seized the king's daughter, cut out her tongue, cut off her hands, and then bade her go call for water and wash her hands.[2] What a picture of woman's position! Robbed of her natural rights, handicapped by law and custom at every turn, yet compelled to fight her own battles, and in the emergencies of life to fall back on herself for protection.

The girl of sixteen, thrown on the world to support herself, to make her own place in society, to resist the temptations that surround her and maintain a spotless integrity, must do all this by native force or superior education. She does not acquire this power by being trained to trust others and distrust herself. If she wearies of the struggle, finding it hard work to swim up stream, and allows herself to drift with the current, she will find plenty of company, but not one to share her misery in the hour of her deepest humiliation. If she tries to retrieve her position, to conceal the past, her life is hedged about with fears lest willing hands should tear the veil from what she fain would hide. Young and friendless, *she* knows the bitter solitude of self.

How the little courtesies of life on the surface of society, deemed so important from man towards woman, fade into utter insignificance in view of the deeper tragedies in which she must play her part alone, where no human aid is possible!

The young wife and mother, at the head of some establishment, with a kind husband to shield her from the adverse winds of life, with wealth, fortune and position, has a certain harbor of safety, secure against the ordinary ills of life. But to manage a household, have a desirable influence in society, keep her friends and the affections of her husband, train her children and servants well, she must have rare common sense, wisdom, diplomacy, and a knowledge of human nature. To do all this, she needs the

---

[2] Act 2.4. Lavinia was also raped.

cardinal virtues and the strong points of character that the most successful statesman possesses. An uneducated woman trained to dependence, with no resources in herself, must make a failure of any position in life. But society says women do not need a knowledge of the world, the liberal training that experience in public life must give, all the advantages of collegiate education, but when for the lack of all this, the woman's happiness is wrecked, alone she bears her humiliation; and the solitude of the weak and the ignorant is indeed pitiable. In the wild chase for the prizes of life, they are ground to powder.

Imag[in]e when the pleasures of youth are passed, children grown up, married and gone, the hurry and bustle of life in a measure over, when the hands are weary of active service, when the old arm chair and the fireside are the chosen resorts, then men and women alike must fall back on their own resources. If they cannot find companionship in books, if they have no interest in the vital questions of the hour, no interest in watching the consummation of reforms with which they might have been identified, they soon pass into their dotage. The more fully the faculties of the mind are developed and kept in use, the longer the period of vigor and active interest in all around us continues. If, from a life-long participation in public affairs, a woman feels responsible for the laws regulating our system of education, the discipline of our jails and prisons, the sanitary condition of our private homes, public buildings and thoroughfares, an interest in commerce, finance, our foreign relations, in any or all these questions, her solitude will at least be respectable, and she will not be driven to gossip or scandal for entertainment.

The chief reason for opening to every soul the doors to the whole round of human duties and pleasures is the individual development thus attained, the resources thus provided under all circumstances to mitigate the solitude that at times must come to every one. I once asked Prince Kropotkin, a Russian Nihilist, how he endured his long years in prison, deprived of books, pen, ink and paper.[3] "Ah!" said he, "I thought out many questions in which I had a deep interest. In the pursuit of an idea, I took no note of time. When tired solving knotty problems, I recited all the beautiful passages in prose and verse I had ever learned. I became acquainted with myself, and my own resources. I had a world of my own, a vast empire, that no Russian jailer or Czar could invade." Such is the value of liberal thought and broad culture, when shut off from all human companionship, bringing comfort and sunshine within even the four walls of a prison cell.

As women ofttimes share a similar fate, should they not have all the consolation that the most liberal education can give? Their suffering in the prisons of St. Petersburg; in the long weary marches to Siberia, and in the mines, working side by side with men, surely call for all the self-support that the most exalted sentiments of heroism can give. When suddenly roused at midnight, with the startling cry of "Fire! Fire!" to find the house over their heads in flames, do women wait for men to point the way to safety? And are the men, equally bewildered, and half suffocated with smoke, in a position to do more than try to save themselves? At such times the most timid women have shown a courage and heroism, in saving their husbands and children, that has surprised everybody. Inasmuch, then, as woman shares equally the joys and sorrows of time and eternity, is it not the height of presumption in man to propose to represent her at the ballot box and the throne of grace, to do her voting in the State, her praying in the

---

[3] Piotr Alekseyevich Kropotkin (1842-1921), a Russian anarchist; his most famous work is *Mutual Aid* (1902).

church, and to assume the position of High Priest at the family altar?

Nothing strengthens the judgment and quickens the conscience like individual responsibility; nothing adds such dignity to character as the recognition of one's self-sovereignty; the right to an equal place, everywhere conceded; a place earned by personal merit, not an artificial attainment by inheritance, wealth, family and position. Seeing, then, that the responsibilities of life rest equally on man and woman, that their destiny is the same, they need the same preparation for time and eternity. The talk of sheltering woman from the fierce storms of life is the sheerest mockery, for they beat on her from every point of the compass, just as they do on man, and with more fatal results, for he has been trained to protect himself, to resist, and to conquer. Such are the facts in human experience, the responsibilities of individual sovereignty. Rich and poor, intelligent and ignorant, wise and foolish, virtuous and vicious, man and woman; it is ever the same, each soul must depend wholly on itself.

Whatever the theories may be of woman's dependence on man, in the supreme moments of her life, he cannot bear her burdens. Alone she goes to the gates of death to give life to every man that is born into the world; no one can share her fears, no one can mitigate her pangs; and if her sorrow is greater than she can bear, alone she passes beyond the gates into the vast unknown.

From the mountain-tops of Judea long ago, a heavenly voice bade his disciples, "Bear ye one another's burdens" [Gal.6:2]; but humanity has not yet risen to that point of self-sacrifice; and if ever so willing, how few the burdens are that one soul can bear for another! In the highways of Palestine; in prayer and fasting on the solitary mountain-top; in the Garden of Gethsemane; before the judgment-seat of Pilate; betrayed by one of his trusted disciples at his last supper; in his agonies on the cross, even Jesus of Nazareth, in those last sad days on earth, felt the awful solitude of self. Deserted by man, in agony he cries, "My God, my God, why hast thou forsaken me?" [Matt. 27:46; Mark 15:34]. And so it ever must be in the conflicting scenes of life, in the long, weary march, each one walks alone. We may have many friends, love, kindness, sympathy and charity, to smooth our pathway in everyday life, but in the tragedies and triumphs of human experience, each mortal stands alone.

But when all artificial trammels are removed, and women are recognized as individuals, responsible for their own environments, thoroughly educated for all positions in life they may be called to fill; with all the resources in themselves that liberal thought and broad culture can give; guided by their own conscience and judgment, trained to self-protection, by a healthy development of the muscular system, and skill in the use of weapons of defense; and stimulated to self-support by a knowledge of the business world and the pleasure that pecuniary independence must ever give; when women are trained in this way, they will in a measure be fitted for those hours of solitude that come alike to all, whether prepared or otherwise. As in our extremity we must depend on ourselves, the dictates of wisdom point to complete individual development.

In talking of education, how shallow the argument that each class must be educated for the special work it proposes to do, and that all those faculties not needed in this special walk must lie dormant and utterly wither for want of use, when, perhaps, these will be the very faculties needed in life's greatest emergencies! Some say, Where is the use of drilling girls in the languages, the sciences, in law, medicine, theology? As wives, mothers, housekeepers, cooks, they need a different curriculum from boys who are to fill all positions. The chief cooks in our great hotels and ocean steamers are men. In our large cities, men run the bakeries; they make our bread, cake and pies. They manage the laundries; they are now considered our best milliners and dressmakers. Because some men fill these departments of usefulness, shall we regulate the curriculum in Harvard and Yale to their present necessities? If not, why this talk in our best colleges of a curriculum for girls who are crowding into the trades and professions, teachers in all our public schools, rapidly filling many lucrative and honorable positions in life?

They are showing, too, their calmness and courage in the most trying hours of human experience. You have probably all read in the daily papers of the terrible storm in the Bay of Biscay, when a tidal wave made such havoc on the shore, wrecking vessels, unroofing houses, and carrying destruction everywhere. Among other buildings, the woman's prison was demolished. Those who escaped saw men struggling to reach the shore. They promptly, by clasping hands, made a chain of themselves, and pushed out into the sea, again and again, at the risk of their lives, until they had brought six men to shore, carried them to a shelter, and done all in their power for their comfort and protection.

What special school training could have prepared these women for this sublime moment in their lives? In times like this, humanity rises above all college curriculums, and recognizes nature as the greatest of all teachers in the hour of danger and death. Women are already the equals of men in the whole realm of thought, in art, science, literature and government. With telescopic vision they explore the starry firmament and bring back the history of the planetary spheres. With chart and compass they pilot ships across the mighty deep, and with skillful fingers send electric messages around the world. In galleries of art the beauties of nature and the virtues of humanity are immortalized by them on canvas, and by their inspired touch dull blocks of marble are transformed into angels of light. In music they speak again the language of Mendelssohn, Beethoven, Chopin, Schumann, and are worthy interpreters of their great thoughts. The poetry and novels of the century are theirs, and they have touched the keynote of reform, in religion, politics and social life. They fill the editor's and professor's chair, and plead at the bar of justice; walk the wards of the hospital, and speak from the pulpit and the platform. Such is the type of womanhood that an enlightened public sentiment welcomes to-day, and such the triumph of the facts of life over the false theories of the past.

Is it, then, consistent to hold the developed woman of this day within the same narrow political limits as the dame with the spinning-wheel and knitting-needle occupied in the past? No! no! Machinery has taken the labors of woman, as well as man, on its tireless shoulders, the loom and the spinning wheel are but dreams of the past; the pen, the brush, the easel, the chisel, have taken their places, while the hopes and ambitions of women are essentially changed.

We see reason sufficient in the outer conditions of human beings for individual liberty and development, but when we consider the self-dependence of every human soul we see the need of courage, judgment and the exercise of every faculty of mind and body, strengthened and developed by use, in woman as well as man.

Whatever may be said of man's protecting power in ordinary conditions, amid all the terrible disasters by land and sea, in the supreme moments of danger, alone woman must ever meet the horrors of the situation. The Angel of Death even makes no royal pathway for her. Man's love and sympathy enter only into the sunshine of our lives. In that solemn solitude of self, that links us with the immeasurable and the eternal, each soul lives alone forever. A recent writer says:

> I remember once, in crossing the Atlantic, to have gone upon the deck of the ship at midnight, when a dense black cloud enveloped the sky, and the great deep was roaring madly under the lashes of demoniac winds. My feeling was not of danger or fear (which is a base surrender of the immortal soul) but of utter desolation and loneliness; a little speck of life shut in by a tremendous darkness. Again I remember to have climbed the slopes of the Swiss Alps, up beyond the point where vegetation ceases, and the stunted conifers no longer struggle against the unfeeling blasts. Around me lay a huge confusion of rocks, out of which the gigantic ice peaks shot into the measureless blue of the heavens; and again my only feeling was the awful solitude.

And yet, there is a solitude which each and every one of us has always carried with him, more inaccessible than the ice-cold mountains, more profound than the midnight sea; the solitude of self. Our inner being which we call ourself, no eye nor touch of man or angel has ever pierced. It is more hidden than the caves of the gnome; the sacred adytum of the oracle; the hidden chamber of Eleusinian mystery,[4] for to it only Omniscience is permitted to enter.

Such is individual life. Who, I ask you, can take, dare take on himself the rights, the duties, the responsibilities of another human soul?

---

[4] A highly venerated part of Greek religion; because the mysteries were secret, little is known of them. They were part of the worship of Demeter (Kore-Persephone), a mother goddess.

20

Ida B. Wells, "Southern Horrors: Lynch Law in All its Phases," 1892, with Mary Church Terrell's Introduction, 1893

Ida B. Wells (1862-1931), teacher, journalist, lecturer, and clubwoman, launched a one-woman, anti-lynching campaign in 1892. She encouraged formation of Afro-American women's clubs. She was a charter member of the National Association for the Advancement of Colored People, and she founded (1914) the first Afro-American woman suffrage organization, the Alpha Suffrage Club of Chicago.

She first delivered this speech at a testimonial in her honor at Lyric Hall in New York City on October 5, 1892. The gathering was said to be "the greatest demonstration ever attempted by race women for one of their number" (Davis 1982, 2:80), *and leading Afro-American women were present with her on the platform. A collection of five hundred dollars, taken at the end of the evening, was used to publish "Southern Horrors"* (Duster 1970, 78).

Wells delivered a similar speech in February 1893, when Frederick Douglass invited her to speak at the Metropolitan African Methodist Episcopal Church, Washington, D.C. On that occasion she was introduced by Mary Church Terrell, whose speech of introduction demonstrates that Afro-Americans believed that if Northern whites were informed of what was being done to Afro-Americans in the South, they would take immediate action. The text of

Church Terrell's introduction is taken from a holograph copy in her papers at the Library of Congress (Terrell 1893). *Wells's speech was printed as a pamphlet and reprinted in 1969* (Wells 1892). *All (?) are Wells's insertions.*

MARY CHURCH TERRELL'S INTRODUCTION (1893)

Chauncey M. Depew in his oration delivered at the dedicatory exercises of the World's Fair a few days ago said, "The United States is a Christian country and a living and practical Christianity is characteristic of its people."[1] In his conviction that this is a Christian country, that a living and practical Christianity is characteristic of its people, we naturally conclude that Mr. Depew, along with other truthful, law-abiding citizens of this great commonwealth is ignorant of the many barbarities, and the fiendish atrocities visited by the Southern Whites upon the defenceless and persecuted Blacks. We must conclude that Mr. Depew is not aware of the knavish methods employed to disfranchise the Negro, or of the scandalous compliances resorted to which transform the courts from seats of justice into veritable haunts of inquisition and corruption wherever the Afro-American is concerned.

A lecture upon Southern Mob Rule is therefore a necessity to night because of the vicious tactics of the South and because it is imperative that the race shall everywhere have their eyes opened to the outrages which the government seems powerless to prevent.

When men whose only crime is the color of their skin are denied even the farce of a trial, are forcibly torn from jails of the largest and wealthiest cities of the South and foully murdered, it is time for a persistent and systematic agitation of the subject of Southern Mob Rule, time for an earnest and comprehensive discussion of ways and means of

---

[1] See p. 369, n 25.

protection. Surely no one can charge us with exaggerating our woes and magnifying the indignities heaped upon us when the murder of colored men is of almost daily occurrence in the South, when you have with you tonight in the person of Miss Wells an exile driven from home, because she dared to raise her voice in defence of her own oppressed and persecuted people.

I can not believe that the great mass of Americans, who fought for freedom and who love justice, are awake to the shocking and systematic subversion of all law and order in the South. To ignorance and not to connivance must we charge the wicked apathy of some of the best citizens of the country. Open their eyes to the magnitude and hideousness of the evil flourishing in the South, blighting the lives and wrecking the happiness of men whose labor has enriched and whose blood has been shed for this country and I can not believe that by their silence and indifference they will continue to be accomplices in crime. Let us impress upon men and women whose hearts are not dead to law and love that there are citizens in the South who are deprived of all the rights of citizenship, denied even the right to life, who are hunted down and butchered like wild animals, and I am persuaded that the inquisition will be throttled to death.

This meeting then is a step in the right direction. We have come to agitate the subject of vital interest to us all. There are two organs through which public opinion may vent itself, the press and the lecture platform. It is our privilege to have with us to night a representative of both.

One of the most important factors in moulding public opinion to day is the newspaper. Into the homes of the rich as well as the poor it goes carrying conviction to thousands by the logic or cunning of its argument. According as it arrays itself on the side of right and justice or of evil and fraud does it elevate or debase public morals.

A great responsibility rests upon the conscientious journalist, a mighty power is wielded by his pen.

In Mr. T. Thomas Fortune of the New York *Age* we possess a journalist who has always felt this responsibility, who has always been a power for good, a journalist whose opinions have been an education and whose sentiments an inspiration to all earnest souls.[2] His paper has always been a credit to himself as well as to his race, full of food for thought and reflection. His stand has been firmly and irrevocably for the right. Against unscrupulous methods, against cowardly submission, against trickery and treachery he has inveighed with unremitting zeal. With an order and energy worthy of emulation he has worked to disseminate truths bearing upon issues and conditions of vital interest to the whole race.

When Miss Wells, a journalist of the South, exiled for daring to use the prerogative of free speech in defence of her own race, fled to the North, it was Mr. Fortune who espoused her cause and made it possible for her to continue the good work so nobly begun. We admire Miss Wells for her undaunted courage, we laud her zeal in so worthy a cause, we encourage her ambition to enlighten the mind and touch the heart by a thrilling and earnest recital of the wrongs heaped upon her oppressed people in the South.

We extend to her a cordial welcome, we offer her our hearty support. In suppressing Miss Wells's paper, the *Free Speech*, tyranny

---

[2] The *Age*, the most prestigious Afro-American newspaper of the period, was edited by T. Thomas Fortune and Jerome B. Peterson, who hired Wells after the offices of the *Free Speech* were destroyed and her life threatened if she returned to Memphis. Fortune was the author of *Black and White: Land, Labor and Politics in the South* (1884) and *The Negro in Politics* (1885).

has wrought a good work of which it little dreamed. The fetters placed upon the truth in the South are here transformed into weapons against itself.

We congratulate ourselves upon having two such efficient and zealous workers as Miss Wells and Mr. Fortune to address us tonight. The harvest truly is great but the labourers [sic] are few. Too much can not be said, too much can not to be to throw full light upon the dark and dangerous passes along which the Afro-American is obliged to grope his way in the South.

IDA B. WELLS'S 1892 SPEECH

Wednesday evening May 24th, 1892, the city of Memphis was filled with excitement. Editorials in the daily papers of that date caused a meeting to be held in the Cotton Exchange Building; a committee was sent for the editors of the "Free Speech," an Afro-American journal published in that city, and the only reason the open threats of lynching that were made were not carried out was because they could not be found. The cause of all this commotion was the following editorial published in the "Free Speech" May 21st, 1892, the Saturday previous.

> Eight Negroes lynched since last issue of the "Free Speech," one at Little Rock, Ark., last Saturday morning where the citizens broke (?) into the penitentiary and got their man; three near Anniston, Ala., one near New Orleans; and three at Clarksville, Ga., the last three for killing a white man, and five on the same old racket--the new alarm about raping white women. The same programme of hanging, then shooting bullets into the lifeless bodies was carried out to the letter.
>
> Nobody in this section of the country believes the old thread bare

> lie that Negro men rape white women. If Southern white men are not careful, they will over-reach themselves and public sentiment will have a reaction; a conclusion will then be reached which will be very damaging to the moral reputation of their women.

"The Daily Commercial" of Wednesday following, May 25th, contained the following leader:

> Those negroes who are attempting to make the lynching of individuals of their race a means for arousing the worst passions of their kind are playing with a dangerous sentiment. The negroes may as well understand that there is no mercy for the negro rapist and little patience with his defenders. A negro organ printed in this city, in a recent issue publishes the following atrocious paragraph: "Nobody in this section of the country believes the old thread-bare lie that Negro men rape white women. If Southern white men are not careful they will over-reach themselves, and public sentiment will have a reaction; and a conclusion will be reached which will be very damaging to the moral reputation of their women."
>
> The fact that a black scoundrel is allowed to live and utter such loathsome and repulsive calumnies is a volume of evidence as to the wonderful patience of Southern whites. But we have had enough of it.
>
> There are some things that the Southern white man will not tolerate, and the obscene intimations of the foregoing have brought the writer to the very outermost limit

> of public patience. We hope we have said enough.[3]

The "Evening Scimitar" of same date, copied the "Commercial's" editorial with these words of comment:

> Patience under such circumstances is not a virtue. If the negroes themselves do not apply the remedy without delay it will be the duty of those whom he has attacked to tie the wretch who utters these calumnies to a stake at the intersection of Main and Madison Sts., brand him in the forehead with a hot iron and perform upon him a surgical operation with a pair of tailor's shears.

Acting upon this advice, the leading citizens met in the Cotton Exchange Building the same evening, and threats of lynching were freely indulged, not by the lawless element upon which the deviltry of the South is usually saddled--but by the leading business men, in their leading business centre. Mr. Fleming, the business manager and owning a half interest [in] the "Free Speech," had to leave town to escape the mob, and was afterwards ordered not to return; letters and telegrams sent me in New York where I was spending my vacation advised me that bodily harm awaited my return. Creditors took possession of the office and sold the outfit, and the "Free Speech" was as if it had never been.

The editorial in question was prompted by the many inhuman and fiendish lynchings of Afro-Americans which have recently taken place

---

[3] The author of the editorial is identified in Wells's autobiography as "a man named [Edward] Carmack, who afterward became an editor in Nashville, Tennessee" (Duster 1970, 66).

and was meant as a warning. Eight lynched in one week and five of them charged with rape! The thinking public will not easily believe freedom and education more brutalizing than slavery, and the world knows that the crime of rape was unknown during four years of civil war, when the white women of the South were at the mercy of the race which is all at once charged with being a bestial one.

Since my business has been destroyed and I am an exile from home because of that editorial, the issue has been forced, and as the writer of it I feel that the race and the public generally should have a statement of the facts as they exist. They will serve at the same time as a defense for the Afro-American Sampsons [sic] who suffer themselves to be betrayed by white Delilahs.[4]

The whites of Montgomery, Ala., knew J.C. Duke sounded the keynote of the situation--which they would gladly hide from the world, when he said in his paper, "The Herald," five years ago: "Why is it that white women attract negro men now more than in former days? There was a time when such a thing was unheard of. There is a secret to this thing, and we greatly suspect it is the growing appreciation of white Juliets for colored Romeos." Mr. Duke, like the "Free Speech" proprietors, was forced to leave the city for reflecting on the "honah" of white women and his paper suppressed; but the truth remains that Afro-American men do not always rape (?) white women without their consent.

Mr. Duke, before leaving Montgomery, signed a card disclaiming any intention of slandering Southern white women. The editor of the "Free Speech" has no disclaimer to enter, but asserts instead that there are many white women in the South who would marry colored men if such an act would not place them at once beyond the pale of society and within the clutches of the law. The miscegna-

---

[4] See Judges 16:4-21.

tion [sic] laws of the South only operate against the legitimate union of the races; they leave the white man free to seduce all the colored girls he can, but it is death to the colored man who yields to the force and advances of a similar attraction in white women. White men lynch the offending Afro-American, not because he is a despoiler of virtue, but because he succumbs to the smiles of white women.

The "Cleveland Gazette" of January 16, 1892, publishes a case in point. Mrs. J.S. Underwood, the wife of a minister of Elyria, Ohio, accused an Afro-American of rape. She told her husband that during his absence in 1888, stumping the State for the Prohibition Party, the man came to the kitchen door, forced his way in the house and insulted her. She tried to drive him out with a heavy poker, but he overpowered and chloroformed her, and when she revived her clothing was torn and she was in a horrible condition. She did not know the man but could identify him. She pointed out William Offett, a married man, who was arrested and, being in Ohio, was granted a trial.

The prisoner vehemently denied the charge of rape, but confessed he went to Mrs. Underwood's residence at her invitation and was criminally intimate with her at her request. This availed him nothing against the sworn testimony of a minister's wife, a lady of the highest respectability. He was found guilty, and entered the penitentiary, December 14, 1888, for fifteen years. Some time afterwards the woman's remorse led her to confess to her husband that the man was innocent.

These are her words:

> I met Offett at the Post Office. It was raining. He was polite to me, and as I had several bundles in my arms he offered to carry them home for me, which he did. He had a strange fascination for me, and I

> invited him to call on me. He called, bringing chestnuts and candy for the children. By this means we got them to leave us alone in the room. Then I sat on his lap. He made a proposal to me and I readily consented. Why I did so, I do not know, but that I did is true. He visited me several times after that and each time I was indiscreet. I did not care after the first time. In fact I could not have resisted, and had no desire to resist.

When asked by her husband why she told him she had been outraged, she said: "I had several reasons for telling you. One was the neighbors saw the fellows [sic] here; another was, I was afraid I had contracted a loathsome disease, and still another was that I feared I might give birth to a Negro baby. I hoped to save my reputation by telling you a deliberate lie." Her husband, horrified by the confession, had Offett, who had already served four years, released and secured a divorce.

There are thousands of such cases throughout the South, with the difference that the Southern white men in insatiate fury wreak their vengeance without intervention of law upon the Afro-Americans who consort with their women. A few instances to substantiate the assertion that some white women love the company of the Afro-American will not be out of place. Most of these cases were reported by the daily papers of the South.

In the winter of 1885-6 the wife of a practicing physician in Memphis, in good social standing whose name has escaped me, left home, husband and children, and ran away with her black coachman. She was with him a month before her husband found and brought her home. The coachman could not be found. The doctor moved his family away from Memphis, and is living in another city under an assumed name.

In the same city last year a white girl

in the dusk of evening screamed at the approach of some parties that a Negro had assaulted her on the street. He was captured, tried by a white judge and jury, that acquitted him of the charge. It is needless to add if there had been a scrap of evidence on which to convict him of so grave a charge he would have been convicted.

Sarah Clark of Memphis loved a black man and lived openly with him. When she was indicted last spring for miscegenation, she swore in court that she was *not* a white woman. This she did to escape the penitentiary and continued her illicit relation undisturbed. That she is of the lower class of whites, does not disturb the fact that she is a white woman. "The leading citizens" of Memphis are defending the "honor" of *all* white women, *demi-monde* included.

Since the manager of the "Free Speech" has been run away from Memphis by the guardians of the honor of Southern white women, a young girl living on Poplar St., who was discovered in intimate relations with a handsome mulatto young colored man, Will Morgan by name, stole her father's money to send the young fellow away from that father's wrath. She has since joined him in Chicago.

The Memphis "Ledger" for June 8th has the following:

> If Lillie Bailey, a rather pretty white girl seventeen years of age, who is now at the City Hospital, would be somewhat less reserved about here disgrace, there would be some very nauseating details in the story of her life. She is the mother of a little coon. The truth might reveal fearful depravity or it might reveal the evidence of rank outrage. She will not divulge the name of the man who has left such black evidence of her disgrace, and, in fact, says it is a matter in which there can be no interest to

> the outside world. She came to Memphis nearly three months ago and was taken in at the Woman's Refuge in the southern part of the city. She remained there until a few weeks ago, when the child was born. The ladies in charge of the Refuge were horrified. The girl was at once sent to the City Hospital, where she has been since May 30th. She is a country girl. She came to Memphis from her father's farm, a short distance from Hernando, Miss. Just when she left there she would not say. In fact she says she came to Memphis from Arkansas, and says her home is in that State. She is rather good looking, has blue eyes, a low forehead and dark red hair. The ladies at the Woman's Refuge do not know anything about the girl further than what they learned when she was an inmate of the institution; and she would not tell much. When the child was born an attempt was made to get the girl to reveal the name of the Negro who had disgraced her, she obstinately refused and it was impossible to elicit any information from her on the subject.

Note the wording. "The truth might reveal fearful depravity or rank outrage." If it had been a white child or Lillie Bailey had told a pitiful story of Negro outrage, it would have been a case of woman's weakness or assault and she could have remained at the Woman's Refuge. But a Negro child and to withhold its father's name and thus prevent the killing of another Negro "rapist." A case of "fearful depravity."

The very week the "leading citizens" of Memphis were making a spectacle of themselves in defense of all white women of every kind, an Afro-American, M. Stricklin, was found in a white woman's room in that city. Although she made no outcry of rape, he was jailed and would have been lynched, but the woman stated she bought curtains of him (he was a furniture dealer) and his business in her room that night was to put them up. A white woman's word was taken as absolutely in this case as when the cry of rape is made, and he was freed.

What is true of Memphis is true of the entire South. The daily papers last year reported a farmer's wife in Alabama had given birth to a Negro child. When the Negro farm hand who was plowing in the field heard it he took the mule from the plow and fled. The dispatches also told of a woman in South Carolina who gave birth to a Negro child and charged three men with being its father, *every one of whom has since disappeared*. In Tuscumbia, Ala., the colored boy who was lynched there last year for assaulting a white girl told her before his accusers that he had met her there in the woods often before.

Frank Weems of Chattanooga who was not lynched in May only because the prominent citizens became his body guard until the doors of the penitentiary closed on him, had letters in his pocket from the white woman in the case, making the appointment with him. Edward Coy, who was burned alive in Texarkana, January 1, 1892, died protesting his innocence. Investigation since, as given by the Bystander in the "Chicago Inter-Ocean," October 1, proves:

1. The woman who was paraded as a victim of violence was of bad character; her husband was a drunkard and a gambler.

2. She was publicly reported and generally known to have been criminally intimate with Coy for more than a year previous.

3. She was compelled by threats, if not by violence, to make the charge against the victim.

4. When she came to apply the match, Coy asked her if she would burn him after they had

"been sweethearting" so long.

5. A large majority of the "superior" white men prominent in the affair are the reputed fathers of mulatto children.

These are not pleasant facts, but they are illustrative of the vital phase of the so-called "race question," which should properly be designated an earnest inquiry as to the best methods by which religion, science, law and political power may be employed to excuse injustice, barbarity and crime done to a people because of race and color. There can be no possible belief that these people were inspired by any consuming zeal to vindicate God's law against miscegnationists [sic] of the most practical sort. The woman was a willing partner in the victim's guilt, and being of the "superior" race must naturally have been more guilty.

In Natchez, Miss., Mrs. Marshall, one of the *crème de la crème* of the city, created a tremendous sensation several years ago. She has a black coachman who was married, and had been in her employ several years. During this time she gave birth to a child whose color was remarked, but traced to some brunette ancestor, and one of the fashionable dames of the city was its godmother. Mrs. Marshall's social position was unquestioned, and wealth showered every dainty on this child which [sic] was idolized with its brothers and sisters by its white papa. In course of time another child appeared on the scene, but it was unmistakably dark. All were alarmed, and "rush of blood, strangulation" were the conjectures, but the doctor, when asked the cause, grimly told them it was a Negro child. There was a family conclave, the coachman heard of it and leaving his own family went West, and has never returned. As soon as Mrs. Marshall was able to travel she was sent away in deep disgrace. Her husband died within the year of a broken heart.

Ebenzer [sic] Fowler, the wealthiest colored man in Issaquena County, Miss., was shot down on the street in Mayersville, January 30, 1885, just before dark by an armed body of white men who filled his body with bullets. They charged him with writing a note to a white woman of the place, which they intercepted and which proved there was an intimacy existing between them.

Hundreds of such cases might be cited, but enough have been given to prove the assertion that there are white women in the South who love the Afro-American's company even as there are white men notorious for their preference for Afro-American women.

There is hardly a town in the South which has not an instance of the kind which is well-known, and hence the assertion is reiterated that "nobody in the South believes the old thread bare lie that Negro men rape white women." Hence there is a growing demand among Afro-Americans that the guilt or innocence of parties accused of rape be fully established. They know the men of the section of the country who refuse this are not so desirous of punishing rapists as they pretend. The utterances of the leading white men show that with them it is not the crime but the *class*. Bishop Fitzgerald has become apologist for lynchers of the rapists of *white* women only. Governor Tillman, of South Carolina, in the month of June, standing under the tree in Barnwell, S.C., on which eight Afro-Americans were hung [sic] last year, declared that he would "lead a mob to lynch a *negro* who raped a *white* woman."[5] So say the pulpits, officials and newspapers of the South. But when the victim is a colored woman it is different.

Last winter in Baltimore, Md., three white

---

[5] Benjamin Ryan Tillman (1847-1918), Governor (1890-94), later U.S. Senator from South Carolina (1895-1918). He dominated the 1895 state constitutional convention, which adopted rules virtually disfranchising Afro-Americans, and defended the use of force to keep Afro-Americans from voting.

ruffians assaulted a Miss Camphor, a young Afro-American girl, while out walking with a young man of her own race. They held her escort and outraged the girl. It was a deed dastardly enough to arouse Southern blood, which gives its horror of rape as an excuse for lawlessness, but she was an Afro-American. The case went to the courts, an Afro-American lawyer defended the men and they were acquitted.

In Nashville, Tenn., there is a white man, Pat Hanifan, who outraged a little Afro-American girl, and, from the physical injuries received, she has been ruined for life. He was jailed for six months, discharged, and is now a detective in that city. In the same city, last May, a white man outraged an Afro-American girl in a drug store. He was arrested, and released on bail at the trial. It was rumored that five hundred Afro-Americans had organized to lynch him. Two hundred and fifty white citizens armed themselves with Winchesters and guarded him. A cannon was placed in front of his home, and the Buchanan Rifles (State Militia) ordered to the scene for his protection. The Afro-American mob did not materialize. Only two weeks before Eph. Grizzard, who had only been *charged* with rape upon a white woman, had been taken from the jail, with Governor Buchanan and the police and militia standing by, dragged through the streets in broad daylight, knives plunged into him at every step, and with every fiendish cruelty a frenzied mob could devise, he was at last swung out on the bridge with hands cut to pieces as he tried to climb up the stanchions. A naked, bloody example of the blood-thirstiness of the nineteenth century civilization of the Athens of the South! No cannon or military was called out in his defense. He dared to visit a white woman.

At the very moment these civilized whites were announcing their determination "to protect their wives and daughters," by murdering Grizzard, a white man was in the same jail for raping eight-year-old Maggie Reese, an Afro-American girl. He was not harmed. The "honor" of grown women who were glad enough to be supported by the Grizzard boys and Ed Coy, as long as the liasion [sic] was not known, needed protection; they were white. The outrage upon helpless childhood needed no avenging in this case; she was black.

A white man in Guthrie, Oklahoma Territory, two months ago inflicted such injuries upon another Afro-American child that she died. He was not punished, but an attempt was made in the same town in the month of June to lynch an Afro-American who visited a white woman.

In Memphis, Tenn., in the month of June, Ellerton L. Dorr, who is the husband of Russell Hancock's widow, was arrested for attempted rape on Mattie Cole, a neighbor's cook; he was only prevented from accomplishing his purpose, by the appearance of Mattie's employer. Dorr's friends says he was drunk and not responsible for his actions. The grand jury refused to indict him and he was discharged.

The appeal of Southern whites to Northern sympathy and sanction, the adroit, insiduous [sic] plea made by Bishop Fitzgerald for suspension of judgment because those "who condemn lynching express no sympathy for the *white* woman in the case," falls to the ground in the light of the foregoing.

From this exposition of the race issue in lynch law, the whole matter is explained by the well-known opposition growing out of slavery to the progress of the race. This is crystalized in the oft-repeated slogan: "This is a white man's country and the white man must rule." The South resented giving the Afro-American his freedom, the ballot box, and the Civil Rights Law.[6] The raids of the Ku-Klux and White Liners to subvert reconstruction government, the Hamburg and Ellerton, S.C., the Copiah County, Miss., and the Lafayette Parish, La., massacres were excused as the natural resentment of intelligence against government by ignorance.

Honest white men practically conceded the necessity of intelligence murdering ignorance to correct the mistake of the general government, and the race was left to the tender mercies of the solid South. Thoughtful Afro-Americans with the strong arm of the government withdrawn and with the hope to stop such wholesale massacres urged the race to sacrifice its political rights for the sake of peace. They honestly believed the race should fit itself for government, and when that should be done, the objection to race participation in politics would be removed.

But the sacrifice did not remove the trouble, nor move the South to justice. One by one the Southern States have legally (?) disfranchised the Afro-American, and since the repeal of the Civil Rights Bill nearly every Southern State has passed separate car laws with a penalty against their infringement. The race regardless of advancement is penned into filthy, stifling partitions cut off from smoking cars. All this while, although the political cause has been removed, the butcheries of black men at Barnwell, S.C., Carrolton, Miss., Waycross, Ga., and Memphis, Tenn., have gone on; also the flaying alive of a man in

---

[6] Passed in 1871, the third of the Civil Rights Acts (1866, 1870, 1871, 1875) attempted to guarantee Afro-Americans those social rights that were still withheld, penalizing owners of public accommodations and conveyances for discriminating against them. It was declared unconstitutional in 1883 on the grounds that these were not properly civil rights and, hence, not a proper field for federal legislation.

Kentucky, the burning of one in Arkansas, the hanging of a fifteen-year-old girl in Louisiana, a woman in Jackson, Tenn., and one in Hollendale, Miss., until the dark and bloody record of the South shows 728 Afro-Americans lynched during the past 8 years. Not 50 of these were for political causes; the rest were for all manner of accusations from that of rape of white women, to the case of the boy Will Lewis who was hanged at Tullahoma, Tenn., last year for being drunk and "sassy" to white folks.

These statistics, compiled by the Chicago "Tribune," were given the first of this year (1892).[7] Since then, not less than one hundred and fifty have been known to have met violent death at the hands of cruel bloodthirsty mobs during the past nine months.

To palliate this record (which grows worse as the Afro-American becomes intelligent) and excuse some of the most heinous crimes that ever stained the history of a country, the South is shielding itself behind the plausible screen of defending the honor of its women. This, too, in the face of the fact that only *one-third* of the 728 victims to mobs have been *charged* with rape, to say nothing of those of that one-third who were innocent of the charge. A white correspondent of the Baltimore Sun declares that the Afro-American who was lynched in Chesterton, Md., in May for assault on a white girl was innocent; that the deed was done by a white man who had since disappeared. The girl herself maintained that her assailant was a white man. When that poor Afro-American was murdered, the whites excused their refusal of a trial on the ground that they wished to spare the white girl the mortification of having to testify in court.

This cry has had its effect. It closed

---

[7] The *Chicago Tribune* began keeping statistics on lynching in 1882; the number reached an all-time high of 255 (155 of them Afro-Americans) in 1892 (McPherson 1975, 303).

the heart, stifled the conscience, warped the judgment and hushed the voice of press and pulpit on the subject of lynch law throughout this "land of liberty." Men who stand high in the esteem of the public for christian character, for moral and physical courage, for devotion to the principles of equal and exact justice to all, and for great sagacity, stand as cowards who fear to open their mouths before this great outrage. They do not see that by their tacit encouragement, their silent acquiescence, the black shadow of lawlessness in the form of lynch law is spreading its wings over the whole country.

Men who, like Governor Tillman, start the ball of lynch law rolling for a certain crime, are powerless to stop it when drunken or criminal white toughs feel like hanging an Afro-American on any pretext.

Even to the better class of Afro-Americans the crime of rape is so revolting they have too often taken the white man's word and given lynch law neither the investigation nor condemnation it deserved.

They forget that a concession of the right to lynch a man for a certain crime, not only concedes the right to lynch any person for any crime, but (so frequently is the cry of rape now raised) it is in a fair way to stamp us a race of rapists and desperadoes. They have gone on hoping and believing that general education and financial strength would solve the difficulty, and are devoting their energies to the accumulation of both.

The mob spirit has grown with the increasing intelligence of the Afro-American. It has left the out-of-the-way places where ignorance prevails, has thrown off the mask and with this new cry stalks in broad daylight in large cities, the centres of civilization, and is encouraged by the "leading citizens" and the press.

The "Daily Commercial" and "Evening Scimitar" of Memphis, Tenn., are owned by leading business men of that city, and yet, in spite of the fact that there had been no white woman in Memphis outraged by an Afro-American, and that Memphis possessed a thrifty law-abiding, property owning class of Afro-Americans, the "Commercial" of May 17th, under the head of "More Rapes, More Lynchings" gave utterance to the following:

> The lynching of three Negro scoundrels reported in our dispatches from Anniston, Ala., for a brutal outrage committed upon a white woman will be a text for much comment on "Southern barbarism" by Northern newspapers; but we fancy it will hardly prove effective for campaign purposes among intelligent people. The frequency of these lynchings calls attention to the frequency of the crimes which causes lynching. The "Southern barbarism" which deserves the serious attention of all people North and South, is the barbarism which preys upon weak and defenseless women. Nothing but the most prompt, speedy and extreme punishment can hold in check the horrible and beastial [sic] propensities of the Negro race. There is a strange similarity about a number of cases of this character which have lately occurred.
>
> In each case the crime was deliberately planned and perpetrated by several Negroes. They watched for an opportunity when the women were left without a protector. It was not a sudden yielding to a fit of passion, but the consummation of a devilish purpose which has been seeking and waiting for the opportunity. This feature of the crime not only makes it the most fiendishly brutal, but it adds to the terror of the situation in the thinly settled country communities. No man can leave his family at night

without the dread that some roving Negro ruffian is watching and waiting for this opportunity. The swift punishment which invariably follows these horrible crimes doubtless acts as a deterring effect upon the Negroes in that immediate neighborhood for a short time. But the lesson is not widely learned nor long remembered. Then such crimes, equally atrocious, have happened in quick succession, one in Tennessee, one in Arkansas, and one in Alabama. The facts of the crime appear to appeal more to the Negro's lustful imagination than the facts of the punishment do to his fears. He sets aside all fear of death in any form when opportunity is found for the gratification of his bestial desires.

There is small reason to hope for any change for the better. The commission of this crime grows more frequent every year. The generation of Negroes which have grown up since the war have lost in large measure the traditional and wholesome awe of the white race which kept the Negroes in subjection, even when their masters were in the army, and their families left unprotected except by the slaves themselves. There is no longer a restraint upon the brute passion of the Negro.

What is to be done? The crime of rape is always horrible, but [for] the Southern man there is nothing which so fills the soul with horror, loathing and fury as the outraging of a white woman by a Negro. It is the race question in the ugliest, vilest, most dangerous aspect. The Negro as a political factor can be controlled. But neither laws nor lynchings can subdue his lusts.

> Sooner or later it will force a crisis. We do not know in what form it will come.

In its issue of June 4th, the Memphis "Evening Scimitar" gives the following excuse for lynch law:

> Aside from the violation of white women by Negroes, which is the outcropping of a bestial perversion of instinct, the chief cause of trouble between the races in the South is the Negro's lack of manners. In the state of slavery he learned politeness from association with white people, who took pains to teach him. Since the emancipation came and the tie of mutual interest and regard between master and servant was broken, the Negro has drifted away into a state which is neither freedom nor bondage. Lacking the proper inspiration of the one and the restraining force of the other he has taken up the idea that boorish insolence is independence, and the exercise of a decent degree of breeding toward white people is identical with servile submission. In consequence of the prevalence of this notion there are many Negroes who use every opportunity to make themselves offensive, particularly when they think it can be done with impunity.
>
> We have had too many instances right here in Memphis to doubt this, and our experience is not exceptional. *The white people won't stand this sort of thing, and whether they be insulted as individuals are [sic] as a race, the response will be prompt and effectual.* The bloody riot of 1866, in which so many Negroes perished, was

> brought on principally by the outrageous conduct of the blacks toward the whites on the streets. It is also a remarkable and discouraging fact that the majority of such scoundrels are Negroes who have received educational advantages at the hands of the white taxpayers. They have got just enough of learning to make them realize how hopelessly their race is behind the other in everything that makes a great people, and they attempt to "get even" by insolence, which is ever the resentment of inferiors. There are well-bred Negroes among us, and it is truly unfortunate that they should have to pay, even in part, the penalty of the offenses committed by the baser sort, but this is the way of the world. The innocent must suffer for the guilty. If the Negroes as a people possessed a hundredth part of the self-respect which is evidenced by the courteous bearing of some that the "Scimitar" could name, the friction between the races would be reduced to a minimum. It will not do to beg the question by pleading that many white men are also stirring up strife. The Caucasian blackguard simply obeys the promptings of a depraved disposition, and he is seldom deliberately rough or offensive toward strangers or unprotected women.
>
> The Negro tough, on the contrary, is given to just that kind of offending, and he almost invariably singles out white people as his victims.

On March 9th, 1892, there were lynched in this same city three of the best specimens of young since-the-war Afro-American manhood.

They were peaceful, law-abiding citizens and energetic business men.[8]

They believed the problem was to be solved by eschewing politics and putting money in the purse. They owned a flourishing grocery business in a thickly populated suburb of Memphis, and a white man named Barrett had one on the opposite corner. After a personal difficulty, which Barrett sought by going into the "People's Grocery" drawing a pistol and was thrashed by Calvin McDowell, he (Barrett) threatened to "clean them out." These men were a mile beyond the city limits and police protection; hearing that Barrett's crowd was coming to attack them Saturday night, they mustered forces and prepared to defend themselves against attack.

When Barrett came, he led a *posse* of officers, twelve in number, who afterward claimed to be hunting a man for whom they had a warrant. That twelve men in citizen's clothes should think it necessary to go in the night to hunt one man who had never before been arrested, or made any record as a criminal has never been explained. When they entered the back door the young men thought the threatened attack was on, and fired into them. Three of the officers were wounded, and when the *defending* party found it was officers of the law upon whom they had fired, they ceased and got away.

Thirty-one men were arrested and thrown in jail as "conspirators," although they all declared more than once they did not know they were firing on officers. Excitement was at fever heat until the morning papers, two days after, announced that the wounded deputy sheriffs were out of danger. This hindered rather than helped the plans of the whites. There was no law on the statute books which would execute an Afro-American for wounding a

---

[8] For a further report of this lynching and its impact on Wells and Church Terrell, see Giddings 1984, 17-20.

white man, but the "unwritten law" did. Three of these men, the president, the manager and clerk of the grocery--"the leaders of the conspiracy"--were secretly taken from jail and lynched in a shockingly brutal manner. "The Negroes are getting too independent," they say, "we must teach them a lesson."

"What lesson?["] The lesson of subordination. "Kill the leaders and it will cow the Negro who dares to shoot a white man, even in self-defense."

Although the race was wild over the outrage, the mockery of law and justice which disarmed men and locked them up in jails where they could be easily and safely reached by the mob--the Afro-American ministers, newspapers and leaders counselled obedience to the law which did not protect them.

Their counsel was heeded and not a hand was uplifted to resent the outrage; following the advice of the "Free Speech," people left the city in great numbers.

The dailies and associated press reports heralded these men to the country as "toughs," and "Negro desperadoes who kept a low dive." This same press service printed that the Negro who was lynched at Indianola, Miss., in May, had outraged the sheriff's eight-year-old daughter. The girl was more than eighteen years old, and was found by her father in this man's room, who was a servant on the place.

Not content with misrepresenting the race, the mob-spirit was not to be satisfied until the paper which was doing all it could to counteract this impression was silenced. The colored people were resenting their bad treatment in a way to make itself felt, yet gave the mob no excuse for further murder, until the appearance of the editorial which is construed as a reflection on the "honor" of the Southern white women. It is not half so libelous as that of the "Commercial" which appeared four days before, and which has been given in these pages. They would have lynched the manager of the "Free Speech" for exercising the right of free speech if they had found him as quickly as they would have hung [sic] a rapist, and glad of the excuse to do so. The owners were ordered not to return. "The Free Speech" was suspended with as little compunction as the business of the "People's Grocery" broken up and the proprietors murdered.

Henry W. Grady in his well-remembered speeches in New England and New York pictured the Afro-American as incapable of self-government.[9] Through him and other leading men the cry of the South to the country has been "Hands off! Leave us to solve our problem." To the Afro-American the South says, "the white man must and will rule." There is little difference between the Ante-bellum South and the New South.

Her white citizens are wedded to any method however revolting, any measure however extreme, for the subjugation of the young manhood of the race. They have cheated him out of his ballot, deprived him of civil rights or redress therefor in the civil courts, robbed him of the fruits of his labor, and are still murdering, burning and lynching him.

The result is a growing disregard of human life. Lynch law has spread its insiduous [sic] influence till men in New York State, Pennsylvania, and on the free Western plains feel they can take the law in their own hands with impunity, especially where an Afro-American is concerned. The South is brutalized to a degree not realized by its own inhabitants, and the very foundation of government, law and order, are imperilled.

Public sentiment has had a slight "reaction" though not sufficient to stop the crusade of lawlessness and lynching. The spirit of christianity of the great M[ethod-

---

[9] Henry W. Grady (1850-89) was editor of the *Atlanta Constitution* and gained fame with his speech "The New South" (1890), delivered in New York in 1886.

ist] E[piscopal] Church was aroused to the frequent and revolting crimes against a weak people, enough to pass strong condemnatory resolutions at its General Conference in Omaha last May. The spirit of justice of the grand old party asserted itself sufficiently to secure a denunciation of the wrongs, and a feeble declaration of the belief in human rights in the Republican platform at Minneapolis, June 7th. Some of the great dailies and weeklies have swung into line declaring that lynch law must go. The President of the United States issued a proclamation that it be not tolerated in the territories over which he has jurisdiction.[10] Governor Northern and Chief Justice Bleckley of Georgia have proclaimed against it. The citizens of Chattanooga, Tenn., have set a worthy example in that they not only condemn lynch law, but her public men demanded a trial for Weems, the accused rapist, and guarded him while the trial was in progress. The trial only lasted ten minutes, and Weems chose to plead guilty and accept twenty-one years sentence, than invite the certain death which awaited him outside that cordon of police if he had told the truth and shown the letters he had from the white woman in the case.

Col. A.S. Colyar, of Nashville, Tenn., is so overcome with the horrible state of affairs that he addressed the following earnest letter to the Nashville "American."

> Nothing since I have been a reading man has so impressed me with the decay of manhood among the people of Tennessee as the dastardly submission to the mob reign. We have

---

[10] Benjamin Harrison (1833-1901), U.S. President (1889-1893), was visited by Mary Church Terrell and Frederick Douglass, who asked him to support an anti-lynching bill in his state of the union message of 1893, but he refused (Davis 1982, 2:79).

> reached the unprecedented low level; the awful criminal depravity of substituting the mob for the court and jury, of giving up the jail keys to the mob whenever they are demanded. We do it in the largest cities and in the country towns; we do it in midday; we do it after full, not to say formal, notice, and so thoroughly and generally is it acquiesced in that the murderers have discarded the formula of masks. They go into the town where everybody knows them, sometimes under the gaze of the governor, in the presence of the courts, in the presence of the sheriff and his deputies, in the presence of the entire police force, take out the prisoner, take his life, often with fiendish glee, and often with acts of cruelty and barbarism which impress the reader with a degeneracy rapidly approaching savage life. That the State is disgraced but faintly expresses the humiliation which has settled upon the once proud people of Tennessee. The State, in its majesty, through its organized life, for which the people pay liberally, makes but one record, but one note, and that a criminal falsehood, "was hung by persons to the jury unknown." The murder at Shelbyville is only a verification of what every intelligent man knew would come, because with a mob a rumor is as good as a proof.

These efforts brought forth apologies and a short halt, but the lynching mania was [sic] raged again through the past three months with unabated fury.

The strong arm of the law must be brought to bear upon lynchers in severe punishment, but this cannot and will not be done unless a healthy public sentiment demands and sustains such action.

The men and women in the South who disapprove of lynching and remain silent on the perpetration of such outrages are *particeps criminis*, accomplices, accessories before and after the fact, equally guilty with the actual law-breakers who would not persist if they did not know that neither the law nor militia would be employed against them.

In the creation of this healthier public sentiment, the Afro-American can do for himself what no one else can do for him. The world looks on with wonder that we have conceded so much and remain law-abiding under such great outrage and provocation.

To Northern capital and Afro-American labor the South owes its rehabilitation. If labor is withdrawn capital will not remain. The Afro-American is thus the backbone of the South. A thorough knowledge and judicious exercise of this power in lynching localities could many times effect a bloodless revolution. The white man's dollar is his god, and to stop this will be to stop outrages in many localities.

The Afro-Americans of Memphis denounced the lynching of three of their best citizens, and urged and waited for the authorities to act in the matter and bring the lynchers to justice. No attempt was made to do so, and the black men left the city by thousands, bringing about great stagnation in every branch of business. Those who remained so injured the business of the street car company by staying off the cars, that the superintendent, manager and treasurer called personally on the editor of the "Free Speech," asked them to urge our people to give them their patronage again. Other business men became alarmed over the situation and the "Free Speech" was run away that the colored people might be more easily controlled. A meeting of white citizens in June, three months after the lynching, passed resolutions for the first time, condemning it. *But they did not punish the lynchers.*[11] Every one of them was known by name, because they had been selected to do the dirty work, by some of the very citizens who passed these resolutions. Memphis is fast losing her black population, who proclaim as they go that there is no protection for the life and property of any Afro-American citizen in Memphis who is not a slave.

The Afro-American citizens of Kentucky, whose intellectual and financial improvement has been phenomenal, have never had a separate car law until now. Delegations and petitions poured into the Legislature against it, yet the bill passed and the Jim Crow Car of Kentucky is a legalized institution. Will the great mass of Negroes continue to patronize the railroad? A special from Covington, Ky., says:

> Covington, June 13th.--The railroads of the State are beginning to feel very markedly, the effects of the separate coach bill recently passed by the Legislature. No class of people in the State have so many and so largely attended excursion as the blacks. All these have been abandoned, and regular travel is reduced to a minimum. A competent authority says the loss to the various roads will reach $1,000,000 this year.

A call to a State Conference in Lexington, Ky., last June had delegates from every county in the State. Those delegates, the ministers, teachers, heads of secret and other orders, and the head of every family should pass the word around for every member of the race in Kentucky to stay off railroads unless

---

[11] The overall record of not convicting known lynchers and of not punishing convicted lynchers severely is detailed by Motley 1966, 516-19.

obliged to ride. If they did so, and their advice was followed persistently the convention would not need to petition the Legislature to repeal the law or raise money to file a suit. The railroad corporations would be so effected [sic] they would in self-defense lobby to have the separate car law repealed. On the other hand, as long as the railroads can get Afro-American excursions they will always have plenty of money to fight all the suits brought against them. They will be aided in so doing by the same partisan public sentiment which passed the law. White men passed the law, and white judges and juries would pass upon the suits against the law, and render judgment in line with their prejudices and in deference to the greater financial power.

The appeal to the white man's pocket has ever been more effectual than all the appeals ever made to his conscience. Nothing, absolutely nothing, is to be gained by a further sacrifice of manhood and self-respect. By the right exercise of his power as the industrial factor of the South, the Afro-American can demand and secure his rights, the punishment of lynchers, and a fair trial for accused rapists.

Of the many inhuman outrages of this present year, the only case where the proposed lynching did *not* occur, was where the men armed themselves in Jacksonville, Fla., and Paducah, Ky., and prevented it. The only times an Afro-American who was assaulted got away has been when he had a gun and used it in self-defense.

The lesson this teaches and which every Afro-American should ponder well, is that a Winchester rifle should have a place of honor in every black home, and it should be used for that protection which the law refuses to give. When the white man who is always the aggressor knows he runs as great risk of biting the dust every time his Afro-American victim does, he will have greater respect for Afro-American life. The more the Afro-American yields and cringes and begs, the more he has to do so, the more he is insulted, outraged and lynched.

The assertion has been substantiated throughout these pages that the press contains unreliable and doctored reports of lynchings, and one of the most necessary things for the race to do is to get these facts before the public. The people must know before they can act, and there is no educator to compare with the press.

The Afro-American papers are the only ones which will print the truth, and they lack means to employ agents and detectives to get at the facts. The race must rally a mighty host to the support of their journals, and thus enable them to do much in the way of investigation.

A lynching occurred at Port Jarvis, N.Y., the first week in June. A white and colored man were implicated in the assault upon a white girl. It was charged that the white man paid the colored boy to make the assault, which he did on the public highway in broad day time, and was lynched. This, too, was done by "parties unknown." The white man in the case still lives. He was imprisoned and promises to fight the case on trial. At the preliminary examination, it developed that he had been a suitor of the girl's. She had repulsed and refused him, yet had given him money, and he had sent threatening letters demanding more.

The day before this examination she was so wrought up, she left home and wandered miles away. When found she said she did so because she was afraid of the man's testimony. Why should she be afraid of the prisoner? Why should she yield to his demands for money if not to prevent him exposing something he knew? It seems explainable only on the hypothesis that a *liason* [sic] existed between the colored boy and the girl, and the white man knew of it. The press is singularly silent. Has it a motive? We owe it to ourselves to find out.

The story comes from Larned, Kansas, Oct.

1st, that a young white lady held at bay until daylight, without alarming any one in the house, "a burly Negro" who entered her room and bed. The "burly Negro" was promptly lynched without investigation or examination of inconsistent stories.

A house was found burned down near Mongomery, Ala., in Monroe County, Oct. 13th, a few weeks ago; also the burned bodies of the owners and melted piles of gold and silver.

These discoveries led to the conclusion that the awful crime was not prompted by motives of robbery. The suggestion of the whites was that "brutal lust was the incentive, and as there are nearly 200 Negroes living within a radius of five miles of the place the conclusion was inevitable that some of them were the perpetrators."

Upon this "suggestion," probably made by the real criminal, the mob acted upon the "conclusion" and arrested ten Afro-Americans, four of whom, they tell the world, confessed to the deed of murdering Richard L. Johnson and outraging his daughter, Jeanette. These four men, Berrell Jones, Moses Johnson, Jim and John Packer, none of them 25 years of age, upon this conclusion, were taken from jail, hanged, shot, and burned while yet alive the night of Oct. 12th. The same report says Mr. Johnson was on the best of terms with his Negro tenants.

The race thus outraged must find out the facts of this awful hurling of men into eternity on supposition, and give them to the indifferent and apathetic country. We feel this to be a garbled report, but how can we prove it?

Near Vicksburg, Miss., a murder was committed by a gang of burglars. Of course it must have been done by Negroes, and Negroes were arrested for it. It is believed that 2 men, Smith Tooley and John Adams, belonged to a gang controlled by white men and, fearing exposure, on the night of July 4th, they were hanged in the Court House yard by those interested in silencing them. Robberies since committed in the same vicinity have been known to be by white men who had their faces blackened. We strongly believe in the innocence of these murdered men, but we have no proof. No other news goes out to the world save that which stamps us as a race of cut-throats, robbers and lustful wild beasts. So great is Southern hate and prejudice, they legally (?) hung [sic] poor little thirteen-year-old Mildrey Brown at Columbia, S.C., Oct. 7th, on the circumstantial evidence that she poisoned a white infant. If her guilt had been proven unmistakably, had she been white, Mildrey Brown would never have been hung.

The country would have been aroused and South Carolina disgraced forever for such a crime. The Afro-American himself did not know as he should have known, as his journals should be in a position to have him know and act.

Nothing is more definitely settled than [that] he must act for himself. I have shown how he may employ the boycott, emigration and the press, and I feel that by a combination of all these agencies can be effectually stamped out lynch law, that last relic of barbarism and slavery. "The gods help those who help themselves."[12]

---

[12] "God loves to help him who strives to help himself," reads Aeschylus, Fragment 223. Similar maxims are found in fragments from the works of Sophocles and Euripedes.

21

Mary Church Terrell, "What It Means to Be Colored in the Capital of the United States," 1906

Mary Church (1863-1954) was the daughter of the South's first Afro-American millionaire. She graduated from Oberlin in 1884, studied in Germany, France, and Italy, taught at Wilberforce University, Xenia, OH, and the M Street High School, Washington, D.C., and was a member of the District of Columbia Board of Education. She became a professional lecturer campaigning against lynching, disfranchisement, and discrimination against Afro-Americans and for woman suffrage and racial pride. She was the first president of the National Association of Colored Women and a charter member of the National Association for the Advancement of Colored People. She spoke frequently to white audiences in the belief that ignorance was a major cause of racism.

This speech was delivered before the Washington, D.C., United Women's Club on October 10, 1906. It was later published in the **Independent** (Terrell 1907).

Washington, D.C., has been called "The Colored Man's Paradise." Whether this sobriquet was given to the national capital in bitter irony by a member of the handicapped race, as he reviewed some of his own persecutions and rebuffs, or whether it was given immediately after the war by an ex-slave-holder who for the first time in his life saw colored people walking about like freemen, minus the overseer and his whip, history saith not. It is certain that it would be difficult to find a worse misnomer for Washington than "The Colored Man's Paradise" if so prosaic a consideration as veracity is to determine the appropriateness of a name.

For fifteen years I have resided in Washington, and while it was far from being a paradise for colored people, when I first touched these shores, it has been doing its level best ever since to make conditions for us intolerable. As a colored woman I might enter Washington any night, a stranger in a strange land, and walk miles without finding a place to lay my head. Unless I happened to know colored people who live here or ran across a chance acquaintance who could recommend a colored boarding-house to me, I should be obliged to spend the entire night wandering about. Indians, Chinamen [sic], Filipinos, Japanese and representatives of any other dark race can find hotel accommodations, if they can pay for them. The colored man alone is thrust out of the hotels of the national capital like a leper.

As a colored woman I may walk from the Capitol to the White House, ravenously hungry and abundantly supplied with money with which to purchase a meal, without finding a single restaurant in which I would be permitted to take a morsel of food, if it was patronized by white people, unless I were willing to sit behind a screen. As a colored woman I cannot visit the tomb of the Father of this country, which owes its very existence to the love of freedom in the human heart and which stands for equal opportunity to all, without being forced to sit in the Jim Crow section of an electric car which starts from the very heart of the city--midway between the Capitol and the White House. If I refuse thus to be humiliated, I am cast into jail and forced to pay a fine for violating the Virginia laws. Every hour in the day Jim Crow cars filled with colored people, many of whom are intelligent and well to do, enter and leave the national capital.

As a colored woman I may enter more than one white church in Washington without receiving that welcome which as a human being I have a right to expect in the sanctuary of God. Sometimes the color blindness of the usher takes on that peculiar form which prevents a dark face from making any impression whatsoever upon his retina, so that it is impossible for him to see colored people at all. If he is not so afflicted, after keeping a colored man or woman waiting a long time, he will ungraciously show these dusky Christians who have had the temerity to thrust themselves into a temple where only the fair of face are expected to worship God to a seat in the rear, which is named in honor of a certain personage, well known in this country, and commonly called Jim Crow.

Unless I am willing to engage in a few menial occupations, in which the pay for my services would be very poor, there is no way for me to earn an honest living, if I am not a trained nurse or a dressmaker or can secure a position as teacher in the public schools, which is exceedingly difficult to do. It matters not what my intellectual attainments may be or how great is the need of the services of a competent person, if I try to enter many of the numerous vocations in which my white sisters are allowed to engage, the door is shut in my face.

From one Washington theater I am excluded altogether. In the remainder certain seats are set aside for colored people, and it is almost impossible to secure others. I once telephoned to the ticket seller just before a matinee and asked if a neat-appearing colored nurse would be allowed to sit in the parquet with her little white charge, and the answer rushed quickly and positively thru [sic] the receiver--NO. When I remonstrated a bit and told him that in some of the theaters colored nurses were allowed to sit with the white children for whom they cared, the ticket seller told me that in Washington it was very poor policy to employ colored nurses, for they were excluded from many places where white girls would be allowed to take children for pleasure.

If I possess artistic talent, there is not a single art school of repute which will admit me. A few years ago a colored woman who possessed great talent submitted some drawings to the Corcoran Art School, of Washington, which were accepted by the committee of awards, who sent her a ticket entitling her to a course in this school. But when the committee discovered that the young woman was colored, they declined to admit her, and told her that if they had suspected that her drawings had been made by a colored woman, they would not have examined them at all. The efforts of Frederick Douglass[1] and a lawyer of great repute who took a keen interest in the affair were unavailing. In order to cultivate her talent this young woman was forced to leave her comfortable home in Washington and incur the expense of going to New York. Having entered the Woman's Art School of Cooper Union, she graduated with honor, and then went to Paris to continue her studies, where she achieved signal success and was complimented by some of the greatest living artists in France.

With the exception of the Catholic University, there is not a single white college in the national capital to which colored people are admitted, no matter how great their ability, how lofty their ambition, how unexceptionable their character or how great their thirst for knowledge may be.

A few years ago the Columbian Law School admitted colored students, but in deference to the Southern white students the authorities have decided to exclude them altogether.

Some time ago a young woman who had already attracted some attention in the

---

[1] See headnote p. 33.

literary world by her volume of short stories answered an advertisement which appeared in a Washington newspaper, which called for the services of a skilled stenographer and expert typewriter. It is unnecessary to state the reasons why a young woman whose literary ability was so great as that possessed by the one referred to should decide to earn money in this way. The applicants were requested to send specimens of their work and answer certain questions concerning their experience and their speed before they called in person. In reply to her application the young colored woman, who, by the way, is very fair and attractive indeed, received a letter from the firm stating that her references and experience were the most satisfactory that had been sent and requesting her to call. When she presented herself there was some doubt in the mind of the man to whom she was directed concerning her racial pedigree, so he asked her point-blank whether she was colored or white. When she confessed the truth the merchant expressed great sorrow and deep regret that he could not avail himself of the services of so competent a person, but frankly admitted that employing a colored woman in his establishment in any except a menial position was simply out of the question.

Another young friend had an experience which, for some reasons, was still more disheartening and bitter than the one just mentioned. In order to secure lucrative employment she left Washington and went to New York. There she worked her way up in one of the largest dry goods stores till she was placed as saleswoman in the cloak department. Tired of being separated from her family, she decided to return to Washington, feeling sure that, with her experience and her fine recommendation from the New York firm, she could easily secure employment. Nor was she overconfident, for the proprietor of one of the largest dry goods stores in her native city was glad to secure the services of a young woman who brought such hearty credentials from New York. She had not been in this store very long, however, before she called upon me one day and asked me to intercede with the proprietor in her behalf, saying that she had been discharged that afternoon because it had been discovered that she was colored. When I called upon my young friend's employer he made no effort to avoid the issue, as I feared he would. He did not say he had discharged the young saleswoman because she had not given satisfaction, as he might easily have done. On the contrary, he admitted without the slightest hesitation that the young woman he had just discharged was one of the best clerks he had ever had. In the cloak department, where she had been assigned, she had been a brilliant success, he said. "But I cannot keep Miss Smith in my employ," he concluded. "Are you not master of your own store?" I ventured to inquire. The proprietor of this store was a Jew, and I felt that it was particularly cruel, unnatural and cold-blooded for the representative of one oppressed and persecuted race to deal so harshly and unjustly with a member of another. I had intended to make this point when I decided to intercede for my young friend, but when I thought how a reference to the persecution of his own race would wound his feelings, the words froze on my lips. "When I first heard your friend was colored," he explained, "I did not believe it and said so to the clerks who made the statement. Finally, the girls who had been most pronounced in their opposition to working in a store with a colored girl came to me in a body and threatened to strike. 'Strike away,' said I, 'your places will be easily filled.' Then they started on another tack. Delegation after delegation began to file down to my office, some of the women my very best customers, to protest against my employing a colored girl. Moreover, they threatened to boycott my store if I did not discharge her at once. Then it became a question of bread and butter and I yielded to the inevitable--that's all. Now," said he, concluding, "if I lived in a great, cosmopolitan city like New York, I should do as I pleased, and refuse to discharge a girl simply because she was colored." But I thought of a similar incident that happened in New York. I remembered that a colored woman, as fair as a lily and as beautiful as a Madonna, who was the head saleswoman in a large department store in New York, had been discharged, after she had held this position for years, when the proprietor accidentally discovered that a fatal drop of African blood was percolating somewhere thru [sic] her veins.

Not only can colored women secure no employment in the Washington stores, department and otherwise, except as menials, and such positions, of course, are few, but even as customers they are not infrequently treated with discourtesy both by the clerks and the proprietor himself. Following the trend of the times, the senior partner of the largest and best department store in Washington, who originally hailed from Boston, once the home of William Lloyd Garrison, Wendell Phillips, and Charles Sumner, if my memory serves me right,[2] decided to open a restaurant in his store. Tired and hungry after her morning's shopping a colored school teacher, whose relation to her African progenitors is so remote as scarcely to be discernible to the naked eye, took a seat at one of the tables in the restaurant of this Boston [sic] store. After sitting unnoticed a long time the colored teacher asked a waiter who passed her by if she would not take her order. She was quickly informed that colored people could not be served in that restaurant and was obliged to leave in confusion and shame, much to the amusement of the waiters and the guests who had noticed the incident. Shortly after that a teacher in Howard University, one of the

---

[2] All three worked actively for the abolition of slavery. See headnote p. 188 and p. 265 n 11.

best schools for colored youth in the country, was similarly insulted in the restaurant of the same store.

In one of the Washington theaters from which colored people are excluded altogether, members of the race have been viciously assaulted several times, for the proprietor well knows that colored people have no redress for such discriminations against them in the District courts. Not long ago a colored clerk in one of the departments who looks more like his paternal ancestors who fought for the lost cause than his grandmothers who were the victims of the peculiar institution, bought a ticket for the parquet of this theater in which colored people are nowhere welcome, for himself and mother, whose complexion is a bit swarthy. The usher refused to allow the young man to take the seats for which his tickets called and tried to snatch from him the coupons. A scuffle ensued and both mother and son were ejected by force. A suit was brought against the proprietor and the damages awarded the injured man and his mother amounted to the munificent sum of one cent. One of the teachers in the Colored High School received similar treatment in the same theater.

Not long ago one of my little daughter's bosom friends figured in one of the most pathetic instances of which I have ever heard. A gentleman who is very fond of children promised to take six little girls in his neighborhood to a matinee. It happened that he himself and five of his little friends were so fair that they easily passed muster, as they stood in judgment before the ticket seller and the ticket taker. Three of the little girls were sisters, two of whom were very fair and the other a bit brown. Just as this little girl, who happened to be last in the procession, went by the ticket taker, that argus-eyed[3] sophisticated gentleman detected something which caused a deep, dark frown to mantle his brow and he did not allow her to pass. "I guess you have made a mistake," he called to the host of this theater party. "Those little girls," pointing to the fair ones, "may be admitted, but this one," designating the brown one, "can't." But the colored man was quite equal to the emergency. Fairly frothing at the mouth with anger, he asked the ticket taker what he meant, what he was trying to insinuate about that particular little girl. "Do you mean to tell me," he shouted in rage, "that I must go clear to the Philippine Islands to bring this child to the United States and then I can't take her to the theater in the National Capital?" The little ruse succeeded brilliantly, as he knew it would. "Beg your pardon," said the ticket taker, "don't know what I was thinking about. Of course she can go in."

"What was the matter with me this afternoon? mother," asked the little brown girl innocently, when she mentioned the affair at home. "Why did the man at the theater let my two sisters and the other girls in and try to keep me out?" In relating this incident, the child's mother told me her little girl's question, which showed such blissful ignorance of the depressing, cruel conditions which confronted her, completely unnerved her for a time.

Altho [sic] white and colored teachers are under the same Board of Education and the system for the children of both races is said to be uniform, prejudice against the colored teachers in the public schools is manifested in a variety of ways. From 1870 to 1900 there was a colored superintendent at the head of the colored schools. During all that time the directors of the cooking, sewing, physical

---

[3] In Greek mythology, Argus, a giant with a thousand eyes, was made guardian of Io and was later slain by Hermes.

culture, manual training, music and art departments were colored people. Six years ago a change was inaugurated. The colored superintendent was legislated out of office and the directorships, without a single exception, were taken from colored teachers and given to the whites. There was no complaint about the work done by the colored directors, no more than is heard about every officer in every school. The directors of the art and physical culture departments were particularly fine. Now, no matter how competent or superior the colored teachers in our public schools may be, they know that they can never rise to the height of a directorship, can never hope to be more than an assistant and receive the meager salary therefor, unless the present regime is radically changed.

Not long ago one of the most distinguished kindergartners in the country came to deliver a course of lectures in Washington. The colored teachers were eager to attend, but they could not buy the coveted privilege for love or money. When they appealed to the director of kindergartens, they were told that the expert kindergartner had come to Washington under the auspices of private individuals, so that she could not possibly have them admitted. Realizing what a loss colored teachers had sustained in being deprived of the information and inspiration which these lectures afforded, one of the white teachers volunteered to repeat them as best she could for the benefit of her colored co-laborers for half the price she herself had paid, and the proposition was eagerly accepted by some.

Strenuous efforts are being made to run Jim Crow streetcars in the national capital. "Resolved, that a Jim Crow law should be adopted and enforced in the District of Columbia," was the subject of a discussion engaged in last January by the Columbian Debating Society of the George Washington University in our national capital, and the decision was rendered in favor of the affirmative. Representative Heflin, of Alabama, who introduced a bill providing for Jim Crow street cars in the District of Columbia last winter, has just received a letter from the president of the East Brookland Citizens' Association "indorsing [sic] the movement for separate street cars and sincerely hoping that you will be successful in getting this enacted into a law as soon as possible."[4] Brookland is a suburb of Washington.

The colored laborer's path to a decent livelihood is by no means smooth. Into some of the trades unions here he is admitted, while from others he is excluded altogether. By the union men this is denied, altho [sic] I am personally acquainted with skilled workmen who tell me they are not admitted into the unions because they are colored. But even when they are allowed to join the unions they frequently derive little benefit, owing to certain tricks of the trade. When the word passes round that help is needed and colored laborers apply, they are often told by the union officials that they have secured all the men they needed, because the places are reserved for white men, until they have been provided with jobs, and colored men must remain idle, unless the supply of white men is too small.

I am personally acquainted with one of the most skilful laborers in the hardware business in Washington. For thirty years he has been working for the same firm. He told me he could not join the union, and that his employer had been almost forced to discharge him, because the union men threatened to boycott his store if he did not. If another man could have been found at the time to take his place he would have lost his job, he said.

---

[4] James Thomas Heflin (1869-1951), U.S. Senator (1920-30), anti-Roman Catholic crusader and supporter of white supremacy, famous for theatrical oratory and distinctive dress.

When no other human being can bring a refractory chimney or stove to its senses, this colored man is called upon as the court of last appeal. If he fails to subdue it, it is pronounced a hopeless case at once. And yet this expert workman receives much less for his services than do white men who cannot compare with him in skill.

And so I might go on citing instance after instance to show the variety of ways in which our people are sacrificed on the altar of prejudice in the Capital of the United States and how almost insurmountable are the obstacles which block his [sic] path to success. Early in life many a colored youth is so appalled by the helplessness and the hopelessness of his situation in this country that, in a sort of stoical despair he resigns himself to his fate. "What is the good of our trying to acquire an education? We can't all be preachers, teachers, doctors and lawyers. Besides those professions, there is almost nothing for colored people to do but engage in the most menial occupations, and we do not need an education for that." More than once such remarks, uttered by young men and women in our public schools who possess brilliant intellects, have wrung my heart.

It is impossible for any white person in the United States, now matter how sympathetic and broad, to realize what life would mean to him if his incentive to effort were suddenly snatched away. To the lack of incentive to effort, which is the awful shadow under which we live, may be traced the wreck and ruin of scores of colored youth. And surely nowhere in the world do oppression and persecution based solely on the color of the skin appear more hateful and hideous than in the capital of the United States, because the chasm between the principles upon which this Government was founded, in which it still professes to believe, and those which are daily practiced under the protection of the flag, yawns so wide and deep.

22

Anna Howard Shaw, "The Fundamental Principle of a Republic," 1915

The Rev. Dr. Anna Howard Shaw (1847-1919) was an ordained Methodist minister (1880), the first woman minister of that denomination. She completed an M.D. at Boston University in 1886, but did not practice medicine. She was a lecturer and organizer for the Massachusetts Woman Suffrage Association (1885-87); superintendent of the Franchise Department of the WCTU (1888-92); a lecturer first for the American Woman Suffrage Association and then for the combined NAWSA; and president of NAWSA from 1904 to 1915. She spoke in every state of the union, and her talents were oratorical.

This speech was given many times over the years; the version reprinted here was delivered during the New York state referendum campaign of 1915, a year in which she made 204 speeches in that state (Linkugel 1963, 166). *It was claimed that Shaw won more people for equal suffrage than any other advocate. This speech illustrates her persuasive talents, particularly her use of humor, her ability to refute opposition arguments, and her skill in making arguments clear and simple. The text is from the* **Ogdensburg Advance and St. Lawrence Weekly Democrat** (Shaw 1915). *Some paragraphing and punctuation have been added.*

When I came into your hall tonight, I thought of the last time I was in your city. Twenty-one years ago I came here with Susan B. Anthony, and we came for exactly the same purpose as that for which we are here tonight. Boys have been born since that time and have become voters, and the women are still trying to persuade American men to believe in the fundamental principles of democracy, and I never quite feel as if it was a fair field to argue this question with men, because in doing it you have to assume that a man who professes to believe in a Republican form of government does not believe in a Republican form of government, for the only thing that woman's enfranchisement means at all is that a government which claims to be a Republic should be a Republic, and not an aristocracy.

The difficulty with discussing this question with those who oppose us is that they make any number of arguments but none of them have anything to do with the subject. I have never heard an argument against Woman's Suffrage which had anything to do with Woman's Suffrage; they always have something to do with something else, therefore the arguments which we have to make rarely ever have anything to do with the subject, because we have to answer our opponents who always escape the subject as far as possible in order to have any sort of reason in connection with what they say.

Now one of two things is true: either a Republic is a desirable form of government, or else it is not. If it is, then we should have it, if it is not then we ought not to pretend that we have it. We ought, at least, to be true to our ideals, and the men of New York have, for the first time in their lives the rare opportunity, on the second day of next November, of making this state truly a part of a Republic. It is the greatest opportunity which has ever come to the men of the state. They have never had so serious a problem to solve before, they will never have a more serious problem to solve in any future year of our Nation's life, and the thing that disturbs me more than anything else in connection with it is that so few people realize what a profound problem they have to solve on November 2. It is not merely a trifling matter; it is not a little thing that does not concern the state, it is the most vital problem that we could have, and any man who goes to the polls on the second day of next November without thoroughly informing himself in regard to this subject is unworthy to be a citizen of this state, and unfit to cast a ballot.

If Woman's Suffrage is wrong, it is a great wrong; if it is right, it is a profound and fundamental principle, and we all know, if we know what a Republic is, that it is the fundamental principle upon which a Republic must rise. Let us see where we are as a people; how we act here and what we think we are. The difficulty with the men of this country is that they are so consistent in their inconsistency that they are not aware of having been inconsistent; because their consistency has been so continuous and their inconsistency so consecutive that it has never been broken, from the beginning of our Nation's life to the present time. If we trace our history back we will find that from the very dawn of our existence as a people, men have been imbued with a spirit and a vision more lofty than they have been able to live; they have been led by visions of the sublimest truth, both in regard to religion and in regard to government that ever inspired the souls of men from the time the Puritans left the old world to come to this country, led by the Divine ideal which is the sublimest and supremest ideal in religious freedom which men have ever known, the theory that a man has a right to worship God according to the dictates of his own conscience, without the intervention of any other man or any other group of men. And it was this theory, this vision of the right of the human soul which led men first to the shores of this country.

Now, nobody can deny that they are [sic] sincere, honest and earnest men. No one can deny that the Puritans were men of profound conviction, and yet these men who gave up everything in behalf of an ideal, hardly established their communities in this new country before they began to practice exactly the same sort of persecutions on other men which had been practiced upon them. They settled in their communities on the New England shores and when they formed their compacts by which they governed their local societies, they permitted no man to have a voice in the affairs unless he was a member of the church, and not a member of any church, but a member of the particular church which dominated the particular community in which he happened to be. In Massachusetts they drove the Baptists down to Rhode Island; in Connecticut they drove the Presbyterians over to New Jersey; they burned the Quakers in Massachusetts and ducked the witches, and no colony, either Catholic or Protestant, allowed a Jew to have a voice. And so a man must worship God according to the conscience of the particular community in which he was located, and yet they called that religious freedom, they were not able to live the ideal of religious liberty, and from that time to this the men of this government have been following along the same line of inconsistency, while they too have been following a vision of equal grandeur and power.

Never in the history of the world did it dawn upon the human mind as it dawned upon your ancestors, what it would mean for men to be free. They got the vision of a government in which the people would be the supreme power, and so inspired by this vision men wrote such documents as were sent from Massachusetts legislature, from the New York legislature and from the Pennsylvania group over to the Parliament of Great Britain, which rang with the profoundest measures of freedom and justice. They did not equivocate in a single word when they wrote the Declaration of Independence; no one can dream that these men had not got the sublimest ideal of democracy which had ever dawned upon the souls of men.

But as soon as the war was over and our government was formed, instead of asking the question, who shall be the governing force in this great new Republic, when they brought those thirteen little territories together, they began to eliminate instead of include the men who should be the great governing forces, and they said, who shall have the voice in this great new Republic, and you would have supposed that such men as fought the Revolutionary war would have been able to answer that every man who has fought, every one who has given up all he has and all he has been able to accumulate shall be free, it never entered their minds. These excellent ancestors of yours had not been away from the old world long enough to realize that a man is of more value than his purse, so they said every man who has an estate in the government shall have a voice; and they said what shall that estate be? And they answered that a man who had property valued at two hundred and fifty dollars will be able to cast a vote, and so they sang "The land of the free and the home of the brave." And they wrote into their Constitution, "All males who pay taxes on $250. shall cast a vote", and they called themselves a Republic, and we call ourselves a Republic, and they were not quite so much of a Republic as we are, and we are not quite so much of a Republic that we should be called a Republic yet. We might call ourselves angels, but that wouldn't make us angels, you have got to be an angel before you are an angel, and you have got to be a Republic before you are a Republic. Now what did we do? Before the word "male" in the local compacts they wrote the word "church-member"; after that they rubbed out "church-member" and they wrote in a word "tax-payer."

Then there arose a great Democrat, Thomas Jefferson, who looked down into the day when you and I are living and saw that the rapidly accumulated wealth in the hands of a few men would endanger the liberties of the people, and he knew what you and I know, that no power under heaven or among men is known in a Republic by which men can defend their liberties except by the power of the ballot, and so the Democratic party took another step in the evolution of a Republic out of a monarchy and they rubbed out the word "tax-payer" and wrote in the word "white," and then the Democrats thought the millennium had come, and they sang "The land of the free and the home of the brave" as lustily as the Republicans had sung it before them and spoke of the divine right of motherhood with the same thrill in their voices and at the same time they were selling mother's babies by the pound on the auction block and mothers apart from their babies.

Another arose who said a man is not a good citizen because he is white, he is a good citizen because he is a man, and the Republican party took out that progressive evolutionary eraser and rubbed out the word "white" from before the word "male" and could not think of another word to put in there--they were all in, black and white, rich and poor, wise and otherwise, drunk and sober; not a man left out to be put in, and so the Republicans could not write anything before the word "male," and they had to let that little word "male" stay alone by itself.

And God said in the beginning "It is not good for man to stand alone" [Gen. 2:18].[1] That is why we are here tonight, and that is all that woman's suffrage means; just to repeat again and again that first declaration of the Divine, "It is not good for man to stand alone," and so the women of this state are asking that the word "male" shall be stricken out of the Constitution altogether and that the Constitution stand as it ought to have stood in the beginning and as it must

---

[1] The actual words are "And the Lord God said, It is not good that the man should be alone; I will make him an help meet for him."

before this state is any part of a Republic. Every citizen possessing the necessary qualifications shall be entitled to cast one vote at every election, and have that vote counted. We are not asking, as our Anti-Suffrage friends think we are, for any of the awful things that we hear will happen if we are allowed to vote; we are simply asking that that government which professes to be a Republic shall be a Republic and not pretend to be what it is not.

Now what is a Republic? Take your dictionary, encyclopedia, lexicon or anything else you like and look up the definition and you will find that a Republic is a form of government in which the laws are enacted by representatives elected by the people. Now when did the people of New York ever elect their representatives? Never in the world. The men of New York have, and I grant you that men are people, admirable people, as far as they go, but they only go half way. There is still another half of the people who have not elected representatives, and you never read a definition of a Republic in which half of the people elect representatives to govern the whole of the people. That is an aristocracy and that is just what we are. We have been many kinds of aristocracies. We have been a hierarchy of church members, then an aristocracy of wealth, then an oligarchy of sex.

There are two old theories which are dying today. Dying hard but dying. One of them is dying on the plains of Flanders and the Mountains of Galicia and Austria and that is the theory of the divine right of kings.[2] The other is dying here in the state of New York and Massachusetts and New Jersey and Pennsylvania and that is the divine right of sex. Neither of them had a foundation in reason, or justice or common sense.

Now I want to make this proposition and I

---

[2] World War I had already begun in Europe.

believe every man will accept it. Of course he will if he is intelligent. Whenever a Republic prescribes the qualifications as applies equally to all the citizens of the Republic, so that when the Republic says in order to vote, a citizen must be twenty-one years of age, it applies to all alike, there is no discrimination against any race or sex. When the government says that a citizen must be a native born citizen or a naturalized citizen, that applies to all; we are either born or naturalized, somehow or other we are here. Whenever the government says that a citizen, in order to vote, must be a resident of a community a certain length of time, and of the state a certain length of time, and of the nation a certain length of time, that applies to all equally. There is no discrimination.

We might go further and we might say that in order to vote the citizen must be able to read his ballot. We have not gone that far yet. We have been very careful of male ignorance in these United States. I was much interested, as perhaps many of you, in reading the Congressional Record this last winter over the debate over the immigration bill, and when that illiteracy clause was introduced into the immigration bill, what fear there was in the souls of men for fear we would do injustice to some of the people who might want to come to our shores, and I was much interested in the language in which the President [Woodrow Wilson] vetoed the bill, when he declared that by inserting the clause we would keep out of our shores a large body of very excellent people. I could not help wondering then how it happens that male ignorance is so much less ignorant than female ignorance. When I hear people say that if women were permitted to vote a large body of ignorant people would vote, and therefore because an ignorant woman would vote, no intelligent women should be allowed to vote. I wonder why we have made it so easy for male ignorance and so hard for female ignorance.

When I was a girl, years ago, I lived in the back woods, and there the number of votes cast at each election depended entirely upon the size of the ballot box. We had what was known as the old tissue ballots and the man who got the most tissue in was the man elected. Now the best part of our community was very much disturbed by this method, and they did not know what to do in order to get a ballot both safe and secret; but they heard that over in Australia, where the women voted, they had a ballot which was both safe and secret, so we went over there and we got the Australian ballot and brought it there [sic].[3] But when we got it over we found it was not adapted to this country, because in Australia they have to be able to read their ballot. Now the question was how could we adapt it to our conditions? Someone discovered that if you should put a symbol at the head of each column, like a rooster, or an eagle, or a hand holding a hammer, that if a man has intelligence to know the difference between a rooster and an eagle he will know which political party to vote for, and when the ballot was adapted it was a very beautiful ballot, it looked like a page from Life.

Now almost any American woman could vote that ballot, or if she had not that intelligence to know the difference between an eagle and a rooster, we could take the eagle out and put in the hen. Now when we take so much pains to adapt the ballot to the male intelligence of the United States, we should be very humble when we talk about female ignorance. Now if we should take a vote and the men had to read their ballot in order to vote it, more women could vote than men.

---

[3] In this system, all candidates' names were printed on a single ballot, placed in polling places at public expense, and the printing, distribution, and marking of the ballot were protected by law, thus assuring a secret vote.

But when the government says not only that you must be twenty-one years of age, a resident of the community and a native born or naturalized, those are qualifications, but when it says that an elector must be a male, that is not a qualification for citizenship; that is an insurmountable barrier between half of the people and the other half, and no government which erects an insurmountable barrier between one half of the citizens and their rights as citizens can call itself a Republic. It is only an aristocracy. That barrier must be removed before that government can become a Republic, and that is exactly what we are asking now, that the last step in this evolutionary process shall be taken on November 2d, and that this great state of New York shall become in fact, as it is in theory, a part of a government of the people, by the people and for the people.

Men know the inconsistencies themselves; they realize it in one way while they do not realize it in another, because you never heard a man make a political speech when he did not speak of this country as a whole as though the thing existed which does not exist and that is that the people were equally free, because you hear them declare over and over again on the Fourth of July "Under God, the people rule." They know it is not true but they say it with a great hurrah, and then they repeat over and over again that clause from the Declaration of Independence, "Governments derive their just powers from the consent of the governed," and then they see how they can prevent half of us from giving our consent to anything, and then they give it to us on the Fourth of July in two languages, so if [it] is not true in one it will be in the other, "vox populi, vox Dei." "The voice of the people is the voice of God," and the orator forgets that in the people's voice there is a soprano as well as a bass. If the voice of the people is the voice of God, how are we ever going to know what God's voice is when we are content to listen to a bass solo? Now if it is true that the voice of the people is the voice of God, we will never know what the Deity's voice in government is until the bass and soprano are mingled together, the result of which will be the divine harmony. Take any of the magnificent appeals for freedom which men make, and rob them of their universal application and you take the very life and soul out of them.

Where is the difficulty? Just in one thing and one thing only, that men are so sentimental. We used to believe that women were the sentimental sex, but they cannot hold a tallow candle compared with the arc light of the men. Men are so sentimental in their attitude about women that they cannot reason about them. Now men are usually very fair to each other. I think the average man recognizes that he has no more right to anything at the hands of the government than has every other man. He has no right at all to anything to which every other man has not an equal right with himself. He says why have I a right to certain things in the government; why have I a right to life and liberty; why have I a right to this or this? Does he say because I am a man? Not at all, because I am human, and being human I have a right to everything which belongs to humanity, and every right which any other human being has, I have. And then he says of his neighbor, and my neighbor he also is human, therefore every right which belongs to me as a human being, belongs to him as a human being, and I have no right to anything under the government to which he is not equally entitled.

And then up comes a woman, and then they say now she's a woman; she is not quite human, but she is my wife, or my sister, or my daughter, or an aunt, or my cousin. She is not quite human, she is only related to a human, and being related to a human, a human will take care of her. So we have had that care-taking human being to look after us, and they have not recognized that women too are equally human with men. Now if men could forget for a minute--I believe the anti-suffragists say that we want men to forget that we are related to them, they don't know me--if for a minute they could forget our relationship and remember that we are equally human with themselves, then they would say--yes, and this human being, not because she is a woman, but because she is human is entitled to every privilege and every right under the government which I, as a human being am entitled to. The only reason why men do not see as fairly in regard to women as they do in regard to each other is because they have looked upon us from an altogether different plane than what they have looked at men; that is because women have been the homemakers while men have been the so-called protectors, in the period of the world's civilization when people needed to be protected. I know that they say that men protect us now and when we ask them what they are protecting us from, the only answer they can give is from themselves. I do not think that men need any very great credit for protecting us from themselves. They are not protecting us from any special thing from which we could not protect ourselves except themselves. Now this old-time idea of protection was all right when the world needed this protection, but today the protection in civilization comes from within and not from without.

What are the arguments which our good Anti friends give us? We know that lately they have stopped to argue and call suffragist all sorts of creatures.[4] If there is anything we believe that we do not believe, we have not heard about them, so the cry goes out of this; the cry of the infant's mind; the cry of a

---

[4] Throughout the text I have substituted "suffragist" for "suffragette" and "anti-suffragist" for "anti-suffragette." Only their opponents referred to them as "suffragettes." These are terms Shaw did not use in other speeches and would not have used here (Linkugel 1960).

little child. The anti-suffragists' cries are all the cries of little children who are afraid of the unborn and are forever crying, "The goblins will catch you if you don't watch out." So that anything that has not been should not be and all that is is right, when as a matter of fact if the world believed that, we would be in a statical [sic] condition and never move, except back like a crab. And so the cries go on.

When suffragists are feminists, and when I ask what that is, no one is able to tell me. I would give anything to know what a feminist is.[5] They say, would you like to be a feminist? If I could find out I would, you either have to be masculine or feminine and I prefer feminine. Then they cry that we are socialists, and anarchists. Just how a human can be both at the same time, I really do not know. If I know what socialism means it means absolute government and anarchism means no government at all. So we are feminists, socialists, anarchists and mormons or spinsters. Now that is about the list. I have not heard the last speech. Now as a matter of fact, as a unit we are nothing, as individuals we are like all other individuals.

We have our theories, our beliefs, but as suffragists we have but one belief, but one principle, but one theory and that is the right of a human being to have a voice in the government under which he or she lives, on that we agree, if on nothing else. Whether we agree or not on religion or politics we are not concerned. A clergyman asked me the other day, "By the way, what church does your official board belong to?" I said I don't know. He said, "Don't you know what religion your official board believes?" I said,

---

[5] Shaw attempted to explain what is meant by feminism and that it was not opposed to cherished traditions and institutions in a speech delivered in 1918 (Linkugel 1960, 667-83).

"Really it never occurred to me, but I will hunt them up and see, they are not elected to my board because they believe in any particular church. We had no concern either as to what we believe as religionists or as to what we believe as women in regard to theories of government, except that one fundamental theory in the right of democracy. We do not believe in this fad or the other, but whenever any question is to be settled in any community, then the people of that community shall settle that question, the women people equally with the men people. That is all there is to it, and yet when it comes to arguing our case they bring up all sorts of arguments, and the beauty of it is they always answer all their own arguments. They never make an argument but they answer it. When I was asked to answer one of their debates I said, "What is the use? Divide up their literature and let them destroy themselves."

I was followed up last year by a young married woman from New Jersey. She left her husband and home for three months to tell the women that their place was at home, and that they could not leave home long enough to go to the ballot box, and she brought all her arguments out in pairs and backed them up by statistics. The anti-suffragist can gather more statistics than any other person I ever saw, and there is nothing so sweet and calm as when they say, "You cannot deny this, because here are the figures, and figures never lie." Well they don't, but some liars figure.

When they start out they always begin the same. She started by proving that it was no use to give the women the ballot because if they did have it they would not use it, and she had statistics to prove it. If we would not use it, then I really cannot see the harm of giving it to us, we would not hurt anybody with it and what an easy way for you men to get rid of us. No more suffrage meetings, never any nagging you again, no one could blame you for anything that went wrong with the town, if it did not run right, all you would have to say is, you have the power, why don't you go ahead and clean up.

Then the young lady, unfortunately for her first argument, proved by statistics, of which she had many, the awful results which happened where women did have the ballot; what awful laws have been brought about by women's vote; the conditions that prevail in the homes and how deeply women get interested in politics, because women are hysterical, and we cannot think of anything else, we just forget our families, cease to care for our children, cease to love our husbands and just go to the polls and vote and keep on voting for ten hours a day 365 days in the year, never let up, if we ever get to the polls once you will never get us home, so that the women will not vote at all, and they will not do anything but vote. Now these are two very strong anti-suffrage arguments and they can prove them by figures.

Then they will tell you that if women are permitted to vote it will be a great expense and no use because wives will vote just as their husbands do; even if we have no husbands, that would not affect the result because we would vote just as our husbands would vote if we had one. How I wish the anti-suffragists could make the men believe that; if they could make men believe that the women would vote just as they wanted them to, do you think we would ever have to make another speech or hold another meeting, we would have to vote whether we wanted to or not.

And then the very one who will tell you that women will vote just as their husbands do will tell you in five minutes that they will not vote as their husbands will and then the discord in the homes, and the divorce. Why, they have discovered that in Colorado there are more divorces than there were before women began to vote, but they have forgotten to tell you that there are four times as many people in Colorado today as there were when women began to vote, and that may have some effect, particularly as these people went from the East.

Then they will tell you all the trouble that happens in the home. A gentleman told me that in California,--and when he was talking I had a wonderful thing pass through my mind, because he said he and his wife had lived together for twenty years and never had a difference in opinion in the whole twenty years and he was afraid if women began to vote that his wife would vote differently from him and then that beautiful harmony which they had had for twenty years would be broken, and all the time he was talking I could not help wondering which was the idiot,--because I knew that no intelligent human beings could live together for twenty years and not have differences of opinion. All the time he was talking I looked at that splendid type of manhood and thought, how would a man feel being tagged up by a little woman for twenty years saying "me too, me too." I would not want to live in a house with a human being for twenty hours who agreed with everything I said. The stagnation of a frog pond would be hilarious compared to that. What a reflection is that on men. If we should say that about men we would never hear the last of it. Now it may be that the kind of men being [sic] that the anti-suffragists live with is that kind, but they are not the kind we live with and we could not do it. Great big overgrown babies! Cannot be disputed without having a row! While we do not believe that men are saints, by any means, we do believe that the average American man is a fairly good sort of a fellow.

In fact my theory of the whole matter is exactly opposite, because instead of believing that men and women will quarrel, I think just the opposite thing will happen. I think just about six weeks before election a sort of honeymoon will start and it will continue until they will think they are again hanging over the gate, all in order to get each other's votes. When men want each other's votes they do not go up and knock them down; they are very solicitous of each other, if they are thirsty or need a smoke, or--well we won't worry about the home. The husband and wife who are quarreling after the vote are quarreling now.

Then the other belief that the women would not vote if they had a vote and would not do anything else; and would vote just as their husbands vote, and would not vote like their husbands; that women have so many burdens that they cannot bear another burden, and that women are the leisure class.

I remember hearing Rev. Dr. Abbott speak before the anti-suffrage meeting in Brooklyn, and he stated that if women were permitted to vote we could not have so much time for charity and philanthropy, and I would like to say, "Thank God, there will not be so much need of charity and philanthropy."[6] The end and aim of the suffrage is not to furnish an opportunity for excellent old ladies to be charitable. There are two words that we ought to be able to get along without, and they are charity and philanthropy. They are not needed in a Republic. If we put in the word "opportunity" instead, that is what Republics stand for. Our doctrine is not to extend the length of our bread lines or the size of our soup kitchens, what we need is the opportunity for men to buy their own bread and eat their own soup. We women have used up our lives and strength in fool charities, and we have made more paupers than we have ever helped by the folly of our charities and philanthropies; the unorganized methods by which we deal with the conditions of society, and instead of giving people charity we must learn to give them an opportunity to develop and make themselves capable of earning the bread; no human being

---

[6] Lyman Abbott (1835-1922), a clergyman, who in 1888 succeeded Henry Ward Beecher as minister of the Plymouth Congregational Church, Brooklyn.

has the right to live without toil; toil of some kind, and that old theory that we used to hear "The world owes a man a living" never was true and never will be true. This world does not owe anybody a living, what it does owe to every human being is the opportunity to earn a living. We have a right to the opportunity and then the right to the living thereafter. We want it, no woman, any more than a man has the right to live an idle life in this world, we must learn to give back something for the space occupied and we must do our duty wherever duty calls, and the woman herself must decide where her duty calls, just as a man does.

Now they tell us we should not vote because we have not the time, we are so burdened that we should not have any more burdens. Then, if that is so, I think we ought to allow the women to vote instead of the men, since we pay a man anywhere from a third to a half more than we do women, it would be better to use up the cheap time of the women instead of the dear time of the men. And talking about time you would think it took about a week to vote.

A dear, good friend of mine in Omaha said, "Now Miss Shaw," and she held up her child in her arms, "is not this my job." I said it certainly is, and then she said, "How can I go to the polls and vote and neglect my baby?" I said, "Has your husband a job?" and she said, "Why, you know he has." I did know it, he was a banker and a very busy one. I said, "Yet your husband said he was going to leave his bank and go down to the polls and vote," and she said, "Oh yes, he is so very interested in election." Then I said, "What an advantage you have over your husband, he has to leave his job and you can take your job with you and you do not need to neglect your job."

Is it not strange that the only time a woman might neglect her baby is on election day, and then the dear old Antis hold up their hands and say, "You have neglected your baby."

A woman can belong to a whist club and go once a week and play whist, she cannot take her baby to the whist club, she has to keep whist herself without trying to keep a baby whist. She can go to the theatre, to church or a picnic, and no one is worrying about that baby, but to vote and everyone cries out about the neglect. You would think on election day that a woman grabbed up her baby and started out and just dropped it anywhere and paid no attention to it.

It used to be asked when we had the question-box, "Who will take care of the babies?" I didn't know what person could be got to take care of all the babies, so I thought I would go out West and find out. So I went to Denver and I found that they took care of their babies just the same on election day as they did on every other day; they took their baby along with them, when they went to put a letter in a box they took their baby along, and when they went to put their ballot in the box they took their baby along. If the mother had to stand in line and the baby got restless she would joggle the go-cart, most every one had a go-cart, and when she went in to vote a neighbor would joggle the go-cart, and if there was no neighbor there was the candidate and he would joggle the cart. That is one day in the year when you could get a hundred people to take care of any number of babies. I have never worried about the babies on election day since that time.

Then the people will tell you that women are so burdened with their duties that they cannot vote, and then they will tell you that women are the leisure class and the men are worked to death; but the funniest argument of the lady who followed me about in the West: Out there they were great on the temperance question, and she declared that we were not prohibition, or she declared that we were. Now in North Dakota, which is one of the first prohibition states, and they are dry because they want to be dry. In that state she wanted to prove to them that if women were allowed to vote they would vote North Dakota wet and she had her figures; that women had not voted San Francisco dry, or Portland dry or Chicago dry. Of course we had not voted on the question in Chicago, but that did not matter. Then we went to Montana, which is wet. They have it wet there because they want it wet, so that any argument that she could bring to bear upon them to prove that we would make North Dakota wet and keep it wet would have given us the state, but that would not work, so she brought out the figures out of her pocket to prove to the men of Montana that if women were allowed to vote in Montana they would vote Montana dry. She proved that in two years in Illinois they had voted ninety-six towns dry, and that at that rate we would soon get over Montana and have it dry. Then I went to Nebraska and as soon as I reached there a reporter came and asked me the question "How are the women going to vote on the prohibition question?" I said "I really don't know. I know how we will vote in North Dakota, we will vote dry [sic] in North Dakota; in Montana we will vote dry, but how we will vote in Nebraska, I don't know, but I will let you know just as soon as the lady from New Jersey comes."

We will either vote as our husbands vote or we will not vote as our husbands vote. We either have time to vote or we don't have time to vote. We will either not vote at all or we will vote all the time. It reminds me of the story of the old Irish woman who had twin boys and they were so much alike that the neighbors could not tell them apart, and the mother always seemed to be able to tell them apart, so one of the neighbors said, "Now Mrs. Mahoney, you have two of the finest twin boys I ever saw in all my life, but how do you know them apart." "Oh," she says, "That's easy enough, anyone could tell them apart. When I want to know which is which I just put my finger in Patsey's mouth and if he bites it is Mikey."

Now what does it matter whether the women will vote as their husbands do or will not vote; whether they have time or have not; or whether they will vote for prohibition or not. What has that to do with the fundamental question of democracy, no one has yet discovered. But they cannot argue on that; they cannot argue on the fundamental basis of our existence so that they have to get off on all these side tracks to get anything approaching an argument. So they tell you that democracy is a form of government. It is not. It was before governments were; it will prevail when governments cease to be; it is more than a form of government; it is a great spiritual force emanating from the heart of the Infinite, transforming human character until some day, some day in the distant future, man by the power of the spirit of democracy, will be able to look back into the face of the Infinite and answer, as man cannot answer today, "One is our Father, even God, and all we people are the children of one family." And when democracy has taken possession of human lives no man will ask for himself any thing which he is not willing to grant to his neighbor, whether that neighbor be a man or a woman; no man will then be willing to allow another man to rise to power on his shoulders, nor will he be willing to rise to power on the shoulders of another prostrate human being. But that has not yet taken possession of us, but some day we will be free, and we are getting nearer and nearer to it all the time; and never in this history of our country had the men and women of this nation a better right to approach it than they have today; never in the history of the nation did it stand out so splendidly as it stands today, and never ought we men and women to be more grateful for anything than that there presides in the White House today a man of peace.

And so our good friends go on with one thing after another and they say if women should vote they will have to sit on the jury and they ask whether we will like to see a woman sitting on a jury. I have seen some juries that ought to be sat on, and I have seen some women that would be glad to sit on anything. When a woman stands up all day behind a counter, or when she stands all day doing a washing, she is glad enough to sit; and when she stands for seventy-five cents, she would like to sit for two dollars a day. But don't you think we need some women on juries in this country? You read your paper and you read that one day last week or the week before or the week before a little girl went out to school and never came back; another little girl was sent on an errand and never came back; another little girl was left in charge of a little sister and her mother went out to work and when she returned the little girl was not there, and you read it over and over again, and the horror of it strikes you. You read that in these United States five thousand young girls go out and never come back, don't you think that the men and women, the vampires of our country who fatten and grow rich on the ignorance and innocence of children would rather face Satan himself than a jury of mothers? I would like to see some juries of mothers. I lived in the slums of Boston for three years and I know the need of juries of mothers.

Then they tell us that if women were permitted to vote that they would take office, and you would suppose that we just took office in this country. There is a difference of getting an office in this country and in Europe. In England a man stands for Parliament and in this country he runs for Congress, and so long as it is a question of running for office I don't think women have much chance, especially with our present hobbles.[7]

There are some women who want to hold office and I may as well own up, I am one of them. I have been wanting to hold office for

---

[7] A hobble skirt was a long skirt, popular between 1910 and 1914, that was so narrow below the knees that it restricted a normal stride.

more than thirty-five years. Thirty-five years ago I lived in the slums of Boston and ever since then I have wanted to hold office. I have applied to the mayor to be made an officer; I wanted to be the greatest office holder in the world, I wanted the position of the man I think is to be the most envied, as far as ability to do good is concerned, and that is a policeman [sic]. I have always wanted to be a policeman and I have applied to be appointed policeman and the very first question that was asked me was, "Could you knock a man down and take him to jail?" That is some people's idea of the highest service that a policeman can render a community. Knock somebody down and take him to jail. My idea is not so much to arrest criminals as it is to prevent crime. That is what is needed in the police force of every community. When I lived for three years in the back alleys of Boston, I saw there that it was needed to prevent crime and from that day to this I believe there is no great public gathering of any sort whatever where we do not need women on the police force; we need them at every moving picture show, every dance house, every restaurant, every hotel, and every great store with a great bargain counter and every park and every resort where the vampires who fatten on the crimes and vices of men and women gather. We need women on the police force and we will have them there some day.

If women vote will they go to war?[8] They are great on having us fight. They tell you that the government rests on force, but there are a great many kinds of force in this world, and never in the history of man were the words of the Scriptures proved to the extent that they are today, that the men of the nation

---

[8] That woman could not fight was a major argument against their being allowed to vote, on the grounds that the threat of force was essential to acceptance of the outcome of balloting.

that lives by the sword shall die by the sword.[9] When I was speaking in North Dakota from an automobile with a great crowd and a great number of men gathered around a man who had been sitting in front of a store whittling a stick called out to another man and asked if women get the vote will they go over to Germany and fight the Germans? I said, "Why no, why should we go over to Germany and fight Germans?" I said, why no, why over here to fight [sic], if German men come over here would you fight?" I said, "Why should we women fight men, but if Germany should send an army of women over here, then we would show you what we would do. We would go down and meet them and say, 'Come on, let's go up to the opera house and talk this matter over.' It might grow wearisome but it would not be death."

Would it not be better if the heads of the governments in Europe had talked things over? What might have happened to the world if a dozen men had gotten together in Europe and settled the awful controversy which is today decimating the nations of Europe? We women got together over there last year, over in Rome, the delegates from twenty-eight different nations of women, and for two weeks we discussed problems which had like interests to us all.[10] They were all kinds of Protestants, both kinds of Catholics, Roman and Greek, there were Jews and Mohammedans, but we were not there to discuss our different religious beliefs, but we were there to discuss the things that were of vital importance to us all, and at the end of the two

---

[9] Rev. 13:10.

[10] Founded in 1888, the International Council of Women (ICW), which counted membership in the millions, held its congress in Rome in 1914. It supported many causes in addition to woman suffrage (Van Voris 1987, 55-56).

weeks, after the discussions were over, we passed a great number of resolutions. We discussed white slavery, the immigration laws, we discussed the spread of contagious and infectious diseases; we discussed various forms of education, and various forms of juvenile criminals, every question which every nation has to meet, and at the end of two weeks we passed many resolutions, but two of them were passed unanimously. One was presented by myself as Chairman on the Committee on Suffrage and on that resolution we called upon all civilizations of the world to give to women equal rights with men and there was not a dissenting vote.

The other resolution was on peace. We believed then and many of us believe today, notwithstanding all the discussion that is going on, we believe and we will continue to believe that preparedness for war is an incentive to war, and the only hope of permanent peace is the systematic and scientific disarmament of all the nations of the world, and we passed a resolution and passed it unanimously to that effect. A few days afterward I attended a large reception given by the American Ambassador, and there was an Italian diplomat there and he spoke rather superciliously and said, "You women think you have been having a very remarkable convention, and I understand that a resolution on peace was offered by the Germans, and the French women seconded it, and the British presiding officer presented it and it was carried unanimously." We none of us dreamed what was taking place at that time, but he knew and we learned it before we arrived home, that awful, awful thing that was about to sweep over the nations of the world. The American Ambassador replied to the Italian diplomat and said, "Yes Prince, it was a remarkable convention, and it is a remarkable thing that the only people who can get together internationally and discuss their various problems without acrimony and without a sword at their side are the women of the world, but we men, even when we go to The

Hague to discuss peace, we go with a sword dangling at our side." It is remarkable that even at this age men cannot discuss international problems and discuss them in peace.

When I turned away from that place up in North Dakota, that man in the crowd called out again, just as we were leaving and said, "Well, what does a woman know about war anyway?" I had read my paper that morning and I knew what the awful headline was, and I saw a gentleman standing in the crowd with a paper in his pocket, and I said, will that gentleman hold the paper up, and he held it up, and the headline read, "250,000 Men Killed Since the War Began." I said you ask me what a woman knows about war? No woman can read that line and comprehend the awful horror; no woman knows the significance of 250,000 dead men, but you tell me that one man lay dead and I might be able to tell you something of its awful meaning to one woman. I would know that years before a woman whose heart beat in unison with her love and her desire for motherhood walked day by day with her face to an open grave, with courage, which no man has ever surpassed, and if she did not fill that grave, if she lived and if there was laid in her arms a tiny little bit of helpless humanity, I would know that there went out from her soul such a cry of thankfulness as none save a mother could know. And then I would know, what men have not yet learned, that women are human; that they have human hopes and human passions, aspirations and desires as men have, and I would know that that mother had laid aside all those hopes and aspirations for herself, but never for one moment did she lay them aside for her boy, and if, after years had passed by, she forgot her nights of sleeplessness and her days of fatiguing toil in her care of her growing boy, and when at last he became a man and she stood looking up into his eyes and beheld him, bone of her bone and flesh of her flesh, for out of her woman's life she had carved twenty beautiful years that went into the making of a man; and there he stands, the most wonderful thing in all the world; for in all the Universe of God there is nothing more sublimely wonderful than a strong limbed, clean hearted, keen brained, aggressive young man, standing as he does on the border line of life, ready to reach out and grapple with its problems. O, how wonderful he is, and he is hers. She gave her life for him, and in an hour this country calls him out and in an hour he lies dead; that wonderful, wonderful thing lies dead; and sitting by his side, that mother looking into the dark years to come knows that when her son died her life's hope died with him, and in the face of that wretched motherhood, what man dare ask what a woman knows of war. And that is not all. Read your papers, you cannot read it because it is not printable; you cannot tell it because it is not speakable, you cannot even think it because it is not thinkable, the horrible crimes perpetrated against women by the blood drunken men of the war.

You read your paper again and the second headline reads, "It Costs Twenty Millions of Dollars a Day," for what? To buy the material to slaughter the splendid results of civilization of the centuries. Men whom it has taken centuries to build up and make into great scientific forces of brain, the flower of the manhood of the great nations of Europe, and we spend twenty millions of dollars a day to blot out all the results of civilization of hundreds and hundreds of years. And what do we do? We lay a mortgage on every unborn child for a hundred and more years to come. Mortgage his brain, his brawn, every pulse of his heart in order to pay the debt, to buy the material to slaughter the men of our country. And that is not all, the greatest crime of war is the crime against the unborn. Read what they are doing. They are calling out every man, every young man, every virile man from seventeen to forty-five or fifty years old, they are calling them out. All the splendid scientific force and energy of the splendid virile manhood are being called out to be food for the cannon, and they are leaving behind the degenerate, defective, imbecile, the unfit, the criminals, the diseased to be the fathers of the children yet to be born. The crime of crimes of the war is the crime against the unborn children that we take from them what every child has a right to, that is a virile father, and we rob women of fit mates to become the fathers of their children. In the face of these crimes against women and against children, and in the face of the fact that women are driven out of the home, shall men ask if women shall fight if they are permitted to vote.

No, we women do not want the ballot in order that we may fight, but we do want the ballot in order that we may help men to keep from fighting, whether it is in war or in peace; whether it is in the home or in the state, just as the home is not without the man, so the state is not without the woman, and you can no more build up homes without men than you can build up the state without women. We are needed everywhere where human life is. We are needed everywhere where human problems are to [be] solve[d] and men and women must go through this world together from the cradle to the grave, it is God's way and it is the fundamental principle of a Republican form of government.

23

Carrie Chapman Catt, Presidential Address, 1902

Carrie Clinton Lane (1859-1947) grew up on the frontier in Iowa. She was graduated from Iowa State College at Ames in 1880, became high school principal in Mason City in 1881, and superintendent of schools in 1883. In 1885 she married Leo Chapman, owner and editor of the **Mason City Republican** *and became its assistant editor. In 1886, Mr. Chapman went to California intending to purchase a newspaper company, but died of typhoid fever before she could join him. She worked for a year on a San Francisco newspaper, but returned to Charles City, Iowa, and began a career on the lecture platform. In 1887 she joined the Iowa Woman Suffrage Association. In 1890 she married George William Catt, who encouraged his wife to remain active in suffrage work.*

In 1895, at Catt's suggestion, the NAWSA set up an organization committee to direct its field work, which she headed, and in this role she participated in a long succession of campaigns to win the vote in individual states. When Susan B. Anthony retired from the NAWSA presidency in 1900, she chose Catt as her successor; Catt remained in that post until 1904, when she left to care for her husband in his final illness. When he died in 1905, he left her financially independent and able to devote herself full time to reform.

In 1909, she consolidated activists in New York City into an Interurban Suffrage Council, which grew into the Woman Suffrage Party in 1910, and in 1913-14, as head of the Empire State Campaign Committee, she directed a brilliant campaign for passage of a state referendum. Although the measure was defeated at the polls in 1915, the campaign laid the groundwork for the successful campaign of 1917 that created the momentum for passage of a federal woman suffrage amendment. Based on her work in the 1915 New York state campaign, Catt was drafted to return to the NAWSA presidency in 1916 for the final effort.

This speech was delivered at the annual national convention of NAWSA, and the first convention of the International Woman Suffrage Alliance, during a period in which the domestic movement was becalmed. It was experiencing major changes in leadership, and was confronting an organized anti-suffrage opposition and a climate of opinion more hostile to reform.

The speech was published as a pamphlet (Catt 1902). *This text is from a copy of the pamphlet in the Sophia Smith Collection of the New York Public Library.*

An International Woman Suffrage Conference deserves to be called "a new thing under the sun."[1] It does not matter whether its immediate results shall prove to be important

---

[1] The International Woman Suffrage Alliance was founded in Washington, D.C., on February 12, 1902, during the thirty-fourth annual convention of the NAWSA. Seven of the eight countries with woman suffrage societies sent delegates. Clara Barton, then age 81, spoke to the assembled women representing the International Red Cross, and pointed out that this was the first time women from several countries had met to oppose the injustice of their position (Van Voris 1987, 57).

or insignificant, it stands as a milepost in the onward progress of a great cause, an unmistakable indication, too, which points in no uncertain manner to the heights beyond where without a question, the banner of equal rights for men and women will one day be planted.

Self-government for men, in its modern acceptance, is in itself a new thing. It is true there were so-called republics of great influence and power in the early centuries of Europe, but in every one the number of those who were authorized to exercise the rights of citizenship was so limited, it is doubtful if they deserved the name. Self-government, based upon the broad claim of individual liberty and individual right, although its evolution may reach far back through the centuries, may justly be claimed as a new idea. The starting point of the modern movement was unquestionably the American Declaration of Independence. The world had been making long and successful preparation for the departure from old ideals. De Tocqueville, in writing of the American Republic, declared that "for seven centuries aristocracies and class privileges had been steadily dissolving,"[2] and John Stuart Mill added in comment, "The noble has been gradually going down on the social ladder and the commoner has been gradually going up. Every half century has brought them nearer to each other."[3] During the centuries in which the repressive customs of Feudalism were gradually receding into the past, while commerce was uniting more closely the destinies of Nations,

---

[2] Alexis De Tocqueville (1805-59), French political figure, traveler, historian, best known for *Democracy in America*, 4 vols., 1835-40, one of the classics of political literature.

[3] See p. 268, n 14.

while education was surely substituting understanding and reason for faith and superstition, while wars for conquest were becoming less common and periods of peace more frequent and of longer duration, there was slowly but steadily growing in the minds of men a self-respect, a self-reliance, an individuality which would sooner or later ask why some men should be born to rule and others to obey. That question chanced to be formulated first by the American Colonists. Had the declaration not come from America it would have come elsewhere. The time was ripe for it and it came as a result of a world movement and a world crisis, and not alone because England had been unjust. It came because the rank and file of men had begun to think and because the glittering tinsel of royal courts, which had once served to hold subjects loyal, had grown transparent.

In quick response to growing intelligence and individualism, the principle of self-government has been planted in every civilized nation of the world. Beneath the force of this onward movement the most cherished ideals of conservatism have fallen. Out of the ashes of the old, Phoenix-like, has arisen a new institution, vigorous and strong, yea, more, an institution which will live as long as men occupy the earth. The little band of Americans who initiated the modern movement would never have predicted that within a century "Taxation (of men) without representation is tyranny" would have been written into the fundamental law of all the monarchies of Europe, except Russia and Turkey, and that even there self-government should obtain in the municipalities. The most optimistic seer among them would not have prophesied that Mongolian Japan, then tightly shutting her gates against the Commerce of the world, and jealously guarding her ancient customs, would before the century closed have welcomed Western Civilization and established universal suffrage for its men. He would not have dreamed that every inch of the great Continent of South America, then chiefly an unexplored region over which bands of savages roved at will, would be covered by written constitutions guaranteeing self-government to men, based upon Declarations of Independence similar to their own; that the settlements in Mexico and Central America and many islands of the Ocean would grow into republics, and least of all that the island Continent of Australia with its associates of New Zealand and Tasmania, then unexplored wildernesses, would become great democracies where self-government would be carried on with such enthusiasm, fervor and wisdom, that they would give lessons in methods and principles to all the rest of the world.

Yet it has come about in a hundred years that civilized nations are governed by the sovereign will of men instead of monarchs. It is true, Kings and Queens still occupy the thrones of Europe, but they are majesties robbed of the power over the lives and liberties of men which belonged to their predecessors, and the power behind every throne is the voice of the people. The monarchies of to-day still display something of the pomp and show and ceremonial of earlier times, but they are no longer offered in hope to cajole the people into loyalty. They are merely the symbols of power which remain after the power is gone, and mean no more than the purple robes worn in the South Carolina Legislature. No careful observer can doubt that real monarchical and aristocratic power have gone forever. Wherever self-government for men exists, it will stay; and where it does not exist it will come.

True, modern democracy is received even yet with not a little skepticism. An English critic much quoted by American doubters, exclaims: "The government of the United States is not the result of democracy, but of the craftiest combination of schemes to defeat the will of democracy ever devised in the world." There are [sic] a considerable number of Americans who are in apparent accord with this belief. Not only do they cry, "democracy is a failure," but they enforce their opinion by doing nothing to make it a success.

If democracy is a failure, what then shall be the government of the future? Monarchy, or some form of aristocracy, alone remain to choose from. Will the future take one of these? Nay, for free schools and free thought, which have educated the commonest minds to new ideals, have rung the death knell of both. The evolution of society pointing to "governments of the people, by the people, and for the people," has made a steady march forward since the days of the English King John,[4] and in all the centuries it has known no serious check. There can be no turning back now.

If it is true, as some would have us think, that the tyranny of empire has only been replaced by the tyranny of democracy which still represses and robs men of rights, it is still the duty of patriots to press ahead. If there are serious problems, intelligence and conscience will solve them. When Americans determine, as Americans will some day, to apply to the political problems which vex us, the intelligence and public spirit which has made this nation what it is, they will find a remedy for every ill, and democracy purified of its errors, will rise triumphant as the only ideal form of government. It does not matter that there are men who perceive rights still unattained, the

---

[4] John (1167-1216), king of England (1199-1216), issued the Magna Charta at Runnymede, under compulsion from the barons and the church in June 1215. This, the most famous document of British constitutional history, implies that there are laws protecting the rights of subjects and communities that the king is bound to observe or, if he fails to do so, that he will be compelled to observe. Later generations interpreted it as guaranteeing trial by jury and habeas corpus.

majority of the civilized men of the world today stand upon a plane of security and power they have never known before and where they are free to carve out their own destiny. Not every individual is free to control his own life, but men as a whole are free to control the destiny of men as a whole. Every man possesses one ballot's share in each law, custom and condition which form the environment of his life. With this weapon of offense and defense he is armed to storm the heights beyond and to take the rights which should be his. While skeptics may sneer at the possibilities of pure politics and pessimists shake their heads in despair as they contemplate its problems, democracy moves triumphantly on, not only the government of the present and the undoubted government of the future, but the crowning attainment in the evolution of the Rights of Man.

Hard upon the track of the man-suffrage movement presses the movement for woman suffrage, a logical step onward. It has come as inevitably and as naturally as the flower unfolds from the bud, or the fruit develops from the flower. Why should woman suffrage not come? Men throughout the world hold their suffrage by the guarantee of two principles of liberty, and for these reasons only. One, "Taxation without representation is tyranny," who dares deny it--and are not women taxed? The other, "Governments derive their just powers from the consent of the governed." How simple and unanswerable that petition of justice! And are not women governed? These axioms have been translated into every tongue and thundered forth in eloquent plea in every civilized land. Before their logic the most cherished of ancient prejudices have yielded, and can their logic fail at last?

More, many students of history, awed by the wonder of changed conditions, have expressed their observations in terse aphorisms which the world at large has adopted for its own and these have put new and still more unanswerable logic into the mouths of our advocates.

"The future belongs to the book, not the sword; it belongs to life and not to death," pealed out the voice of Victor Hugo.[5] The world, nodded and explained, "True, the sword is passing and the rule of the book is coming in." Then, we may ask, since woman may read the book and write the book, why should she have no share in the government of which the book stands the chief prop and support? And who can answer?

The President of Stanford University said: "The function of democracy is not to make governments good. It is to make men strong."[6] The world approves and adds, that statement is the clearest possible definition of the differences between the old, when men existed for the government, and the new, when governments exist for men. But we may ask, if democracy is a means of making men strong, is there any good reason for keeping women weak, that we should deny them the same chance to grow strong?

Balzac makes a character say: "Empires began with the sword and ended with the inkstand; we have reached the inkstand" and the world cries "good!"[7] But, we ask, since

---

[5] Victor Hugo (1802-85), French poet, dramatist, and novelist, whose greatest works are his novels *Notre Dame de Paris* (1831) and *Les Misérables* (1862).

[6] Stanford University opened in 1891; David Starr Jordan (1851-1931), a leading ichthyologist, served as its first president (1891-1913) and later as its chancellor (1913-16).

[7] Honoré de Balzac (1799-1850), French writer who ranks among the great masters of the novel; he produced a vast collection of novels and stories called "*La comedie humaine*."

women may dip judgement and wisdom from that inkstand upon their pen points, why should they have no share in an empire based upon the inkstand?

Said Ingersoll: "The method of the settlement of disputes is the chief test of civilization. It began with a contest of clubs and ended with a plea before a jury and a judge" and the lawyers say, "True."[8] Then if the woman in her cap and gown may make the plea before the jury, why should she not make the law she expounds?

A campaigner in the recent New York municipal campaign plead eloquently with the women to lend their aid. Said he: "It is the proud duty of the women of this City to advise men how to vote, since they have more time than men to intelligently learn to comprehend the situation," and every Low follower echoed: "True!"[9] But, if women are competent to teach men how to vote, why may they not vote themselves? These are the arguments the world has put into our mouths. Their logic can no more be disputed than can that of the multiplication table. Surely, the world cannot long withstand the force of it!

The question of woman suffrage is a very simple one. The plea is dignified, calm and logical. Yet, great as is the victory over conservatism which is represented in the accomplishment of man suffrage, infinitely greater will be the attainment of woman suffrage. Man suffrage exists through the

---

[8] Robert Green Ingersoll (1833-99), orator, lawyer, and agnostic, a brilliant speaker whose lectures drew large audiences.

[9] Seth Low (1850-1916), reform mayor of Brooklyn (1882-86); president of Columbia (1889-1901); mayor of New York City (1901-03).

surrender of many a stronghold of ancient thought, deemed impregnable, yet these obstacles were the veriest Don Quixote windmills compared with the opposition which has stood arrayed against woman suffrage.

Woman suffrage must meet precisely the same objections which have been urged against man suffrage, but in addition, it must combat sex-prejudice, the oldest, the most unreasoning, the most stubborn of all human idiosyncracies. What *is* prejudice? An opinion, which is not based upon reason; a judgment, without having heard the argument; a feeling, without being able to trace from whence it came. And sex-prejudice is a pre-judgment against the rights, liberties and opportunities of women. A belief, without proof, in the incapacity of women to do that which they have never done. Sex-prejudice has been the chief hindrance in the rapid advance of the woman's rights movement to its present status, and it is still a stupendous obstacle to be overcome.

In the United States, at least, we need no longer argue woman's intellectual, moral and physical qualification for the ballot with the intelligent. The Reason of the best of our citizens has long been convinced. The justice of the argument has been admitted, but sex-prejudice is far from conquered.

When a great church official exclaims petulantly, that if women are not more modest in their demands men may be obliged to take to drowning female infants again; when a renowned United States Senator declares no human being can find an answer to the arguments for woman suffrage, but with all the force of his position and influence he will oppose it; when a popular woman novelist speaks of the advocates of the movement as the "shrieking sisterhood;" when a prominent politician says "to argue against woman suffrage is to repudiate the Declaration of Independence," yet he hopes it may never come, the question flies entirely outside the domain of reason, and retreats within the realm of sex-prejudice, where neither logic nor common sense can dislodge it.

Sex-prejudice is the chief tower and fortress of the opposition to equal rights for women, and we may ask from whence came this sex-prejudice? Why does it control the universal understanding? Is there a real foundation for the belief? Are women in reality, inevitably, and permanently the inferiors of men?

Sex-prejudice is the outgrowth of a theory practically universal throughout the world for many centuries past. It may be briefly stated as a belief that men were the units of the human race. They performed the real functions of the race; all the responsibilities and duties of working out the destiny of the race were theirs. Women were auxiliaries, or dependents, with no race responsibilities of their own. In the perpetuation of the race the contribution of the mother was negative and insignificant; that of the father vital and all-important. A favorite figure among writers for several centuries was the comparison of the father of the race to the seed, and the mother of the race to the soil. Man was considered the real creator of the race. Grant Allen states fairly the belief which dominated the thought of the world for many centuries when he said that women were simply "told off" for the express purpose of procreation, in the same manner as are drones in a hive of bees, and have no other place in society.[10]

The world rarely inquires into the origin of a universal belief. It proceeds upon the theory that "whatever is, is right," and the very fact of the universality of any belief is accepted as a sufficient guarantee of its truth. Such a belief becomes a blind faith. Its defense is not reason, but feeling.

Add to a universal belief of this character, of which no one knows the origin, a

---

[10] See p. 373, n 1.

supposed Divine authority for its existence, and it becomes well-nigh unmovable. The wildest fanaticisms of the race have been aroused through appeals to this kind of unreason. Curiously enough, whenever an unreasoning belief of this kind has been questioned humanity has invariably claimed Divine authority for it, and often without the slightest grounds. It has been quoted in support of every departing theory from the flatness of the earth to human slavery, and has been hurled in defiance at the advocates of every new discovery from the printing press to the administration of chloroform. Such a belief has been the basis of the theory that man is the race and woman is the dependent. To question its authority or truth was considered for centuries a sacrilege and a blasphemy and consequently all honest investigation into its truth was forestalled at the beginning.

The subordination of women is directly traceable to this theory. Every repressive law and custom concerning them is an outgrowth of it and all opposition to the rights of women receives its strength from the surviving remains of it. Four chief causes led to the subjection of women, each the logical deduction from the theory that men were the units of the race--obedience, ignorance, the denial of personal liberty, and the denial of right to property and wages. These forces united in cultivating a spirit of egotism and tyranny in men and weak dependence in women. The details of their enforcement have filled the pages of history with records of cruelty and tragedy which form the saddest commentary upon the ignorance and superstition of past centuries. The sickening details of the brutality which accompanied the enforcement of obedience and the denial of personal liberty upon women, surpasses all understanding. In fastening these disabilities upon women, the world acted logically when reasoning from the premise that man is the race and woman his dependent. The perpetual tutelage and subjection robbed women of all freedom of thought and action, and all incentive for growth, and they logically became the inane weaklings the world would have them, and their condition strengthened the universal belief in their incapacity. This world taught woman nothing skillful and then said her work was valueless. It permitted her no opinions and then said she did not know how to think. It forbade her to speak in public, and said the sex had no orators. It denied her the schools, and said the sex had no genius. It robbed her of every vestige of responsibility, and then called her weak. It taught her that every pleasure must come as a favor from men, and when to gain it she decked herself in paint and fine feathers, as she had been taught to do, it called her vain.

This was the woman enshrined in literature. She was immortalized in song and story. Chivalry paid her fantastic compliments. As Diderot said, "when woman is the theme, the pen must be dipped in the rainbow, and the pages must be dried with a butterfly's wing."[11] Surrounded by a halo of this kind of mysticism woman was encouraged to believe herself adored. This woman who was pretty, coquettish, affectionate, obedient, self effacive, now gentle and meek, now furious and emotional, always ignorant, weak and silly, became the ideal woman of the world.

When at last the New Woman came, bearing the torch of truth and with calm dignity asked a share in the world's education, opportunities and duties, it is no wonder these untrained weaklings should have shrunk away in horror. As a French writer (Clavière) in speaking of the women of the middle ages, says: "It might be supposed that married women, handed over like so many sheep, would pitifully cry out against their sacrifice. But such was not the case; humanity is so

---

[11] Denis Diderot (1713-84), French encyclopedist, philosopher, and critic of art and literature.

constituted that, sunk in abject slavery, with no glimpse of anything beyond, it will hug its chains, while the more freedom it enjoys, the keener grows its appetite for freedom."[12] Nor was it any wonder that man should arise to defend the woman of the past, whom he had learned to love and cherish. Her very weakness and dependence were dear to him and he loved to think of her as the tender clinging vine, while he was the strong and sturdy oak. He had worshiped her ideal through the age of chivalry as though she were a goddess, but he had governed her as though she were an idiot. Without the slightest comprehension of the inconsistency of his position, he believed this relation to be in accordance with God's command.

The fate of the woman question turns upon the truth or falsity of the premise from which the world has reasoned throughout the ages past. If the ancient premise is true, the problem is a complicated one. If it is false, then nothing but prejudice can stand in the way of the fullest individual liberty for women. Women are either inferior to men, or they are not.

Von Baer, a German scientist, pricked the bubble of the fallacy that "man is the race" in 1827 when he demonstrated that father and mother contribute equally to the physical, mental and moral characteristics of their children.[13] This discovery was received

---

[12] Etienne Clavière (1735-93), French financier who participated in the popular revolution at Geneva in 1782 and who advised the Comte de Mirabeau during the French Revolution.

[13] Karl Ernst von Baer (1792-1876), Estonian biologist, founder of modern embryology, whose identification of the mammalian egg led to an awareness that the sperm and the egg were equal contributors to the inherited characteristics of a child.

reluctantly by scientists, but the fact is no longer questioned by those competent to judge. What a flood of light it throws upon the problem. In the perpetuation of the race the function of motherhood is not the negative, insignificant thing it was once thought, but equal in importance with fatherhood. More, as the race obeys that still higher law which compels humanity to climb onward and upward to newer ideals and nobler conceptions, the hereditary traits of each generation come equally from the father and mother. Can it be that Nature is so poor an economist that she commands the mother of the race to infuse into posterity half its efficiency and then denies her equal efficiency with the father of the race? It is unthinkable.

If we find woman inferior to man we must find the reason not in her natural endowment, but in the environment which warped her growth. But religion, say the doubters, the Word of God, the Creator of all, and Guide of all human destiny, commands the subjection of women and this could not be true if she were not a natural dependent. True, the sacred word of the four great religious systems of the world commands obedience and subjection, the Christian Scriptures according to common interpretation no less than the others. The Christian world is finding itself in much the position of the minister in Wyoming, who after an election in which the contest had been fairly fought between the moral and immoral elements of the town, and morality had won clearly because of the votes of women, gave a hearty prayer of thanksgiving in his prayer meeting, in which he fervently pleaded in defense of his attitude of mind, "O Lord, we have not forgotten Paul. We remember all he said. But O God, we do not know what he meant. Surely it was not this!" Every father who has permitted a liberal education to his daughter has violated the Pauline law, for she will not "ask her husband at home" [1 Cor. 14:35] that which she known [sic] as well herself. Every minister who has permitted a woman's voice in his choir, or in his prayer meeting, and every church which has ordained a woman has violated the command that women shall "keep silence in the churches" [1 Cor. 14:34], and more, every church which permits a Woman's Aid Society to raise the money to pay the minister's salary and the church debts, violates the command to subjection. Every minister who is importuning women members to follow the example of theatre attendants and remove their bonnets, is violating the command of St. Paul that women should not "pray with uncovered heads" [1 Cor. 11:5]. In fact, the women in the more intelligent classes of Christendom are no longer in subjection. The Pauline commands are forgotten, and verily in each violation, the world "does not know what he meant, but surely not this."

It is only brought forward now to oppose the political emancipation for women because it is the only freedom asked for which has not yet been gained. It remains for future students to discover why the commands are there; whether they were interpolated by later centuries, as has been claimed, or whether they may be "explained away." However, one thing is certain, and that is that all the Christian world will some day reach the point occupied by many Christians to-day where it will see that any Scripture which commands one class of human beings to remain in perpetual tutelage to another, which commands that one human being from birth owes obedience to another, does not represent the Divine Will. Instead, such command is on a plane with the understanding of justice in barbaric ages, and is shocking to modern human ideals. How little then can it represent the Divine conception which must be all-wise and all-just!

Nevertheless, the apparent Biblical endorsement of the subjection of women weighed mightily in the balance against all liberty for women for full eighteen hundred years. Ah, the pity of it! What a cruel mistake it all seems to have been! We may well paraphrase Madame Roland's celebrated utterance and say, "O, religion, what crimes have been committed in they name!"[14]

We are told these subjected earlier women were content. No doubt, content liked the imprisoned bird which sings in its cage in forgetfulness of the freedom which is its birthright. But how quickly these imprisoned ones learn to lift their wings and to fly when the bars are no longer there! Throughout the ages, when for any reason the tutelage over them grew lenient, when ever so little encouragement was given them, these women grew, and unfolded and blossomed, until like the lilies of the field, they filled the air with the fragrance of their well doing.

We find them teaching in universities, practicing medicine, writing books and governing empires under the ameliorating influence of the Revival of Learning, and the petition of one lady in 1555 has been preserved, who in true "Twentieth Century" fashion, implored "virtuous ladies to raise their minds a little above their distaffs and their spindles. The hour has now struck," says she, "when man can no longer shackle the honest liberty which our sex has so long yearned for." How many sorrowful souls longed for better things and beat their wings in pitiful struggle against the bars of their life prisons we may never know, for the historians were men. As few men to-day comprehend even faintly the depths of humiliation and anguish of the awakened woman who comprehends her restrictions, how much less could the historians of that day have cared for the experiences of women they believed to be born to perpetual dependence. It matters little, however, whether the woman of the past was contented or restless. The chief injury

---

[14] See p. 116, n 5.

of her subjection did not come to her but to the race. No people can rise higher than its source and we now know that source is men and women, not men alone. The punishment of belittled motherhood comes unerringly to every people. There was once a time when China had free women, but their freedom was gradually stolen under the cover of the mandates of Confucius.[15] China subjected its women more than any other people since she dwarfed their feet as well as their minds, and with the weight of this enslaved motherhood hanging like a millstone about its neck, the nation has stood still for hundreds of years. They say commerce, railroads, and liberal ideas might yet save her from the final downfall which seems threatening. These would help, doubtless, but the one remedy which could bring back the breath of life, and start her climbing upward on the ladder of civilization once more would be freedom for the women who are the mothers of China.

If the punishment of the subjection of women is certain, the reward for liberality is equally sure. There are doubtless many reasons for the dominance of the Anglo-Saxon race, but none more important than the fact that the Anglo-Saxons have permitted to their women a larger individuality and independence than any other people.

In fact, if we would give to the world races fitted to solve the mighty problems time is bringing, we must begin by utterly shattering the old fallacy that man is the race and woman his subject. That the subjection of motherhood operates to the injury of the race is a fact which must be cried from the house

---

[15] Confucianism promulgates four cardinal virtues for females: obedience, chastity, mercy, and quietness, virtues not unlike the tenets of the cult of true womanhood. These are embodied in a Confucian moral text, in Japan, the *Onna Daigaku* or *Greater Learning for Women* (1672) (Robins-Mowry 1983, 24).

tops. It must be taught in schools and colleges. It must be sent with every band of Christian missionaries, to be taught as their first precept. We must educate and agitate, agitate and educate until a full understanding of the race responsibility of motherhood shall have reached the remotest man and woman.

The Confucians have a proverb that "a woman owes three obediences: first to her father, second to her husband, and after his death to her son."[16] It is but a little time when this might have been claimed as the proverb of all peoples, for it represented the world's conception of the just and natural relation of the sexes. At no period in her life did the woman gain her freedom.

The whole aim of the woman movement has been to destroy the idea that obedience is necessary to women; to train women to such self-respect that they would not grant obedience and to train men to such comprehension of equity they would not exact it. The movement has traveled far when the world conceives the new opportunities which are now so freely offered. Education extends its hope to women in the remotest quarters of the globe. Even the prejudices of Mohammedans and Buddhists have yielded sufficiently to permit graduated physicians among the women of their religion. Occasional women in China and Japan are college educated. Women are beginning to realize among all peoples that self-abnegation is no more the duty of women than of men. They are learning that self-development and self-reliance are obligations equally imposed upon both. In every quarter of the globe the old theory is showing signs of dissolution.

A few men still expect obedience from their wives, a few wives willingly grant it

---

[16] In Confucianism, peace comes through order; hence, it established hierarchies that set of rigid codes of moral and social behavior, of which this is an example. See note 15.

and a few churchmen still preach it as the command of God, but that which remains is the mere shadow where once the substance existed.

As John Stuart Mill said in speaking of the conditions which preceded the enfranchisement of men: "The noble has been gradually going down on the social ladder and the commoner has been gradually going up. Every half century has brought them nearer to each other;"[17] so we may say, for the past five hundred years, man as the dominant power in the world has been going down the ladder and woman has been climbing up. Every decade has brought them nearer together. The opposition to the enfranchisement of women is the last defense of the old theory that obedience is necessary for women, because man alone is the creator of the race.

The whole effort of the woman movement has been to destroy obedience of woman in the home. That end has been very generally attained, and the average civilized woman enjoys the right of individual liberty in the home of her father, her husband, and her son. The individual woman no longer obeys the individual man. She enjoys self-government in the home and in society. The question now is, shall all women as a body obey all men as a body? Shall the woman who enjoys the right of self-government in every other department of life be permitted the right of self-government in the State? It is no more right for all men to govern all women that it was for one man to govern one woman. It is no more right for men to govern women that it was for one man to govern other men.

A little more than a century ago men asked, "why are some men born to rule and others to obey?" The world answered by making sovereigns of those who had been subjects, and now we ask, "Why are men born to rule and women to obey?" There is but one answer and that is, to lift the subject woman to the

---

[17] See p. 265, n 14.

throne by the side of the sovereign man.

A milepost marking vast progress is an International Woman Suffrage Conference, with nine Nations sending official delegates, while fourteen Nations have well-defined woman-suffrage movements.[18] Our question is clearly International in its scope and object. Sex-prejudice, with the old scientific blunder for its basis; sex-prejudice with its unreason and its intolerance, is our common enemy. We must win by the use of the same arguments, the same appeals to justice. We shall hope that the deliberations of the Conference will result in some form of International Alliance which will hasten the day when the women of all civilized Nations will possess the right of self-government in the home, the church and the State. We shall at least learn to know each other and join hands in fraternal helpfulness. That the old doctrine of obedience will be entirely obliterated, both for the individual woman in her home, and women as a whole in the State, among all the peoples of the world, is as certain as the rising of the sun to-morrow.

Yet before the attainment of equal rights for men and women there will be years of struggle and disappointment. We of a younger generation have taken up the work where our noble and consecrated pioneers left it. We in turn, are enlisted for life, and generations yet unborn will take up the work where we lay it down. So, through centuries if need be, the education will continue, until a regenerated race of men and women who are equal before man and God shall control the destinies of the earth. It will be the proud duty of the new International Alliance, if one shall be formed, to extend its helping hand to the women of every nation and every people, and its complete duty will not have been performed until the last vestige of the old obedience of

---

[18] For information on the number of nations with woman suffrage organizations see Van Voris 1987 (188-9, n. 5).

one human being to another shall have been permanently destroyed. God give us wisdom and courage to face the disappointment and the struggle of the contest, and above all, God grant us patience and tolerance for our opponents.

24

Carrie Chapman Catt, *"The Crisis,"* *Atlantic City, NJ, 1916*

National American Woman Suffrage Association president Carrie Chapman Catt made this address at the special 1916 convention of the NAWSA at Atlantic City, at which she also presented her "Winning Plan" for passage of a federal suffrage amendment. The plan was highly pragmatic; it called for pressure from women voters in states where they had the franchise for passage of a federal amendment by Congress; for passage of suffrage referenda in states where that was feasible; and for obtaining presidential suffrage or primary suffrage by act of the state legislatures where referenda were doomed. Suffrage workers were sworn to secrecy to prevent anti-suffragists from mounting organized opposition.

This speech is a classic example of a convention address designed to raise the morale of discouraged adherents who have worked for decades for a cause. The speech was the kickoff of the final campaign that resulted in passage and ratification of a federal amendment. The text is from a typewritten and edited copy in the author's papers at the New York Public Library (Catt 1916).

I have taken for my subject, "The Crisis," because I believe that a crisis has come in our movement which, if recognized and the opportunity seized with vigor, enthusiasm and will, means the final victory of our great cause in the very near future. I am aware that some suffragists do not share this belief; they see no signs nor symptoms today which were not present yesterday; no manifestations in the year 1916 which differ significantly from those in the year 1910. To them, the movement has been a steady, normal growth from the beginning and must so continue until the end. I can only defend my claim with the plea that it is better to *imagine* a crisis where none exists than to fail to recognize one when it comes; for a crisis is a culmination of events which calls for new considerations and new decisions. A failure to answer the call may mean an opportunity lost, a possible victory postponed.

The object of the life of an organized movement is to secure its aim. Necessarily, it must obey the law of evolution and pass through the stages of agitation and education and finally through the stage of realization. As one has put it: "A new idea floats in the air over the heads of the people and for a long, indefinite period evades their understanding but, by and by, when through familiarity, human vision grows clearer, it is caught out of the clouds and crystalized into law." Such a period comes to every movement and is its crisis. In my judgment, that crucial moment, bidding us to renewed consecration and redoubled activity has come to our cause. I believe our victory hangs within our grasp, inviting us to pluck it out of the clouds and establish it among the good things of the world.

If this be true, the time is past when we should say: "Men and women of America, look upon that wonderful idea up there; see, one day it will come down." Instead, the time has come to shout aloud in every city, village and hamlet, and in tones so clear and jubilant that they will reverberate from every mountain peak and echo from shore to shore: "The

Woman's Hour has struck."[1] Suppose suffragists as a whole do not believe a crisis has come and do not extend their hands to grasp the victory, what will happen? Why, we shall all continue to work and our cause will continue to hang, waiting for those who possess a clearer vision and more daring enterprise. On the other hand, suppose we reach out with united earnestness and determination to grasp our victory while it still hangs a bit too high? Has any harm been done? None!

Therefore, fellow suffragists, I invite your attention to the signs which point to a crisis and your consideration of plans for turning the crisis into victory.

FIRST: We are passing through a world crisis. All thinkers of every land tell us so; and that nothing after the great war will be as it was before. Those who profess to know, claim that 100 millions of dollars are being spent on the war every day and that 2 years of war have cost 50 billions of dollars or 10 times more than the total expense of the American Civil War. Our own country has sent 35 millions of dollars abroad for relief expenses.

Were there no other effects to come from the world's war, the transfer of such unthinkably vast sums of money from the usual avenues to those wholly abnormal would give so severe a jolt to organized society that it would vibrate around the world and bring untold changes in its wake.

But three and a half millions of lives have been lost. The number becomes the more impressive when it is remembered that the entire population of the American Colonies was

---

[1] This phrase refers to the frustration of woman's rights activists in the post-Civil War period who were told to defer the demand for woman suffrage because this was "the Negro's hour."

little more than three and one-half millions. These losses have been the lives of men within the age of economic production. They have been taken abruptly from the normal business of the world and every human activity from that of the humblest, unskilled labor to art, science and literature has been weakened by their loss. Millions of other men will go to their homes, blind, crippled and incapacitated to do the work they once performed. The stability of human institutions has never before suffered so tremendous a shock. Great men are trying to think out the consequences but one and all proclaim that no imagination can find color or form bold enough to paint the picture of the world after the war. British and Russian, German and Austrian, French and Italian agree that it will lead to social and political revolution throughout the entire world. Whatever comes, they further agree that the war presages a total change in the status of women.

A simple-minded man in West Virginia, when addressed upon the subject of woman suffrage in that State, replied, "We've been so used to keepin' our women down, 'twould seem queer not to." He expressed what greater men feel but do not say. Had the wife of that man spoken in the same clear-thinking fashion, she would have said, "We women have been so used to being kept down that it would seem strange to get up. Nature intended women for door-mats." Had she so expressed herself, these two would have put the entire anti-suffrage argument in a nut-shell.

In Europe, from the Polar Circle to the Aegean Sea, women have risen as though to answer that argument. Everywhere they have taken the places made vacant by men and in so doing, they have grown in self-respect and in the esteem of their respective nations. In every land, the people have reverted to the primitive division of labor and while the men have gone to war, women have cultivated the fields in order that the army and nation may be fed. No army can succeed and no nation can endure without food; those who supply it are a war power and a peace power.

Women by the thousands have knocked at the doors of munition factories and, in the name of patriotism, have begged for the right to serve their country there. Their services were accepted with hesitation but the experiment once made, won reluctant but universal praise. An official statement recently issued in Great Britain announced that 660,000 women were engaged in making munitions in that country alone. In a recent convention of munition workers, composed of men and women, a resolution was unanimously passed informing the government that they would forego vacations and holidays until the authorities announced that their munition supplies were sufficient for the needs of the war and Great Britain pronounced the act the highest patriotism. Lord Derby addressed such a meeting and said, "When the history of the war is written, I wonder to whom the greatest credit will be given; to the men who went to fight or to the women who are working in a way that many people hardly believed that it was possible for them to work." Lord Sydenham added his tribute. Said he, "It might fairly be claimed that women have helped to save thousands of lives and to change the entire aspect of the war. Wherever intelligence, care and close attention have been needed, women have distinguished themselves." A writer in the *London Times* of July 18, 1916, said: "But, for women, the armies could not have held the field for a month; the national call to arms could not have been made or sustained; the country would have perished of inanition and disorganization. If, indeed, it be true that the people have been one, it is because the genius of women has been lavishly applied to the task of reinforcing and complementing the genius of men. The qualities of steady industry, adaptability, good judgement and concentration of mind which men do not readily associate with women have been conspicuous features."

On fields of battle, in regular and improvised hospitals, women have given tender and skilled care to the wounded and are credited with the restoration of life to many, many thousands. Their heroism and self-sacrifice have been frankly acknowledged by all the governments; but their endurance, their skill, the practicality of their service, seem for the first time, to have been recognized by governments as "war power". So, thinking in war terms, great men have suddenly discovered that women are "war assets". Indeed, Europe is realizing, as it never did before, that women are holding together the civilization for which men are fighting. A great search-light has been thrown upon the business of nation-building and it has been demonstrated in every European land that it is a partnership with equal, but different responsibilities resting upon the two partners.

It is not, however, in direct war work alone that the latent possibilities of women have been made manifest. In all the belligerent lands, women have found their way to high posts of administration where no women would have been trusted two years ago and the testimony is overwhelming that they have filled their posts with entire satisfaction to the authorities. They have dared to stand in pulpits (once too sacred to be touched by the unholy feet of a woman) and there, without protest, have appealed to the Father of All in behalf of their stricken lands. They have come out of the kitchen where there was too little to cook and have found a way to live by driving cabs, motors and streetcars. Many a woman has turned her hungry children over to a neighbor and has gone forth to find food for both mothers and both families of children and has found it in strange places and occupations. Many a drawing-room has been closed and the maid who swept and dusted it is now cleaning streets that the health of the city may be conserved. Many a woman who never before slept in a bed of her own making, or ate food not prepared by paid labor, is now sole mistress of parlor and kitchen.

In all the warring countries, women are postmen [sic], porters, railway conductors, ticket, switch and signal men. Conspicuous advertisements invite women to attend agricultural, milking and motor-car schools. They are employed as police in Great Britain and women detectives have recently been taken on the government staff. In Berlin, there are over 3,000 women streetcar conductors and 3,500 women are employed on the general railways. In every city and country, women are doing work for which they would have been considered incompetent two years ago.

The war will soon end and the armies will return to their native lands. To many a family, the men will never come back. The husband who returns to many a wife, will eat no bread the rest of his life save of her earning.

What, then, will happen after the war? Will the widows left with families to support cheerfully leave their well-paid posts for those commanding lower wages? Not without protest! Will the wives who now must support crippled husbands give up their skilled work and take up the occupations which were open to them before the war? Will they resignedly say: "The woman who has a healthy husband who can earn for her, has a right to tea and raisin cake, but the woman who earns for herself and a husband who has given his all to his country, must be content with butterless bread?" Not without protest! On the contrary, the economic axiom, denied and evaded for centuries, will be blazoned on every factory, counting house and shop: "Equal pay for equal work"; and common justice will slowly, but surely enforce that law. The European woman has risen. She may not realize it yet, but the woman "door-mat" in every land has unconsciously become a "door-jamb"! She will have become accustomed to her new dignity by the time the men come home. She will wonder how she ever could have been content lying across the threshold now that she discovers the upright jamb gives so much broader and more normal a vision of things. The men returning may find the new order a bit queer but everything else will be strangely unfamiliar too, and they will soon grow accustomed to all the changes together. The "jamb" will never descend into a "door-mat" again.

The male and female anti-suffragists of all lands will puff and blow at the economic change which will come to the women of Europe. They will declare it to be contrary to Nature and to God's plan and that somebody ought to do something about it. Suffragists will accept the change as the inevitable outcome of an unprecedented world's cataclysm over which no human agency had any control and will trust in God to adjust the altered circumstances to the eternal evolution of human society. They will remember that in the long run, all things work together for good, for progress and for human weal.

The economic change is bound to bring political liberty. From every land, there comes the expressed belief that the war will be followed by a mighty, oncoming wave of democracy for it is now well known that the conflict has been one of governments, of kings and Czars, Kaisers and Emperors; not of peoples. The nations involved have nearly all declared that they are fighting to make an end of wars. New and higher ideals of governments and of the rights of the people under them, have grown enormously during the past two years. Another tide of political liberty, similar to that of 1848, but of a thousandfold greater momentum, is rising from battlefield and hospital, from camp and munitions factory, from home and church which, great men of many lands, tell us, is destined to sweep over the world. On the continent, the women say, "It is certain that the vote will come to men and women after the war, perhaps not immediately but soon. In Great Britain, which was the storm centre of the suffrage movement for some years before the war, hundreds of bitter, active opponents have confessed their conversion on account of the war services of women. Already, three great provinces of Canada, Manitoba, Alberta, and Saskatchawan [sic], have given universal suffrage to their women in sheer generous appreciation of their war work. Even Mr. Asquith, world renouned [sic] for his immovable opposition to the Parliamentary suffrage for British women, has given evidence of a change of view.[2] Some months ago, he announced his amazement at the utterly unexpected skill, strength and resource developed by the women and his gratitude for their loyalty and devotion. Later, in reply to Mrs. Henry Fawcett, who asked if woman suffrage would be included in a proposed election bill, he said that when the war should end, such a measure would be considered without prejudice carried over from events prior to the war.[3] A public statement issued by Mr. Asquith in August, was couched in such terms as to be interpreted by many as a pledge to include women in the next election bill.

In Great Britain, a sordid appeal which may prove the last straw to break the opposition to woman suffrage, has been added to the enthusiastic appreciation of woman's patriotism and practical service and to the sudden comprehension that motherhood is a national asset which must be protected at any price. A new voters' list is contemplated. A parliamentary election should be held in September

---

[2] Herbert Henry Asquith (1852-1928), British prime minister (1908-1916) and leader of the Liberal party until 1925, when he was raised to the peerage; he opposed woman suffrage (Harrison 1978).

[3] Millicent Garrett Fawcett, the leading figure in the National Union of Women's Suffrage Societies, which began in 1867 and stood apart from the more militant suffrage organizations.

but the voters are scattered far and wide. The whole nation is agitated over the questions involved in making a new register. At the same time, there is a constant anxiety over war funds, as is prudent in a nation spending 50 millions of dollars per day. It has been proposed that a large poll tax be assessed upon the voters of the new lists, whereupon a secondary proposal of great force has been offered and that is, that twice as much money would find its way into the public coffers were women added to the voters' list. What nation, with compliments fresh spoken concerning women's patriotism and efficiency, could resist such an appeal?

So it happens that above the roar of cannon, the scream of shrapnel and the whirr of aeroplanes, one who listens may hear the cracking of the fetters which have long bound the European woman to outworn conventions. It has been a frightful price to pay but the fact remains that a womanhood, well started on the way to final emancipation, is destined to step forth from the war. It will be a bewildered, troubled and grief-stricken womanhood with knotty problems of life to solve, but it will be freer to deal with them than women have ever been before.

"The Woman's Hour has struck." It has struck for the women of Europe and for those of all the world. The significance of the changed status of European women has not been lost upon the men and women of our land; our own people are not so unlearned in history, nor so lacking in National pride that they will allow the Republic to lag long behind the Empire, presided over by the descendant of George the Third. If they possess the patriotism and the sense of nationality which should be the inheritance of an American, they will not wait until the war is ended but will boldly lead in the inevitable march of democracy, our own American specialty. Sisters, let me repeat, the Woman's Hour has struck!

SECOND: As the most adamantine rock gives

way under the constant dripping of water, so the opposition to woman suffrage in our own country has slowly disintegrated before the increasing strength of our movement. Turn backward the pages of our history! Behold, brave Abbie Kelley rotten-egged because she, a woman, essayed to speak in public.[4] Behold the Polish Ernestine Rose startled that women of free America drew aside their skirts when she proposed that they should control their own property.[5] Recall the saintly Lucretia Mott and the legal-minded Elizabeth Cady Stanton, turned out of the [W]orld's Temperance Convention in London and conspiring together to free their sex from the world's stupid oppressions.[6] Remember the gentle, sweet-voiced Lucy Stone, egged because she publicly claimed that women had brains capable of education.[7] Think upon Dr. Elizabeth

---

[4]Abigail ("Abby") Kelley [Foster] (1810-1887), abolitionist and woman's rights lecturer, spoke first in 1838 to a mixed audience in Philadelphia's Pennsylvania Hall. A powerful agitator, she was attacked as a Jezebel and faced angry mobs outraged at a woman speaking effectively to mixed audiences against slavery.

[5] An allusion to the 1836 effort to petition the New York Legislature to amend the Married Woman's Property Act. See Volume I, chapter 6.

[6] Lucretia Coffin Mott and other women were not seated as delegates at the World Anti-Slavery Convention in 1840. Cady Stanton was present but not a delegate.

[7] Lucy Stone (1818-93), the first Massachusetts woman to take a college degree (Oberlin, 1847). She became a lecturer for the American Anti-Slavery Society, but also spoke on woman's rights prior to the emergence of a movement, fearlessly facing hostile

Blackwell, snubbed and boycotted by other women because she proposed to study medicine.[8] Behold Dr. Antoinette Brown Blackwell, standing in sweet serenity before an Assembly of howling clergymen, angry that she, a woman dared to attend a Temperance Convention as a delegate.[9] Revere the intrepid Susan B. Anthony mobbed from Buffalo to Albany because she demanded fair play for women. These are they who builded with others the foundation of political liberty for American women.

Those who came after only laid the stones in place. Yet, what a wearisome task even that has been! Think of the wonderful woman who has wandered from village to village, from city to city, for a generation compelling men and women to listen and to reflect by her matchless eloquence. Where in all the world's history has any movement among men produced so invincible an advocate as our own Dr. Anna Howard Shaw? Those whom she has led to the light are Legion. Think, too, of the consecration, the self-denial, the never-failing constancy of that other noble soul set in a frail but unflinching body,--the heroine we

---

audiences. Defying convention, she kept her own name after her marriage to Henry Blackwell in 1855. She became the leader of the New England wing of the suffrage movement, a founder of the American Woman Suffrage Association and of the *Woman's Journal* (1870), which after 1872 she and her husband, and later her daughter, Alice Stone Blackwell, edited.

[8] Elizabeth Blackwell (1821-1910), the first woman of modern times to graduate in medicine. She received her degree in 1849 from Geneva College, and founded the New York Infirmary for Women and Children in 1857, and the Woman's Medical College of the New York Infirmary in 1868.

[9] See headnote p. 188 and p. 367, n 24.

know as Alice Stone Blackwell![10] A woman who never forgets, who detects the slightest flaw in the weapons of her adversary, who knows the most vulnerable spot in his armor, presides over the *Woman's Journal* and, like a lamp in a lighthouse, the rays of her intelligence, far-sightedness and clear-thinking have enlightened the world concerning our cause. The names of hundreds of other brave souls spring to memory when we pause to review the long struggle.

The hands of many suffrage master-masons have long been stilled; the names of many who laid the stones have been forgotten. That does not matter. The main thing is that the edifice of woman's liberty nears completion. It is strong, indestructible. All honor to the thousands who have helped in the building.

The four Corner-stones of the foundations were laid long years ago. We read upon the first: "We demand for women education, for not a high school or college is open to her"; upon the second, "We demand for women religious liberty for in few churches is she permitted to pray or speak"; upon the third, "We demand for women the right to own property and an opportunity to earn an honest living. Only six, poorly-paid occupations are open to her, and if she is married, the wages she earns are not hers"; upon the fourth, "We demand political freedom and its symbol, the vote."

The stones in the foundation have long been overgrown with the moss and mould of time, and some there are who never knew they were laid. Of late, four cap-stones at the top have been set to match those in the base, and we read upon the first: "The number of

---

[10] Daughter of Lucy Stone and Henry Blackwell (1857-1950). Following graduation from Boston University in 1881, she bore the main burdens of editing the *Woman's Journal*, the country's leading woman's rights newspaper founded by her parents, for the next thirty-five years.

women who are graduated from high schools, colleges and universities is legion"; upon the second, "The Christian Endeavor, that mighty, undenominational church militant, asks the vote for the women and the Methodist Episcopal Church, and many another, joins that appeal"; upon the third, "Billions of dollars worth of property are earned [and] owned by women; more than 8 millions of women are wage-earners. Every occupation is open to them"; upon the fourth: "Women vote in 12 States; they share in the determination of 91 electoral votes."

After the cap-stones and cornice comes the roof. Across the empty spaces, the roof-tree has been flung and fastened well in place. It is not made of stone but of two *planks*,--planks in the platform of the two majority parties, and these are well supported by planks in the platforms of all minority parties.

And we who are the builders of 1916, do we see a crisis? Standing upon these planks which are stretched across the top-most peak of this edifice of woman's liberty, what shall we do? Over our heads, up there in the clouds, but tantalizing [sic] near, hangs the roof of our edifice,--the vote. What is our duty? Shall we spend time in admiring the capstones and cornice? Shall we lament the tragedies which accompanied the laying of the cornerstones? Or, shall we, like the builders of old, chant, "Ho! all hands, all hands, heave to! All hands, heave to!" and while we chant, grasp the overhanging roof and with a long pull, a strong pull and a pull together, fix it in place forevermore?

Is the crisis real or imaginary? If it be real, it calls for action, bold, immediate and decisive.

Let us then take measure of our strength. Our cause has won the endorsement of all political parties. Every candidate for the presidency is a suffragist. It has won the endorsement of most churches; it has won the hearty approval of all great organizations of women. It was won the support of all reform movements; it has won the progressives of every variety. The majority of the press in most States is with us. Great men in every political party, church and movement are with us. The names of the greatest men and women of art, science, literature and philosophy, reform, religion and politics are on our lists.

We have not won the reactionaries of any party, church or society, and we never will. From the beginning of things, there have been Antis. The Antis drove Moses out of Egypt; they crucified Christ who said, "Love thy neighbor as thyself" [Matt. 19:19, 22:39]; they have persecuted Jews in all parts of the world; they poisoned Socrates, the great philosopher; they cruelly persecuted Copernicus[11] and Galileo,[12] the first great scientists; they burned Giordano Bruno at the stake because he believed the world was round;[13]

---

[11] Nicholas Copernicus (1473-1543), Polish astronomer, whose great work, the foundation of modern astronomy, was *De revolutionibus orbium coelestium* (1543), dedicated to Pope Paul III.

[12] Galileo Galilei (1564-1642), Italian astronomer, mathematician, and physicist, who constructed the first complete astronomical telescope, and whose investigations confirmed the Copernican theory of the solar system. In 1616 that theory was denounced as dangerous to faith, but in 1632 Galileo published a work which supported it, and was tried in 1633 by the Inquisition and forced to recant all beliefs and writings holding that the earth and other planets revolved about the sun.

[13] Giordano Bruno (1548-1600), Italian philosopher. His major metaphysical works were *De la causa, principio, et uno* (1584) and *De l'infinito, universo et mondi* (1584). Tried for heresy in Venice in 1591 by the Inquisition, he was imprisoned, then burned to

they burned Savonarola who warred upon church corruption;[14] they burned Eufame McIlyane [sic] because she used an anaesthetic;[15] they burned Joan d'Arc for a heretic; they have sent great men and women to Siberia to eat their hearts out in isolation; they burned in effigy William Lloyd Garrison;[16] they egged Abbie Kelley and Lucy Stone and mobbed Susan B. Anthony. Yet, in proportion to the enlightenment of their respective ages, these Antis were persons of intelligence and honest purpose. They were merely deaf to the call of Progress and were enraged because the world insisted upon moving on. Antis male and female there still are and will be to the end of time. Give to them a prayer of forgiveness for they know not what they do; and prepare for the forward march.

We have not won the ignorant and illiterate and we never can. They are too undeveloped mentally to understand that the institutions of today are not those of yesterday nor will be those of tomorrow.

We have not won the forces of evil and we

---

death at Rome.

[14] Girolamo Savonarola (1452-98), Italian religious reformer, prior of San Marco, the Dominican house in Florence. He was excommunicated by Pope Alexander VI for disobedience after he continued to preach against the scandalously corrupt papal court. Under torture he supposedly confessed to being a false prophet and was hanged for schism and heresy.

[15] Euphemia MacCalyean was sentenced to be burned in Scotland on June 15, 1591, for attempting to relieve her pains in giving birth to twins and for other charges related to witchcraft.

[16] See headnote p. 188 and vol. I, chps. 2 and 5.

never will. Evil has ever been timorous and suspicious of all change. It is an instinctive act of self-preservation which makes it fear and consequently oppose votes for women. As the Hon. Champ Clark said the other day: "Some good and intelligent people are opposed to woman suffrage; but all the ignorant and evil-minded are against it."[17]

These three forces are the enemies of our cause.

Before the vote is won, there must and will be a gigantic final conflict between the forces of progress, righteousness and democracy and the forces of ignorance, evil and reaction. That struggle may be postponed, but it cannot be evaded or avoided. There is no question as to which side will be the victor.

Shall we play the coward, then, and leave the hard knocks for our daughters, or shall we throw ourselves into the fray, bare our own shoulders to the blows, and thus bequeath to them a politically liberated womanhood? We have taken note of our gains and of our resources, and they are all we could wish. Before the final struggle, we must take cognizance of our weaknesses. Are we prepared to grasp the victory? Alas, no! Our movement is like a great Niagara with a vast volume of water tumbling over its ledge but turning no wheel. Our organized machinery is set for the propagandistic stage and not for the seizure of victory. Our supporters are spreading the argument for our cause; they feel no sense of responsibility for the realization of our hopes. Our movement lacks cohesion, organization, unity and consequent momentum.

Behind us, in front of us, everywhere

---

[17] James Beauchamp Clark (1850-1921), member U.S. House of Representatives (1893-95, 1897-1921). He became Democratic leader (1907) and Speaker (1911-19), and in 1912 was the leading Democratic candidate for the presidency until William Jennings Bryan shifted his support to Woodrow Wilson.

about us are suffragists,--millions of them, but inactive and silent. They have been "agitated and educated" and are with us in belief. There are thousands of women who have at one time or another been members of our organization but they have dropped out because, to them the movement seemed negative and pointless. Many have taken up other work whose results were more immediate. Philanthropy, charity, work for corrective laws of various kinds, temperance, relief for working women and numberless similar public services have called them. Others have turned to the pleasanter avenues of clubwork, art or literature.

There are thousands of other women who have never learned of the earlier struggles of our movement. They found doors of opportunity open to them on every side. They found well-paid posts awaiting the qualified woman and they have availed themselves of all these blessings; almost without exception they believe in the vote but they feel neither gratitude to those who opened the doors through which they have entered to economic liberty nor any sense of obligation to open other doors for those who come after.

There are still others who, timorously looking over their shoulders to see if any listeners be near, will tell us they hope we will win and win soon but they are too frightened of Mother Grundy to help.[18] There are others too occupied with the small things of life to help. They say they could find time to vote but not to work for the vote. There are men, too, millions of them, waiting to be called. These men and women are our reserves. They are largely unorganized and untrained soldiers with little responsibility toward our movement. Yet these reserves must be mobilized. The final struggle needs their numbers and the momentum those numbers will bring. Were never another convert made, there

---

[18] Public opinion personified.

are suffragists enough in this country, if combined, to make so irresistible a driving force that victory might be seized at once.

How can it be done? By a simple change of mental attitude. If we are to seize the victory, that change must take place in this hall, here and now!

The old belief, which has sustained suffragists in many an hour of discouragement, "woman suffrage is bound to come," must give way to the new, "The Woman's Hour has struck." The long drawn out struggle, the cruel hostility which, for years was arrayed against our cause, have accustomed suffragists to the idea of indefinite postponement but eventual victory. The slogan of a movements sets its pace. The old one counseled patience; it said, there is plenty of time; it pardoned sloth and half-hearted effort. It set the pace of an educational campaign. The "Woman's Hour has struck" sets the pace of a crusade which will have its way. It says: "Awake, arise, my sisters, let your hearts be filled with joy,--the time of victory is here. Onward March."

If you believe with me that a crisis has come to our movement,--if you believe that the time for final action is now, if you catch the rosy tints of the coming day, what does it mean to you? Does it not give you a thrill of exaltation; does the blood not course more quickly through your veins; does it not bring a new sense of freedom, of joy and of determination? Is it not true that you who wanted a little time ago to lay down the work because you were weary with long service, now, under the compelling influence of a changed mental attitude, are ready to go on until the vote is won. The change is one of spirit! Aye, and the spiritual effect upon you will come to others. Let me borrow an expression from Hon. John Finlay: What our great movement needs now is a "mobilization of spirit",--the jubilant, glad spirit of victory. Then let us sound a bugle call here and now to the women of the Nation: "The Woman's Hour has struck." Let the bugle sound from the suffrage headquarters of every State at the inauguration of a State campaign. Let the call go forth again and again and yet again. Let it be repeated in every article written, in every speech made, in every conversation held. Let the bugle blow again and yet again. The political emancipation of our sex call[s] you, women of America, arise! Are you content that others shall pay the price of your liberty?

Women in schools and counting house, in shops and on the farm, women in the home with babes at their breasts and women engaged in public careers will hear. The veins of American women are not filled with milk and water. They are neither cowards nor slackers. They will come. They only await the bugle call to learn that the final battle is on.

25

Carrie Chapman Catt, "Address to the United States Congress," 1917

This address was delivered to the 1917 National American Woman Suffrage Association national convention following the successful referendum campaign that conferred the ballot on the women of New York. This victory clearly signaled that success on the federal level was finally within their grasp. Catt's "Address" initiated the final campaign targeted at the U.S. Congress for passage of a federal suffrage amendment. It was published as a pamphlet (Catt 1917), *and suffragists considered it an absolutely conclusive statement of their case* (**HWS** 5: 522). *Tightly structured, the force of the speech comes from its logic and its realistic assessment of the situation. Its arguments and the implicit threat of its conclusions may have influenced legislators: on January 10, 1918, the House of Representatives passed the suffrage amendment 274 to 136. On October 1, 1918, however, it failed to achieve the two-thirds majority required for passage in the Senate, by a vote of 62 to 34.*

Woman suffrage is inevitable. Suffragists knew it before November 6, 1917; opponents afterward.[1] Three distinct causes make it inevitable:

1. *The history of our country*. Ours is a nation born of revolution; of rebellion against a system of government so securely entrenched in the customs and traditions of human society that in 1776 it seemed impregnable. From the beginning of things nations had been ruled by kings and for kings, while the people served and paid the cost. The American Revolutionists boldly proclaimed the heresies:

"Taxation without representation is tyranny."

"Governments derive their just powers from the consent of the governed."

The colonists won and the nation which was established as a result of their victory has held unfailingly that these two fundamental principles of democratic government are not only the spiritual source of our national existence but have been our chief historic pride and at all times the sheet anchor of our liberties.

Eighty years after the Revolution Abraham Lincoln welded those two maxims into a new one:

"Ours is a government of the people, by the people and for the people."[2]

Fifty years more passed and the President of the United States, Woodrow Wilson, in a mighty crisis of the nation, proclaimed to the world:

"We are fighting for the things which we have always carried nearest our hearts--for

---

[1] *Date of passage of the New York state referendum on woman suffrage.*

[2] *In his address at the dedication of the cemetery at Gettysburg, PA, November 19, 1863, Lincoln concluded saying "that government of the people, by the people, for the people, shall not perish from the earth."*

democracy, for the right of those who submit to authority to have a voice in their own government."[3]

All the way between these immortal aphorisms political leaders have declared unabated faith in their truth. Not one American has arisen to question their logic in the one hundred and forty-one years of our national existence. However stupidly our country may have evaded the logical application at times, it has never swerved from its devotion to the theory of democracy as expressed by those two axioms.

Not only has it unceasingly upheld the THEORY but it has carried these theories into PRACTICE whenever men made application.

Certain denominations of Protestants, Catholics, Jews, non-land holders, workingmen, Negroes, Indians, were at one time disfranchised in all, or in part, of our country. Class by class they have been admitted to the electorate. Political motives may have played their part in some instances but the only reason given by historians for their enfranchisement is the unassailability of the logic of these maxims of the Declaration.

Meantime the United States opened wide its gates to men of all the nations of earth. By the combination of naturalization granted the foreigner after a five-years' residence by our national government and the uniform provision of the State constitutions which extends the vote to *male citizens*, it has been the custom in our country for three generations that any male immigrant, accepted by the national government as a citizen, automatically becomes a voter in any State in which he chooses to reside, subject only to the minor qualifications prescribed by the State. Justifiable exceptions to the general principle might have been entered. Men just emerging from slavery, untrained to think or

---

[3] Woodrow Wilson, "Request for a Declaration of War," April 12, 1917.

act for themselves and in most cases wholly illiterate, were not asked to qualify for voting citizenship. Not even as a measure of national caution has the vote ever been withheld from immigrants until they have learned our language, earned a certificate of fitness from our schools or given definite evidence of loyalty to our country. When such questions have been raised, political leaders have replied: "What! Tax men and in return give them no vote; compel men to obey the authority of a government to which they may not give consent! Never. That is un-American." So, it happens that men of all nations and all races, except the Mongolian, may secure citizenship and automatically become voters in any State in the Union, and even the Mongolian born in this country is a citizen and has the vote.[4] With such a history behind it, how can our nation escape the logic it has never failed to follow, when its last unenfranchised class calls for the vote? Behold our Uncle Sam floating the banner with one hand, "Taxation without representation is tyranny," and with the other seizing the billions of dollars paid in taxes by women to whom he refuses "representation." Behold him again, welcoming the boys of twenty-one and the newly-made immigrant citizen to "a voice in their own government" while he denies that fundamental right of democracy to thousands of women public school teachers from whom many of these men learn all they know of citizenship and patriotism, to women college presidents, to women who preach in our pulpits, interpret law in our courts, preside over our hospitals, write books and magazines and serve in every uplifting moral and social enterprise.

Is there a single man who can justify such inequality of treatment, such outrageous discriminations? Not one.

---

[4] The 1868 Burlingame Treaty with China guaranteed the right of Chinese immigration, but not the right of naturalization.

Woman suffrage became an assured fact when the Declaration of Independence was written. It matters not at all whether Thomas Jefferson and his compatriots thought of women when they wrote that immortal document. They conceived and voiced a principle greater than any man. "A Power not of themselves which makes for righteousness" gave them the vision and they proclaimed truisms as immutable as the multiplication table, as changeless as time. The Hon. Champ Clark announced that he had been a woman suffragist ever since he "got the hang of the Declaration of Independence."[5] So it must be with every other American. The amazing thing is that it has required so long a time for a people, most of whom know how to read, "to get the hang of it." Indeed, so inevitable does our history make woman suffrage that any citizen, political party, Congress or Legislature that now blocks its coming by so much as a single day, contributes to the indefensible inconsistency which threatens to make our nation a jest among the onward-moving peoples of the world.

2. *The suffrage for women already established in the United States makes woman suffrage for the nation inevitable*. When Elihu Root, as President of the American Society of International Law, at the eleventh annual meeting in Washington, April 26, 1917, said, "The world cannot be half democratic and half autocratic. It must be all democratic or all Prussian. There can be no compromise," he voiced a general truth.[6] Precisely the same intuition has already taught the blindest and most hostile foe of woman suffrage that our nation cannot long continue a condition under which government in half its territory rests

---

[5] See p. 499, n 17.

[6] Elihu Root (1845-1937), U.S. Secretary of War (1899-1909), U.S. Senator from New York (1909-15), and 1912 Nobel Peace Prize winner 1912; he actively opposed woman suffrage.

upon the consent of half the people and in the other half upon the consent of all the people; a condition which grants representation to the taxed in half its territory and denies it in the other half; a condition which permits women in some States to share in the election of the President, Senators and Representatives and denies them that privilege in others. It is too obvious to require demonstration that woman suffrage, now covering half our territory, will eventually be ordained in all the nation. No one will deny it; the only question left is when and how will it be completely established.

3. *The leadership of the United States in world democracy compels the enfranchisement of its own women.*

The maxims of the Declaration were once called "fundamental principles of government." They are now called "American principles" or even "Americanisms." They have become the slogans of every movement toward political liberty the world around; of every effort to widen the suffrage for men or women in any land. Not a people, race or class striving for freedom is there, anywhere in the world, that has not made our axioms the chief weapon of the struggle. More, all men and women the world around, with far-sighted vision into the verities of things, know that the world tragedy of our day is not now being waged over the assassination of an Archduke, nor commercial competition, nor national ambitions, nor the freedom of the seas--it is a death grapple between the forces which deny and those which uphold the truths of the Declaration of Independence.

Our "Americanisms" have become the issue of the great war!

Every day the conviction grows deeper that a world humanity will emerge from the war, demanding political liberty and accepting nothing less. In that new struggle there is little doubt that men and women will demand and attain political liberty together. To-day they are fighting the world's battle for

Democracy together. Men and women are paying the frightful cost of war and bearing its sad and sickening sorrows together. To-morrow they will share its rewards together in democracies which make no discriminations on account of sex.

These are new times and, as an earnest of its sincerity in the battle for democracy, the government of Great Britain has not only pledged votes to its disfranchised men and to its women, but the measure passed the House of Commons in June, 1917, by a vote of 7 to 1 and will be sent to the House of Lords in December with the assurances of Premier Lloyd George that it will shortly become a national law. The measure will apply to England, Scotland, Ireland, Wales and all the smaller British islands.

Canada, too, has enfranchised the women of all its provinces stretching from the Pacific Coast to Northern New York, and the Premier has predicted votes for all Canadian women before the next national election.

Russia, whose opposing forces have made a sad farce of the new liberty, is nevertheless pledged to a democracy which shall include women. It must be remembered that no people ever passed from absolute autocracy into a smoothly running democracy with ready-made constitution and a full set of statutes to cover all conditions. Russia is no exception. She must have time to work out her destiny. Except those maxims of democracy put forth by our own country, it is interesting to note that the only one worthy of immortality is the slogan of the women of New Russia, *"Without the participation of women, suffrage is not universal."*

France has pledged votes to its women as certainly as a Republic can. Italian men have declared woman suffrage an imperative issue when the war is over and have asked its consideration before. The city of Prague (Bohemia) has appointed a Commission to report a new municipal suffrage plan which shall include women. Even autocratic Germany has debated the question in the Imperial Reichstag.

In the words of Premier Lloyd George: "There are times in history when the world spins along its destined course so leisurely that for centuries it seems to be at a standstill. Then come awful times when it rushes along at so giddy a pace that the track of centuries is covered in a single year. These are the times in which we now live."[7]

It is true; democracy, votes for men and votes for women, making slow but certain progress in 1914, have suddenly become established facts in many lands in 1917. Already our one-time Mother Country has become the standard bearer of our Americanisms, the principles she once denied, and--cynical fact--Great Britain, not the United States, is now leading the world on to the coming democracy.[8] Any man who has red American

---

[7] David Lloyd George (1863-1945) entered Parliament in 1890; he became chancellor, then minister of munitions (1908-15) and minister of war (1916), before ousting Herbert Asquith to form his own coalition government, which lasted until 1922.

[8] [*Note in original.*] The present bill provides that the parliamentary vote shall be extended to women. All other suffrage rights on equal terms with men have long been enjoyed by the women of England, Scotland, Ireland and Wales; the women of Canada too have had municipal suffrage for many years, the qualifications varying in different provinces, and the women of Australia and New Zealand have long had full suffrage on equal terms with men. The Scandinavian countries, too, have outstripped us in applied democracy and have taken the second lead. Universal suffrage including women is already established in Finland, Norway, Denmark and Iceland, while Sweden long ago gave women equal political rights with men, except the

blood in his veins, any man who has gloried in our history and has rejoiced that our land was the leader of world democracy, will share with us the humbled national pride that our country has so long delayed action upon this question that another country has beaten us in what we thought was our especial world mission.

Is it not clear that American history makes woman suffrage inevitable? That full suffrage in twelve States makes its coming in all forty-eight States inevitable? That the spread of democracy over the world, including votes for the women of many countries, in each case based upon the principles our Republic gave to the world, compels action by our nation? Is it not clear that the world expects such action and fails to understand its delay?

In the face of these facts we ask you, Senators and Members of the House of Representatives of the United States, is not the immediate enfranchisement of the women of our nation the duty of the hour?

Why hesitate? Not an inch of solid ground is left for the feet of the opponent. The world's war has killed, buried and pronounced the obsequies upon the hard-worked "war argument." Mr. Asquith, erstwhile champion anti-suffragist of the world, has said so and the British Parliament has confirmed it by its enfranchisement of British women.[9] The million and fifteen thousand women of New York who signed a declaration that they wanted the vote, plus the heavy vote of women in every State and country where women have the franchise, have finally and completely disposed of the familiar "they don't want it" argument. Thousands of women annually emerging from the schools and

---

vote for Parliament. The King has twice recommended that this disability be removed and action is promised soon.

[9] See p. 491, n 2.

colleges have closed the debate upon the one-time serious "they don't know enough" argument. The statistics of police courts and prisons have laid the ghost of the "too bad to vote" argument. The woman who demanded the book and verse in the Bible which gave men the vote, declaring that the next verse gave it to women, brought the "Bible argument" to a sudden end. The testimony of thousands of reputable citizens of our own suffrage States and of all other suffrage lands that woman suffrage has brought no harm and much positive good, and the absence of reputable citizens who deny these facts, has closed the "women only double the vote" argument. The increasing number of women wage-earners, many supporting families and some supporting husbands, has thrown out the "women are represented" argument. One by one these pet misgivings have been relegated to the scrap heap of all rejected, cast-off prejudices. Not an argument is left. The case against woman suffrage, carefully prepared by the combined wit, skill and wisdom of opponents, including some men of high repute, during sixty years, has been closed. The jury of the New York electorate heard it all, weighed the evidence and pronounced it "incompetent, irrelevant and immaterial." Historians tell us that the battle of Gettysburg brought our Civil War to an end, although the fighting went on a year longer, because the people who directed it did not see that the end had come. Had their sight been clearer, a year's casualties of human life, desolated homes, high taxes and bitterness of spirit, might have been avoided. The battle of New York is the Gettysburg of the woman suffrage movement. There are those too blind to see that the end has come, and others, unrelenting and unreasoning, who stubbornly deny that the end has come although they know it. These can compel the women of the nation to keep a standing suffrage army, to finance it, to fight on until these blind and stubborn ones are gathered to their fathers and men with clearer vision come to take their places, but the casualties will be sex antagonism, party antagonism, bitterness, resentment, contempt, hate and the things which grow out of a rankling grievance autocratically denied redress. These things are not mentioned in the spirit of threat, but merely to voice well known principles of historical psychology.

Benjamin Franklin once said "The cost of war is not paid at the time, the bills come afterwards." So too the nation, refusing justice when justice is due, finds the costs accumulating and the bills presented at unexpected and embarrassing times. Think it over.

If enfranchisement is to be given to women now, how is [it] to be done? Shall it be by amendment of State constitutions or by amendment of the Federal Constitution? There are no other ways. The first sends the question from the Legislature by referendum to all male voters of the State; the other sends the question from Congress to the Legislatures of the several States.

We elect the Federal method. There are three reasons why we make this choice and three reasons why we reject the State method. We choose the Federal method (1) because it is the quickest process and justice demands immediate action. If passed by the Sixty-fifth Congress, as it should be, the amendment will go to forty-one Legislatures in 1919, and when thirty-six have ratified it, will become a national law. In 1869 Wyoming led the way and 1919 will round out half a century of the most self-sacrificing struggle any class ever made for the vote. It is enough. The British women's suffrage army will be mustered out at the end of their half century of similar endeavor. Surely men of the land of George Washington will not require a longer time than those of the land of George the Third to discover that taxation without representation is tyranny no matter whether it be men or women who are taxed! We may justly expect American men to be as willing to grant to the women of the United States as generous consideration as those of Great Britain have done.

(2) Every other country dignifies woman suffrage as a national question. Even Canada and Australia, composed of self-governing states like our own, so regard it. Were the precedent not established our own national government has taken a step which makes the treatment of woman suffrage as a national question imperative. For the first time in our history Congress has imposed a direct tax upon women and has thus deliberately violated the most fundamental and sacred principle of our government, since it offers no compensating "representation" for the tax it imposes. Unless reparation is made it becomes the same kind of tyrant as was George the Third. When the exemption for unmarried persons under the Income Tax was reduced to $1,000 the Congress laid the tax upon thousands of wage-earning women--teachers, doctors, lawyers, bookkeepers, secretaries and the proprietors of many businesses.[10] Such women are earning their incomes under hard conditions of economic inequalities largely due to their disfranchisement. Many of these, while fighting their own economic battle, have been contributors to the campaign for suffrage that they might bring easier conditions for all women. Now those contributions will be deflected from suffrage treasuries into government funds through taxation. Women realize the dire need of huge government resources at this time and will make no protest against the tax, but it must be understood, and understood clearly, that the protest is there just the same and that women income taxpayers with few exceptions harbor a genuine grievance against the government of

---

[10] The Sixteenth Amendment to the U.S. Constitution, adopted in 1913, permitted both corporate and individual income tax to become a lawful element in the Federal tax structure.

the United States. The national government is guilty of the violation of the principle that the tax and the vote are inseparable; it alone can make amends. Two ways are open: exempt the women from the Income Tax or grant them the vote--there can be no compromise. To shift responsibility from Congress to the States is to invite the scorn of every human being who has learned to reason. A Congress which creates the law and has the power to violate a world-acknowledged axiom of just government can also command the law and the power to make reparation to those it has wronged by the violation. To you, the Congress of the United States, we must and do look for this act of primary justice.

(3) If the entire forty-eight States should severally enfranchise women, their political status would still be inferior to that of men, since no provision for national protection in their right to vote would exist. The women of California or New York are not wholly enfranchised, for the national government has not denied the States the right to deprive them of the vote. This protection can come only by Federal action. Therefore, since women will eventually be forced to demand Congressional action in order to equalize the rights of men and women, why not take such action now and thus shorten and ease the process? When such submission is secured, as it will be, forty-eight simultaneous State ratification campaigns will be necessary. By the State method thirty-six States would be obliged to have individual campaigns, and those would still have to be followed by the forty-eight additional campaigns to secure the final protection in their right to vote by the national government. We propose to conserve money, time and woman's strength by the elimination of the thirty-six State campaigns as unnecessary at this stage of the progress of the woman suffrage movement.

The three reasons why we object to the State amendment process are: (1) The constitutions of many States contain such difficult provisions for amending that it is practically impossible to carry an amendment at the polls. Several States require a majority of all the votes cast at an election to insure the passage of an amendment. As the number of persons voting on amendments is usually considerably smaller than the number voting for the head of the ticket, the effect of such provision is that a majority of those men who do not vote at all on the amendment are counted as voting against it. For example, imagine a State casting 100,000 votes for Governor and 80,000 on a woman suffrage amendment. That proportion would be a usual one. Now suppose there were 45,000 votes in favor and 35,000 against woman suffrage. The amendment would have been carried by 10,000 majority in a State which requires only a majority of the votes cast on the amendment, as in the State of New York. If, however, the State requires a majority of the votes cast at the election, the amendment would be lost by 10,000 majority. The men who were either too ignorant, too indifferent or too careless to vote on the question would have defeated it. Such constitutions have rarely been amended and then only on some non-controversial question which the dominant powers have agreed to support with the full strength of their "machines."

New Mexico, for example, requires three-fourths of those voting at an election, including two-thirds from each county. New Mexico is surrounded by suffrage States but the women who live there probably can secure enfranchisement only by federal action. The Indiana constitution provides that a majority of all voters is necessary to carry an amendment; thus the courts may decide that registered voters who did not go to the polls at all may be counted in the number, a majority of whom it is necessary to secure. The constitution cannot be amended. The courts have declared that the constitution prohibits the Legislature from granting suffrage to women. What then can the women of Indiana do? They have no other hope than the Federal Amendment. Several State constitutions stipulate that a definite period of time must elapse before an amendment defeated at the polls can again be submitted. New York has no such provision and the second campaign of 1917 immediately followed the first in 1915; but Pennsylvania and New Jersey, both voting on the question in 1915, cannot vote on it again before 1920. New Hampshire has no provision for the submission of an amendment by the Legislature at all. A Constitutional Convention alone has the right to submit an amendment, and such conventions can not be called oftener than once in seven years. The constitutional complications in many of the States are numerous, varied and difficult to overcome.

All careful investigators must arrive at the same conclusion that the only hope for the enfranchisement of the women of several States is through Congressional action. Since this is true, we hold it unnecessary to force women to pass through any more referenda campaigns. The hazards of the State constitutional provisions which women are expected to overcome in order to get the vote, as compared with the easy process by which the vote is fairly thrust upon foreigners who choose to make their residence among us, is so offensive an outrage to one's sense of justice that a woman's rebellion would surely have been fomented long ago had women not known that the discrimination visited upon them was without deliberate intent. The continuation of this condition is, however, the direct responsibility now of every man who occupies a position authorized to right the wrong. You are such men, Honorable Senators and Representatives. To you we appeal to remove a grievance more insulting than any nation in the wide world has put upon its women.

2. The second reason why we object to the State process is far more serious and important than the first. It is because the

statutory laws governing elections are so inadequate and defective as to vouchsafe little or no protection to a referendum in most States. The need for such protection seems to have been universally overlooked by the lawmakers. Bipartisan election boards offer efficient machinery whereby the representatives of one political party may check any irregularities of the other. The interests of all political parties in an election are further protected by partisan watchers. None of these provisions is available to those interested in a referendum. In most States women may not serve as watchers and no political party assumes responsibility for a non-partisan question. In the State of New York women may serve as watchers. They did so serve in 1915 and in 1917; nearly every one in the more than 5,000 polling places was covered by efficiently trained women watchers. The women believe that this fact had much to do with the favorable result.

In twenty-four States there is no law providing for a recount on a referendum. Voters may be bribed, colonized, repeated and the law provides for no possible redress. In some States corrupt voters may be arrested, tried and punished, but that does not remove their votes from the total vote cast nor in any way change the results. When questions which are supported by men's organizations go to referendum, such as prohibition, men interested may secure posts as election officials or party watchers and thus be in position to guard the purity of the election. This privilege is not open to women.

That corrupt influences have exerted their full power against woman suffrage, we know well. I have myself seen blocks of men marched to the polling booth and paid money in plain sight, both men and bribers flaunting the fact boldly that they were "beating the ______ women," I have myself seen men who could not speak a word of English, nor write their names in any language, driven to the polls like sheep to vote against woman suffrage and no law at the time could punish them for the misuse of the vote so cheaply extended to them, nor change the result.

It is our sincere belief based upon evidence which has been completely convincing to us that woman suffrage amendments in several States have been won on referendum, but that the returns were juggled and the amendment counted out. We have given to such campaigns our money, our time, our strength, our very lives. We have believed the amendment carried and yet have seen our cause announced as lost. We are tired of playing the State campaign game with "the political dice loaded and the cards stacked" against us before we begin. The position of such an amendment is precisely like that of the defendant in a case brought before an inexperienced judge. After having heard the plaintiff, he untactfully remarked that he would listen to the defendant's remarks but he was bound to tell him in advance that he proposed to give the verdict to the plaintiff. From this lower court, often unscrupulous in its unfairness, we appeal to the higher, the Congress and the Legislatures of the United States.

(3) The third reason why we object to the State method is even more weighty than either or both of the others. It is because the State method fixes responsibility upon no one. The Legislatures pass the question on to the voters and have no further interest in it. The political parties, not knowing how the election may decide the matter, are loth [sic] to espouse the cause of woman suffrage, lest if it loses, they will have alienated from their respective parties the support of enemies of woman suffrage.

Contributors to campaign funds have at times stipulated the return service of the party machinery to defeat woman suffrage, and as such contributors are wily enough to make certain of their protection, they often contribute to both dominant parties. Thousands of men in every State have become so accustomed to accept party nominations and platforms as their unquestioned guide that they refuse to act upon a political question without instruction from their leaders. When the leaders pass the word along the line to defeat a woman suffrage amendment, it is impossible to carry it. It is not submitted to an electorate of thinking voters whose reason must be convinced, but to such voters, plus political "machines" skillfully organized, servilely obedient, who have their plans laid to defeat the question at the polls even before it leaves the Legislature. From a condition where no one is responsible for the procedure of the amendment through the hazards of an election, where every enemy may effectively hide his enmity and the methods employed behind the barriers of constitutions and election laws, we appeal to a method which will bring our cause into the open where every person or party, friend or foe involved in the campaign, may be held responsible to the public. We appeal from the method which has kept the women of this country disfranchised a quarter of a century after their enfranchisement was due, to the method by which the vote has been granted to the men and women of other lands. We do so with the certain assurance that every believer in fair play, regardless of party fealties, will approve our decision.

These are the three reasons why we elect the federal method, and the three reasons why we reject the State method. We are so familiar with the objections Congressional opponents urge against suffrage by the federal method that we know those objects also, curiously, number three.

Objection No. 1. *War time is not the proper time to consider this question.* Two neutral countries, Iceland and Denmark, and three belligerent countries, Canada, Russia and Great Britain, have enfranchised their women during war time and they have been engaged in war for three and a half years. That which is a proper time for such countries is surely proper enough for us.

More, it is not our fault, you will admit, that this question is still unsettled in 1917. If our urgent advice had been taken it would have been disposed of twenty-five years ago and our nation would now be proudly leading the world to democracy instead of following in third place. Had Congress "got the hang of the Declaration of Independence" then, more men today would know the definition of democracy than do and more men would understand what a world's war "to make the world safe for democracy" means.

In 1866 an Address to Congress was adopted by a Suffrage Convention held in New York and presented to Congress later by Susan B. Anthony and Elizabeth Cady Stanton.[11] They protested against the enfranchisement of Negro men while women remained disfranchised and asked for Congressional action. That was fifty-one years ago. In 1878 the Federal Suffrage Amendment now pending was introduced in Congress at the request of the National Woman Suffrage Association and has been reintroduced in each succeeding Congress.

The representatives of this Association have appeared before the Committees of every Congress since 1878 to urge its passage. The women who made the first appeal, brave, splendid souls, have long since passed into the Beyond, and every one died knowing that the country she loved and served classified her as a political pariah. Every Congress has seen the Committee Rooms packed with anxious women yearning for the declaration of their nation that they were no longer to be classed with idiots, criminals and paupers. Every State has sent its quota of woman [sic] to those Committees. Among them have been the daughters of Presidents, Governors, Chief Justices, Speakers of the House, leaders of political parties and leaders of great movements. List the women of the last century

---

11 HWS 2: 168-171.

whose names will pass into history among the immortals and scarcely one is there who has not appeared before your committees--Susan B. Anthony, Elizabeth Cady Stanton, Lucy Stone, Mary A. Livermore,[12] Lillie Devereux Blake,[13] Julia Ward Howe,[14] Harriet Beecher Stowe,[15] Frances Willard, Clara Barton[16] and hundreds

---

[12] Mary Ashton Rice Livermore (1820-1905) volunteered her services to the Chicago (later Northwestern) Sanitary Commission in 1861 and, as a result of her experiences during the war, became a suffragist, founding and becoming president of the Illinois Woman Suffrage Association in 1868. She edited the *Woman's Journal* (1870-72) and was president of the American Woman Suffrage Association (1875-78), of the Massachusetts Woman Suffrage Association (1893-1903), and of the Massachusetts WCTU (1875-85). From 1872 to 1895 she averaged 150 lectures annually on the lyceum lecture circuit.

[13] Lillie Devereux Blake (1833-1913), author of many stories and novels. After 1869 she devoted herself to the woman suffrage movement and was president of the New York State Woman Suffrage Association (1879-90) and of the New York City Woman Suffrage League (1886-1900). From 1870 to 1900 her speeches were a regular feature of the national conventions and congressional lobbying of the NWSA/NAWSA.

[14] See pp. 337-38, n 18.

[15] Harriet Beecher Stowe (1811-96), prolific author best known for her novel *Uncle Tom's Cabin* (1852).

[16] Clara Barton (1821-1912), founder and for twenty-three years president of the American Red Cross (1882-1904). From 1866 to 1868, she described her experiences caring for soldiers during the Civil War on lecture

more. There are hundreds of women in the suffrage convention now sitting who have paid out more money in railroad fare to come to Washington in order to persuade men that "women are people" than all the men in the entire country ever paid to get a vote.

Perhaps you think our pleas in those Committee Rooms were poor attempts at logic. Ah, one chairman of the committee long ago said to a fellow member: "There is no man living or dead who could answer the arguments of those women," and then he added, "but I'd rather see my wife dead in her coffin than going to vote." Yet, there are those of you who have said that women are illogical and sentimental! Since Congress has already had fifty-one years of peace in which to deal with the question of woman suffrage, we hold that a further postponement is unwarranted.

Objection No. 2. *A vote on this question by Congress and the Legislatures is undemocratic; it should go to the "people" of the States*. You are wrong, gentlemen, as your reason will quickly tell you, if you will reflect a moment. When a State submits a constitutional amendment to male voters, it does a legal, constitutional thing, but when that amendment chiefly concerns one-half the people of the State and the law permits the other half to settle it, the wildest stretch of the imagination could not describe the process as democratic. Democracy means "the rule of the people," and, let me repeat, women are people. No State referendum goes to the people; it goes to the male voters. Such referenda can never be democratic. Were the question of woman suffrage to be submitted to a vote of both sexes, the action would be democratic, but in that case it would not be legal nor constitutional.

Male voters have never been named by any

---

platforms throughout the North and West. She was a lifelong woman suffragist and advocate of equal pay for equal work (Pryor 1987, 150-53).

constitution or statute as the representatives of women; we therefore decline to accept them in that capacity. The nearest approach to representation allowed voteless women are the members of Congress and the Legislatures. These members are apportioned among the several States upon the basis of population and not upon the basis of numbers of voters. Therefore every Congressman theoretically represents the women of his constituency as well as the male voters. He is theoretically responsible to them and they may properly go to him for redress of such grievances as fall within his jurisdiction. More, every member of Congress not only represents the small constituency confined to his district, but all the people of the country, since his vote upon national questions affects them all. Women, whether voters or non-voters, may properly claim members of Congress as the only substitution for representation provided by the constitution. We apply to you, therefore, to correct a grievous wrong which your constitutional jurisdiction gives you authority to set right.

Objection No. 3. *States Rights.*[17] You pronounce it unfair that thirty-six States should determine who may vote in the remaining twelve; that possible [sic] Republican Northern States should decide who may vote in Democratic Southern States. It is no more unfair than that some counties within a State should decide who may vote in the remaining counties; no more unfair than that the Democratic city of New York should enfranchise the women of the Republican cities of Albany and Rochester, as it has just done.

Forty-eight States will have the opportunity to ratify the Federal Amendment and every State, therefore, will have its oppor-

---

[17] Combined with objection 2, this was a source of serious disagreements among suffragists, which led to the defection from NAWSA of Laura Clay of Kentucky.

tunity to enfranchise its own women in this manner. If any State fails to do it, we may agree that that State would probably not enfranchise its own women by the State method; but if it would not so enfranchise them that State is behind the times and is holding our country up to the scorn of the nations. It has failed to catch the vision and the spirit of Democracy sweeping over the world. This nation cannot, must not, wait for any State, so ignorant, so backward. That State more than all others needs woman suffrage to shake its dry bones, to bring political questions into the home and set discussion going. It needs education, action, stimulation to prevent atrophy. In after years posterity will utter grateful thanks that there was a method which could throw a bit of modernity into it from the outside.

It is urged that the women of some such States do not want the vote. Of course if the thought of an entire State is antiquated, its women will share the general stagnation, but there is no State where there is not a large number of women who are working, and working hard, for the vote. The vote is permissive, a liberty extended. It is never a burden laid upon the individual, since there is no obligation to exercise the right. On the other hand, the refusal to permit those who want the vote to have and to use it is oppression, tyranny--and no other words describe the condition. When, therefore, men within a State are so ungenerous or unprogressive or stubborn as to continue the denial of the vote to the women who want it, men on the outside should have no scruples in constituting themselves the liberators of those women.

Despite these truths there are among you those who still harbor honest misgivings. Please remember that woman suffrage is coming; you know it is. In this connection, have you ever thought that the women of your own families who may tell you now that they do not want the vote are going to realize some day that there is something insincere in your protestations of chivalry, protection and "you are too good to vote, my dear," and are going to discover that the trust, respect, and frank acknowledgment of equality which men of other States have given their women are something infinitely higher and nobler than you have ever offered them? Have you thought that you may now bestow upon them a liberty that they may not yet realize they need, but that tomorrow they may storm your castle and demand? Do you suppose that any woman in the land is going to be content with unenfranchisement when she once comprehends that men of other countries have given women the vote? Do you not see that when that time comes to her she is going to ask why you, her husband, her father, who were so placed, perhaps, that you could observe the progress of world affairs, did not see the coming change of custom and save her from the humiliation of having to beg for that which women in other countries are already enjoying? Have you known that no more potent influence has aroused the sheltered and consequently narrow-visioned woman into a realization that she wanted to be a part of an enfranchised class than the manner in which men treat enfranchised women? There is no patronizing "I am holier than thou" air, but the equality of "fellow citizens." One never sees that relation between men and women except where women vote. Some day that woman who doesn't know the world is moving on and leaving her behind, will see and know these things. What will she say and do then? What will you do for her now?

There are many well known men in Great Britain who frankly confess that their desire to give British women the vote is founded upon their sense of gratitude for the loyal and remarkable war service women have performed. They speak of suffrage as a reward. For years women have asked the vote as a recognition of the incontrovertible fact that they are responsible, intelligent citizens of the country and because its denial has been an outrageous discrimination against their sex. British women will receive their enfranchisement with joyous appreciation but the joy will be lessened and the appreciation tempered by the perfect understanding that "vote as a reward" is only an escape from the uncomfortable corner into which the unanswerable logic of the women had driven the government. Mutual respect between those who give and those who receive the vote would have been promoted had the inevitable duty not been deferred. We hope American men will be wiser.

Many of you have admitted that "State's Rights" is less a principle than a tradition--a tradition, however, which we all know is rooted deep in the memory of bitter and, let us say, regrettable incidents of history. But the past is gone. We are living in the present and facing the future. Other men of other lands have thrown aside traditions as tenderly revered as yours in response to the higher call of Justice, Progress and Democracy. Can you, too, not rise to this same call of duty? Is any good to be served by continuing one injustice in order to resent another injustice? We are one nation and those of us who live now and make our appeal to you are like yourselves not of the generation whose difference created the conditions which entrenched the tradition of State's Rights. We ask you, our representatives, to right the wrong done us by the law of our land as the men of other lands have done.

Our nation is in the extreme crisis of its existence and men should search their very souls to find just and reasonable causes for every thought and act. If you, making this search shall find "State's Rights" a sufficient cause to lead you to vote "no" on the Federal Suffrage Amendment, then, with all the gentleness which should accompany the reference to a sacred memory, let us tell you that your cause will bear neither the test of time nor critical analysis, and that your vote will compel your children to apologize for your act.

Already your vote has forwarded some of the measures which are far more distinctly State's Rights questions than the fundamental demand for equal human rights. Among such questions are the regulation of child labor, the eight-hour law, the white slave traffic, moving pictures, questionable literature, food supply, clothing supply, prohibition. All of these acts are in the direction of the restraint of "personal liberty" in the supposed interest of the public good. Every instinct of justice, every principle of logic and ethics is shocked at the reasoning which grants Congress the right to curtail personal liberty but no right to extend it. "Necessity knows no law" may seem to you sufficient authority to tax the incomes of women, to demand exhausting amounts of volunteer military service, to commandeer women for public work and in other ways to restrain their liberty as war measures. But by the same token the grant of more liberty may properly be conferred as a war measure. If other lands have been brave enough to extend suffrage to women in war time, our own country, the mother of democracy, surely will not hesitate. We are told that a million or more American men will be on European battle-fields ere many months. For every man who goes, there is one loyal woman and probably more who would vote to support to the utmost that man's cause. The disloyal men will be here to vote. Suffrage for women now as a war measure means suffrage for the loyal forces, for those who know what it means "to fight to keep the world safe for democracy."

The framers of the Constitution gave unquestioned authority to Congress to act upon woman suffrage. Why not use that authority and use it now to do the big, noble, just thing of catching pace with other nations on this question of democracy? The world and posterity will honor you for it.

In conclusion, we know, and you know that we know, that it has been the aim of both dominant parties to postpone woman suffrage as long as possible. A few men in each party have always fought with us fearlessly, but the party machines have evaded, avoided, tricked and buffeted this question from Congress to Legislatures, from Legislatures to political conventions. I confess to you that many of us have a deep and abiding distrust of all existing political parties--they have tricked us so often and in such unscrupulous fashion that our doubts are natural. Some of you are leaders of those parties and all are members. Your parties we also know have a distrust and suspicion of new women voters. Let us counsel together. Woman suffrage is inevitable--you know it. The political parties will go on--we know it. Shall we then be enemies or friends? Can party leaders in twelve States really obtain the loyal support of women voters when those women know that the same party is ordering the defeat of amendments in States where campaigns are pending, or delaying action in Congress on the Federal Amendment? Gentlemen, we ask you to put yourselves in our places. What would you do? Would you keep on spending your money and your lives on a slow, laborious, clumsy State method, or would you use the votes you have won to complete your campaign on behalf of suffrage for all women in the nation? Would you be content to keep a standing army of women, told off for the special work of educating men in the meaning of democracy; would you raise and spend millions of dollars in the process; would you give up every other thing in life you hold dear in order to keep State campaigns going for another possible quarter of a century? Would you do this and see the women of other countries leaving you behind, or would you make "a hard pull, a long pull and a pull altogether" and finish the task at once? You know you would choose the latter. We make the same choice.

Do you realize that in no other country in the world with democratic tendencies is suffrage so completely denied as in a considerable number of our own States? There are 13 black States where no suffrage for women exists, and 14 others where suffrage for women is more limited than in many foreign countries.

Do you realize that no class of men in our own or in any other land have been compelled to ask their inferiors for the ballot?

Do you realize that when you ask women to take their cause to State referendum you compel them to do this; that you drive women of education, refinement, achievement, to beg men who cannot read for their political freedom?

Do you realize that such anomalies as a College President asking her janitor to give her a vote are overstraining the patience and driving women to desperation?

Do you realize that women in increasing numbers indignantly resent the long delay in their enfranchisement?

Your party platforms have pledged woman suffrage. Then why not be honest, frank friends of our cause, adopt it in reality as your own, make it a party program and "fight with us"? As a party measure--a measure of all parties--why not put the amendment through Congress and the Legislatures? We shall all be better friends, we shall have a happier nation, we women will be free to support loyally the party of our choice and we shall be far prouder of our history.

"There is one thing mightier than kings and armies"--aye, than Congresses and political parties--"the power of an idea when its time has come to move." The time for woman suffrage has come. The woman's hour has struck. If parties prefer to postpone action longer and thus do battle with this idea, they challenge the inevitable. The idea will not perish; the party which opposes it may. Every delay, every trick, every political dishonesty from now on will antagonize the women of the land more and more, and when the party or parties which have so delayed woman suffrage finally let it come, their sincerity will be doubted and their appeal to the new voters will be met with suspicion. This is the psychology of the situation. Can you afford the risk? Think it over.

We know you will meet opposition. There are a few "woman haters" left, a few "old males of the tribe," as Vance Thompson calls them, whose duty they believe it to be to keep women in the places they have carefully picked out for them.[18] Treitschke, made world famous by war literature, said some years ago: "Germany, which knows all about Germany and France, knows far better what is good for Alsace-Lorraine than that miserable people can possibly know."[19] A few American Treitschkes we have who know better than women what is good for them. There are women, too, with "slave souls" and "clinging vines" for backbones. There are female dolls and male dandies. But the world does not wait for such as these, nor does Liberty pause to heed the plaint of men and women with a grouch. She does not wait for those who have a special interest to serve, nor a selfish reason for depriving other people of freedom. Holding her torch aloft, Liberty is pointing the way onward and upward and saying to America, "Come."

To you the supporters of our cause, in Senate and House, and the number is large, the

---

[18] [Charles] Vance Thompson (1863-1925), author and playwright, who in 1895 established and edited *M'lle New York*, a fortnightly review.

[19] Heinrich von Treitschke (1834-96), German historian and political writer. As a member of the Reichstag, he supported the government in its attempts to subdue Socialists, Poles, and Roman Catholics by legislation, and he was one of the few men of eminence who sanctioned attacks on Jews which began in 1878. His masterpiece was the *History of Germany in the Nineteenth Century* (7 vols., 1915-19).

suffragists of the nation express their grateful thanks. This address is not meant for you. We are more truly appreciative of all you have done than any words can express. We ask you to make a last, hard fight for the amendment during the present session. Since last we asked a vote on this amendment your position has been fortified by the addition to suffrage territory of Great Britain, Canada and New York.

Some of you have been too indifferent to give more than casual attention to this question. It is worthy of your immediate consideration--a question big enough to engage the attention of our Allies in war time, is too big a question for you to neglect.

Some of you have grown old in party service. Are you willing that those who take your places by and by shall blame you for having failed to keep pace with the world and thus having lost for them a party advantage? Is there any real gain for you, for your party, for the nation by delay? Do you want to drive the progressive men and women out of your party?

Some of you hold to the doctrine of State's rights, as applying to woman suffrage. Adherence to that theory will keep the United States far behind all other democratic nations in action upon this question. *A theory which prevents a nation from keeping up with the trend of world progress cannot be justified*.

Gentlemen, we hereby petition you, our only designated representatives, to redress our grievances by the immediate passage of the Federal Suffrage Amendment and to use your influence to secure its ratification in your own state, in order that the women of our nation may be endowed with political freedom before the next presidential election, and that our nation may resume its world leadership in democracy.

Woman suffrage is coming--you know it. Will you, Honorable Senators and Members of the House of Representatives, help or hinder it?

26

Crystal Eastman, "Now We Can Begin," 1920

Crystal Eastman (1881-1928) was a lawyer and writer, a socialist and a feminist. She participated in the "Pittsburgh Survey," the first attempt in the United States to study in detail the effects of industrialism on urban workers, and published her findings in **Work Accidents and the Law** (1910), *a work that did much to advance the movement for workmen's compensation laws. With Alice Paul, Lucy Burns, and others, she founded the Congressional Union, which later became the National Woman's Party. In 1917 she became managing editor of her brother Max Eastman's radical journal, the* **Liberator,** *and wrote articles on labor problems and feminism. In March 1919 she was one of the organizers of a feminist congress in New York City. There, in the name of women, she demanded not only the vote but equal employment opportunities, birth control, economic independence, and a single moral standard* (**Liberator**, May 1919, p. 37).

After moving to England in 1921, she helped found a London branch of the NWP. She returned to the United States in 1927, but her political radicalism and her feminist views prevented her from being employed by any agency concerned with women's problems, despite her proven abilities as a social investigator. The only job she could find was a temporary position with the liberal journal,

Nation (O'Neill 1971, 288). *She died shortly afterward in 1928. In Freda Kirchwey's memorial, she wrote that when Crystal Eastman "spoke to people . . . hearts beat faster and nerves tightened as she talked. She was simple, direct, dramatic. Force poured from her strong body and her rich voice, and people followed where she led"* (**Nation**, August 8, 1928).

Eastman held a virtually unique position as an active socialist who was also a dedicated feminist. In the months following ratification of the Nineteenth Amendment, she made this speech, "Now We Can Begin." It not only illustrates her synthesis of the economic concerns of socialism with the emphasis on self-development among feminists, it also shows the clear link between the early movement and the issues which still dominate contemporary feminism. The text is reproduced here as published in the **Liberator** (Eastman 1920).

Most women will agree that August 23, the day when the Tennessee legislature finally enacted the Federal suffrage amendment, is a day to begin with, not a day to end with. Men are saying perhaps "Thank God, this everlasting woman's fight is over!" But women, if I know them, are saying, "Now at last we can begin." In fighting for the right to vote most women have tried to be either non-committal or thoroughly respectable on every other subject. Now they can say what they are really after; and what they are after, in common with all the rest of the struggling world, is *freedom*.

Freedom is a large word.

Many feminists are socialists, many are communists, not a few are active leaders in these movements. But the true feminist, no matter how far to the left she may be in the revolutionary movement, sees the woman's battle as distinct in its objects and different in its methods from the workers' battle for industrial freedom. She knows, of course, that the vast majority of women as well as men are without property, and are of necessity bread and butter slaves under a system of society which allows the very sources of life to be privately owned by a few, and she counts herself a loyal soldier in the working-class army that is marching to overthrow that system. But as a feminist she also knows that the whole of woman's slavery is not summed up in the profit system, nor her complete emancipation assured by the downfall of capitalism.

Woman's freedom, in the feminist sense, can be fought for and conceivably won before the gates open into industrial democracy. On the other hand, woman's freedom, in the feminist sense, is not inherent in the communist ideal. All feminists are familiar with the revolutionary leader who "can't see" the women's movement. "What's the matter with the women? My wife's all right," he says. And his wife, one usually finds, is raising his children in a Bronx flat or a dreary suburb, to which he returns occasionally for food and sleep when all possible excitement and stimulus have been wrung from the fight. If we should graduate into communism tomorrow this man's attitude to his wife would not be changed. The proletarian dictatorship may or may not free women. We must begin now to enlighten the future dictators.

What, then, is "the matter with women"? What is the problem of women's freedom? It seems to me to be this: how to arrange the world so that women can be human beings, with a chance to exercise their infinitely varied gifts in infinitely varied ways, instead of being destined by the accident of their sex to one field of activity--housework and child-raising. And second, if and when they choose housework and child-raising, to have that occupation recognized by the world as work, requiring a definite economic reward and not merely entitling the performer to be dependent on some man.

This is not the whole of feminism, of course, but it is enough to begin with. "Oh!

don't begin with economics," my friends often protest, "Woman does not live by bread alone. What she needs first of all is a free soul." And I can agree that women will never be great until they achieve a certain emotional freedom, a strong healthy egotism, and some un-personal sources of joy--that in this inner sense we cannot make woman free by changing her economic status. What we can do, however, is to create conditions of outward freedom in which a free woman's soul can be born and grow. It is these outward conditions with which an organized feminist movement must concern itself.

Freedom of choice in occupation and individual economic independence for women: How shall we approach this next feminist objective? First, by breaking down all remaining barriers, actual as well as legal, which make it difficult for women to enter or succeed in the various professions, to go into and get on in business, to learn trades and practice them, to join trades unions. Chief among these remaining barriers is inequality in pay. Here the ground is already broken. This is the easiest part of our program.

Second, we must institute a revolution in the early training and education of both boys and girls. It must be womanly as well as manly to earn your own living, to stand on your own feet. And it must be manly as well as womanly to know how to cook and sew and clean and take care of yourself in the ordinary exigencies of life. I need not add that the second part of this revolution will be more passionately resisted than the first. Men will not give up their privilege of helplessness without a struggle. The average man has a carefully cultivated ignorance about household matters--from what to do with the crumbs to the grocer's telephone number--a sort of cheerful inefficiency which protects him better than the reputation for having a violent temper. It was his mother's fault in the beginning, but even as a boy he was quick to see how a general reputation for being "no good around the house" would serve him throughout life, and half-consciously he began to cultivate that helplessness until to-day it is the despair of feminist wives.

A growing number of men admire the woman who has a job, and, especially since the cost of living doubled, rather like the idea of their own wives contributing to the family income by outside work. And of course for generations there have been whole towns full of wives who are forced by the bitterest necessity to spend the same hours at the factory that their husbands spend. But these bread-winning wives have not yet developed home-making husbands. When the two come home from the factory the man sits down while his wife gets supper, and he does so with exactly the same sense of fore-ordained right as if he were "supporting her." Higher up in the economic scale the same thing is true. The business or professional woman who is married, perhaps engages a cook, but the responsibility is not shifted, it is still hers. She "hires and fires," she order meals, she does the buying, she meets and resolves all domestic crises, she takes charge of moving, furnishing, settling. She may be, like her husband, a busy executive at her office all day, but unlike him, she is also an executive in a small way every night and morning at home. Her noon hour is spent in planning, and too often her Sundays and holidays are spent in "catching up."

Two business women can "make a home" together without either one being over-burdened or over-bored. It is because they both know how and both feel responsible. But it is a rare man who can marry one of them and continue the home-making partnership. Yet if there are no children, there is nothing essentially different in the combination. Two self-supporting adults decide to make a home together: if both are women it is a pleasant partnership--more fun than work; if one is a man, it is almost never a partnership--the woman simply adds running the home to her regular outside job. Unless she is very strong, it is too much for her, she gets tired and bitter over it, and finally perhaps gives up her outside work and condemns herself to the tiresome half-job of housekeeping for two.

Cooperative schemes and electrical devices will simplify the business of home-making, but they will not get rid of it entirely. As far as we can see ahead, people will always want homes, and a happy home cannot be had without a certain amount of rather monotonous work and responsibility. How can we change the nature of man so that he will honorably share that work and responsibility and thus make the home-making enterprise a song instead of a burden? Most assuredly not by laws or revolutionary decrees. Perhaps we must cultivate or simulate a little of that highly prized helplessness ourselves. But fundamentally it is a problem of education, of early training--we must bring up feminist sons.

Sons? Daughters? They are born of women--how can women be free to choose their occupation, at all times cherishing their economic independence, unless they stop having children? This is a further question for feminism. If the feminist program goes to pieces on the arrival of the first baby, it is false and useless. For ninety-nine out of every hundred women want children, and seventy-five out of every hundred want to take care of their own children, or at any rate so closely superintend their care as to make any other full-time occupation impossible for at least ten or fifteen years. Is there any such thing then as freedom of choice in occupation for women? And is not the family the inevitable economic unit and woman's individual economic independence, at least during that period, out of the question?

The feminist must have an answer to these questions, and she has. The immediate feminist program must include voluntary motherhood. Freedom of any kind for women is hardly worth considering unless it is assumed that they will know how to control the size of their families. "Birth control" is just as elementary an essential in our propaganda as "equal pay." Women are to have children when they want them, that's the first thing. That ensures some freedom of occupational choice; those who do not wish to be mothers will not have an undesired occupation thrust upon them by accident, and those who do wish to be mothers may choose in a general way how many years of their lives they will devote to the occupation of child-raising.

But is there any way of insuring a woman's economic independence while child-raising is her chosen occupation? Or must she sink into that dependent state from which, as we all know, it is so hard to rise again? That brings us to the fourth feature of our program--motherhood endowment. It seems that the only way we can keep mothers free, at least in a capitalist society, is by the establishment of a principle that the occupation of raising children is peculiarly and directly a service to society, and that the mother upon whom the necessity and privilege of performing this service naturally falls is entitled to an adequate economic reward from the political government. It is idle to talk of real economic independence for women unless this principle is accepted. But with a generous endowment of motherhood provided by legislation, with all laws against voluntary motherhood and education in its methods repealed, with the feminist ideal of education accepted in home and school, and with all special barriers removed in every field of human activity, there is no reason why woman should not become almost a human being.

It will be time enough then to consider whether she has a soul.

References

American Equal Rights Association Convention, 10 May 1866. *Proceedings*. 1866. New York: Robert J. Johnston.

Anderson, Judith. 1984. *Outspoken Women: Speeches by American Women Reformers, 1635-1935*. Dubuque, IA: Kendall/Hunt.

Anthony, Susan B. 1874; rpt. 1974. Address of Susan B. Anthony, Delivered in twenty-nine of the Post Office Districts of Monroe, and twenty-one of Ontario, in her canvass of those Counties, prior to her trial in June, 1873. In *An Account of the Proceedings on the Trial of Susan B. Anthony on the Charge of Illegal Voting, at the Presidential Election in Nov., 1872*, 151-78. New York: Arno Press.

Anti-Slavery Convention of American Women held in the City of New York, May 9, 10, 11, 12, 1837. *Proceedings*. 1837. New York: William S. Dorr.

Anti-Slavery Convention of American Women [Third], held in Philadelphia, May 1, 2, and 3, 1839. *Proceedings*. 1839. Philadelphia: Merrihew and Thompson.

Aptheker, Bettina. Ed. 1901; rpt. 1977. *Lynching and Rape: An Exchange of Views* [between Jane Addams and Ida B. Wells]. New York: American Institute for Marxist Studies.

Aristotle's Politics. 1923. Trans. Benjamin Jowett. Oxford: Clarendon Press.

Armstrong, Richard. 1965. *Grace Darling: Maid and Myth*. London: J.M. Dent.

Arnold, Carroll C. 1958. Lord Thomas Erskine: Modern Advocate. *Quarterly Journal of Speech* 44:17-30.

Bacon, Margaret Hope. 1969. *The Quiet Rebels: The Story of the Quakers in America*. New York: Basic Books.

Bacon, Margaret Hope. 1980. *Valiant Friend: The Life of Lucretia Mott*. New York: Walker and Company.

Bacon, Margaret Hope. 1986. *Mothers of Feminism: The Story of Quaker Women in America*. New York: Harper & Row.

Banner, Lois. 1980. *Elizabeth Cady Stanton: A Radical for Woman's Rights*. Boston: Little, Brown.

Barnes, G. H. and D. W. Dumond., eds. 1934. *Letters of Theodore Dwight Weld, Angelina Grimké Weld and Sarah Grimké, 1822-1844*. 2 vols. New York: Appleton-Century.

Bartlett, Elizabeth Ann. Ed. 1988. *Sarah Grimké: Letters on the Equality of the Sexes*

and Other Essays. New Haven, CT: Yale University Press.
Basch, Norma. 1986. The Emerging Legal History of Women in the United States: Property, Divorce, and the Constitution. *Signs* 12:97-117.
Becker, Susan Deubel. 1975. An Intellectual History of the National Woman's Party, 1920-1941. Ph.D. diss., Case Western Reserve University.
Beecher, Catharine. 1829. *Suggestions Respecting Improvements in Education, Presented to the Trustees of the Hartford Female Seminary and Published at Their Request*. Hartford, CT: Packard & Butler.
Beecher, Catharine. 1837. *An Essay on Slavery and Abolition with Reference to the Duty of American Females*. Philadelphia: Henry Perkins.
Berg, Barbara. 1978. *The Remembered Gate: Origins of American Feminism, The Woman and the City, 1800-1860*. New York: Oxford University Press.
Berg, Christine and Philippa Berry. 1981. "Spiritual Whoredom": An Essay on Female Prophets in the Seventeenth Century. In *Literature and Power in the Seventeenth Century: Proceedings of the Essex Conference on the Sociology of Literature, July 1980*, ed. Francis Barker et al., 37-54. Essex, England: University of Essex.
Berry, Mary Frances. 1988. *Why ERA Failed: Politics, Women's Rights, and the Amending Process of the Constitution*. Bloomington: Indiana University Press.
Birney, Catherine. 1885; rpt. 1969. *The Grimké Sisters: Sarah and Angelina Grimké, the First American Women Advocates of Abolition and Woman's Rights*. Westport, CT: Greenwood Press.
Bitzer, Lloyd. 1968. The Rhetorical Situation. *Philosophy & Rhetoric* 1:1-14.
Black, John W. 1943; rpt. 1960. Rufus Choate. In *A History and Criticism of American Public Address*, ed. William Norwood Brigance, 1:434-58. New York: Russell and Russell.
[Blackwell], Antoinette Brown. 1849. Exegesis of I Corinthians, XIV, 34, 35; and II Timothy, 11, 12. *Oberlin Quarterly Review*, July.
Blackwell, Henry B. 1870a. Political Organization. The *Woman's Journal*, 8 January, p. 8.
Blackwell, Henry B. 1870b. Political Exclusiveness. The *Woman's Journal*, 19 March, p. 85.
Blackwell, Henry B. 1870c. "Thou Shalt Not Bear False Witness." The *Woman's Journal*, 16 April, p. 113.
Blackwell, Henry B. 1870d. "Why Demand Suffrage Alone?" The *Woman's Journal*, 16 July, p. 220.
Blackwell, Henry B. 1871. Simply to Equalize. The *Woman's Journal*, 24 June, p. 197.
Blackwell, Henry B. 1873. Why the Delay. The *Woman's Journal*, 9 August, p. 252.
Blackwell, Henry B. 1875. Another Dissatisfied Friend. The *Woman's Journal*, 4 December, p. 388.
Blake, Nelson Manfred. 1962. *The Road to Reno: A History of Divorce in the United States*. New York: Macmillan.
Bland, Sidney Roderick. 1972. Techniques of Persuasion: The National Woman's Party and Woman Suffrage, 1913-1919. Ph.D. diss., George Washington University.
Blocker, Jack S., Jr. 1985. Separate Paths: Suffragists and the Women's Temperance Crusade. *Signs* 10:460-75.
Booth, Wayne C. 1982. Freedom of Interpretation: Bakhtin and the Challenge of

Feminist Criticism. *Critical Inquiry* 9:45-76.

Bordin, Ruth. 1981. *Woman and Temperance: The Quest for Power and Liberty, 1873-1900*. Philadelphia, PA: Temple University Press.

Bordin, Ruth. 1986. *Frances Willard: A Biography*. Chapel Hill: University of North Carolina Press.

Brigance, William Norwood. 1943; rpt. 1960. Jeremiah S. Black. In *A History and Criticism of American Public Address*, ed. William Norwood Brigance, 1:459-82. New York: Russell and Russell.

Bryant, Donald C. 1953. Rhetoric: Its Functions and Its Scope. *Quarterly Journal of Speech* 39:401-24.

Buhle, Mari Jo. 1981. *Women and American Socialism, 1870-1920*. Urbana: University of Illinois Press.

Burke, Kenneth. 1961. *The Rhetoric of Religion: Studies in Logology*. Boston: Beacon.

Camhi, Jane Jerome. 1973. Women Against Women: Antisuffragism, 1880-1920. Ph.D. diss., Tufts University.

Campbell, Karlyn Kohrs. 1980. "The Solitude of Self": A Humanistic Rationale for Feminism. *Quarterly Journal of Speech* 66:304-12.

Campbell, Karlyn Kohrs. 1983a. Contemporary Rhetorical Criticism: Genres, Analogs, and Susan B. Anthony. In *The Jensen Lectures: Contemporary Communication Studies*, ed. John I. Sisco, 117-32. Tampa: University of South Florida.

Campbell, Karlyn Kohrs. 1983b. Femininity and Feminism: To Be or Not to Be a Woman. *Communication Quarterly* 31:101-8.

Campbell, Karlyn Kohrs. 1985. The Communication Classroom: A Chilly Climate for Women? *ACA Bulletin*, no. 51:68-72.

Campbell, Karlyn Kohrs. 1986. Style and Content in the Rhetoric of Early Afro-American Feminists. *Quarterly Journal of Speech* 72:434-45.

Campbell, Karlyn Kohrs. 1987. Elizabeth Cady Stanton. In *American Orators Before 1900: Critical Studies and Sources*, ed. Bernard K. Duffy and Halford R. Ryan, 340-49. Westport, CT: Greenwood Press.

Catt, Carrie Chapman. 4 April 1899. Letter to Contributors to Territorial Funds. In Catherine Waugh McCullough Papers, Schlesinger Library, Radcliffe College, Box 3, Folder 37.

Catt, Carrie Chapman. 1902. *President's Annual Address Delivered by Mrs. Carrie Chapman Catt before the 34th Annual Convention of the National-American Woman-Suffrage Association and the First International Woman-Suffrage Conference, held in Washington, D.C., Feb. 12, 13, 14, 15, 16, 17 and 18, 1902*. Washington, D.C.: Hayworth Publishing.

Catt, Carrie Chapman. 1916. The Crisis. In Carrie Chapman Catt papers, New York Public Library.

Catt, Carrie Chapman. 1917. *An Address to the Congress of the United States by Carrie Chapman Catt*. New York: National Woman Suffrage Publishing Company.

Catt, Carrie Chapman and Nettie Rogers Shuler. 1923; rpt. 1969. *Woman Suffrage and Politics: The Inner Story of the Suffrage Movement*. Bellingham: University of Washington Press.

Cazden, Elizabeth. 1983. *Antoinette Brown Blackwell: A Biography*. Old Westbury, NY: Feminist Press.

Chafe, William H. 1972. *The American Woman: Her Changing Social, Economic, and Political Roles, 1920-1970*. New York: Oxford University Press.

Chester, Ronald. 1984. *Women Lawyers in a Changing America*. MA: Bergin & Garvey.
Christiansen, Adrienne E. 1987. Clarina Howard Nichols: A Rhetorical Criticism of Selected Speeches. M.A. thesis, University of Kansas.
Clark, Thomas D. 1977. An Exploration of Generic Aspects of Contemporary American Christian Sermons. *Quarterly Journal of Speech* 63:384-94.
Clarke, Edward H. 1873. *Sex in Education: A Fair Chance for the Girls*. Boston: James R. Osgood and Co.
Clevenger, Ima Fuchs. 1955. Invention and Arrangement in the Public Address of Carrie Chapman Catt. Ph.D. diss., University of Oklahoma.
Coleman, Willie Mae. 1981. Keeping the Faith and Disturbing the Peace: Black Women from Anti-Slavery to Women's Suffrage. Ph.D. diss., University of California, Irvine.
Conrad, Charles. 1978. Agon and Form: A Dramatistic Analysis of the "Old Feminist" Movement. M.A. thesis, University of Kansas.
Conrad, Charles. 1981. The Transformation of the "Old Feminist" Movement. *Quarterly Journal of Speech* 67:284-97.
Cook, Blanche Wiesen, ed. 1978. *Crystal Eastman on Women and Revolution*. New York: Oxford University Press.
Cott, Nancy F. 1977. *The Bonds of Womanhood: "Woman's Sphere" in New England, 1780-1835*. New Haven: Yale University Press.
Cott, Nancy F. 1987. *The Grounding of Modern Feminism*. New Haven: Yale University Press.
Cowper, William. 1835. *The Task, A Poem in Six Books*. Philadelphia: Joseph M'Dowell.
Cromwell, Otelia. 1958. *Lucretia Mott*. Cambridge, MA: Harvard University Press.
Daly, Mary. 1978. *Gyn/Ecology: The Metaethics of Radical Feminism*. Boston: Beacon Press. chp. 3 "Indian *Suttee*: The Ultimate Consummation of Marriage," pp. 113-33.
Mr. Dana's Lecture on Woman. 9 March 1850. The [New York] *Literary World*, p. 224.
Davis, Angela Y. 1981. *Woman, Race & Class*. New York: Random House.
Davis, Marianna W., ed. 1982. *Contributions of Black Women to America*. 2 vols. Columbia, SC: Kenday Press.
Davis, Paulina Wright. 1871; rpt. 1970. *A History of the National Woman's Rights Movement for Twenty Years*. New York: Source Book Press.
The Declaration of Sentiments and Constitution of the American Anti-Slavery Society of 1833. 1835. New York: American Anti-Slavery Society, Wm. Dorr, Printer.
Dow, Bonnie. 1987. The Reformist Rhetoric of Frances E. Willard: The Romantic Appeal of Mother, God, and Home. M.A. thesis, University of Kansas.
Drescher, Seymour. 1982. Public Opinion and the British Colonial Slavery. In *Slavery and British Society, 1776-1846*, ed. James Walvin, ch. 1. Baton Rouge: Louisiana State University Press.
Drish, Ruth Ellen Williamson. 1985. Susan B. Anthony De-radicalizes, Re-organizes, and Re-unites the American Woman Suffrage Movement, 1880-1890. Ph.D. diss., University of Iowa.
DuBois, Ellen, ed. 1981. *Elizabeth Cady Stanton, Susan B. Anthony: Correspondence, Writings, Speeches*. New York: Schocken.
Duster, Alfreda M., ed. 1970. *Crusade for Justice: The Autobiography of Ida B. Wells*. Chicago: University of Chicago Press.
Eastman, Crystal. 1920. Now We Can Begin. The *Liberator* 3 (December): 23-24.

Engels, Friedrich. 1884; rpt. 1972. *The Origin of the Family, Private Property, and the State*. Trans. Robert Vernon. Intro. by Evelyn Reed. New York: Pathfinder Press.

Farrell, Thomas J. 1979. The Female and Male Modes of Rhetoric. *College English* 40:909-21.

Fauset, Arthur Huff. 1938. *Sojourner Truth: God's Faithful Pilgrim*. Chapel Hill: University of North Carolina Press.

Fell, Margaret. 1667; rpt. 1979. Womens [sic] Speaking Justified. In *Womens Speaking Justified*, intro. David J. Latt, 1-19, Publication no. 194. The Augustan Reprint Society, William Andrew Clark Memorial Library, University of California, Los Angeles.

Fell, Sarah (?). 1975. A Seventeenth-Century Quaker Woman's Declaration. Eds. Milton D. Speizman and Jane C. Kronick. *Signs* 1:231-45.

Fitzgerald, Tracey A. 1985. *The National Council of Negro Women and the Feminist Movement, 1935-1975*. Georgetown Monographs in American Studies. Washington, D.C.: Georgetown University Press.

Flexner, Eleanor. 1959; rpt. 1974. *Century of Struggle: The Woman's Rights Movement in the United States*. New York: Atheneum.

Flexner, Eleanor. 1971. Anna Howard Shaw. In *Notable American Women: A Biographical Dictionary*, ed. Edward T. James, 3:274-77. Cambridge, MA: Belknap Press of Harvard University Press.

Foner, Philip S., ed. 1976. *Frederick Douglass on Women's Rights*. Westport, CT: Greenwood Press.

Ford, Linda G. 1984. American Militants: An Analysis of the National Woman's Party, 1913-1919. Ph.D. diss., Syracuse University.

Forster, Margaret. 1985. *Significant Sisters: The Grassroots of Active Feminism, 1839-1939*. New York: Alfred A. Knopf.

Fowler, Robert Booth. 1986. *Carrie Catt: Feminist Politician*. Boston: Northeastern University Press.

Freeman, Jo. 1971. The Building of the Gilded Cage. *The Second Wave: A Magazine of the New Feminism* 1:7-9, 33-39.

Freeman, Jo. 1975. *The Politics of Women's Liberation*. New York: Longman.

Friedman, Lawrence M. 1985. *A History of American Law*. 2d ed. New York: Simon and Schuster.

Fry, Amelia R. 1986. Alice Paul and the ERA. In *Rights of Passage: The Past and Future of the ERA*, ed. Joan Hoff-Wilson, 8-24. Bloomington: Indiana University Press.

Frye, Northrop. 1957. *Anatomy of Criticism: Four Essays*. Princeton, NJ: Princeton University Press.

Frye, Northrop. 1963. *The Well-Tempered Critic*. Bloomington: Indiana University Press.

Fulkerson, Richard P. 1979. The Public Letter as Rhetorical Form: Structure, Logic, and Style in King's "Letter from Birmingham Jail." *Quarterly Journal of Speech* 65:121-34.

Gage, Matilda Joslyn. 1890. The Dangers of the Hour. Delivered 24 February, Woman's National Liberal Convention. Matilda Joslyn Gage Papers, Schlesinger Library, Radcliffe College, MC 377, folder 45.

Gambone, Joseph G. 1973. The Forgotten Feminist of Kansas: The Papers of Clarina I. H. Nichols, 1854-1885. *Kansas Historical Quarterly* 39:12-28.

Giddings, Paula. 1984. *When and Where I Enter: The Impact of Black Women on Race and Sex in America*. New York: William Morrow.

Giele, Janet Zollinger. 1961. Social Change in the Feminine Role: A Comparison of Woman's Suffrage and Woman's Temperance, 1870-1920. Ph.D. diss., Radcliffe College.

Gifford, Carolyn De Swarte. 1986. Home Protection: The WCTU's Conversion to Woman Suffrage. In *Gender, Ideology, and Action: Historical Perspectives on Women's Public Lives*, ed. Janet Sharistanian, 95-120. Westport, CT: Greenwood Press.

Gilman, Charlotte Perkins. 1898; rpt. 1966. *Woman and Economics: A Study of the Economic Relation Between Men and Women as a Factor in Social Evolution*. New York: Harper and Row.

Gilman, Charlotte Perkins. 1903; rpt. 1972. *The Home: Its Work and Influence*, ed. William L. O'Neill. Urbana: University of Illinois Press.

Gilman, Charlotte Perkins. 1909-1916; rpt. 1968. *The Forerunner, Vols. 1-7*. Intro. Madeleine B. Stern. Westport, CT: Greenwood Press.

Gilman, Charlotte Perkins. 1935; rpt. 1972. *The Living of Charlotte Perkins Gilman: An Autobiography*, eds. Annette K. Baxter and Leon Stein. New York: Arno Press.

Goodman, James E. 1985. The Origins of the "Civil War" in the Reform Community: Elizabeth Cady Stanton on Woman's Rights and Reconstruction. *Critical Matrix: Princeton Working Papers in Women's Studies* 1:1-29.

Gornick, Vivian 1978. Alice Paul. In *Essays in Feminism*, 171-78. New York: Harper & Row.

Grady, Henry W. 1890. The New South. In *Life of Henry W. Grady, Including His Writings and Speeches*, ed. Joel Chandler Harris, 83-93. Cassell Company.

Grant, Donald L. 1975. The Function and Mythology of Lynching, 1–19. In *The Anti-Lynching Movement: 1883–1932*. San Francisco: R & E Associates.

Greeley, Horace and Robert Dale Owen. 1860; rpt. 1972. *Divorce: Being a Correspondence Between Horace Greeley and Robert Dale Owen, Originally Published in the New York Daily Tribune*. New York: Source Book Press.

Greene, Dana, ed. 1980. *Lucretia Mott: Her Complete Speeches and Sermons*. New York: Edwin Mellen Press.

Griffith. Elisabeth. 1984. *In Her Own Right: The Life of Elizabeth Cady Stanton*. New York: Oxford University Press.

Grimké, Angelina E. 1836. *Appeal to the Christian Women of the Southern States*. New York: American Anti-Slavery Society.

Grimké, Angelina E. 1838. *Letters to Catharine E. Beecher, in Reply to an Essay on Slavery and Abolitionism, Addressed to A.E. Grimké, revised by the author.* Boston: Isaac Knapp.

Grimké, Sarah Moore. 1838. *Letters on the Equality of the Sexes and the Condition of Woman, Addressed to Mary Parker, President of the Boston Female Anti-Slavery Society*. Boston: Isaac Knapp.

Grossberg, Michael. 1985. *Governing the Hearth: Law and the Family in Nineteenth-Century America*. Chapel Hill: University of North Carolina Press.

Gurko, Miriam. 1976. *The Ladies of Seneca Falls: The Birth of the Woman's Rights Movement*. New York: Schocken Books.

Guy-Sheftall, Beverly Lynn. 1984. Daughters of Sorrow: Attitudes Toward Black Women, 1880-1920. Ph.D. diss., Emory University.

Hall, Jacqueline Dowd. 1978. "A Truly Subversive Affair": Women Against Lynching in the Twentieth-Century South. In *Women of America: A History*, eds. Carol Ruth Berkin and Mary Beth Norton, 370-88. Boston: Houghton-Mifflin.

Hall, Jacqueline Dowd. 1979. *Revolt Against Chivalry: Jessie Daniel Ames and the Women's Campaign Against Lynching*. New York: Columbia University Press.

Hallowell, Anna Davis, ed. 1884. *James and Lucretia Mott: Life and Letters*. Boston: Houghton-Mifflin.

Hamilton, Tullia Brown. 1978. The National Association of Colored Women, 1896-1970. Ph.D. diss., Emory University.

Hardesty, Nancy A. 1984. *Women Called to Witness: Evangelical Feminism in the 19th Century*. Nashville, TN: Abingdon Press.

Harper, Ida Husted. 1898–1908. *The Life and Work of Anthony*. 3 Vols. Indianapolis: Bowen-Merrill, Hollenbeck Press.

Harrison, Brian. 1978. *Separate Spheres: The Opposition to Women's Suffrage in Britain*. New York: Holmes and Meier.

Hayden, Dolores. 1981. *The Grand Domestic Revolution: A History of Feminist Designs for Contemporary Homes, Neighborhoods and Cities*. Cambridge, MA: Massachusetts Institute of Technology.

Hersh, Blanche Glassman. 1978. *The Slavery of Sex: Feminist Abolitionists in America*. Urbana: University of Illinois Press.

Herttell, Thomas. 1839. *The Right of Married Women to Hold and Contract Property Sustained by the Constitution of the State of New York*. New York: Henry Durrell.

Higginson, Thomas Wentworth. 1870a. Turn Your Guns upon the Enemy. The *Woman's Journal*, 19 November, p. 361.

Higginson, Thomas Wentworth. 1870b. Remarks at the Annual Meeting of the American Woman Suffrage Association. The *Woman's Journal*, 3 December, p. 378.

History of Pennsylvania Hall, Which was Destroyed by a Mob on the 17th of May, 1838. 1838. [Ed. Samuel Webb.] Philadelphia: Merrihew and Gunn.

History of Woman Suffrage, 1848–1861, vol. 1. 1881. Eds. Elizabeth Cady Stanton, Susan B. Anthony, and Matilda Joslyn Gage. New York: Fowler and Wells. Cited as HWS 1.

History of Woman Suffrage, 1861–1876, vol. 2, 1882. Eds. Elizabeth Cady Stanton, Susan B. Anthony, and Matilda Joslyn Gage. New York: Fowler and Wells. Cited as HWS 2.

History of Woman Suffrage, 1876–1885, vol. 3. 1887. Eds. Susan B. Anthony and Ida Husted Harper. Rochester, NY: Susan B. Anthony. Cited as HWS 3.

History of Woman Suffrage, 1883–1900, vol. 4. 1906. Eds. Susan B. Anthony and Ida Husted Harper. Rochester, NY: Susan B. Anthony. Cited as HWS 4.

History of Woman Suffrage, 1900–1913, vol. 5. 1922. Ed. Ida Husted Harper. New York: J. J. Little and Ives. Cited as HWS 5.

History of Woman Suffrage, 1913–1920, vol. 6. 1922. Ed. Ida Husted Harper. New York: J. J. Little and Ives. Cited as HWS 6.

Hodes, W. William. 1970. Women and the Constitution: Some Legal History and a New Approach to the Nineteenth Amendment. *Rutgers Law Review* 25:26-53.

Hoff-Wilson, Joan. 1987. The Unfinished Revolution: The Changing Legal Status of U.S. Women. *Signs* 13:7-36.

Homer. *Odyssey* [*The Authoress of the Odyssey*]. 1897; rpt. 1967. Trans. Samuel Butler.

Chicago: University of Chicago Press.

Homer. *Odyssey*. 1932. Trans. T. Shaw [T. E. Lawrence]. New York: Oxford University Press.

Homer. *Odyssey*. 1935. Trans. S. H. Butcher and Andrew Lang. New York: Modern Library.

Homer. *Odyssey*. 1946. Trans. E.V. Rieu. London: Allen Lane/Penguin.

Homer. *Odyssey*. 1980. Trans. Walter Shewring. New York: Oxford University Press.

Hooks, Bell. 1981. *Ain't I A Woman: Black Women and Feminism*. Boston: South End Press.

Howell, Wilbur S. and Hoyt H. Hudson. 1943; rpt. 1960. Daniel Webster. In *A History and Criticism of American Public Address*, ed. William Norwood Brigance, 2:665-734. New York: Russell and Russell.

Hurwitz, Edith F. 1978. Carrie Chapman Catt's "Suffrage Militancy" [7 April 1913]. *Signs* 3:739-43.

Irwin, Inez Haynes. 1964; rpt. 1977. *The Story of Alice Paul and the National Woman's Party*. Fairfax, VA: Denlinger's Publishers.

James, Henry, et al. 1853; rpt. 1972. *Love, Marriage and Divorce and the Sovereignty of the Individual*. New York: Source Book Press.

Janeway, Elizabeth. 1971. *Man's World; Woman's Place: A Study in Social Mythology*. New York: Dell.

Janis, Irving L. 1972. Effects of Fear Arousal on Attitude Change: Recent Developments in Theory and Experimental Research. In *The Process of Social Influence: Readings in Persuasion*, eds. Thomas D. Beisecker and Donn W. Parson, 277-302. Englewood Cliffs, NJ: Prentice-Hall.

Japp, Phyllis M. 1985. Esther or Isaiah?: The Abolitionist-Feminist Rhetoric of Angelina Grimké. *Quarterly Journal of Speech* 71:335-48.

Jerry, E. Claire. 1986. Clara Bewick Colby and the *Woman's Tribune*: Strategies of a Free Lance Movement Leader. Ph.D. diss., University of Kansas.

Jones, Rufus M. 1921; rpt. 1970. *The Later Periods of Quakerism*. 2 vols. Westport, CT: Greenwood Press.

Katz, David Howard. 1973. Carrie Chapman Catt and the Struggle for Peace. Ph.D. diss., Syracuse University.

Kerber, Linda K. 1980. *Women of the Republic: Intellect and Ideology in the American Revolution*. Chapel Hill: University of North Carolina Press.

Kettler, Ernestine Hara. 1976. In Prison. In *From Parlor to Prison: Five American Suffragists Talk About Their Lives*, ed. Sherna Gluck, 227-70. New York: Vintage.

Kierkegaard, Søren. 1941; rpt. 1954. *Fear and Trembling: A Dialectical Lyric*. Trans. Walter Lowrie. New York: Anchor.

Kraditor, Aileen. 1965; rpt. 1981. *The Ideas of the Woman Suffrage Movement, 1890-1920*. New York: W. W. Norton.

Lane, Margaret. 1972. *Frances Wright and the "Great Experiment."* Manchester, England: Manchester University Press.

Langer, Susanne K. 1953. *Feeling and Form*. NY: Scribner's.

Laws of the State of New York Passed at the Eighty-Third Session of the Legislature. 1860. Albany, NY: William Gould.

Leach, William. 1980. *True Love and Perfect Union: The Feminist Reform of Sex and Society*. New York: Basic Books.

Leff, Michael C. and G. P. Mohrmann. 1974. Lincoln at Cooper Union: A Rhetorical

Analysis of the Text. *Quarterly Journal of Speech* 60:346-58.
Lemons, J. Stanley. 1973. *The Woman Citizen: Social Feminism in the 1920s*. Urbana: University of Illinois Press.
Lender, Mark Edward and James Kirby Martin. 1983. *Drinking in America*. New York: Free Press.
Lerner, Gerda. 1967. *The Grimké Sisters from South Carolina: Pioneers for Woman's Rights and Abolition*. New York: Schocken Books.
Lerner, Gerda. 1969. The Lady and the Mill Girl: Changes in the Status of Women in the Age of Jackson. *Midcontinent American Studies Journal* 10:515.
Lerner, Gerda. 1971. *Women in American History*. Reading, MA: Addison-Wesley.
Linkugel, Wilmer A. 1960. The speeches of Anna Howard Shaw, Collected and Edited with Introduction and Notes. 2 vols. Ph.D. diss., University of Wisconsin.
Linkugel, Wilmer A. 1963. The Woman Suffrage Argument of Anna Howard Shaw. *Quarterly Journal of Speech* 49:165-74.
Linkugel, Wilmer A. 1987. Anna Howard Shaw. In *American Orators of the Twentieth Century: Critical Studies and Sources*, eds. Bernard K. Duffy and Halford R. Ryan. Westport, CT: Greenwood Press.
Lipking, Lawrence. 1983. Aristotle's Sister: A Poetics of Abandonment. *Critical Inquiry* 10:61-81.
Lorant, Stefan. 1953. *The Presidency: A Pictorial History of Presidential Elections from Washington to Truman*. New York: Macmillan.
Lougee, Robert W. 1972. *Midcentury Revolution, 1848: Society and Revolution in France and Germany*. Lexington, MA: D. C. Heath.
Lucas, Stephen. 1988. The Renaissance of American Public Address: Text and Context in Rhetorical Criticism. *Quarterly Journal of Speech* 72:241-60.
Lumpkin, Katharine Du Pre. 1974. *The Emancipation of Angelina Grimké*. Chapel Hill: University of North Carolina Press.
Lunardini, Christine A. 1986. *From Equal Suffrage to Equal Rights: Alice Paul and the National Woman's Party, 1910–1928*. New York: New York University Press.
Lutz, Alma. 1931. *Emma Willard: Pioneer Educator of American Women*. Boston: Beacon Press.
Lutz, Alma. 1940. *Created Equal: A Biography of Elizabeth Cady Stanton*. New York: John Day.
Lutz, Alma. 1959. *Susan B. Anthony: Rebel, Crusader, Humanitarian*. Boston: Beacon Hill.
Lutz, Alma. 1971. Susan Brownell Anthony. In *Notable American Women, 1607–1950*, 1:51-57. 3 vols. Cambridge, MA: Belknap Press of Harvard University.
McClelland, David C. 1964. Wanted: A New Self-Image for Women. In *The Woman in America*, ed. Robert Jay Lifton, 173-92. Boston: Beacon Press.
Mack, Phyllis. 1982. Women as Prophets During the English Civil War. *Feminist Studies* 8:19-47.
Mack, Phyllis. 1986. Feminine Behavior and Radical Action: Franciscans, Quakers, and the Followers of Gandhi. *Signs* 11:457-77.
McMillan, Carol. 1982. *Woman, Reason and Nature: Some Philosophical Problems with Feminism*. Princeton, NJ: Princeton University Press.
McPherson, James M. 1975. *The Abolitionist Legacy: From Reconstruction to the NAACP*. Princeton, NJ: Princeton University Press.
Mäsel-Walters, Lynne. 1980. To Hustle With the Rowdies: the Organization and

Functions of the American Suffrage Press. *Journal of American Culture* 3:167-83.

Maloney, Martin. 1947. The Forensic Speaking of Clarence Darrow. *Speech Monographs* 14:111-26.

Maloney, Martin. 1955. Clarence Darrow. In *A History and Criticism of American Public Address*, ed. Marie Kathryn Hochmuth, 3:262-312. New York: Longmans, Green.

Martineau, Harriet. 1848. *Eastern Life, Past and Present*. Philadelphia: Lea and Blanchard.

Martyn, Henry. 1846. *Deceitfulness of the Heart*. Boston: Tract Committee of the Diocese of Massachusetts.

Martyn, Henry. 1851. *Journals and Letters of the Rev. Henry Martyn, B.D.* New York: M. W. Dodd.

Mills, Glen E. 1942. Webster's Principles of Rhetoric. *Speech Monographs* 9:124-40.

Mills, Glen E. 1943. Misconceptions Concerning Daniel Webster. *Quarterly Journal of Speech* 29:423-38.

Mohrmann, G. P. and Michael C. Leff. 1974. Lincoln at Cooper Union: A Rationale for Neo-Classical Criticism. *Quarterly Journal of Speech* 60:459-67.

Mossell, Mrs. Nathan Francis [Gertrude E. H. Bustill]. 1894; rpt. 1988. *The Work of Afro-American Women*. 2d ed. Intro. Joanne Braxton. New York: Oxford University Press.

Motley, Constance Baker. 1966. The Legal Status of the Negro in the United States. In *The American Negro Reference Book*, ed. John P. Davis, 484-521. Englewood Cliffs, N.J.: Prentice-Hall.

Mott, Lucretia [Coffin]. 1850. *Discourse on Woman*. Delivered at the Assembly Buildings, December 17, 1849. Philadelphia: T. B. Peterson.

National Woman's Rights Convention, held at Worcester, October 15, 16, 1851. *Proceedings*. 1852. New York: Fowler and Wells.

National Woman's Rights Convention, held at the Broadway Tabernacle, New York, on Tuesday, Sept. 6th and 7th, 1853. *Proceedings*. 1853. New York: Fowler and Wells.

National Woman's Rights Convention, held at Cleveland, Ohio, on Wednesday, Thursday, and Friday, October 5th, 6th, and 7th, 1853. *Proceedings*. 1854. Cleveland, OH: Beardsley, Spear and Co., Printers, Plain Dealer Office.

National Woman's Rights Convention [Seventh], held at the Broadway Tabernacle, New York, on Tuesday and Wednesday, November 25th and 26th, 1856. *Proceedings*. 1856. New York: Edward O. Jenkins, Printer.

National Woman's Rights Convention, 1859. *Proceedings*. 1859. Rochester, NY: Steam Press.

Nelson, Marjory. 1976. Ladies in the Streets: A Sociological Analysis of the National Woman's Party, 1910–1930. Ph.D. diss., State University of New York at Buffalo.

Nichols, Clarina Howard. 3 December 1852. Woman's Property Rights [Synopsis of Speech to Vermont Legislature]. In Woman's Rights and Wrongs. *New York Daily Tribune*, p. 4.

Nichols, Clarina Howard. 1853. *The Responsibilities of Woman* [1851]. Series of Woman's Rights Tracts. Rochester, NY: Steam Press of Curtis, Butts, and Co.

Nies, Judith. 1977. *Seven Women: Portraits from the American Radical Tradition*. New

York: Viking Press.
O'Neill, William L. 1967. *Divorce in the Progressive Era*. New Haven: Yale University Press.
O'Neill, William L. 1971. *Everyone Was Brave: A History of Feminism in America*. New York: Quadrangle/New York Times.
Peck, Mary Gray. 1944. *Carrie Chapman Catt: A Biography*. New York: H. W. Wilson.
Phillips, Brenda D. 1985. The Decade of Origin: Resource Mobilization and Women's Rights in the 1850s. Ph.D. diss., Ohio State University.
Pleck, Elizabeth. 1983. Feminist Responses to "Crimes Against Women," 1868-1896. *Signs* 8:451-70.
Pryor, Elizabeth Brown. 1987. *Clara Barton: Professional Angel*. Philadelphia: University of Pennsylvania Press.
Quarles, Benjamin. 1969. *Black Abolitionists*. New York: Oxford University Press.
Rabkin, Peggy A. 1975. The Silent Feminist Revolution: Women and the Law in New York State from Blackstone to the Beginnings of the American Women's Rights Movement. Ph.D. diss., State University of New York at Buffalo.
Rabkin, Peggy A. 1980. *Fathers to Daughters. The Legal Foundations of Female Emancipation*. Westport, CT: Greenwood Press.
Redding, Saunders. 1971. Sojourner Truth. In *Notable American Women, 1607–1950*, ed. Edward T. James, 3:479-81. Cambridge, MA: Belknap Press of Harvard University.
Richardson, Marilyn, ed. 1987. *Maria W. Stewart, America's First Black Woman Political Writer: Essays and Speeches*. Bloomington: Indiana University Press.
Robins-Mowry, Dorothy. 1983. *The Hidden Sun: Women of Modern Japan*. Boulder, CO: Westview Press.
Rorabaugh, W. J. 1980. *The Alcoholic Republic: An American Tradition*. New York: Oxford University Press.
Sanbonmatsu, Akira. 1971. Darrow and Rorke's Use of Burkeian Identification Strategies in *New York vs. Gitlow*. *Communication Monographs* 38:36-48.
Sartre, Jean-Paul. 1956. Existentialism is a Humanism. In *Existentialism from Dostoevsky to Sartre*, ed. Walter Kaufmann, 287-311. Cleveland: Meridian.
Sartre, Jean-Paul. 1962. Introduction to *Les Temps Modernes*. Trans. Françoise Ehrmann. In *Paths to the Present: Aspects of European Thought from Romanticism to Existentialism*, ed. Eugen Weber, 432-41. New York: Dodd, Mead.
Scott, Ann Firor. 1970. *The Southern Lady: From Pedestal to Politics, 1830–1930*. Chicago: University of Chicago Press.
Scott, Ann Firor. 1978. What, Then, is the American: This New Woman? *Journal of American History* 65:679-703.
Scott, Robert L. and Donald K. Smith. 1969. The Rhetoric of Confrontation. *Quarterly Journal of Speech* 55:1-8.
Shaw, Anna Howard. 1 July 1915. The Fundamental Principle of a Republic. The *Ogdenburg Advance and St. Lawrence Weekly Democrat*, pp. 2-3.
Shaw, Anna Howard. 1915. *Story of a Pioneer*. With Elizabeth Jordan. New York: Harper & Brothers.
Simons, Herbert W. 1970. Requirements, Problems, and Strategies: A Theory of Persuasion for Social Movements. *Quarterly Journal of Speech* 56:1-11.
Sklar, Kathryn Kish. 1986. Why Were Most Politically Active Women Opposed to the ERA in the 1920s? In *Rights of Passage: The Past and Future of the ERA*, ed. Joan Hoff-Wilson, 25-35. Bloomington: Indiana University Press.

Smith, Page. 1970. *Daughters of the Promised Land: Women in American History*. Boston: Little, Brown.

Smith-Rosenberg, Carroll. 1975. The Female World of Love and Ritual: Relations Between Women in Nineteenth-Century America. *Signs* 1:1-30.

Snow, Malinda. 1985. Martin Luther King's "Letter from Birmingham Jail" as Pauline Epistle. *Quarterly Journal of Speech* 71:318-34.

Sochen, June. 1973. *Movers and Shakers: American Women Thinkers and Activists, 1900–1970*. New York: Quadrangle/New York Times.

Solomon, Martha. 1988. Ideology as Rhetorical Constraint: The Anarchist Agitation of "Red Emma" Goldman. *Quarterly Journal of Speech* 74:184-200.

Stanton, Elizabeth Cady. 1854. *Address to the Legislature of New York, Adopted by the State Woman's Rights Convention, held at Albany, Tuesday and Wednesday, February 14 and 15, 1854*. Albany, NY: Weed, Parsons.

Stanton, Elizabeth Cady. 18 May 1860. Speech to the Anniversary of the American Anti-Slavery Society, May 1860. The *Liberator*, p. 78.

Stanton, Elizabeth Cady. 1861. *Address of Elizabeth Cady Stanton on the Divorce Bill, before the Judiciary Committee of the New York Senate, in the Assembly Chamber, Feb. 8, 1861*. Albany, NY: Weed, Parsons and Company.

Stanton, Elizabeth Cady. 1867. First speech in the Kansas State Referendum Campaign. Holograph. Topeka: Kansas State Historical Society.

Stanton, Elizabeth Cady. 19 May 1870. President's Address to the National Woman Suffrage Association Convention, 10 May 1870. *Revolution* 5:305-7.

Stanton, Elizabeth Cady. 1888. Statement. Hearing before the Committee on Woman Suffrage, United States Senate, April 2, 1888. 50th Cong. 2d sess. Report no. 2543, 9-17.

Stanton, Elizabeth Cady. 1892a. The Solitude of Self. The *Woman's Journal*, 23 January, pp. 1, 32.

Stanton, Elizabeth Cady. 1892b. Solitude of Self. *Hearings of the Woman Suffrage Association before the Committee on the Judiciary, 18 January 1892, House of Representatives*, 1-5. Washington, D.C.: U.S. Government Printing Office.

Stanton, Elizabeth Cady. 1983. Solitude of Self. In *We Shall Be Heard: Women Speakers in America*, eds. Patricia Scileppi Kennedy and Gloria Hartmann O'Shields, 66-74. Dubuque, IA: Kendall/Hunt.

Stanton, Elizabeth Cady. 1898; rpt. 1971. *Eighty Years and More: Reminiscences, 1815–1897*. New York: Schocken.

Stanton, Elizabeth Cady and the Revising Committee. 1892, 1895; rpt. 1974. *The Woman's Bible*. Seattle, WA: Seattle Coalition Task Force on Women and Religion.

Stanton, Theodore and Harriot Stanton Blatch, eds. 1922. *Elizabeth Cady Stanton: As Revealed in Her Letters, Diaries, and Reminiscences*. 2 vols. New York: Harper & Brothers.

Sterling, Dorothy. 1979. *Black Foremothers: Three Lives*. Old Westbury, New York: The Feminist Press.

Stewart, Maria W. Miller. 1835. *Productions of Mrs. Maria W. Stewart*. Boston: Friends of Freedom and Virtue.

Stewart, Maria W. Miller. 1879. *Meditations from the Pen of Mrs. Maria W. Stewart*. Washington, D.C.

Stewart, Maria W. Miller. 1971. Religion and the Pure Principles of Morality, Boston, October 1831. In *Early Negro Writing, 1760–1837*, ed. Dorothy Porter, 460-71. Boston: Beacon Press.

Stowe, Harriet Beecher. 1863. The Libyan Sibyl. *Atlantic Monthly* 11:473-81.

Stratton, Joanna L. 1981. *Pioneer Women: Voices from the Kansas Frontier*. Intro. Arthur M. Schlesinger, Jr. New York: Simon and Schuster.

Suhl, Yuri. 1959. *Ernestine L. Rose and the Battle for Human Rights*. New York: Reynal.

Terborg-Penn, Rosalyn. 1977. Afro-Americans in the Struggle for Woman Suffrage. Ph.D. diss., Howard University.

Terrell, Mary Church. 1893. Introduction of Ida B. Wells. In Mary Church Terrell Papers, Library of Congress Ms. 16976, Reel 20, container 28, 507-509.

Terrell, Mary Church. 1898. *The Progress of Colored Women* [Speech to NAWSA National Convention February 18, 1898]. Washington, D.C.: Smith Brothers.

Terrell, Mary Church. 1904. Speech at the 1904 International Congress of Women in Berlin. *Voice of the Negro* 1:454-461.

Terrell, Mary Church. 24 January 1907. What It Means to Be Colored in the Capital of the United States [1906]. The *Independent*, pp. 181-86.

Terrell, Mary Church. 1912; rpt. 1983. The Justice of Woman Suffrage. The *Crisis* 90:6.

Terrell, Mary Church. c.1913-1919. The Effects of Disfranchisement Upon the Colored Women of the South. 13 typed pp. Library of Congress, Ms. 16976, Reel 23, container 32, 385–397.

Terrell, Mary Church. 1940. *A Colored Woman in a White World*. Washington, D.C.: Ransdell.

Terrell, Mary Church. September 1943. If I Were Young Again. *Negro Digest*, pp. 57, 59.

Terrell, Mary Church. 1948. Something About Our Name. The *Delta* 18:57.

Tick, Judith. 1983. *American Women Composers before 1870*. Ann Arbor, MI: UMI Research Press.

Truth, Sojourner. 1 June 1867. Speeches delivered on May 9 and 10 at the First Annual Meeting of the American Equal Rights Association. *National Anti-Slavery Standard*, p. 3.

Truth, Sojourner. 1878; rpt. 1968. *Narrative of Sojourner Truth*. With Olive Gilbert. New York: Arno Press.

Van Voris, Jacqueline. 1987. *Carrie Chapman Catt: A Public Life*. New York: The Feminist Press at the City University of New York.

Vicinus, Martha. 1985. *Independent Women: Work and Community for Single Women, 1850–1920*. Chicago: University of Chicago Press.

Wagner, Sally Roesch. 1978. "That Word is Liberty": A Biography of Matilda Joslyn Gage. Ph.D. diss., University of California, Santa Cruz.

Wagner, Sally Roesch. 1987. *A Time of Protest: Suffragists Challenge the Republic, 1870–1887*. Sacramento, CA: Spectrum Publications.

Walker, Lola Carolyn. 1951. The Speeches and Speaking of Carrie Chapman Catt. Ph.D. diss., Northwestern University.

Wallace, John William. 1887. Silver v. Ladd. *Cases Argued and Adjudged in the Supreme Court of the United States, December term, 1868*, 7:219-28. New York: Banks and Brothers.

Washington, Booker T. 1901. Atlanta Exposition Address. In *Up from Slavery: An Autobiography*, 217-25. New York: Doubleday Page.

Wells, Ida B. 1892; rpt. 1969. Southern Horrors: Lynch Law in All Its Phases. In *On Lynchings: Southern Horrors, A Red Record, Mob Rule in New Orleans*, 4-24. New York: Arno Press.

Welter, Barbara. 1976. *Dimity Convictions: The American Woman in the Nineteenth*

Century. Athens: Ohio University Press.

Willard, Emma. 1819, rpt. 1893. A Plan for Improving Female Education. In *Woman and Higher Education*, ed. Anna Callender Brackett, 1-46. New York: Harper & Brothers.

Willard, Frances E. 1883. Temperance and Home Protection. Delivered at the Third Annual WCTU Convention in 1876. In Frances Willard, *Woman and Temperance*, 452-59. Hartford, CT: J. Betts.

Willard, Frances E. 6 August 1886. The White Cross and Social Purity. Delivered 4 August 1886. The *Chautauqua Assembly Herald*, p. 2.

Willard, Frances E. 1888. Presidential Address. *Minutes of the National Woman's Temperance Union, 14th Annual Meeting, 1887*. Chicago: Woman's Temperance Publication Association.

Willard, Frances E. 1889a. *Glimpses of Fifty Years, 1839–1889*. Chicago: Woman's Temperance Publication Association, H. J. Smith.

Willard, Frances E. 1889b. *Woman in the Pulpit*. Chicago: Woman's Temperance Publication Association.

Willard, Frances E. 1890. *A White Life for Two*. Chicago: Woman's Temperance Publishing Association.

Willard, Frances E. 2 August 1891. A White Life for Two, a lecture delivered in the Amphitheatre, August 1, 1891. *Chautuqua Assembly Herald*, p. 5.

Willard, Frances E. 7 December 1895. A White Life for Two. The *Lexington Church Record*. 1:2.1.

Wollstonecraft, Mary. 1792; rpt. 1976. *A Vindication of the Rights of Woman*. Ed. C.H. Poston. New York: Norton.

Woman's Rights Convention, held at Worcester, October 23 and 24, 1850. *Proceedings*. 1851. Boston: Prentiss and Sawyer.

Woman's Rights Conventions, held at Seneca Falls and Rochester, New York, July and August, 1848. *Proceedings*. 1870. New York: Robert J. Johnston.

Woman's Rights Convention, held at Syracuse, New York, September 8-10, 1852. *Proceedings*. 1852. Syracuse, NY: J. E. Masters.

Woman's Rights Convention, May 12, 1860. *Proceedings*. 1860. New York: Robert J. Johnston, Printer.

Woman's Rights Convention, May 10, 1866. *Proceedings*. 1866. New York: Robert J. Johnston.

Woodhull, Victoria Claflin. 1871. *A Lecture on Constitutional Equality delivered at Lincoln Hall, Washington, D.C., February 16, 1871*. New York: Journeymen Printers' Cooperative Association.

Yates, Gayle Graham. 1985. *Harriet Martineau on Women*. New Brunswick, NJ: Rutgers University Press.

Index

ABOUT THE COMPILER

KARLYN KOHRS CAMPBELL is Professor of Speech-Communication at the University of Minnesota at Minneapolis. Her publications include *Critiques of Contemporary Rhetoric*, *Interplay of Influence*, and *The Rhetorical Act*.